International Trade and the Protection of the Environment

T0320277

Globalisation has brought in its wake an increasing tension between the goals of free trade and environmental protection.

Since the Seattle Riots in 1999 anxiety has grown as to the potential for the WTO system, as well as the variety of investment treaties, most notably NAFTA, to threaten a 'regulatory chill', with the threat of adverse arbitral awards inhibiting the ability of nation states to deal adequately with the challenges to the domestic and global environment.

The autonomy of the nation state in applying the precautionary principle to GM foods has recently come under challenge in the WTO award in the *EC–Biotech* dispute. Furthermore, trade and investment treaties entrench corporate privilege without imposing any corresponding environmental obligations. The Bhopal disaster of 1984 revealed the inadequacy of civil litigation in obtaining adequate compensation for environmental harm caused by the activities of foreign subsidiaries of multinational corporations.

International Trade and the Protection of the Environment provides a comprehensive and detailed legal analysis, both at national and international level, of what looks set to become the new legal order of the twenty-first century. The intention has been to state the law as of 25 April 2007.

Simon Baughen, a former practitioner in shipping law, is a Reader in law at the University of Bristol where he has worked since 1989. He is the author of *Shipping Law*. His research areas are: trade, investment and environmental protection; maritime law; trusts and equity.

International Trade and the Protection of the Environment

Simon Baughen

Routledge·Cavendish
Taylor & Francis Group
LONDON AND NEW YORK

First published 2007 by Routledge-Cavendish
2 Park Square, Milton Park, Abingdon, Oxon OX14 4RN

Simultaneously published in the USA and Canada
by Routledge-Cavendish
270 Madison Ave, New York, NY 10016

*Routledge-Cavendish is an imprint of the Taylor & Francis Group,
an informa business*

© 2007 Baughen, Simon

Typeset in Times by
RefineCatch Limited, Bungay, Suffolk
Printed and bound in Great Britain by
The Cromwell Press, Trowbridge, Wiltshire

British Library Cataloguing in Publication Data
A catalogue record for this book is available from the British Library

Library of Congress Cataloging-in-Publication Data
Baughen, Simon.
    International trade and the protection of the environment /
Simon Baughen.
        p. cm.
    ISBN13: 978-1-84568-009-1 (1)
    ISBN10: 1-84568-009-X
    ISBN13: 978-0-415-44810-9 (9)
    ISBN10: 0-415-44810-7 (7)
1. Environmental law, International—Economic aspects.
2. Foreign trade regulation.   I. Title.
    K3585.B38   2007
    382′.92—dc22   2007018713

This book is dedicated to the memory of Pamela Baughen (1928–2006).

Table of Contents

Preface

Globalisation has brought in its wake an increasing tension between the goals of free trade and environmental protection. There is a growing public perception that business interests have far too much power in a globalised economy and far too little accountability for the adverse effects of their activities. This perception has led to increased mistrust, and even hostility, towards the World Trade Organisation (WTO), most notably in the Seattle riots of 1999. This tension is particularly evident in three areas. First, there is the prospect that the free trade principles of the WTO will restrict the autonomy of nation states to promote environmental goals by regulating business activity, as well as hampering their ability to work collectively to this end through multilateral environmental agreements. Secondly, there is the potential impact on environmental protection of bilateral and multilateral investment treaties, most notably the North American Free Trade Agreement (NAFTA). Such treaties extend many of the key free trade disciplines of the WTO agreements into the area of investment. Moreover, they give foreign investors a direct right to proceed against state parties by way of arbitration in respect of breaches of these provisions. This has led to a fear that the threat of such litigation may create a 'regulatory chill' whereby states which are parties to such agreements are inhibited from legislating for the public good. Thirdly, there is the issue of investor obligations in respect of their business activities in foreign states. Unlike the question of investor rights, this issue falls outside the scope of treaties such as NAFTA. Instead, it falls to be dealt with entirely by domestic law. The litigation that followed the Bhopal disaster of December 1984 illustrates the complex jurisdictional and substantive law issues that claimants need to surmount when seeking compensation in respect of loss or damage sustained as a result of the activities of foreign investors.

The first of these issues will be examined in the first four chapters of this book which will analyse the balance between trade and the environment that has been struck within the WTO. Although these issues arise against the background of international law, the book is not about international environmental law. Rather, its focus is on how environmental concerns, whether expressed through national legislation or through international agreements, have been accommodated within the *lex specialis* that has developed through international agreements – such as the WTO agreements – whose concern is primarily economic. A comparison will then be made, in Chapter 5, with the way in which these issues have been addressed within the European Union. The focus of the book will then shift to the rights of foreign investors and the potential impact these have on environmental protection. Chapter 6 will examine the protection afforded to foreign investors under customary international law, as well as under the European Convention on Human Rights. Chapter 7 will then consider the protection afforded to investors under Chapter Eleven of NAFTA. The book then moves on, in Chapters 8, 9 and 10 to examine how national legal systems, primarily those of the United States of America and the United Kingdom, have dealt with suits against their domestic corporations in respect of environmental harm caused by the overseas activities of their subsidiaries. The book concludes, in Chapter 11, by considering alternative approaches to transnational pollution, such as the regulatory and compensatory regimes that have been developed to deal with the problem of maritime pollution.

Acknowledgements

I would like to take this opportunity to thank Professor Panos Koutrakos of the School of Law at the University of Bristol for his comments on Chapter 5, and to Vicky Keramida who prepared the table of cases. Any errors and omissions are my own. Thanks, too, are due to my family for their support during the very long gestation of this work.

Table of Cases, Awards and Reports

Decisions of US courts

International arbitration awards

NAFTA, Chapter Eleven awards

WTO and GATT reports

Table of Abbreviations

Ad Hoc Group	Open-ended Ad Hoc Working Group of Legal and Technical Experts on Liability and Redress
AIA	Advance Informed Agreement procedure
AIT	Canadian Agreement on Internal Trade
ARMG	Antibiotic resistance marker genes
ATCA	Alien Tort Claims Act 1789
ATS	Alien Tort Statute
Basel Protocol	Basel Protocol on Liability and Compensation for Damage 1999
BIT	Bilateral Investment Treaty
Brussels Regulation	EC Regulation 44/2001
BSE	Bovine spongiform encephalopathy
Bt	bacillus thuringiensis
CAFTA	Central American Free Trade Agreement 2004
CBD	Convention on Biological Diversity 1992
CEC	Committee on Environmental Co-operation
CERCLA	Comprehensive Environmental Response, Compensation, and Liability Act of 1980
CGIAR	Consultative Group on International Agricultural Research
CIEL	Centre for International Environmental Law
CITES	Washington Convention on International Trade in Endangered Species 1973
CLC	International Convention on Civil Liability for Oil Pollution 1969
CMVA	Canadian Motor Vehicles Association
CNL	Chevron Nigeria Limited
COPI	Chevron Overseas Petroleum, Inc
COPPR	Convention on Oil Pollution Preparedness Response and Co-operation 1990
CRISTAL	Contract Regarding an Interim Supplement to Tanker Liability for Oil Pollution

CTE	WTO Committee on Trade and Environment
CTOP	Chevron Texaco Overseas Petroleum, Inc
CVX	Chevron Texaco Corporation
DBCP	dibromochloropropane
DSB	Dispute Settlement Board
DSU	Dispute Settlement Understanding
EC	European Community
ECHR	European Court of Human Rights
ECJ	European Court of Justice
EEC	European Economic Community
EEZ	exclusive economic zone
EFSA	European Food Safety Authority
EPA	Environmental Protection Agency (US)
EU	European Union
European Convention on Human Rights	Convention for the Protection of Human Rights and Fundamental Freedoms 1950
FAO	Food and Agriculture Organisation of the United Nations
FDA	US Food and Drug Administration
FIPA	Foreign Investment Promotion and Protection Agreement
FRCP	Federal Rules of Civil Procedure
FTC	Free Trade Commission
Fund Convention	International Convention on the Establishment of an International Fund for Compensation for Oil Pollution Convention 1971
GATS	General Agreement on Trade and Services
GATT	General Agreement on Tariffs and Trade
GM	Genetically modified
GMO	genetically modified organism
GNPOC	Greater Nile Petroleum Operating Company Ltd
GURT	Genetic Use Restriction Technology
HCFC	hydrochlorofluorocarbons
HNS Convention	International Convention on Liability and Compensation for Damage in Connection with the Carriage of Hazardous and Noxious Substances by Sea 1996
ICJ	International Court of Justice
ICSID	International Centre for Settlement of Investment Disputes
IMO	International Maritime Organisation
INBio	National Biodiversity Institute (Costa Rica)
IP	intellectual property
IRO	Investment Relations Office
ITO	International Trade Organisation

ITOPF	International Tanker Owners Pollution Federation
Joint Protocol	Joint Protocol Relating to the Application of the Vienna Convention and the Paris Convention (Vienna) 1988
LLMC	Convention on Limitation of Liability for Maritime Claims 1976
LMO	living modified organism
MAI	Multilateral Agreement on Investment
MARPOL	International Convention for the Prevention of Pollution from Ships 1973/78
MEA	multilateral environmental agreement
MGA	Melengestrol acetate
MGTC	Myanmar Gas Transportation Company
MOGE	Myanmar Oil and Gas Enterprise
MTBE	methyl tertiary-butyl ether
NAAC	North American Asbestos Company
NAAEC	North American Agreement on Environmental Co-operation
NAFTA	North American Free Trade Agreement
Nuclear Convention	Convention Relating to Civil Liability in the Field of Maritime Carriage of Nuclear Material (Brussels) 1971
OECD	Organisation for Economic Co-operation and Development
OPA	Oil Pollution Act
Paris Convention	OECD Convention on Third Party Liability in the Field of Nuclear Energy 1960
PCBs	polychlorinated biphenyls
PCG fibres	polyvinyl alcohol fibres, cellulose and glass fibres
PCIJ	Permanent Court of International Justice
PNGDF	Papua New Guinea Defence Force
PPM	process and production measure
PVPA	Plant Variety Protection Act 1970
RICO	Racketeer Influenced and Corrupt Organisations Act
SCVMPH	Scientific Committee on Veterinary Measures relating to Public Health
SDMI	SD Myers Incorporated
SDRs	special drawing rights
SLD	Softwood Lumber Division (Canada)
SLORC	State Law and Order Restoration Committee
SPS	sanitary and phyto-sanitary measures
SPS Agreement	Agreement on the Application of Sanitary and Phyto-Sanitary Measures

STOPIA 2006	Small Tanker Oil Pollution Indemnification Agreement 2006
TBT	technical barriers to trade
TBT Agreement	Agreement on Technical Barriers to Trade
TEDs	turtle-excluder devices
TOPIA 2006	Tanker Oil Pollution Indemnification Agreement 2006
TOVALOP	Tanker Owners Voluntary Agreement Concerning Liability for Oil Pollution
TRIMS	Trade Related Investment Measures Agreement
TRIPS	Agreement on Trade-Related Aspects of Intellectual Property Rights
TVPA	Torture Victims Protection Act 1991
UK	United Kingdom
UN	United Nations
UNATRA	Union Nationale des Transports
UNCITRAL	United Nations Centre for Trade Law
UNCLOS	United Nations Convention on the Law of the Sea 1982
UNCTAD	UN Conference on Trade and Development
UNESCO World Heritage Convention	Convention Concerning the Protection of the World Cultural and Natural Heritage 1972
UPOV	International Union for the Protection of New Varieties of Plant
US	United States of America
USDA	United States Department of Agriculture
Vienna Convention	International Atomic Energy Agency Convention on Civil Liability for Nuclear Damage 1963
WHO	World Health Organisation
WIPO	World Intellectual Property Organisation
WPDR	Working Party on Domestic Regulation
WTO	World Trade Organisation
WWF	World Wildlife Fund

Introduction

We live, it is said, in a shrinking world – a world of globalisation. The internet and cheap air travel have shrunk the geographic barriers that previously kept peoples apart. The fall of communism has torn down the political barriers that had divided humanity since the end of the Second World War. However, perhaps the most important factor in this shrinking world is the economic one. From the Reagan-Thatcher era of the 1980s a new global consensus has emerged in favour of ever-greater liberalisation of trade and investment. The Mumbai call centre, the 'made in China' label on our children's toys (how quaint a 'made in Britain' label now seems) are the everyday manifestations of this new consensus. Overseeing it all is a new global institution, the World Trade Organisation (WTO). Created in 1994 the WTO has a truly global reach and 150 countries now are members. The most notable accession has been that of the Peoples' Republic of China on 11 December 2001.

The distinguishing feature of the WTO agreements, which came into force on 1 January 1995, is their binding legal force. Unlike the position under the General Agreement on Tariffs and Trade (GATT) 1947, a losing party no longer has the right to block the adoption of the recommendations of an arbitral panel. The WTO Agreement includes the Dispute Settlement Understanding (DSU), which provides for recommendations of panels hearing disputes under any of the WTO agreements to have binding effect on the members involved. Panels now have the power to impose sanctions, in the form of withdrawal of trade concessions, on a member that fails to bring its measure into conformity with the recommendations of a panel. Another important innovation of the DSU is the creation of an appeal process to the appellate body. It is an article of faith of this new consensus that progressive liberalisation of trade and investment will lead to growing economic prosperity on a global scale. Its most optimistic acolytes also believe that global liberalisation will open up previously closed societies and lead to the replacement of despotism by Western-style democracies. This optimism was succinctly expressed by Mr Renato Ruggiero, the then Director General of the WTO on 8 October 1996. When addressing the UN Conference on Trade and Development (UNCTAD) Trade and Development Board, he stated: 'We are no longer writing the rules of interaction among separate national economies. We are writing the constitution of a single global economy.'

Globalisation, however, has proved to be Janus-like in nature, for globalisation also has its dark side. This manifests itself in the environmental damage caused by all this relentless expansion in human economic activity. This damage, which may prove to be irreversible, is now occurring on a truly global scale. Humanity's 'carbon footprint' relentlessly trails behind our new prosperity, threatening a new dark age within our lifetime. Instead of reaching the promised land of universal global prosperity, the current odds are on humanity becoming sucked into a quagmire of a hotter, increasingly inhospitable, earth.

The principal focus of this book will be on the extent to which environmental protection plays a role in Mr Ruggiero's new 'constitution of a single global economy'. How has the pressing need to protect our environment been dealt with in the new legal instruments that aim to promote free trade and investment? After all, most measures of environmental protection will inevitably involve restrictions on trade and investment. The legal balance that is being struck internationally between these competing values is the fundamental enquiry of this book.

The first part of the book examines the international legal disciplines that have emerged, first, in limited fashion, through the GATT 1947, and, since 1995, through the WTO agreements. Trade restrictions that are aimed at environmental protection are likely to be challenged under one of three WTO agreements. The first of these is the GATT 1994. The GATT is primarily directed at securing free trade in goods through two principles of non-discrimination. The first, in GATT, Art I is that of 'most favoured nation' whereby members must afford non-discriminatory treatment to 'like' goods of all other members. Members must not, for instance, afford more favourable treatment to the goods of one member than they afford to the 'like' goods of another member. The second, in GATT, Art III is that of 'national treatment' which requires members to afford to the goods of other members treatment no less favourable than that which they accord to 'like' goods of domestic producers. These two principles are explicitly directed at non-discrimination.

However, the WTO agreements go beyond non-discrimination to outlaw certain forms of non-discriminatory measures, essentially on the grounds that there is no objective justification for a particular measure that restricts trade. The GATT, for instance, contains a prohibition, in Art XI, on quantitative restrictions on imports that contains no reference to the threshold concept of 'likeness' that is found in Arts I and III. This approach outlaws obstacles to free trade, irrespective of whether or not they are discriminatory, and finds concrete expression in the other two WTO agreements that bear on the trade/environment debate. These are the Agreement on Technical Barriers to Trade (TBT Agreement) and the Agreement on the Application of Sanitary and Phyto-Sanitary Measures (SPS Agreement).

Environmental protection measures are of two basic types. First, there are those that restrict or prohibit imports of goods because of concerns as to the adverse impact such goods may have on the environment of the importing state, including their impact on the public health of its citizens. For example, in *EC–Asbestos* Canada unsuccessfully challenged a French prohibition on the import of products containing asbestos, on the ground of protecting public health. However, similar measures have been successfully challenged, in *Thailand–Cigarettes* (under the GATT 1947) and in *US–Reformulated Gasoline*, on the ground that the public health objectives behind the measures could have been realised in a manner which was less restrictive of trade.

There is also a problematic category of cases that involve scientific uncertainty in relation to the introduction of novel processes and technologies. In *EC–Beef Hormones* the measure in question was a prohibition on the sale of meat that had been reared using growth-promoting hormones. In 1998 the appellate body ruled that the measure was not in conformity with the SPS Agreement in that it had not been based on a 'risk assessment' as required by Art 5.1. The appellate body required a very high degree of specificity in determining this issue. The risk assessment had to be directed not at the use of such hormones on human beings but on the risk to human beings through eating meat that had been reared with the aid of such hormones. A similar issue recently came up in *EC–Biotech* where the panel had to consider the conformity with the SPS Agreement of various national prohibitions on genetically modified organisms (GMOs) that had been approved at European Community (EC) level. The panel found that it was not enough to point to scientific studies that showed that various environmental harms 'might' result as a result of the introduction of such GMOs. The scientific studies must also evaluate the potential for such risks materialising. As this had not been done, the measures were, therefore, not in conformity with the EC's obligations under the SPS Agreement. The problem with such technologies is that to require such a degree of specificity may be to demand the impossible. It might be thought that such measures could be justified under the 'precautionary principle' which has arguably reached the status of a norm of customary international law. However, in both cases the findings were based exclusively on an application of the relevant provisions of the SPS Agreement.

The second category of cases is that involving so-called process and production measures (PPMs). These are measures which involve a restriction on imports based not on the potentially harmful characteristics of the product, but rather by reference to the environmental harm that has been caused by the way in which it has been produced. Such measures have been held to violate not only the non-discrimination principles contained in GATT, Arts I and III, but also the prohibition on quantitative restrictions on imports to be found in Art XI. Different production methods will not affect the nature of the product, as a product, and therefore a product produced in one way will be treated as 'like' the same product that has been treated in another, environmentally harmful, way.

To justify such measures, the focus must shift to two of the exceptions contained in Art XX. The first, contained in para b, applies to measures 'necessary to protect human, animal or plant life or health'. This has been interpreted very narrowly, so as to require the member relying on the exception to show that there was no alternative, less trade-restrictive, way of achieving such protection. The second exception, contained in para g, applies to measures 'relating to the conservation of exhaustible natural resources if such measures are made effective in conjunction with restrictions on domestic production or consumption'. This has been interpreted less restrictively and its scope received exhaustive analysis by the appellate body in *US–Shrimp Turtle*. This dispute involved a US prohibition of imports of shrimp from countries that were unable to show that the shrimp had been caught with the use of turtle-excluder devices (TEDs). The measure was designed to protect sea turtles by preventing them from being caught during shrimp fishing. The appellate body did not find that such a PPM could not, by definition, come within Art XX(g). However, the appellate body identified various administrative flaws in the way in which the US had sought to achieve its aims. These meant that the measure did not satisfy the requirements of the introductory *chapeau* to Art XX which provides that such measures are not to be applied 'in a manner which would constitute a means of arbitrary or unjustifiable discrimination between countries where the same conditions prevail, or a disguised restriction on international trade . . .'. Caution as regards PPMs is perhaps understandable, in that they can be seen as a one member's attempt to impose its environmental standards on other members. However, the issue of PPMs may, in future, come up in the rather different context of transboundary spillovers, where the objection to the way in which a product is manufactured is based on adverse environmental consequences felt in the member state imposing the measure. This could well occur in the context of the contribution to global warming made by the carbon emissions produced from a particular mode of production adopted by a member.

The appellate body in *US–Shrimp Turtle* expressed a clear preference for issues relating to PPMs, particularly those relating to protected migratory species that form part of the global commons, to be resolved by negotiation and, wherever possible, by the conclusion of multilateral agreements. The global nature of pollution requires global solutions and a variety of international agreements over the last two decades have attempted to provide them. For example, the Montreal Protocol 1987 addresses the issue of global ozone pollution, while the Kyoto Protocol has attempted to deal with the issue of global warming. A feature of many such multilateral environmental agreements (MEAs) is their use of trade restrictions as one of the instruments used to secure their objectives. This raises the question of how such MEAs fit into the WTO system. The issue is currently under review within the WTO, as part of the Doha Declaration 2001, but only as regards the issue of the effect on the WTO obligations of members who are also party to an MEA. This review does not extend to the issue of whether the WTO obligations of members are affected by an MEA as against another member that is not a party to that MEA. This issue came up in *EC–Biotech* where the panel, rather curtly, ruled that the provisions of the Cartagena Biosafety Protocol 2000 could not be invoked by the EC as against the complainants who were not parties to this MEA.

The WTO agreements are not exclusively directed at promoting free trade. Investment, in a limited fashion, is covered by the Trade Related Investment Measures Agreement (TRIMS). It is the General Agreement on Trade and Services (GATS), though, which has the greater potential for expanding the trade disciplines of the GATT into this area. This is an unusual agreement in that it is two-tiered. There are a limited number of obligations of general application, namely those requiring transparency and the application of most favoured nation treatment in the field of services. There are also a larger number of obligations which will apply only if a member has entered into specific commitments in certain service sectors. Both the GATS itself and the Doha Declaration 2001 urge WTO members to enter into these specific commitments with each other. The GATS obligations applicable to specific commitments include provisions on national treatment and market access. However, the most far-reaching provisions are those on domestic regulation which are contained in Art VI, the relevant disciplines for which are currently being developed by a Working Party on Domestic Regulation.

Another important side agreement is the Agreement on Trade-Related Aspects of Intellectual Property Rights (TRIPS), which aims to secure a base level of protection for intellectual property (IP) rights within the WTO. This book examines three areas in which TRIPS has the potential to conflict with environmental protection, in the wider sense of ensuring global equity within the WTO between the interests of its members which are developed countries, and those of its members which are developing, and least developed, countries. The first is the issue of the farmer's traditional right to save, use, exchange and sell seed. This is under threat from a biotechnology industry which is aggressively promoting the use of genetically modified (GM) seeds whose use it rigorously controls through licensing agreements. This control is backed up by the IP protection afforded by TRIPS, which can be deployed even against third parties who come to use such seeds, as demonstrated by Monsanto's recent litigation against the Saskatchewan farmer, Percy Schmeiser, before the Canadian courts. The second is the issue of how traditional knowledge should be treated under TRIPS. This involves the practice whereby biotechnology and pharmaceutical companies from the developed world make use of the traditional knowledge of the developing world in developing new products. This raises a fundamental issue of global equity. Why should traditional knowledge be regarded as part of the common heritage of mankind, available free of charge, when the products which are derived from that knowledge are entitled to the full protection of the patent laws of the developed world? The issue raises potential conflicts between TRIPS and another MEA, the Convention on Biodiversity 1992. The third issue is the extent to which TRIPS allows the manufacture of generic copies of in-patent pharmaceuticals to provide an affordable source of medication for developing countries. The issue is particularly acute with respect to pharmaceuticals directed at controlling HIV and AIDS.

Having completed our survey of the WTO agreements, the book moves on, in Chapter 5, to consider how the trade and environment debate has played out within the EC. Under the EC Treaty, restrictions on trade in goods fall under Art 28 for imports and Art 29 for exports. Unlike the position under GATT, neither provision makes reference to any threshold concept of 'likeness'. Instead, they are directed at quantitative restrictions on imports or exports. The first of these provisions, Art 28, also covers 'indistinctly applicable' measures where an even-handed measure has the effect of restricting imports. Restrictions on imports and exports between member states may, however, be justified on two grounds. The first is by reference to Art 30 which provides a list of exceptions which include 'the protection of health and life of humans, animals or plants'. The second is by reference to the case law developed by the European Court of Justice whereby 'indistinctly applicable' measures may be justified if they are necessary for the effectiveness of mandatory measures on, *inter alia*, the protection of the environment. A member state's ability to rely on either of these grounds of justification is subject to its ability to satisfy a threefold test. The measure must be necessary. It must be proportionate to the objective pursued. The measure must be the least restrictive of the internal market.

These provisions, although different in structure from those in the WTO agreements, perform essentially the same role – that of protecting free trade in goods with environmental considerations coming into play by way of an exception. However, the distinguishing feature of the EU is that is has for some time had an extensive legislative competence in the sphere of environmental protection. Environmental protection, therefore, has a positive role to play, which is not the case within the WTO. The principal manifestation of this positive role is through legislation which seeks to impose harmonised environmental standards throughout the EU. There are two different legislative grounds on which this might be introduced. On the one hand, harmonising legislation directed at the functioning of the internal market is introduced under Art 95. Most of the harmonised legislation on GMOs has been introduced on this basis. On the other hand, harmonising legislation directed at the protection of the environment is introduced under Art 175. Harmonised legislation gives rise to a problem not seen under the WTO agreements, and that is the extent to which member states may introduce national safeguard measures that introduce more stringent standards than those contained in the harmonising measure. Different principles apply depending on whether the harmonised measure was introduced under Art 95 or under Art 175, whose provisions give more leeway for the introduction of national safeguard measures.

The validity, or otherwise, of national safeguard measures, therefore, adds another layer of complexity to the trade-environment balance within the EU. It also affects the external relations of the EU, as a member of the WTO. This can be seen in the recent WTO dispute in *EC–Biotech* which, in part, involved the existence of national safeguard measures prohibiting the use of GMOs whose use had already been approved at EC level. This led the panel to find that the EC was in breach of its obligations under the SPS Agreement. At the date of writing, the EC is unlikely to be able to conform with the panel's recommendations, as the Council of the Environment has rejected the Commission's recommendation that Austria withdraw its national measure prohibiting one of the GMOs in issue in the WTO dispute. The EC's membership of the WTO also has internal repercussions. The provisions of the WTO agreements do not in themselves have direct effect. However, the European Court of Justice in *Biret* has recently held that a failure to comply with the recommendations of a WTO panel may give rise to a claim in damages against the EC, which adds an additional layer of complication to the relationship between the EU and the WTO.

In Chapters 6 and 7 the book turns its attention to the way in which environmental protection may be affected by international treaties on investment. This involves an examination of the norm of customary international law against the expropriation without compensation of the property of aliens. In particular, these chapters analyse whether the development of the norm to cover 'creeping' or 'indirect' expropriation has the capacity of affecting bona fide, non-discriminatory, measures of environmental protection that have an adverse economic impact on a foreign investor. By way of comparison, the book will analyse the protection accorded to property rights by Art 1 of the First Protocol of the European Convention on Human Rights.

Traditionally, foreign investors whose property has been expropriated have had to look to their home state to take proceedings against the host state for compensation in accordance with customary international law. However, the position has changed substantially over the last 30 years with the emergence of the Bilateral Investment Treaty (BIT). Most BITs provide for investor-state arbitration in respect of breaches of their provisions, which gives the adversely affected investor a direct right of action against the expropriating state. Moreover, the substantive protection afforded to investors under BITs is not limited to protection against expropriations. Many BITs include 'most favoured nation' and 'national treatment' provisions which are similar to those found in the GATT. The most important development in this area has undoubtedly been the creation of the NAFTA in 1994. Its parties are the US, Canada and Mexico. BITs tend to be between a developed nation and a developing nation and, although their provisions are bilateral, in practice suits tend to be brought by investors of the developed nation. NAFTA, however, opens up the possibility of suits being brought by foreign investors against a developed nation. Many such suits have been brought under Chapter Eleven in which NAFTA's provisions on investor-state arbitration are to be found. In Chapter 7, these investor-state provisions will be subject to detailed scrutiny with a view to testing the claims of those who feared that NAFTA would lead to a 'regulatory chill' within its three state parties.

So far, the book has been concerned with the protection afforded to business through international agreements on trade, such as the WTO agreements, and through international agreements on investment, such as NAFTA. However, what about the potential liability of foreign investors for environmental harm they cause in a foreign jurisdiction? This issue arose in dramatic fashion with the Bhopal gas explosion of the night of 2/3 December 1984, which remains the world's most serious chemical disaster – 45 tons of toxic gas were released into a city of 500,000 people, 2,660 people died and between 30,000 to 40,000 people were seriously injured, giving rise to claims in tort totalling US$3.3 billion. As well as causing environmental harm, multinational corporations may also become implicated in human rights abuses committed by foreign governments who are also their commercial partners. For example, horrendous abuses were said to have been committed by the Myanmar military in the mid-1990s while providing security for the creation of a gas pipeline as part of the Yadana Project in which a Californian oil company, Unocal, was a participant.

The potential liability of multinational corporations in these situations falls outside the scope of international law, and is unregulated by any international agreements. Instead, the issue of civil accountability has to be fought through private claims in national courts. To date, most of the litigation has been brought before the US courts, although, recently, similar cases have started to come before the English courts. The pattern that invariably emerges is that the overseas activity of the multinational corporation has been conducted by a subsidiary company which has insufficient assets to satisfy any judgment. In the light of this fact, claimants naturally direct their fire at the parent company and commence suit in its home jurisdiction. However, such litigation will be met by a determined effort by the parent company to have the proceedings stayed, usually on the grounds of *forum non conveniens*, but also on other grounds such as act of state. There is also the problem of finding a way to make the parent company liable for defaults of its subsidiary, either by piercing the corporate veil, or by finding that the subsidiary acted as the agent of its parent. Alternatively, the claimant may attempt to show that the parent is directly liable in respect of its own acts and omissions.

The book will examine the course of such litigation in the US, with jurisdictional issues being dealt with in Chapter 8, and substantive law issues in Chapter 9. US litigation has a distinguishing dimension in that the Alien

Tort Claims Act 1789 (ATCA) allows aliens to bring tort claims in the federal courts where the tort involves a violation of the law of nations. This means that as well as suing in tort, claims can be founded on the breach of a norm of customary international law. Although the scope of ATCA has been somewhat reduced as a result of the Supreme Court's decision in *Sosa v Alvarez-Machain* in 2004, it still remains an important avenue for human rights litigation against defendants that are present in the US. Chapter 10 will examine English law on the potential liability of English parent corporations in respect of the defaults of their overseas subsidiaries. Although English law has no equivalent of ATCA, it may, nonetheless, be possible to found a cause of action on the violation of a norm of customary international law. For example, in both *Al-Adsani v Govt of Kuwait* and *Jones v Saudi Arabia* claims in respect of torture suffered at the hand of a foreign state, or its officials, were pleaded both as conventional tort claims and as claims arising out of a violation of the international prohibition on torture embodied in the UN Torture Convention 1984. Another distinguishing feature of English law is that the preliminary hurdle of *forum non conveniens*, that has seen the death of so many claims in the US, no longer applies where a claim is brought against a defendant which is domiciled in England. This is the result of the European Court of Justice's recent decision in *Owusu v Jackson* as to the scope of EC Regulation 44/2001 (the Brussels Regulation), Art 2.

The book concludes, in Chapter 11, with a look at the problem of marine pollution which raises many of the transnational issues associated with civil litigation against multinational corporations in respect of 'exported' environmental harm. However, this is an area which is extensively covered by international conventions. Regulation of marine pollution falls under the International Convention for the Prevention of Pollution from Ships 1973/78 (MARPOL), while civil liability falls under the International Convention on Civil Liability for Oil Pollution 1969 (CLC) and Fund Convention 1971, as updated by the 1992 protocols. The book ends with a consideration of whether these conventions provide a useful template for any future attempts at addressing the issue of the accountability of multinational corporations for transnational environmental harm.

Chapter 1

Trade and environment within the GATT

One country's environmental regulation can become another's barrier to trade. This can be most clearly seen when country A bans the import of goods from country B on environmental grounds yet allows the sale within its jurisdiction of similar goods produced domestically. Such a regulation is patently discriminatory against country B. However, discriminatory trade barriers may not always be so obvious. What if country A provides that a class of goods can only be sold within its jurisdiction if they meet a specified health and safety standard? If the standard is applied to all goods, whether imported or produced domestically, there would appear to be no discrimination between domestic and foreign producers. However, foreign producers may nonetheless argue that *de facto* discrimination exists if the standards are pitched unreasonably high. Another problem exists when the standards applied do not relate to the possible effects of the product within the jurisdiction of the regulating country, but rather to the possible adverse affects caused by the manufacture of the product *outside* the jurisdiction of the regulating country, in other words, process and production methods (PPMs).

These issues are currently resolved through the WTO which was established on 1 January 1995 to replace the GATT that had existed since 1947. After the Second World War, the 'Bretton Woods' process attempted to set up three new multilateral institutions dedicated to international economic co-operation. This process successfully established two of these institutions, the World Bank and the International Monetary Fund. The third of these was to be the International Trade Organisation (ITO). This was to have been a new specialised agency of the United Nations (UN). Its Charter was intended to provide not only world trade disciplines, but also rules relating to employment, commodity agreements, restrictive business practices, international investment and services. In 1946 the 23 founding members of the GATT opened a round of tariff negotiations which led to agreement on substantial tariff concessions affecting about one-fifth of world trade. To protect these concessions it was agreed to enter a 'provisional' acceptance of some of the trade rules in the draft ITO Charter. This resulted in GATT 1947 which came into force in January 1948. In March 1948 the ITO Charter was agreed at a UN conference in Havana. The ITO, however, was to remain still-born following the announcement in 1950 by the US Government that it would not seek congressional ratification of the Havana Charter. The GATT, on the other hand, remained – despite its 'provisional' nature – the only multilateral trading agreement until the establishment of the WTO on 1 January 1995. This was the result of the negotiations between the GATT parties which was known as the 'Uruguay Round'. These began in September 1986 and were concluded on 15 April 1994 when ministers from most of the 125 participating governments signed the agreement establishing the WTO at a meeting in Marrakesh, Morocco.

As of 11 January 2007, 150 countries were WTO members and 31 governments have observer status. Trade disputes between members are regulated by a variety of treaties which appear under the aegis of the GATT 1994. This incorporates the original 1947 GATT (the GATT). The GATT is built upon two principles which aim to liberalise world trade. The first, under Art I, is 'most-favoured nation' treatment under which each member is to be accorded equal trading rights with every other member.[1] The second, under Art III, is 'national treatment' whereby each member is obliged to treat 'like products' of other members no less favourably than it treats domestic products.

In addition, Art XI also provides for the general elimination of quantitative restrictions on imports and exports, whilst Art XIII requires any legitimate quantitative restriction to be administered in a non-discriminatory manner to 'like products' of the contracting parties. The aim is twofold. First, to provide a 'level playing field' for trade which prevents discrimination in favour of one WTO member at the expense of other WTO members, or in favour of domestic traders at the expense of traders in other WTO members. Secondly, to remove measures which constitute unnecessary obstacles to trade, even if these are non-discriminatory. Transparency and even-handedness in the publication and administration of trade regulations is provided for under Art X. A measure that violates one or more provisions of the GATT may, nonetheless, be maintained if falls within the exceptions provided in Art XX. However, in exceptional circumstances, Art XXIII.1(b) allows compensation to be claimed in respect of the nullification or impairment of an advantage under the GATT, 'whether or not it [the measure] conflicts with the provisions of this Agreement'.

Measures that contravene these provisions can be challenged by a member by a reference to a panel of experts convened under the WTO Dispute Settlement Understanding (DSU). Unlike the position under NAFTA, and bilateral investment treaties, there is no provision in the DSU for suit by persons within member states who are adversely affected by measures of other member states. Only members may bring proceedings, and their right to

---

1   The term 'contracting party' appears in GATT 1947. GATT 1994 replaces it by 'member'.

do so are not subject to any 'legal interest' requirement.[2] DSU, Art 3.7 merely requires a member, before bringing a case, to 'exercise its judgement as to whether action under these procedures would be fruitful'. As long as the member has a potential interest in the trade in goods or services affected by the disputed measure, it will have the right to have recourse to the DSU. In *EC–Bananas III* the appellate body upheld the panel's finding that the US was entitled to take proceedings against the EC in respect of alleged violations of the GATT and of GATS arising out of the EC's preferential treatment of bananas imported from the Caribbean.[3] Although the US produced only small quantities of bananas, which it did not export, the WTO rules were not concerned with actual trade, but rather with competitive opportunities. It could not be excluded that the US might become an exporter of bananas. In any event, its internal market for bananas could be affected by the EC regime and its effect on world supplies and prices.

The DSU has introduced several important changes to the previous practice of dispute resolution under GATT. It provides for the automatic adoption of panel and appellate body reports unless there is a consensus decision by the Dispute Settlement Board (DSB) to the contrary.[4] In contrast, GATT panel reports had to be adopted by a consensus decision of the contracting parties and the losing party could block the adoption of a report in the GATT Council. The DSU also provides for an appeal stage from a panel decision and allows for a single panel to hear disputes under all the various GATT agreements, such as the SPS and technical barriers to trade (TBT) Agreements. Furthermore, the DSU explicitly requires the losing party to implement the recommendations of the panel within a reasonable time. Failure to do so entitles the complainant to request authorisation from the DSB, under Art 22, to take retaliatory trade measures by suspending concessions or other obligations under the covered agreements. The DSB, however, has no power to award any financial compensation. Where the parties cannot agree as to whether or not the measure in dispute has been brought into compliance with the covered agreements, Art 21.5 provides for the issue to be determined by compliance proceedings before a panel, preferably the original panel.

The net effect of these changes has been greatly to increase the authority of panel reports and to encourage WTO members to refer disputes to panels. This has lead to the development of a truly international law relating to trade

---

2   In contrast, DSU, Art 10 gives third-party members with a 'substantial interest' in the dispute a right to be heard.

3   *EC–Bananas III. European Communities–Regime for the Importation, Sale and Distribution of Bananas.* WT/DS/27/R/ECU, WT/DS/27/R/GTM, WT/DS/27/R/HND, WT/DS/27/R/MEX, WT/DS/27/R/US. Panel report 22 May 1997. WT/DS27/AB/R. Appellate body report 9 September 1997.

4   DSU, Art 19 provides that where there is a finding that a measure is inconsistent with one of the WTO agreements, the panel or appellate body shall recommend that the member concerned bring the measure into conformity with that agreement.

disputes between nations. In addition, the WTO has put in place an institutional framework within which members can discuss issues arising out of its agreements. There are at least five committees, whose competences overlap, in which issues relating to trade and the environment may be addressed. They are the Committee on Trade and Environment, the Committee on Sanitary and Phyto-sanitary Measures, the Committee on Technical Barriers to Trade, the TRIPS Council, and the Committee on Agriculture.[5] The Preamble to the WTO Agreement affords recognition to environmental considerations in its reference to:

> . . . allowing for the optimal use of the world's resources in accordance with the objective of sustainable development, seeking both to protect and preserve the environment and to enhance the means for doing so in a manner consistent with their respective needs and concerns at different levels of economic development.

The Preamble also recognises the need for 'positive efforts designed to ensure that developing countries, and especially the least developed among them, secure a share in the growth in international trade commensurate with the needs of their economic development . . .'. By way of contrast, the Preamble to GATT 1947 contained no such references and was wholly centred on economic and social factors.[6]

This chapter will now analyse the extent to which this emerging WTO jurisprudence has focused on trade issues to the exclusion of non-economic issues, such as public health and the protection of the environment.[7] This will involve an analysis of four issues. First, it must be established whether the measure in question actually violates one of the provisions of the GATT. Secondly, if a violation is established, it will be necessary to examine whether the measure can be justified by reference to the exceptions contained in

5 Discussions between members on these issues will also take place in *fora* outside the WTO, such as the Convention on Biological Diversity, the *Codex Alimentarius* Commission and the Food and Agriculture Organisation.
6 Such as, 'raising standards of living, ensuring full employment and a large and steadily growing volume of real income and effective demand, developing the full use of the resources of the world and expanding the production and exchange of goods . . .'.
7 On the general issue of the conflict between trade and the environment, see Charnovitz, S, 'Exploring the environmental exceptions in GATT Art XX' (1991) 25(5) JWT 37; Cameron, J, Demaret, P and Geradined, D, *Trade and the Environment. The Search for Balance*, 1994, London: Cameron & May Ltd; Ward, H, 'Common but differentiated debates. Environment, Labour and the World Trade Organisation' [1996] ICLQ 592, esp pp 601–6–7; Cameron, J and Campbell, K, 'Challenging the boundaries of the DSU through trade and environment disputes', in Cameron, J and Campbell, K (eds), *Dispute Resolution in the WTO*, 1998, London: Cameron & May Ltd, Chapter 10; Macmillan, F, *WTO and the Environment*, 2001, London: Sweet & Maxwell.

Art XX. Thirdly, a measure that is not in violation of the GATT may still generate a right to compensation by reference to the provisions of Art XXIII.1(b) on impairment of advantages. Fourthly, there is the issue of the relationship between trade restrictive measures that are imposed pursuant to a MEA and the rights of members under the WTO agreements.

1.1 Article I. Most-favoured-nation treatment

This article provides that 'any advantage, favour, privilege or immunity granted by any member to any product originating in or destined for any other country shall be accorded immediately and unconditionally to the like product originating in or destined for the territories of all other members'. This obligation applies with respect to 'customs duties and charges of any kind imposed on or in connection with importation or exportation or imposed on the international transfer of payments for imports or exports, and with respect to the method of levying such duties and charges'. It applies also with respect to 'all rules and formalities in connection with importation and exportation, and with respect to all matters referred to in paragraphs 2 and 4 of Article III'.

1.2 Article III. National treatment

Article III provides for national treatment on internal taxation and regulation. The basic principle is set out in Art III.1, as follows:

> The members recognize that internal taxes and other internal charges, and laws, regulations and requirements affecting the internal sale, offering for sale, purchase, transportation, distribution or use of products, and internal quantitative regulations requiring the mixture, processing or use of products in specified amounts or proportions, should not be applied to imported or domestic products so as to afford protection to domestic production.

The focus of Art III is on products rather than persons, but restrictions on persons may still come within its ambit if they have an affect on products. In *US–Section 337*[8] Art III applied because a factor determining whether or not a person was susceptible to US s 337 proceedings was the source of the challenged products. With PPM measures the panels in *US–Tuna Dolphin I*[9]

---

8   *US–Section 337 of the Tariff Act 1930.* BISD 36S/345. Panel report adopted 7 November 1989.
9   *US–Tuna Dolphin I. US–Restrictions on Imports of Tuna.* Panel report 16 August 1991. (1991) 30 ILM 1594.

and *US–Tuna Dolphin II*[10] were unclear as to whether Art III only covered product measures or whether it only permitted them. In *US–Auto Taxes* there was held to be no need to regulate the product directly.[11] It would be enough if the measure affected the conditions of competition between domestic and imported products. Therefore, measures which applied directly to producers or importers could affect the product. However, the panel also noted that the measures listed in Art III.4 related to the product as a product, from its introduction onto the market to its final consumption and did not relate directly to its producer. A similar principle applies to Art III.2 as regards taxes. The 1970 Working Party on Border Taxes stated that domestic taxes which applied to imports based on factors directly related to the product would be acceptable, but not those related to other factors, such as the income of producers. In *US–Auto Taxes* differential treatment was based on factors relating to the ownership and control of producers or importers and therefore violated Art III.2. The panel in *US–Reformulated Gasoline* held that to distinguish between refiners on the one hand and importers and blenders on the other hand, by reference to the data each held, was not permissible under Art III.4.[12]

Article III.2 then provides specific provisions relating to national treatment on taxes and internal charges. Article III.4 does likewise with regards to laws, regulations and requirements. How does the general principle in Art III.1 relate to these specific provisions? In *US–Beer* the GATT panel found that it was not appropriate to consider the more general provisions in Art III.1 if the measures were inconsistent with the more specific measures in Art III.2 and Art III.4.[13] The appellate body in *Japan–Alcohol*[14] was of the view that Art III.1 informs the interpretation of these provisions, but it also held in *EC–Bananas III*[15] that there was no need to determine a separate violation of Art III.1 in the event that there had been a violation of Art III.4. In *EC–Asbestos* the appellate body held that the reference to 'less favourable' treatment in Art III.4 expressed the general principle contained in Art III.1 that

10 *US–Tuna Dolphin II. US–Restrictions on Imports of Tuna.* DS29/R. Panel report 16 June 1994. (1994) 33 ILM 839.
11 *US–Auto Taxes. US–Taxes on Automobiles.* Panel report 11 October 1994. (1994) 33 ILM 1397.
12 *US–Reformulated Gasoline. US–Standards for reformulated and conventional gasoline.* WT/DS2/R. Panel report 29 January 1996. WT/DS2/AB/R. Appellate body report 29 April 1996.
13 *US–Beer. US–Measures affecting alcoholic and malt beverages.* DS23/R – 39S/206. Panel report 16 March 1992, adopted 19 June 1992, para 5.
14 *Japan–Taxes on Alcoholic Beverages.* WT/DS/8, 10–11/AB/R. Appellate body report 4 October 1996.
15 *EC–Bananas III. European Communities–Regime for the Importation, Sale and Distribution of Bananas.* WT/DS/27/R/ECU, WT/DS/27/R/GTM, WT/DS/27/R/HND, WT/DS/27/R/MEX, WT/DS/27/R/US. Panel report 22 May 1997. WT/DS27/AB/R. Appellate body report 9 September 1997.

internal regulations 'should not be applied . . . so as to afford protection to domestic production'.[16]

1.2.1 Article III.2. Internal taxes and charges

The general principle is applied to internal taxes and charges in Art III.2, the first sentence of which provides:

> The products of the territory of any member imported into the territory of any other member shall not be subject, directly or indirectly, internal taxes or other internal charges of any kind in excess of those applied, directly or indirectly, to like domestic products.

The first sentence requires a finding that a comparison can be made between a 'like' imported and domestic product and that taxes on imported products exceed those on their domestic equivalents. The second sentence then continues thus:

> Moreover, no member shall otherwise apply internal taxes or other internal charges to imported or domestic products in a manner contrary to the principles set forth in paragraph 1.

Annex 1 clarifies the effect of the second sentence of Art III.2 as follows:

> A tax conforming to the first sentence of paragraph 2 would be considered to be inconsistent with the provisions of the second sentence only in cases where competition was involved between, on the one hand, the taxed product and, on the other hand, a directly competitive or substitutable product that was not similarly taxed.

The second sentence also requires a finding of protective application in the way in which the measure is applied. The appellate body in *Japan–Alcohol* held that the magnitude of dissimilar taxation might evidence such protective application.[17]

Article III.2 has been considered in two disputes involving US taxes based on environmental criteria. The first case, *US–Taxes on Petroleum*,[18] arose out

---

16 *EC–Asbestos. European Communities–Measures Affecting Asbestos and Products Containing Asbestos.* WT/DS/135/R. Panel report 19 September 2000. WT/DS/135/AB/R. Appellate body report 12 March 2001.
17 *Japan–Taxes on Alcoholic Beverages.* WT/DS/8, 10–11/AB/R. Appellate body report 4 October 1996.
18 *US–Taxes on Petroleum and Certain Imported Substances.* 34th Supp. BISD 136, 1987. (1988) 27 ILM 1601.

of the US Superfund Amendments and Reauthorisation Act 1986. The Act aimed to tax polluting products to provide for their clean-up costs and contained a border tax adjustment to ensure that foreign importers of such products paid an amount equivalent to that paid by their US competitors. Domestic crude oil would be taxed at 8.2 cents per barrel, but imported petroleum products were taxed at 11.7 cents per barrel. Feedstock would be taxed in relation to imported downstream chemicals, namely the tax which would have been due on the chemical inputs had they been sold in the US. In the absence of information necessary to enable the US tax authorities to calculate this, there would be a penalty rate tax of 5 per cent of the value of the product as imported or, at the discretion of the Secretary of State for Trade, a rate equal to the amount due if the product were manufactured using its predominant mode of production.

The European Economic Community (EEC), Canada and Mexico jointly challenged the two taxes in 1987 as being inconsistent with Art III.2. As regards the differential tax rates on petroleum products, the panel adopted the suggestion of the 1970 Working Party on Border Taxes that in determining whether products were 'like' a comparison should be made of the end uses of the products in question. Domestic and foreign petroleum products were clearly 'like' as they had the same end uses.[19] The violation of Art III.2 then gave rise to a rebuttable presumption that there had been a nullification or impairment of benefits under Art XXIII. The panel found that in practice this presumption was irrebutable and rejected the US argument that the petroleum differential did not violate this provision as it had no, or only minimal, trade effects. The trade effects of a measure were irrelevant to the question of whether Art III.2 had been violated. Article III, instead, was focused on the establishment of certain competitive conditions as between imported and domestic products.

Turning now to the feedstock regulations, although these would not come into effect until 1 January 1989, Art III.2 required predictability and an immediate analysis of this prospective tax was required. The panel then held that the regulations constituted a valid border tax adjustment under Arts II and III. The panel rejected the argument made by the EEC that border tax adjustments did not apply to a tax to finance a specific service to benefit domestic producers or made necessary by their activities and which did not benefit foreign producers, who had not caused the need for the service. Nor did it matter that the tax departed from the 'polluter pays' principle adopted by the Organisation for Economic Co-operation and Development (OECD).[20] The GATT did not distinguish between the different policy purposes behind

---

19 *Report of the Working Party on Border Tax Adjustments.* BISD 18S/97. Adopted 2 December 1970.

20 The US argued that environmental taxes had to take account of the cost of disposing of imported chemicals.

a tax, and allowed, but did not mandate, the operation of the 'polluter pays' principle, for example, by taxing domestic producers only. Therefore, the tax was eligible for border adjustment. The penalty tax, however, was inconsistent with GATT's provisions on national treatment. However, the mere existence of the penalty did not amount to a violation, given that the US tax authorities were given authority to avoid the power to levy a penalty, by issuing regulations setting a tax based on the predominant mode of production.

The second decision is that in *US–Auto Taxes*.[21] Three measures were involved: a luxury tax imposed on cars above a $30,000 threshold; a gas-guzzler tax progressively imposed on cars that were unable to achieve 22.5 mpg; and a fleet averaging requirement. The panel held that Art III.1 informed both sub-rules 2 and 4. Article III.1 prohibited fiscal or regulatory distinctions between different products so as to afford protection to domestic production, but it did not prohibit fiscal or regulatory distinctions which were applied to achieve another policy goal. The first part of the analysis was to determine whether the particular distinction was made on the national origin of a product, in which case there would clearly be a violation of this principle. Assuming that was not the case, the next step was to ascertain whether the distinction was made on a product basis. If that was a case, one should then apply an aims and effect test to see if the measure tended to promote domestic production over foreign production as proscribed by Art III.1. Ascertaining the 'aims' of a measure meant analysing the instruments available to achieve the domestic policy goal and to see whether the change in competitive opportunities for domestic products was a desired outcome and not merely an incidental consequence of the pursuit of a legitimate policy goal. The 'effects' of a measure were to be ascertained by considering whether the measure afforded greater competitive opportunities to domestic products than to imports, although its impact on trade flows would not be relevant. This analysis would continue through into the next part of the test which involved consideration of whether the measure was 'so as to afford protection' to domestic production.

Applying this test, the panel held that the luxury tax on cars above a $30,000 threshold did not violate Art III.2. A determination of the aim behind the measure could not be based solely on preparatory statements by legislators that a threshold intentionally targetted foreign cars. One also had to examine the wording of the legislation as a whole. The policy objectives of raising revenue from the sale of luxury goods was consistent with setting a price threshold at a level at which only a small proportion of cars sold in the US would be taxed. The fact that a large percentage of cars imported from the EC, as opposed to imported cars generally, would fall over the threshold did not necessarily show a protectionist aim. The competitive conditions for

---

21 *US–Taxes on Automobiles*. Panel report 11 October 1994. (1994) 33 ILM 1397.

goods just above and just below the threshold did not differ markedly and it was very difficult to assess the proportion of foreign and domestic cars being sold in these bands, which indicated that the measure was not protectionist in its aim. As regards its effect, it did not create an inherent division of products into two categories, domestic and imported, there being no evidence that foreign car makers could not or did not manufacture and market cars below the threshold. Similar reasoning applied to the 22.5 mpg threshold. When the gas-guzzler tax was first introduced in 1978 most domestic cars were unable to meet the target. There was no evidence that the technology for meeting the target was inherent to the US and the regulatory distinction was consistent with the goal of reducing fuel consumption.

These findings meant that the wider, second sentence of Art III.2 was not violated, given the finding that these measures did not have the aim of affording protection to domestic production. This focus on intent has subsequently disappeared. Thus, in *EC–Asbestos* it was not a factor taken into account in assessing whether or not the measure had violated Art III.[22] However, the fleet averaging scheme, which was classified as a regulation rather than a tax, was held to violate Art III.4 in that it distinguished between cars, not as products, but on the basis of the location of their manufacturer. The decision in *US–Auto Taxes* therefore shows that 'eco-taxes' based on product criteria are acceptable, but not those based on production criteria, such as a carbon tax based on the energy consumed in manufacturing a product, even it were applied equally to domestic and imported products. This mirrors the findings of the Panel in *US–Tuna Dolphin II*, discussed below, that PPM criteria are not to be considered in determining the likeness of a product for the purpose of Art III.4.[23] The WTO Committee on Trade and Environment (CTE), on its website, summarises the position as follows:

> Under existing GATT rules and jurisprudence, 'product' taxes and charges can be adjusted at the border (i.e. when products are imported or exported), but 'process' taxes and charges by and large cannot. For example, a domestic tax on fuel can be applied perfectly legitimately to imported fuel. But a tax on the energy consumed in producing a ton of steel (a tax on the production process) cannot be applied to imported steel, even if it is charged on domestically produced steel, which could make the imported steel cheaper (and presumably less environmentally friendly). For this reason, there is some concern that the WTO rules

---

22 *EC–Asbestos. European Communities–Measures Affecting Asbestos and Products Containing Asbestos.* WT/DS/135/R. Panel report 19 September 2000. WT/DS/135/AB/R. Appellate body report 12 March 2001.

23 *US–Tuna Dolphin II. US–Restrictions on Imports of Tuna.* DS29/R. Panel report 16 June 1994. (1994) 33 ILM 839.

could affect the competitiveness of domestic producers when they face environmental process taxes and charges. Indeed, these concerns about competitiveness were widely reported to have been behind the European Commission's decision to abandon its proposal for a carbon tax in 1992.[24]

1.2.2 Article III.4. 'Laws, regulations and requirements'

Regulations are dealt with in Art III.4 as follows:

> The products of the territory of any member imported into the territory of any other member shall be accorded treatment no less favourable than that accorded to like products of national origin in respect of all laws, regulations and requirements affecting their internal sale, offering for sale, purchase, transportation, distribution or use.

The provision operates in a twofold manner. First, one must compare the imported product with a 'like' domestic equivalent. Secondly, one must determine whether or not the imported product is accorded treatment 'no less favourable' than that accorded to the domestic comparator.[25] Article III.4 has a wide scope, covering 'all laws, regulations and internal regulations affecting their internal sale . . .'. It covers all laws which govern the use and sale of the imported product once it has cleared customs and entered the country. The panel in *EC–Bananas III* stated that this provision goes beyond laws directly regulating or governing the sale of domestic and like imported products.[26] Account is to be taken of the Interpretative Note *ad* Art III which means that the mere fact that an internal charge is collected or a regulation enforced on an imported product at the time or point of importation does not necessarily take it outside the scope of Art III.

Until recently, environmental measures challenged under these provisions involved measures directed at the environmental harm involved in the production of the product, so called PPMs, rather than at any environmental harm that might follow from the introduction of the product into the importing state. The two GATT awards in the *US–Tuna Dolphin* dispute involved primary and secondary embargoes by the US on the import of tuna that had been caught by use of 'purse seine' nets which were of a type likely to catch Dolphins as well. The award in *US–Tuna Dolphin II* proceeded on the basis that the measure involved a breach of Art III.4 in that the embargoed tuna

---

24 www.wto.org/english/tratop_e/envir_e/cte03_e.htm (accessed 19 March 2007).
25 There then follows a proviso that: 'The provisions of this paragraph shall not prevent the application of differential internal transportation charges which are based exclusively on the economic operation of the means of transport and not on the nationality of the product.'
26 *EC–Bananas III*, para 7.175.

was 'like' the permitted tuna, notwithstanding the difference in the method by which it had been harvested.[27] The panel noted that: 'Article III calls for a comparison between the treatment accorded to domestic and imported like *products*, not for a comparison of the policies or practices of the country of origin with those of the country of importation.'[28] The panel, therefore, concluded that a distinction based on the differing harvesting policies of the importing and exporting countries had no effect on the inherent character of tuna as a product. Similarly in *US–Reformulated Gasoline*[29] imported gasoline was held to be 'like' domestic gasoline notwithstanding that there might be difficulties in obtaining data from the country of export regarding its quality.

Recently, the issue of whether well-substantiated concerns about the public health and environmental implications of the import of a product *within* the jurisdiction of the member imposing the measure could affect the analysis of its 'likeness' to substitute products came under scrutiny before the appellate body in *EC–Asbestos*.[30] The dispute involved a challenge by Canada to French Decree No 96–1133 concerning asbestos and products containing asbestos. Articles 1 and 2 contained prohibitions on asbestos and on products containing asbestos fibres, together with limited and temporary exceptions. Canada claimed that the Decree was inconsistent with GATT, Arts III and XI.[31] It also claimed that, under GATT, Art XXIII.1(b), the Decree, directly or indirectly, nullified or impaired advantages to Canada under the WTO Agreement or impeded the attainment of an objective of that agreement.

The panel ruled that the measure violated Art III.4 and that, having come to this conclusion, there was no need to consider the alternative claim of violation of Art XI. For the purposes of Art III.4 chrysotile asbestos fibres were 'like' polyvinyl alcohol fibres, cellulose and glass fibres (PCG fibres) and cement-based products containing chrysotile asbestos fibres were 'like' cement-based products containing one of the PCG fibres. In coming to this conclusion the panel used the four criteria set out in the *Report of the Working*

---

27 *US–Tuna Dolphin II. US–Restrictions on Imports of Tuna.* DS29/R. Panel report 16 June 1994. (1994) 33 ILM 839. In contrast, the panel in *US–Tuna Dolphin I* made its finding that the measure was inconsistent with GATT 1947 solely by reference to the fact that it violated Art XI. *US–Tuna Dolphin I. US–Restrictions on Imports of Tuna.* Panel report 16 August 1991. (1991) 30 ILM 1594.

28 Paragraph 5.8.

29 *US–Reformulated Gasoline. US–Standards for reformulated and conventional gasoline.* WT/DS2/R. Panel report 29 January 1996. WT/DS2/AB/R. Appellate body report 29 April 1996.

30 *EC–Asbestos. European Communities–Measures Affecting Asbestos and Products Containing Asbestos.* WT/DS/135/R. Panel report 19 September 2000. WT/DS/135/AB/R. Appellate body report 12 March 2001.

31 Canada also advanced a claim based on violation of TBT Agreement, Art 2, which is considered in the next chapter. Initially, Canada also argued that the Decree was inconsistent with SPS Agreement, Arts 2 and 5 but this claim was not pursued before the panel.

Party on Border Tax Adjustments,[32] namely: (i) the properties, nature and quality of the products; (ii) the end-uses of the products; (iii) consumers' tastes and habits; and (iv) the tariff classification of the products. The panel focused on market access and whether the products had the same applications and could replace each other for some industrial uses and concluded that chrysotile asbestos fibres were 'like' PCG fibres. The panel declined to introduce a criterion on the risk of the product. The fact that the products being compared did not have the same structure of chemical composition was not decisive of the issue of 'likeness' and neither was the unique nature of asbestos. The panel declined to apply a criterion relating to the health risks of the product.

The appellate body noted that this was its first opportunity to consider the meaning of 'like' in Art III.4, although the term appeared in many different provisions of the WTO agreements, and had been addressed in many GATT and WTO references. It was particularly important to note that in Art III.2, dealing with the internal tax treatment of imported and domestic products, the word 'like' had been narrowly construed so as to give effect to the second distinct obligation it imposes in respect of 'directly competitive or substitutable' products, an obligation which does not appear in Art III.4. The appellate body made the following analogy regarding the relationship between the different paragraphs in Art III. 'Given the textual difference between [the] Articles ... the "accordion" of "likeness" stretches in a different way in Article III.4.'[33]

Instead, the starting point for interpretation should be Art III.1 in which the general principle was set out. This was previously articulated by the appellate body in *Japan–Taxes on Alcoholic Beverages*, as imposing an obligation on members of the WTO, as follows:

> ... to provide *equality of competitive conditions for imported products in relation to domestic products* ... Article III protects expectations not of any particular trade volume but rather of the equal competitive relationship between imported and domestic products ...[34] (emphasis added)

Thus 'likeness' fundamentally depends on a determination about the nature and extent of a competitive relationship between and among products. A finding of 'likeness' on its own is not, however, sufficient to establish inconsistency with Art III.4. The complainant must also establish that the measure affords to the group of like imported products 'less favourable treatment' than it affords to the group of like domestic products. The drawing of distinctions

---

32 *Report of the Working Party on Border Tax Adjustments*. BISD 18S/97. Adopted 2 December 1970.

33 Paragraph 96.

34 *Japan–Taxes on Alcoholic Beverages*. WT/DS8/AB/R, 10–11/AB/R, paras 109 and 110. Appellate body report 4 October 1996.

between like products would not necessarily entail according to the group of 'like' *imported* products 'less favourable treatment than that accorded to the group of "like" *domestic* products'.[35]

The appellate body first stressed that the four criteria in the *Report of the Working Party on Border Tax Adjustments* merely provided a framework for analysing the 'likeness' of particular products on a case-by-case basis. The panel's use of this framework was criticised in that it had based its conclusion after examining only the first of the four criteria. In doing so, the panel had adopted a 'market access' approach that relied on the 'end-uses' of the products being compared, to overcome the fact that, based on physical properties alone, the products were not 'like'. Physical properties, however, deserved separate consideration from end-uses. The panel was also wrong in excluding from consideration risks posed by the product to human health. While this factor did not constitute a further criterion, evidence relating to it needed to be evaluated under the existing criteria of physical properties as well as of consumers' tastes and habits. The fact that chrysotile asbestos fibres were highly carcenogenic while PCG fibres did not share these properties to the same extent was a highly important physical difference between the products that had to be taken into account. Where the products at issue were physically quite different a higher burden was placed on the complainant 'to establish that, despite the pronounced physical differences, there is a competitive relationship between the products such that *all* of the evidence, taken together, demonstrates that the products are "like" . . .'.

The panel's analysis of the second criterion was flawed in that it essentially referred back to its analysis of 'properties' under the first criterion. It had declined to make a finding on the third criterion on the grounds that it would not provide clear results. The appellate body criticised this on the grounds that a panel could not come to such a conclusion without examining *any* evidence relating to this criterion. The tastes of consumers, even if defined as manufacturers, would be very likely to be shaped by the health risks of a product known to be highly carcinogenic, particularly bearing in mind their own potential civil liability arising out of the marketing of such a product. Canada had argued that this criterion was irrelevant to this dispute because the measure had disturbed normal conditions of competition between the products. The appellate body rejected this argument and said that it was always open to the complainant to submit evidence of latent, or suppressed, consumer demand in that market, or evidence of substitutability from some relevant third market.

The appellate body then criticised, on similar grounds, the panel's findings on the likeness of cement-based products containing chrsyotile and those containing PCG fibres. As regards physical properties, 'it cannot be ignored that one set of products contains a fibre known to be highly carcinogenic

---

35 Paragraph 100.

while the other does not'.[36] It then proceeded to complete the analysis of Art III.4. Taking into account the fact that since 1977 chrysotile asbestos fibres have been recognised internationally as a known carcinogen, and that PCG fibres are not classified by the World Health Organisation (WHO) at the same level of risk as them, it followed that physically the two substances are very different. In the absence of any evidence as to the nature and extent of the many end-uses for the two products that were not overlapping, the appellate body could not determine the significance of the fact that the two products shared a small number of similar end-uses.

Turning now to cement-based products, the fact that one class of product contained a known carcinogen, while the other did not, rendered them quite different, despite the apparent similarity in their physical properties. As regards end-uses, the appellate body stated:

> Thus, while we accept that the two different types of cement-based products may perform largely similar end-uses, in the absence of evidence, we cannot determine whether each type of cement-based product can perform with *equal* efficiency, *all* of the functions performed by the other type of cement-based product.

In the absence of any evidence as to consumer tastes, the appellate body could only speculate that 'the presence of a known carcinogen in one of the products will have an influence on consumers' tastes and habits regarding that product'.[37]

The decision in *EC–Asbestos* is significant in that it introduces health risks into the analysis of 'likeness'. The differing incidence of the burden of proof makes it important that such considerations form part of the analysis of Art III.4, where the burden lies on the party challenging the measure, and are not confined to the analysis of the exceptions under Art XX(b), where the burden falls on the party defending the measure.

However, the decision can be criticised in that the health risks involved were so well established that they should have been decisive of the issue of likeness. If Canada had produced more cogent evidence on 'end-uses', the second criterion, is it conceivable that the balance may have been shifted back towards a finding of 'likeness'? This point was picked up by one of the members of the appellate body who stated:

> It is difficult for me to imagine what evidence relating to economic competitive relationships as reflected in end-uses and consumers' tastes and habit could outweigh and set at naught the undisputed deadly nature of

36 Paragraph 128.
37 Paragraph 145.

chrysotile asbestos fibres, compared with PCG fibres, when inhaled by humans, and thereby compel a characterisation of 'likeness' of chrysotile asbestos and PCG fibres . . .[38]

1.3 Article XI. Quantitative restrictions on imports

This covers border measures which forbid importation as such. It states that:

> . . . no prohibitions or restrictions other than duties, taxes or other charges, whether made effective through quotas, import or export licenses or other measures, shall be instituted or maintained by any member on the importation of any product of the territory of any other member or on the exportation or sale for export of any product destined for the territory of any other member.

Unlike the provisions in Arts I and III this provision is of general application and makes no references to the 'likeness' of products. Exceptions are provided in Art XI.2, but these would not appear to cover an import ban based on public health or environmental risks associated with the product covered by the measure. It is, therefore, important to determine whether a measure falls under this heading or under Art III because Art XI contains no reference to 'like' products and forbids all quantitative restrictions on imports and exports, subject to its own limited list of exceptions, without reference to whether or not they are discriminatory.

With taxation, this issue involves a comparison between Art II which deals with tariffs and Art III.2 which deals with internal taxes and charges, and has entailed a formalistic approach focussing on whether the charge is due on importation or whether it is collected internally. As regards internal regulations, the issue arose in the two *US–Tuna Dolphin* awards.[39] The US argued that Art III.4 applied because the Interpretative Note *ad* Art III, in Annex 1 meant that the measures were to be regarded as internal regulations. The note states that:

> Any internal tax or other internal charge, or any law, regulation or requirement of the kind referred to in [Art III.1] which applies to an imported product and the like domestic product and is collected or enforced in the case of the imported product at the time or point of importation, is nevertheless to be regarded as an internal tax or other internal charge, or a law, regulation or requirement of the kind referred to in [Article III.1], and is accordingly subject to the provisions of Article III.

---

38 Paragraph 152.
39 *US–Tuna Dolphin I.* Panel report 16 August 1991. (1991) 30 ILM 1594. *US–Tuna Dolphin II* DS29/R. Panel report 16 June 1994. (1994) 33 ILM 839.

The panel, in both awards, disagreed. The note did not cover a measure applying equally to domestic producers, as opposed to products, and to imports. The import ban and the restriction on domestic producers did not lead to the same result for imported and domestically produced tuna. The note would cover only a border prohibition on imports to enforce an internal sales ban on both domestic and imported goods.[40] A measure of this nature was involved in *EC–Asbestos* where the import ban on asbestos was part of a wider measure banning the use of asbestos in France. The panel held that the note did not require an identical measure to be applied to the import and to its domestic equivalent, nor did it matter that domestic production of asbestos no longer existed. The measure led to the same result for both imported and domestic asbestos.[41] It was in everyone's interest to prohibit the entry of the like product, rather than letting it in and then banning its sale.

1.4 Article XX

If a complainant manages to establish that a measure is inconsistent with one or more of the provisions of the GATT, the respondent may still be entitled to maintain the measure provided it can proved that it falls within the terms of Art XX, the relevant parts of which read as follows:

> *General Exceptions*
> Subject to the requirement that such measures are not applied in a manner which would constitute a means of arbitrary or unjustifiable discrimination between countries where the same conditions prevail, or a disguised restriction on international trade, nothing in this Agreement shall be construed to prevent the adoption or enforcement by any member of measures:
>
> (a) necessary to protect public morals;
> (b) necessary to protect human, animal or plant life or health; . . .
> (d) necessary to secure compliance with laws or regulations which are not inconsistent with the provisions of this Agreement . . .
> (g) relating to the conservation of exhaustible natural resources if such measures are made effective in conjunction with restrictions on domestic production or consumption . . .

The opening paragraph, the *chapeau*, has proved to be just a significant as the individual exceptions contained in the separate sub-headings.

---

40 In *US–Shrimp Turtle*, WT/DS 58 R.1. (1998) 37 ILM 832, the US conceded that it had violated Art XI through a similar measure by which it refused permission for the import of shrimp from countries who had harvested shrimp without the use of TEDs.
41 *EC–Asbestos*. WT/DS/135/R. Panel report 18 September 2000, paras 8.91–8.96.

The limitations of Art XX in the context of environmental protection were made clear in three GATT references. The first, *Thailand–Cigarettes*,[42] involved a measure designed to protect human health *within* the territory of the state imposing the measure. Thailand had imposed restrictions on the import of foreign, mainly US, cigarettes on the ground that they contained chemicals and other additives that made them more harmful than cigarettes produced in Thailand.[43] While noting that the measure prima facie fell within the scope of sub-heading (b) and that Thailand was permitted to accord priority to human health over trade liberalisation, the panel found that the measure in question was not 'necessary'. The panel stated that:

> the import restrictions imposed by Thailand could be considered to be 'necessary' in terms of article XX(b) only if there were no alternative measures consistent with the General Agreement, or less inconsistent with, which Thailand could reasonably be expected to employ to achieve its health policy objectives.[44]

On the facts, Thailand's health policy objectives could reasonably have been met by alternative measures. Non-discriminatory labelling and a ban on imports of cigarettes containing harmful additives would satisfy its health policy objectives as regards the quality of cigarettes on sale in Thailand.[45] Its other objective of reducing the quantity consumed in Thailand would be met as effectively by a ban on advertising. In consequence, the measure in question could not be regarded as 'necessary'.

In contrast, the next two GATT references involved the applicability of Art XX (b) and (g) to trade regulations to achieve *extra-territorial* environmental objectives. They arose out of the *Tuna Dolphin* dispute between the US and Mexico and resulted in two unadopted awards. The US banned the import of tuna that had been caught by use of 'purse seine' nets which were of a type likely to catch Dolphins as well. Mexico, whose fishermen used this type of net, challenged the ban in *Tuna Dolphin 1*. The GATT panel held that Art XX(b) was limited to measures necessary to protect 'human, animal or plant life or health' *within* the territory of the state seeking to claim an exception for its regulation under this heading. Moreover, it did not cover an import ban based on the *process* by which the product was manufactured. A

---

42 *Thailand–Cigarettes. Thailand–Restrictions on importation of and internal taxes on cigarettes.* BISD 37 S/200–228. Panel report 7 November 1990. (1991) 30 ILM 1122. The panel adopted the reasoning used by a previous panel in *US–Section 337.* (1989) BISD 36S/345, para 5.26.

43 Thailand also relied on the fact that the US provided a composite list of additives contained in US cigarettes but did not give a breakdown for each brand.

44 Paragraph 75.

45 Although not mentioned by the panel, such a policy would be effective only once the US provided full information on additives for each brand exported.

similar result was reached in *Tuna Dolphin 2* in which US restrictions on the import of tuna from intermediary producers came under scrutiny, but for different reasons. The GATT panel found that Art XX (b) and (g) did not need to be construed so as to be limited to measures concerning 'human, animal or plant life or health' or 'conservation of exhaustible natural resources' *within* the territory of the regulating state. However, the panel found that because the measures adopted by the US would conserve dolphins only if exporting countries changed their fishing practices, the measure was neither 'necessary' under (b) nor related to 'the conservation of exhaustible natural resources' under (g).

Following the establishment of the WTO, the appellate body has had the opportunity, on three occasions, to consider the applicability of Art XX to trade restrictive measures whose justification is sought on environmental grounds. Each of these decisions will now be examined in some detail to show how they have contributed to the emergence of a more sophisticated analysis of the scope of Art XX that is better equipped to take account of legitimate policy decisions as regards public health and environmental protection.

1.4.1 US–Reformulated Gasoline[46]

The first of the three decisions involved a challenge by Venezuela and Brazil to the US in respect of its standards for reformulated and conventional gasoline. To implement the Clean Air Act 1990 the Environmental Protection Agency (EPA) introduced regulations to ensure that pollution from gasoline combustion did not exceed 1990 levels. Domestic refiners were required to set pollution baseline levels for 1990 and to ensure that these were not exceeded. However, such a system would work only if there existed easily available data from which to set each refiner's individual 1990 baseline levels. Accordingly, an alternative system was adopted for foreign refiners, where such data might be difficult to obtain, and for domestic refiners who commenced operations after 1990 or who had operated for less than 6 months in 1990. These two classes of refiners had to meet a statutory baseline calculated by reference to average gasoline quality in the US in 1990. Venezuela and Brazil challenged the statutory baseline system on the ground that it prevented them exporting gasoline that was in fact as clean as gasoline being produced by domestic refineries under the system of individual baselines. They alleged breaches of Arts I.1, III.1 and III.4 and claimed that the regulation was also contrary to TBT Agreement, Art 2. In response, the US argued that the regulation fell within subheadings (b), (d) and (g) of Art XX.

The panel found that the regulation violated Art III.4 as imported and

---

46 *US–Reformulated Gasoline. US–Standards for reformulated and conventional gasoline.* WT/DS2/R. Panel report 29 January 1996. WT/DS2/AB/R. Appellate body report 29 April 1996.

domestic gasoline were like products with the same physical characteristics, end-use and tariff classification. It was therefore unnecessary to rule on whether the regulation also breached Arts I.1 and III.1, and on its conformity with TBT Agreement, Arts 2.1 and 2.2. It also held that the measure could not be justified under by Art XX. As regards Art XX(b), although the measures were directed at the protection of human, animal or plant life or health they were not 'necessary' because there existed other possible methods of achieving the same goals that were less inconsistent with GATT, such as a single statutory baseline for all refiners or a more detailed examination of the production of foreign refiners.[47] Nor were the baseline rules covered by Art XX(d), as they were not themselves 'necessary' to secure compliance with the clean air laws. As regards Art XX(g), the panel accepted that clear air was a natural resource that could be depleted and so the measures were capable of falling under this sub-heading. However, the panel interpreted the words 'relating to' as meaning 'primarily aimed at'. On this basis the panel distinguished between the regulation itself and the baseline system by which it was to be implemented, stating that it saw 'no direct connection between less favourable treatment of imported gasoline that was chemically identical to domestic gasoline and the US objective of improving air quality in the US'. Accordingly, the baseline system fell outside Art XX(g).

The appeal was limited to the interpretation of Art XX(g). The appellate body held that the panel had erred in law in concluding that the baseline rules did not fall within this provision. It was of the view that the baseline rules could 'scarcely be understood if scrutinised strictly by themselves, totally divorced from other sections of the Gasoline Rule which certainly constitute part of the context of these provisions'. The appellate body also criticised the panel's decision on this point in that it appeared to have been influenced by its previous conclusions on the applicability of Art XX (b) and (d). It stressed that the words 'relating to' in (g) must bear a different meaning from the word 'necessary' in (b) and (d). In addition, the panel had erred in allowing its findings on Art XX (g) to be influenced by its initial finding that the measure did not comply with Art III.4.

However, the fact that a measure fell under Art XX(g) gave it only prima facie validity. The respondent still bore the burden of proving that the measure fell within the wording of the *chapeau* and the panel had also erred in failing to consider this issue. The appellate body's conclusion on this point was that the measure amounted to 'unjustifiable discrimination' and a 'disguised restriction on international trade' in the following two respects. First, the United States had failed adequately to explore means of mitigating the

---

47 Following the same reasoning used in *Thailand–Cigarettes. Thailand–Restrictions on importation of and internal taxes on cigarettes.* BISD 37S/200–228. Panel report 7 November 1990. (1991) 30 ILM 1122.

administrative problems in relation to data that had led the EPA to reject a system of individual baselines for foreign refiners. In this respect, it is worth noting that in 1994 Congress denied further funding requested by the EPA to enable it to define criteria by which foreign refiners could establish individual baselines. Secondly, the EPA had failed adequately to consider the costs to foreign refiners that a system of statutory baselines would entail. Both these factors had been cited by the panel as justifying its conclusion was not 'necessary' under Art XX (b) and (d). The effect of the appellate body's conclusion on the application of the *chapeau* is to remove much, if not all, of the force of its decision maintaining the linguistic distinction between 'relating to' and 'necessary'.

The decision shows just how difficult in can be to initiate environmental regulation that is 'WTO-proof'. The EPA's system represented a compromise between the interests of domestic and foreign refiners. It is ironic that had the EPA opted for a universal system of individual baselines, which Venezuela and Brazil strenuously opposed when it was mooted in 1994, that system would probably have lowered the amount of imported gasoline entering the US due to inability of foreign refineries to produce the data required to establish their individual baseline, and yet would probably not have contravened Art III.4 in the first place. In identifying two crucial omissions by the US, the appellate body gave little weight to the practical and administrative difficulties identified by the EPA. This highlights the difficulties of establishing a balance between trade and environment concerns in a treaty which is geared exclusively towards trade. A true balance can be achieved only in the context of a wider debate. Identifying alternative means of advancing environmental objectives should only one part of this process. One also needs to take into account the political, financial and administrative costs to the member state in adopting such alternative courses, and to consider whether such costs would be likely to result in the abandonment of the environmental measures altogether.

On 27 August 1997 the EPA reacted to the decision by promulgating revised guidelines that would allow, but not compel, foreign refiners to establish and use individual baselines. To avoid adverse environmental effects from the use of this option, the average quality of imported gasoline would be monitored, and in the event of a specified benchmark being exceeded, remedial action would be taken. The individual baseline option is dependent on the refineries' governments agreeing to subject the refineries to US inspection and enforcement authority. Alternatively, their gasoline could be regulated through their importer and subject to the importer's baseline which would probably be the statutory baseline.

1.4.2 US–Shrimp/turtle[48]

The second decision of the appellate body concerned the vexed question of the jurisdictional limits of the general environmental exceptions in Art XX. Whereas the regulation in *US–Reformulated Gasoline* was designed to achieve a domestic clean air policy, that in *US–Shrimp/Turtle* was designed to promote and international policy to promote the conservation of sea turtles.

US–Shrimp/Turtle concerned the US import ban, under US Endangered Species Act, s 609, on shrimps from countries who did not require their fisherman to use TEDs to prevent sea turtles from being accidentally caught in shrimping nets. The complainants, Thailand, India, Pakistan and Malaysia argued that the ban was inconsistent with GATT, Art XI which prohibited quantitative restrictions which were not duties, taxes or charges. The US response was to accept that there had been a violation of Art XI, but to justify the measure by reliance on Art XX (b) and (g). In contrast to the measures in the *Tuna Dolphin* references, the US could justify its extra-territorial measures as furthering the aims of an international convention on the environment to which the complainants were party. All seven species of sea turtles covered by the measure were classified as an endangered species under the Washington Convention on International Trade in Endangered Species 1973 (CITES). Although CITES neither permitted nor prohibited such measures and was geared solely to prohibition of *trade* in protected species, the US argued that its measures were clearly promoting the underlying purpose of the treaty in protecting endangered species.

The panel held that the 'Subject to . . .' proviso at the start of Art XX, the *chapeau*, required its exceptions to be interpreted in the light of the overall purpose of the treaty of securing trade liberalisation. A measure might appear to fall within the categories set out in Art XX, but still fall at the first hurdle if it fails to satisfy this initial requirement. The panel found that the overall purpose of GATT in facilitating liberalisation of world trade would be undermined by such measures because:

> . . . if one WTO member were allowed to adopt such measures, then other members would also have the right to adopt similar measures on the same subject but with differing, or even conflicting, requirements. If that happened, it would be impossible for exporting Members to comply at the same time with multiple conflicting policy requirements . . .[49]

---

48 *US–Shrimp/Turtle. United States–Import Prohibition of Certain Shrimp and Shrimp Products.* WT/DS/58/R. Panel report 15 May 1998. WT/DS/58/AB/R. Appellate body report 12 October 1998. See also, Mavroidis, P, 'Trade and the Environment after the Shrimp-Turtles legislation' (2000) 34(1) JWT 73.

49 In practice, compliance would generally be secured by conformity with the most demanding requirements enforced by importing states.

The panel was firmly of the view that extra-territorial environmental measures should be confined to international treaties. In this respect, it took a literal view of CITES as being strictly limited to prohibitions on trade in endangered species. The existence of the treaty did not, of itself, justify trade restrictions on non-protected species, even if the effect of such restrictions was to increase the protection of endangered species covered by CITES.

The appellate body rejected the panel's '*chapeau* first' approach of considering compliance with the *chapeau* before dealing with the question of whether the disputed measure was covered by the exceptions of Art XX. Instead, the proper approach was to consider whether a measure fell within an Art XX exception. If it did, it would have provisional validity, but it then needed to be tested to see whether the *manner* of its application was consistent with the chapeau. In adopting this approach, the appellate body reiterated the views it expressed in *US–Reformulated Gasoline*, where it stated:

> The analysis is, in other words, two-tiered: first, provisional justification by reason of characterisation of the measure under Article XX(g); second, further appraisal of the same measure under the introductory clauses of Article XX.

Applying these principles, the appellate body first turned to the question of whether s 609 fell within Art XX(g). This involved consideration of whether living creatures, such as sea turtles, could be considered as 'exhaustible natural resources'. The complainants argued that this term should be limited to finite resources such as minerals and that the protection of living creatures should be confined to Art XX(b). The appellate body was not convinced by these arguments. Textually, Art XX(g) was not limited to the conservation of mineral, or 'non-living' resources. The appellate body observed that:

> One lesson that modern biological sciences teach us is that living species, though in principle, capable of reproduction and, in that sense, 'renewable', are in certain circumstances susceptible of depletion, exhaustion and extinction, frequently because of human activities. Living resources are just as 'finite' as petroleum, iron ore and other non-living resources.[50]

Although Art XX(g) had been drafted more than 50 years ago and had not been modified in the Uruguay Round, its terminology was not static, but, rather, evolutionary. Support for this approach was derived from the wording in the preamble of WTO Agreement, which covered not only GATT, but also the side agreements, which explicitly acknowledged 'the objective of sustainable development, seeking both to protect and preserve the environment and

50 Paragraph 133.

to enhance the means for doing so'. The appellate body reinforced its conclusions by references to the fact that many modern international conventions make frequent references to natural resources as embracing both living and non-living resources. They pointed in particular to Arts 56, 61 and 62 of the United Nations Convention on the Law of the Sea 1982 (UNCLOS) as well as to the Convention on Biological Diversity 1992 and to Agenda 21. These provisions demonstrated a recent acknowledgment by the international community 'of the importance of concerted bilateral or multilateral action to protect living natural resources'. Taking this into account, together with the reference to 'sustainable development' in the preamble to the WTO Agreement, the appellate body held that 'in line with the principle of effectiveness in treaty interpretation, measures to conserve exhaustible natural resources, whether *living* or *non-living*, may fall within Article XX(g)'.

The analysis then turned to the question of whether the living natural resources which the measure sought to conserve could be considered 'exhaustible'. The appellate body held that it would be very difficult to controvert such a proposition given that all seven recognised species of sea turtle were currently listed in Appendix 1 of CITES which includes 'all species threatened with extinction which are or may be affected by trade'. The appellate body then observed that the sea turtle species covered by s 609 were highly migratory animals and were all known to occur in waters over which the US exercised jurisdiction. It stated:

> We do not pass upon the question of whether there is an implied jurisdictional limitation in Article XX(g), and if so, the nature or extent of that limitation. We note only that in the specific circumstances of the case before us, there is a sufficient nexus between the migratory and endangered marine populations involved and the US for the purpose of Article XX(g).

The appellate body then moved to the issue of whether s 609 could be said to be a measure 'relating to' the conservation of sea turtles. This required an examination of the proportionality of the measure in its scope and reach in relation to the policy objective of protection and conservation of sea turtles. The appellate body concluded that s 609 was in principle reasonably related to the legitimate policy of conserving an exhaustible and, in fact, endangered species. Section 609 was also even-handed in that since 1990 regulations had required US shrimp trawlers to use approved TEDs 'in areas and at times when there is a likelihood of intercepting sea turtles'. Accordingly, s 609 was a measure made effective in conjunction with the restrictions on domestic harvesting of shrimp. Having concluded that s 609 prima facie fell within Art XX(g) there was no need to consider the application of Art XX(b) as the US had invoked this exception only as a fall back position in the event that the measure was found not to fall within Art XX(g).

Once s 609 was found to have prima facie validity under Art XX(g), its conformity with the *chapeau* then fell to be tested. The appellate body concluded that the measure was not entitled to the protection of Art XX for the following reasons. First, s 609 had been applied in a manner constituting 'unjustifiable discrimination between countries where the same conditions prevail'. The practical application of the measure, under the 1996 Guidelines for the application of s 609, required harvesting countries to have not merely comparable regulatory programmes to those of the US but identical ones. The US should have taken into account different considerations which might occur in the territories of other countries. The appellate body pointed to the fact that shrimp caught using TEDs comparable in effectiveness to those required in the US would be denied entry into the US if originating in the waters of a country not certified under s 609.

The US was also criticised for failing to make adequate efforts to secure international agreement before introducing its embargo. Although the US did negotiate the 1996 Inter-American Convention with Brazil, Costa Rica, Mexico, Nicaragua and Venezuela to deal with the protection of sea turtles, it made no efforts to negotiate similar agreements with other harvesting countries. Furthermore, s 609 was applied in a way that resulted in differential treatment among members requiring certification in that the 1991 and 1993 Guidelines had allowed 14 countries in the wider Caribbean/West Atlantic region a three-year phase-in period whereas the 1996 Guidelines gave only a four-month period. Although the latter were the direct result of a decision of the US Court of International Trade, the US as a WTO member was held responsible for the actions of its judiciary. Furthermore, the US had made greater efforts to transfer TED technology to those 14 countries than to other members.

Secondly, the inflexible requirements for certification contained in the 1996 Guidelines, coupled with the singularly informal certification process adopted by the US amounted to 'arbitrary discrimination between countries where the same conditions prevail'. In reaching this conclusion, the appellate body was strongly influenced by the lack of any formal opportunity for an applicant country to be heard or respond to any arguments made against it in the course of the certification process, contrary to the 'due process' requirements of Art X.3 which required transparency and procedural fairness in the administration of trade regulation.

The US reacted to the decision of the appellate body by amending its 1996 Guidelines on 8 July 1999 so as to permit greater flexibility in allowing imports of shrimp from countries that had put in place regulatory programmes *comparable in effectiveness* to those of the US. The US also continued to make concerted international efforts to conclude an international agreement on turtle conservation, along the lines of the Inter-American Convention, for the Indian Ocean and South East Asian Regions.

In October 2001 the appellate body upheld the decision of the panel, in compliance proceedings brought by Malaysia, to the effect that the measure was now in conformity with the GATT.[51] The appellate body stressed that, for the purposes of the *chapeau*, there was no requirement that an international environmental agreement be concluded with the complainant; it was sufficient that the US had made substantial efforts towards negotiating such an agreement. The flexibility in the Revised Guidelines was such that the US would be enabled to take into account the particular conditions prevailing in Malaysia, if and when Malaysia applied for certification. The *chapeau* did not require the Revised Guidelines to provide explicitly for the specific conditions prevailing in Malaysia. The appellate body's finding was not altered by the fact that the US Court of International Trade had ruled that the part of the Revised Guidelines which permitted TED-caught shrimp to be imported from non-certified countries was contrary to s 609. As stated by the panel, the ruling was declaratory and the Court of International Trade had not ordered the US Department of State to modify either the content or the interpretation of the Revised Guidelines.[52]

1.4.3 EC–Asbestos[53]

The third decision has already been discussed in connection with the issue of initial inconsistency with the GATT. The panel had found that the French measure prohibiting the import and use of products containing asbestos involved a breach of Art III.4, but could be justified under Art XX(b). The appellate body overruled the first part of this finding, but upheld the second part, providing a useful clarification as to the scope of Art XX(b).

First, the appellate body dealt with the evidential burden imposed on a member that seeks to rely on this exception. Members were not required to place automatic reliance the current majority scientific opinion, when setting health policy. Instead reliance might be placed, 'in good faith, on scientific sources which, at that time, may represent a divergent, but qualified and respected, opinion'. It followed that the panel was not necessarily obliged to decide whether or not Art XX(b) applied, on the basis of the 'preponderant' weight of the evidence.[54] Nor was the panel itself required to quantify the risk of the products affected by the measure. Article XX(b) did not require the quantification, as such, of the risk to human life or health. A risk may be evaluated in either quantitative or qualitative terms. The panel had not merely

---

51 *US–Shrimp/Turtle. United States–Import Prohibition of Certain Shrimp and Shrimp Products. Recourse to Article 21.5 by Malaysia.* WT/DS58/RW. Panel report 15 June 2001. WT/DS58/AB/RW. Appellate body report 22 October 2001.

52 Paragraph 95.

53 *EC–Asbestos. European Communities–Measures Affecting Asbestos and Products Containing Asbestos.* WT/DS/135/R. Panel report 19 September 2000. WT/DS/135/AB/R. Appellate body report 12 March 2001.

54 Paragraph 178.

relied on the 'hypotheses' of the risk presented by the French authorities, but had found, on the basis of the scientific evidence before it that 'no minimum threshold of level of exposure or duration of exposure has been identified with regard to the risk of pathologies associated with chrysotile, except for asbestosis'.

Secondly, members were entitled to determine their chosen level of health protection and France had determined that this should be such as to effect a complete 'halt' to the spread of asbestos-related health risks. It was entitled to set this level of protection, even though the substitute product, PCG fibres, might also pose a threat to health. In any event the scientific evidence before the panel showed that this health risk was less than that posed by chrysolite asbestos fibres.

Thirdly, members were not obliged to accept an alternative measure that would have the effect of negating their chosen level of public health protection. Canada had argued that 'controlled use' of the prohibited products was a reasonably available alternative to the decree. The appellate body rejected Canada's argument that 'controlled use' would only cease to be 'reasonably available' if it proved impossible to implement. In *US–Reformulated Gasoline* the panel had merely held that a measure did not cease to be reasonably available merely because it would involve administrative difficulties for a member.[55] The appellate body then referred to its previous decision *Korea–Beef*[56] in which the meaning of 'necessary' under Art XX(d) had come under scrutiny. This involved a 'weighing and balancing process' which required determination of the extent to which the alternative measure 'contributes to the realisation of the end pursued'.[57] The 'more vital or important [the] common interests or values pursued' the easier it would be to accept as 'necessary' measures designed to achieve those ends.[58] In the present case, the value pursued by France in its measure was 'both vital and important in the highest degree'. France could not be expected to use Canada's alternative 'controlled use' measure as this would prevent France from achieving its chosen level of health protection in securing the halt of asbestos-related illness. The scientific evidence before the panel showed that the efficacy of 'controlled use' remained to be demonstrated. Its efficacy was particularly doubtful for the building industry and DIY enthusiasts, the most important users of cement-based products containing chrysotile asbestos.

---

55 The panel's findings on this point were not appealed so the appellate body did not have the opportunity to address the point in the case.
56 *Korea–Beef. Korea–Measures affecting imports of fresh, chilled and frozen beef.* WT/DS161/AB/R, WT/DS169/AB/R. Appellate body report 11 December 2000.
57 Paragraphs 166 and 163.
58 Paragraph 162.

1.5 Article XXIII:1(b)

In *EC–Asbestos* the panel found that Canada was entitled to make a claim under this article, notwithstanding that the measure involved no violation of GATT 1994, given that it fell within Art XX(b). The threshold question of whether a measure which involved no breach of the GATT, and, in particular, one which fell within Art XX(b) was appealed to the appellate body which upheld the finding of the panel on the following two analyses of the wording of the article. First, the text stipulates that a claim under Art XXIII.1(b) stipulates that a claim thereunder arises when a 'benefit' is being 'nullified or impaired' through the 'application of . . . any measure, *whether or not it conflicts with the provisions of this Agreement*' (emphasis added). Secondly, there could be no exception carved out in favour of measures pursuing health, rather than commercial, objectives because of the use of the words '*any measure*' (emphasis added) in the article. In any event such a distinction would be very difficult to draw in practice.

As Canada did not appeal the panel's finding that its claim failed on the merits, this issue was not considered by the appellate body. However, the panel's reasons for its decision merit close examination. While not accepting the EC's argument that a measure falling within Art XX could never be the subject of a claim under Art XXIII:1(b), the panel nevertheless regarded recourse to this article as particularly exceptional in these circumstances. Where the measure was within Art XX the complainant would be subject to a stricter burden of proof than would otherwise be the case, particularly with regard to the establishment of its legitimate expectations and whether or not the measure could reasonably have been anticipated. In this regard the panel rejected Canada's argument that it should be entitled to the presumption referred to in *Japan–Films*[59] that, if a measure is shown to have been introduced after the conclusion of the tariff negotiations in question, the complainant should not be considered as having anticipated the measure.[60]

Applying *Japan–Films* a complainant had to prove first the application of a measure by a member of the WTO. This was not in dispute in this case. Secondly, it had to establish the existence of a benefit accruing under the applicable agreement. 'Benefit' referred to a legitimate expectation of improved market access opportunities resulting from the relevant tariff concessions. In considering the issue of whether Canada could reasonably have anticipated the French Decree, the panel decided it would focus on those circumstances that had led France to adopt a measure that was justified under Art XX(b). It was clear that any import ban must upset the competitive relationship between products containing Canadian chrysotile and products containing

---

59 *Japan–Films. Japan–Measures affecting consumer photographic film and paper*. WT/DS44/R. Panel report 31 March 1998.
60 Indeed, this was only one of the tests applied by the panel in *Japan–Films*.

substitute fibres. The panel therefore moved onto consider whether the measure could reasonably have been anticipated by the Canadian Government at the time it was negotiating the tariff concessions. These were the concessions established in 1947 with the establishment of the GATT and those established in 1994 and the conclusion of the Uruguay Round leading to the establishment of the WTO. In addition, there were concessions with the EC negotiated in 1962.

The panel pointed to the substantial time lag between the 1947 and 1962 concessions and the implementation of the decree. It was up to Canada to present detailed evidence as to why in 1947 and 1962 it could not reasonably have anticipated that such measures might be brought into force after 50 or 35 years respectively. Canada had failed to present such evidence.

As regards the 1994 concessions, the presumption in *Japan–Films* would not be applied. There the measure concerned the organisation of the Japanese domestic market which a third party might find surprising and hard to anticipate. In contrast, the French Decree was a health measure which fell within Art XX(b). At the time of the 1994 concessions the hazardous nature of asbestos was well known. In 1977 the WHO had classified it as a category I carcinogen. In 1990, Commission Directive (90/394/EEC) provided for the replacement of asbestos. The substance was banned by other WTO members long before the French Decree. In these circumstances in 1994 Canada could have reasonably anticipated not only some restriction on the import of asbestos by another WTO member, but also a complete ban. Nor was the decree invalidated by the inconsistency alleged by Canada in that an import ban had not been imposed on products containing other similarly hazardous material, such as lead and copper. To accept this argument would require of a member an 'all or nothing' approach that would be impossible to realise in practice and would considerably facilitate the bringing of claims under Art XXIII.1(b). Given these findings there was no need for the panel to consider the third element that had to be shown to establish a claim under this article, namely, the nullification or impairment of a benefit as a result of the application of the measure.

The appellate body's finding is welcome but still raises the possibility that, in exceptional circumstances, Art XXIII.1(b) will still apply to a measure, notwithstanding that it falls within Art XX(b). A key feature of the finding was that the risks associated with asbestos and the likely changes in policy relating to it in member states were foreseeable due to the advance in scientific knowledge over a substantial period of time. However, if there were to be an unexpected discovery of a health risk and a sudden, *unforeseeable*, import prohibition, it is likely that such a measure would be caught by Art XXIII.1(b).

1.6 The WTO agreements and MEAs

The relationship between the WTO Agreements and other international agreements relating to the environment, such as CITES,[61] the Montreal Convention[62] and the Basel Convention is a vexed and uncertain issue.[63] There is no provision in the WTO Agreements equivalent to NAFTA, Art 104 which expressly subordinates its provisions to those contained in these other international agreements.[64] GATT, Art XXV.5 provides a procedure for members to waive the obligations of a member. Alternatively, each MEA could be the subject of a waiver pursuant to WTO Treaty, Art IX.3. To date, neither of these provisions has been utilised to effect a waiver in respect of a MEA and the position is unlikely to change in the future.

The problem arises when the MEA mandates measures such as a prohibition on imports or exports of a product. A party to the MEA which gives effect to this requirement will, at the same time, be involved in a breach of its obligations towards other members under the WTO agreements. Moreover, the MEA may go further than mandating certain trade restrictions. It may also authorise a party to apply stricter restrictions than those mandated. CITES, Art XIV.1 has this effect and in recent years has led to parties such as Zimbabwe considering recourse to arbitration under the DSU to challenge restrictions which are not mandated by CITES but are justified only by reference to this provision. The problem with MEAs becomes more acute when they impose prohibitions on trade in certain products with states that are not a party to the MEA.

The Doha Ministerial Declaration of November 2001, para 31 mandated an examination of this issue, but limited its scope to the applicability of existing WTO rules as between parties to the MEA in question. There will be no negotiations regarding the WTO rights of any member that is not a party to the MEA in question. These negotiations have been conducted in the Committee on Trade and Environment, which has produced a comprehensive summary of selected MEAs with an analysis of their possible impact on members' rights under the WTO agreements.[65]

---

61 Convention on International Trade and Endangered Species of Wild Fauna and Flora 1973.
62 Montreal Protocol on Substances that Deplete the Ozone Layer 1987.
63 Basel Convention on the Control of Transboundary Movements of Hazardous Waste and their Disposal 1989.
64 However, Art 104 is subject to the proviso that 'where a Party has a choice among equally effective and reasonably available means of complying with those obligations', that party must choose 'the means that is least inconsistent with the other provisions of this Agreement'. The proviso probably has an effect similar to that imported into GATT, Art XX(b) by the word 'necessary'.
65 WT/CTE/W/160/Rev.4 TN/TE/S/5/Rev.2 Matrix on Trade measures pursuant to selected Multilateral Environmental Agreements. Current revision, 14 March 2007.

1.6.1 Jurisdictional overlap

A country affected by a trade restrictive measure, for which justification was claimed under the provisions of a MEA, would be faced with a choice between challenging it either under the dispute settlement proceedings of the MEA in question or under the DSU. The factual material before the tribunals might be identical but the legal regime to be applied would be very different. In the first example, the issue would be whether the measure was in conformity with the MEA in question. In the second example, the issue would be whether or not the measure was compliant with the WTO agreements. Although the issue of the measure's conformity with the MEA might well have a significant impact on the panel's analysis of its conformity with the WTO agreements, the fact remains that the two situations would require an analysis of the measure with reference to two different international agreements.[66]

The CTE in its 1996 Report[67] recommended that 'if a dispute arises between WTO Members, Parties to an MEA, over the use of trade measures they are applying between themselves pursuant to the MEA, they should consider trying to resolve it through the dispute settlement mechanisms available under the MEA'. This is thoroughly sensible advice, but there is nothing in the DSU that requires the exhaustion of a mechanism in a MEA before commencing proceedings in which it claimed a violation of its rights under one of the WTO agreements.[68] Once proceedings are underway, there is nothing in the DSU that would entitle a panel to delay a hearing until conclusion of the proceedings under the MEA. Indeed, Art 23.1 of the DSU obliges members who 'seek the redress of a violation of obligations or other nullification or impairment of benefit under the covered agreements' to 'have recourse to, and abide by, the rules and procedure of this understanding'. This is reinforced by Art 23.2(a), which provides that members shall:

> not make a determination to the effect that a violation has occurred, that benefits have been nullified or impaired or that the attainment of any objective of the covered agreements has been impeded, *except through recourse to dispute settlement in accordance with the rules and proceedings of this Understanding* . . . (emphasis added).

---

66 For a detailed analysis of this point, see Marceau, G, 'Conflicts of Norms and Conflicts of Jurisdictions – The Relationship between the WTO Agreements and MEAs and Other Treaties' (2001) 35(6) JWT 1081.

67 WT/CTE/1, para 178.

68 SPS Agreement, Art 11.3 preserves the rights of members under 'other international agreements, including the right to resort to the good offices of the dispute settlement mechanism of other international organisations or established under any international agreement'. However, the wording is permissive and does not preclude a reference under the DSU by one member in the event that another member has exercised its rights to invoke the dispute settlement mechanism provided for under another treaty to which both members are party.

This leaves open the possibility that a WTO panel might come to a different conclusion on the validity of a measure under the MEA, as part of the process of determining whether or not there had been a violation of the complainant's rights under the WTO agreements, from that subsequently reached under the MEA proceedings. This embarrassing possibility nearly materialised in *Chile–Swordfish*,[69] which involved a challenge to a Chilean swordfish conservation measure under GATT, Art V and a Chilean response by initiating the dispute settlement provisions of UNCLOS. The parties subsequently reached an agreement to suspend both references.

One way in which such an impasse might be resolved would be by reference to the obligation set out in Vienna Convention 1969, Art 26 that: 'Every treaty in force is binding upon the parties to it and must be performed by them in good faith.' DSU, Art 3.10 also provides that 'if a dispute arises, all Members will engage in these procedures in good faith in an effort to resolve the dispute'. If the complainant in the WTO proceedings were to argue that the non-conformity of the measure under the MEA was the reason why there had been a violation of its rights under the WTO agreements, a panel might accept that 'good faith' required deferral of a hearing until a determination of the issue under the MEA proceedings. However, such an argument would not apply if the complainant were to argue that, irrespective of the conformity or otherwise of the measure with the MEA, there had still been a violation of its rights under the WTO agreements.

The problem is not so acute where the matter comes before a WTO panel after an adjudication on the issue by the MEA tribunal. In this situation it is likely that a panel would take advantage of its right under Art 13.1 'to seek information and technical advice from any individual or body which it deems appropriate'. This would enable it to take account of the adjudication of the MEA tribunal as evidence in the dispute before it, to the extent to which the allegation of violation of rights under the WTO agreements is dependent upon the issue of whether the measure was in conformity with the MEA.

1.6.2 Substantive conflict

The DSU makes it clear that the law to be applied by panels is exclusively that provided in the WTO agreements. Article 3.2 provides that:

> Members recognise that it serves to preserve the rights and obligations of Members *under the covered agreements*, and to clarify the existing provisions of those agreements in accordance with customary rules of interpretation of public international law. Recommendations and rulings of

---

69 *Chile–Swordfish. Chile–Measures affecting the transit and importation of swordfish.* WT/DS 193.

the DSB *cannot add or diminish the rights and obligations* provided in the covered agreements. (emphasis added)

This is reinforced by Art 7.2 which states that: 'Panels shall address the relevant provisions in any covered agreement or agreements cited by the parties to the dispute.' Article 11 provides that:

The function of panels is to assist the DSB in discharging its responsibilities under this Understanding and the covered agreements. Accordingly, a panel should make an objective assessment of the matter before it ... and make such other findings as will assist the DSB in making the recommendations or in giving the rulings provided for *in the covered agreements*. (emphasis added)

These provisions would prevent a panel from making a ruling that a MEA constituted a modification of the WTO agreements when the parties to the WTO dispute were both parties to the MEA, in accordance with Vienna Convention 1969, Art 41. Nor would there be any scope for the application of Vienna Convention, Art 30.2[70] as, unlike NAFTA,[71] none of the WTO agreements contains any savings provision in favour of any MEA. It is also highly probable that there would be no scope for the application of the principle of *lex posterior* under Vienna Convention, Art 30.3. The wording of the DSU would seem to rule out a panel concluding that, as between the parties before it, provisions of a WTO agreement no longer applied, because provisions of an MEA that was concluded later in time prevailed. Although DSU, Art 3.2 contains a reference to the 'customary rules of interpretation of public international law', it is questionable whether *lex posterior* can be regarded as such a rule of interpretation, given that it does not appear in section three of the Vienna Convention that deals with *interpretation* of treaties, appearing instead in section two which deals with the *application* of treaties.

One must also take into account the attitude of the appellate body to customary international law. Although in *US–Shrimp/Turtle* it interpreted GATT, Art XX(g) in the light of other international conventions, in *EC–Beef Hormones* it also stated that, if the precautionary principle had become part of customary international law, it would not override the specific provisions of the SPS Agreement.[72] In any event, there could be no question of

---

70 This provides that: 'When a treaty specifies that it is subject to, or that it is not to be considered as incompatible with, an earlier or later treaty, the provisions of that other treaty prevail.'
71 Under Art 104.
72 See, also, *Korea–Measures affecting government procurement*. WT/DS163/R. Panel report 1 May 2000. The panel stated at para 7.96 that: 'Such international law applies to the extent that the WTO treaty agreements do not "contract out" from it.'

the application of *lex posterior* where only one of the parties to the WTO proceedings was also a party to a MEA.[73]

That would still leave a panel with recourse to 'customary rules of interpretation of public international law'. It is arguable that *lex specialis*, whereby specific provisions in one treaty prevail over general provisions in another, constitutes one such rule. Reference could also be made to Vienna Convention, Art 31 of which provides a 'General rule of interpretation'. Paragraph 3 provides:

> There shall be taken into account, together with the context:
>
> (a) any subsequent agreement between the parties regarding the interpretation of the treaty or the application of its provisions;
> (b) any subsequent practice in the application of the treaty which establishes the agreement of the parties regarding its interpretation;
> (c) any relevant rules of international law applicable in the relations between the parties.

Sub-headings (a) and (b) could be regarded as re-introducing a diluted version of *lex posterior* into treaty interpretation. A WTO panel could 'take into account' the provisions of a subsequent MEA for the purposes of interpreting the parties' rights and obligations under a MEA. Sub-heading (c) could also justify such a conclusion, irrespective of whether the MEA was concluded before or after the relevant WTO agreement.[74] Having taken the provisions into account, it could then conclude, on a case-by-case basis, that a measure taken in conformity with the MEA could be presumed to be compliant with the WTO agreements, without coming to a formal conclusion that those agreements had been modified, as between the parties to the dispute.

Applying these rules of interpretation, a panel could apply a *de facto* presumption that a measure that was justified in conformity with a MEA to which both disputants were a party would fall within the ambit of the exceptions provided in GATT, Art XX. This would obviate the need of finding that there was an irreconcilable conflict between the two treaties that would require the panel to make a finding that the MEA prevailed over one of the WTO agreements, a finding it would lack the capacity to make under the DSU. This conclusion can be supported by the fact that in *US–Shrimp/Turtle*, when considering the ambit of the *chapeau*, the appellate body stressed the importance of attempting to conclude multilateral agreements before

---

73 Vienna Convention, Art 30.4(b).
74 The establishment of the WTO in 1994 causes some difficulty in establishing which would be the 'later' treaty in a conflict between a MEA and one of the WTO agreements. Suppose the MEA was the Basel Convention 1989 and the complainant alleged a breach of the provisions of GATT, would the Basel Convention be the later treaty in that it was concluded after GATT 1947, or would GATT 1947 as it forms part of the agreements under GATT 1994?

taking unilateral measures, without actually stating that the existence of such an agreement would be definitive for the purposes of the analysis required under Art XX. If a bona fide attempt at negotiation is sufficient to satisfy the requirements of the *chapeau*, then, *a fortiori*, so must a successfully concluded negotiation of a MEA with the complainant.

It must be stressed, however, that such an approach can be applied only on a case-by-case basis. The facts of a particular dispute might still lead a panel to conclude that the measure, although authorised by the MEA, fell foul of the *chapeau* in that there existed less trade-restrictive means of achieving the environmental objective behind the measure. This might particularly be so in the case of measures justified by reference to permissive provisions of a MEA such as CITES, Art XIV.1.[75] If an importing member relied on this provision to continue to refuse entry to products from a species, trade in which was permitted under CITES, a panel might well conclude that protection of that species was better served by limited trade in it rather than by a complete embargo on importation.

Where only one of the parties to the WTO dispute is also a party to a MEA, there is much less likelihood that justification of the measure under the MEA will affect the analysis brought to bear on the alleged violation of rights under the WTO agreements. Vienna Convention, Art 34 provides that: 'A treaty does not create either obligations or rights for a third State without its consent.' However, there may be such a widespread adherence to a MEA in the global community that its provisions become part of customary international law, in which case, Vienna Convention, Art 38 provides that: 'Nothing in articles 34 to 37 precludes a rules set forth in a treaty from becoming binding upon a third State as a customary rule of international law.' Even if a rule in a MEA has not yet become part of customary international law, the existence of a MEA, to which the complainant is not a party, might form part of the factual material considered by the panel in deciding whether or not the measure fell within the scope of one of the exceptions provided for in GATT, Art XX. Some limited support for this proposition can be derived from the approach adopted by the appellate body in *US–Shrimp/Turtle* in taking into account a variety of international instruments in determining whether the US measure could prima facie be regarded as a measure 'relating to the conservation of exhaustible natural resources'. In particular, the appellate body took into account the conservation aims of CITES, even though this dealt solely with trade in endangered species, and did not extend to their protection through measures such as the TED requirement in the US measure.

---

75 This authorises parties to adopt '(a) stricter domestic measures regarding the conditions for trade, taking, possession or transport of specimens of species included in Appendices I, II and III, or the complete prohibition thereof, or (b) domestic measures restricting or prohibiting trade, taking possession or transport of species'.

This issue recently came to be considered in *EC–Biotech*. The dispute arose out of the EC's moratorium on approval of GMOs between 1998 and 2003 and the existence of prohibitions at national level on GMOs for which approval had been granted at EC level. The EC is a party to the Cartagena Protocol on Biosafety 2000 which came into force on 11 September 2003. The protocol covers GMOs and Arts 10.6 and 11.8 authorise parties to base decisions on a precautionary approach. However, as none of the three complainants, the US, Canada and Argentina, were parties to the protocol, the panel found that the protocol could have no relevance to the issue of whether a measure was in conformity with the SPS Agreement.

Chapter 2

The WTO side agreements (1). The TBT and SPS Agreements

The WTO Agreement includes a variety of side agreements. Two of these are particularly important as regards trade restrictions that are mandated by considerations of environmental protection. These are the Agreement on Technical Barriers to Trade and the Agreement on the Application of Sanitary and Phyto-Sanitary Measures.

2.1 The TBT Agreement

GATT 1947 contained only a general reference to technical regulations and standards in Arts III, XI and XX. At the end of the Tokyo Round in 1979, 32 GATT contracting parties signed the plurilateral Agreement on Technical Barriers to Trade. This forms the basis of the new WTO TBT Agreement, which was negotiated during the Uruguay Round and came into force on 1 January 1995. The TBT Agreement applies to any 'technical regulation', defined in Annex 1.1 as a:

> Document which lays down product characteristics or their related processes and production methods, including the applicable administrative provisions, with which *compliance is mandatory* (emphasis added). It may also include or deal exclusively with terminology, symbols, packaging, marking or labelling requirements as they apply to a product, process or production method.

It also applies to a 'standard' which is a non-mandatory equivalent of a 'technical regulation'. A 'standard' is defined in Annex 1.2 as a:

> Document approved by a recognised body, that provides, for common and repeated use, rules, guidelines or characteristics for products or related processes and production methods, with which compliance is not mandatory. It may also include or deal exclusively with terminology, symbols, packaging, marking or labelling requirements as they apply to a product, process or production method.

SPS measures are specifically taken out of the scope of the TBT Agreement by Art 1.5. Instead, they are dealt with under the SPS Agreement, which is discussed later in this chapter.

As is the case with the SPS Agreement, the TBT Agreement encourages members to adopt the use of relevant international standards. This is reflected in Art 2.4 which provides that members are to use such standards, 'except when such international standards or relevant parts would be an ineffective or inappropriate means for the fulfilment of the legitimate objectives pursued, for instance because of fundamental climatic or geographical factors or fundamental technological problems'. Article 2.9 provides a notification procedure in respect of a technical regulation that 'may have a significant effect on trade of other members' in cases where a relevant international standard does not exist or 'the technical content of [the] proposed regulation is not in accordance with the technical content of relevant international standards'.

Article 2.1 applies 'most favoured nation' and 'national treatment' principles to the treatment of imported products in respect of technical regulations. Article 2.2 goes onto require members not to prepare, adopt or apply technical regulations 'with a view to or with the effect of creating unnecessary obstacles to international trade'.[1] It further requires that technical regulations should not be more trade-restrictive than necessary to fulfil a 'legitimate objective', taking account of the risks that non-fulfilment would create.

A 'legitimate objective' is defined to include '*inter alia:* national security requirements; the prevention of deceptive practices; protection of human health or safety, animal or plant life or health, or the environment'. These objectives are similar, but not identical, to the exceptions specified in GATT, Art XX. For instance, Art XX(g) refers to measures 'relating to the conservation of exhaustible resources' whereas Art 2.2 refers to protection of 'the environment'. Article 2.5 provides that a technical regulation that is adopted in accordance with a legitimate objective and is based on an international standard 'shall be rebuttably presumed not to create an unnecessary obstacle to international trade'.

Article 2.2 then sets out the criteria for assessing the risks of non-fulfilment, as follows, '*inter alia:* available scientific and technical information, related processing technology or intended end-uses of products'. The last two criteria suggest that a technical regulation based on PPM criteria would be easier to justify under the TBT Agreement than would a measure under the GATT. However, given the lack of a textual link between of Arts 2.1 and 2.2, it is unlikely that a 'technical regulation' that violates Art 2.1 could be justified by reference to the 'legitimate objectives' specified in Art 2.2. It is also unlikely that such a technical regulation could be justified by reference to

---

1   This language is wide enough to cover technical regulations on investment provided they have an effect on international trade.

GATT, Art XX, given the reference in the *chapeau* to 'this agreement', that is to say, to the GATT.

As regards 'standards', a Code of Good Practice is set out in Annex 3. The code requires the standardising body to comply with 'most favoured nation' and 'national treatment' (heading D); to ensure that standards 'are not prepared, adopted or applied with a view to, or with the effect of, creating unnecessary obstacles to international trade' (heading E) and provides for the adoption of international standards in terms similar to those used in Art 2.4 (heading F). Article 4.1 obliges members to ensure that their central government standardising bodies accept and comply with the code. Furthermore, members are obliged to take 'such reasonable measures as may be available to them' to ensure compliance with the code by local government and non-governmental standardising bodies within their territories.

The most obvious environmental application of the TBT code is in the field of 'eco-labelling'. Following, the panel's findings in *EC–Biotech*,[2] it is likely that the US will challenge current EC labelling requirements with respect to food containing GMOs, and this will be discussed in more detail in the next chapter.

To date, however, there has been only one decision of the appellate body, in *EC–Asbestos*,[3] on the application of the TBT Agreement as it relates to measures mandated by public health and environmental concerns. The panel addressed the threshold question of whether the French Decree No 96–1133, concerning asbestos and products containing asbestos, constituted a 'technical regulation' under Annex 1.1 by examining the measure in two stages. First, there was that part of the measure that prohibited the marketing of asbestos and asbestos-containing products. It concluded that this part was not a 'technical regulation' and so fell outside the TBT Agreement. However, it also concluded that the part of the decree containing the exceptions did satisfy this definition and so fell within the TBT Agreement. However, the panel did not explore this point further given that Canada's claims related solely to the prohibitions which fell outside the scope of the TBT Agreement.

The appellate body held that the proper legal character of the measure could only be determined by looking at the measure as a whole. The scope and generality of the prohibitions could only be understood in light of the exceptions to it, which would also have no autonomous legal significance in the absence of the prohibitions. It then went on to consider the definition of a 'technical regulation' in Annex 1.1. The heart of the definition

---

2 *EC–Biotech. European Communities–Measures Affecting the Approval and Marketing of Biotech Products.* WT/DS291/R, WT/DS292/R, WT/DS293/R. Panel report 29 September 2006.

3 *EC–Asbestos. European Communities–Measures Affecting Asbestos and Products Containing Asbestos.* WT/DS/135/R. Panel report 19 September 2000. WT/DS/135/AB/R. Appellate body report 12 March 2001.

is that a 'document' must lay down 'product characteristics' including the 'applicable administrative provisions' with which 'compliance is mandatory'. Annex 1.1 gives certain examples of 'product characteristics', namely, 'terminology, symbols, packaging, marking or labelling requirements' which indicate that this definition covers not only features and qualities intrinsic to the product itself but also related characteristics, such as 'the means of identification, the presentation and the appearance of the product'.[4] Taken together with the requirement of 'mandatory' compliance, the appellate body stated that: 'It follows that, with respect to products, a "technical regulation" has the effect of *prescribing* or *imposing* one or more "characteristics" – "features", "qualities", "attributes", or "other distinguishing mark".'[5] The document might provide that products must possess certain characteristics or might provide that they must not possess certain characteristics.

A 'technical regulation' must be applied to an *identifiable* product, or group of products, which is consonant with the formal obligation in TBT Agreement, Art 2.9.2 for members to notify other members of the products to be covered by a proposed technical regulation. However, nothing in the TBT Agreement requires that products covered by the TBT need be named or expressly identified in a technical regulation. There may be perfectly sound administrative reasons for simply making them identifiable through the 'characteristic' that is the subject of regulation.

Applying these principles, the appellate body found the decree to be aimed primarily at the regulation of a named product, asbestos. The prohibition on asbestos fibres did not, in itself, prescribe or impose any 'characteristics' on them, but simply banned them in their natural state. If this was all there was to the measure then it might not constitute a 'technical regulation'. However, asbestos fibres have no known use in their raw mineral form. Asbestos regulation, therefore, could only be achieved through the regulation of products that contain asbestos. The products covered by the measure were clearly identifiable – *all* products must be free of asbestos fibres. This prohibition was mandatory and backed up by criminal sanctions.

The scope of the exceptions was determined by an 'exhaustive list' of products that were permitted to contain chrysotile asbestos fibres. The criterion for inclusion of a product in this list was the absence of an acceptable alternative fibre for incorporation into a particular product, and the demonstrable provision of 'all technical guarantees of safety'. Viewing the measure as an integrated whole it laid down 'characteristics' for all products that might contain asbestos and prescribed the 'applicable administrative provisions' for certain products containing chrysotile asbestos fibres which were

---

4   Paragraph 7.
5   Paragraph 68.

included in the list of exceptions. The measure as a whole was therefore a 'technical regulation'.

However, the appellate body was unable to complete the analysis of whether the measure fell foul of TBT Agreement, Arts 2.1, 2.2, 2.4, 2.8, as claimed by Canada, given that the panel had made no findings at all regarding any of Canada's four claims under the TBT Agreement. The appellate body noted the 'novel nature' of these claims in that the TBT Agreement, and its predecessor under the Tokyo Round, had never once been subject to arbitral scrutiny either at panel or appellate body level. The appellate body also pointed out that although the TBT Agreement is intended to further the objectives of GATT 1994, it does so through a specialised legal regime that applies solely to a limited class of measures, observing that:

> For these measures, the TBS Agreement imposes obligations on Members that seem to be *different* from, and *additional* to, the obligations imposed on Members under the GATT 1994.[6]

It is unfortunate that the appellate body felt unable to complete the analysis of the decree's conformity with the TBT Agreement. The relationship between the TBT Agreement and the GATT must await further clarification. Previously, in *US – Reformulated Gasoline*, both the panel and the appellate body avoided this issue by making their initial analysis of the measure under the GATT. Once the measure was found not to be in conformity with the GATT, there was no need to consider whether it was also in conformity with the TBT Agreement.

However, what of a measure, such as that in *EC–Asbestos*, that is in conformity with the GATT? Could such a measure still fail to conform with the TBT Agreement? The Preamble to the TBT Agreement contains no reference to any specific provision of GATT, nor does it contain any presumption that conformity with the agreement entails conformity with GATT, of the sort found in SPS Agreement, Art 2.4. TBT Agreement, Art 2.2 imposes the obligation not to create unnecessary obstacles to trade, which entails a wider interference with regulatory powers than the non-discrimination provisions in GATT, Art III. The TBT Agreement applies to all technical regulations, whereas Art XI is limited to border measures. It is, therefore, possible for a measure to be in conformity with the GATT, but not with the TBT Agreement. It is also possible, but unlikely, for a measure to be in conformity with the TBT Agreement and not to be in conformity with the GATT.

However, it is likely that, on the facts in *EC–Asbestos*, there would have been no violation of the TBT Agreement. Given the findings on 'likeness' for the purpose of Art III.4, there would have been no 'likeness' for the purposes

---

6   Paragraph 80.

of, and hence no violation of, Art 2.1 of the TBT Agreement. The findings on GATT, Art XX(b) also make it likely that there would have been no violation of TBT Agreement, Art 2.2. Given these findings, the decree would probably not have been viewed as 'more trade restrictive than necessary to fulfil a legitimate objective', namely 'protection of human health or safety'. As regards Art 2.4, the factual evidence before the panel as to the international recognition of the health risks associated with asbestos makes it likely either that the decree was in accordance with 'international standards' or that 'controlled use' as argued for by Canada did not constitute such a standard. Finally, the reference to public health risks in the analysis of 'likeness' for the purpose of GATT, Art III.4 makes it likely that, for the purposes of TBT Agreement, Art 2.8, the decree was based on a product requirement 'in terms of performance, rather than design or descriptive characteristics' in that the performance of the products subject to the decree could not be examined in isolation from the health risks associated with use of the product.

As well as illustrating the possible overlap between the TBT Agreement and the GATT, *EC–Asbestos* also highlights another possible overlap between the TBT Agreement and the SPS Agreement. The conformity of the measure with the latter agreement was no longer in issue between the parties by the time the matter came before the panel. However, it is important to delineate the boundary between the two agreements because TBT Agreement, Art 1.5 provides that its provisions do not apply to 'sanitary and phytosanitary measures as defined in Annex A of [the SPS Agreement]'. Should the decree, therefore, have been regarded as having been taken out of the ambit of the TBT Agreement altogether? The answer to this would depend on whether it matched the definitions provided in SPS Agreement, Annex A, which were expansively interpreted in *EC–Biotech*.[7] The risks at which the decree was directed could not be said to relate to 'the entry, establishment or spread of pests' within sub-heading (d). Nor could they be said to relate to 'diseases carried by animals, plants or products thereof, or from the entry, establishment or spread of pests' within sub-heading (c). Sub-heading (b) relates to risks arising from 'additives, contaminants, toxins or disease-causing organisms', but would still not apply to the decree as this heading only covers these risks as they occur 'in foods, beverages or feedstuffs'. That leaves sub-heading (a) which relates to 'the entry, establishment or spread of pests, diseases, disease-carrying organisms or disease-causing organisms'. It is possible that the decree could fall within this sub-heading in that it aimed to halt the spread of 'diseases' caused by exposure to asbestos. However, it is also possible

---

7 *EC–Biotech. European Communities–Measures Affecting the Approval and Marketing of Biotech Products.* WT/DS291/R, WT/DS292/R, WT/DS293/R. Panel report 29 September 2006.

that 'diseases' might be subject to a limited construction so as to cover only infectious diseases.

2.2 The SPS Agreement

The Preamble to the SPS Agreement refers to the desire to elaborate the rules for the application of GATT 1994 which relate to SPS measures, in particular Art XX(b). SPS Agreement, Art 2.4 states that measures in conformity with the agreement are presumed to be in accordance with the 'obligations of the Members under the provisions of GATT 1994 which relate to the use of sanitary or phytosanitary measures, in particular the provisions of Article XX(b)'. However, the SPS Agreement is a free-standing set of obligations and its engagement is not conditional on a prior violation of GATT. It is likely that a measure which falls under the SPS Agreement will also fall under the GATT, as occurred in *Australia–Salmon.*[8] The panel decided that it would be more efficient to consider the SPS Agreement first and only proceed to consider GATT if the measure was in conformity with the agreement. This approach has subsequently been adopted by the appellate body in *EC–Beef Hormones*[9] and by the panel in *EC–Biotech.*[10] In all three cases a GATT analysis has not been required due to the finding that the measure in question was not in conformity with the SPS Agreement. In the event that a measure was found to be in conformity with the SPS Agreement, the panel would then have to proceed to an analysis of the position under the GATT. Due to the presumption of conformity contained in Art 2.4 of the SPS Agreement, it is unlikely that such an analysis would lead to a finding that the measure was not also in conformity with the provisions of the GATT. Overlap with the TBT Agreement is precluded by the exclusion of SPS measures from its ambit provided for in Art 1.5. However, the panel in *EC–Biotech* noted that there may be situations where a measure is only partly an SPS measure. In such a case the SPS part of the measure would be considered under the SPS Agreement, while the non-SPS parts would be considered under another WTO agreement, such as the TBT Agreement or the GATT.[11]

SPS Agreement, Art 1 provides for its application to 'all sanitary and

8 *Australia–Salmon. Australia–Measures affecting the importation of salmon.* WT/DS18/R. Panel report 12 June 1998. WT/DS18/AB/R. Appellate body report 20 October 1998. WT/DS18/RW. Article 21.5 panel report 18 February 2000.

9 *EC–Beef Hormones. European Communities–Measures Concerning Meat and Meat Products (Hormones).* WT/ DS/48/R/CAN, WT/DS/26/R/US. Panel report 18 August 1997. WT/ DS/48/AB/R, WT/DS/26/AB/R. Appellate body report 16 January 1998.

10 *EC–Biotech. European Communities–Measures Affecting the Approval and Marketing of Biotech Products.* WT/DS291/R, WT/DS292/R, WT/DS293/R. Panel report 29 September 2006.

11 Regulation 258/97/EC was just such a measure as it was directed at three purposes, only one of which would fall within the definition of an SPS measure.

phytosanitary measures which may, directly or indirectly, affect international trade'. Sanitary and phytosanitary measures are defined in Annex A.1 as any measure applied:

(a) to protect animal or plant life or health within the territory of the Member from risks arising from the entry, establishment or spread of pests, diseases, disease-carrying organisms or disease-causing organisms;
(b) to protect human or animal life or health within the territory of the Member from risks arising from additives, contaminants, toxins or disease-causing organisms in foods, beverages or feedstuffs;
(c) to protect human life or health within the territory of the Member from risks arising from diseases carried by animals, plants or products thereof, or from the entry, establishment or spread of pests; or
(d) to prevent or limit other damage within the territory of the Member from the entry, establishment or spread of pests.

All four of these categories contain the phrase 'within the territory of the Member'. It follows that a measure that it aims to protect human, animal or plant life or health in outside its own territory cannot constitute a 'sanitary and phytosanitary measure' and must, therefore, fall outside the ambit of the SPS Agreement.

To conform with the SPS Agreement, a measure must comply with Art 2.2 and Arts 5.1–5.8. The burden falls on the complainant to establish a prima facie case that the measure is inconsistent with the SPS Agreement. If this burden is discharged, then the burden transfers to the party seeking to justify the retention of the measure. The agreement is structured in two ways. First, there are provisions that deal with the scientific evidence that is required to justify an SPS measure. These provisions endeavour to make explicit the evidential threshold that a measure must cross if it is to fall within the scope of GATT, Art XX(b). Secondly, there are provisions that require the SPS measure to be implemented in such a manner as to avoid unnecessary restrictions on international trade. These provisions can be seen as reflecting the word 'necessary' in GATT, Art XX(b), as well as the wording of the *chapeau*.

The obligations in the first category are defined by Art 2.2 that requires any measure to be applied 'only to the extent necessary to protect human, animal or plant life or health' and must be 'based on scientific principles' and 'not maintained without sufficient scientific evidence'. Article 5.1 requires members to base measures on an assessment 'as appropriate to the circumstances, of the risks to human, animal or plant life or health, taking into account risk assessment techniques developed by the relevant international organisations'. Annex A.4 then defines a 'risk assessment' in two ways. First, there is 'the evaluation of the likelihood of entry, establishment or spread of a pest or disease within the territory of an importing member according to the sanitary or phytosanitary measures which might be applied, and of the associated potential biological and economic consequences'. Alternatively there is 'the evaluation of the potential for adverse effects on human or animal health arising from the presence of additives, contaminants, toxins, disease-causing organisms in food, beverages or feedstuffs'.

Article 5.2 requires 'available scientific evidence' to be taken into account by members when assessing risk. Article 5.3 then provides various economic factors that can be taken into account when assessing the risk to animal or plant life or health, and determining 'the measure to be applied for achieving the appropriate level of [SPS] protection from such risk'.[12] Article 5.7 allows measures to be provisionally adopted in the absence of sufficient scientific evidence. In such circumstances, members must 'seek to obtain the additional information necessary for a more objective assessment of risk and review the sanitary or phytosanitary measure accordingly within a reasonable period of time'.

Turning now to the second category of provisions, Art 5.4 requires members when determining the appropriate level of SPS protection to 'take into account the objective of minimising negative trade effects'. Article 5.5 then goes on to provide that the measure must avoid arbitrary or unjustifiable distinctions in the levels considered appropriate in different situations if such distinctions result in discrimination or a disguised restriction on international trade'. Article 5.6 provides that the measure must not be more trade restrictive than required to achieve their appropriate level of sanitary or phytosanitary protection, taking into account technical and economic feasibility. Footnote 3 provides that for the purposes of Art 5.6 'a measure is not more trade restrictive than required unless there is another measure, reasonably available taking into account technical and economic feasibility, that achieves the appropriate level of [SPS] protection and is significantly less restrictive to trade'.

Compliance with the above requirements is dispensed with where a measure conforms to international standards[13] as Art 3.2 provides that these are to be presumed to be consistent with the SPS Agreement.[14] But what of measures that are more stringent than those prescribed by international standards?

---

12 These factors are first 'the potential damage in terms of loss of production or sales in the event of the entry, establishment or spread of a pest or disease'; secondly, 'the costs of control or eradication in the territory of the importing Member'; and, thirdly, 'the relative cost-effectiveness of alternative approaches to limiting risks'.

13 These are defined in Annex A, para 3. For food safety the relevant standardising body is the *Codex Alimentarius* Commission. For animal health the relevant body is the International Office of Epizootics, while for plant health it is the Secretariat of the International Plant Protection Convention in cooperation with regional organisations operating within its framework. Article 3.4 mandates members to play a full part 'within the limits of their resources' in these organisations.

14 The presumption would be rebuttable where, e.g. a member enforced *Codex* standards against imports, but not against domestic products.

Article 3.1 specifies that SPS measures are to be 'based' on 'international standards, guidelines or recommendations, where they exist' except as otherwise provided for in the agreement, in particular Art 3.3. This provision gives permission to introduce/maintain *higher* SPS protection than available by adopting 'measures based on the relevant international standards'. However, there must be 'a scientific justification' for doing so or else conformity with the provisions of Arts 5.1–5.8, which provide for SPS measures to be justified by a 'risk assessment'. Notwithstanding this, all measures not based on international standards, 'shall not be inconsistent with any other provision of this Agreement'.

Where a measure is not based on international standards, two further issues remain to be dealt with by the agreement. First, there is the issue of equivalence. Article 4 requires members to accepts SPS measures of other members as equivalent 'even if these measure differ from their own or from those used by other members trading in the same product' providing the exporting member 'objectively demonstrates to the importing Member that its measures achieve the importing Member's appropriate level of [SPS] protection'.

Secondly, there is the issue of transparency. Article 7 requires members to 'notify changes in their [SPS] measures' and to 'provide information on their [SPS] measures in accordance with the provisions of Annex B'. Paragraph 1 of this Annex requires members to ensure that all SPS regulations which have been adopted 'are published promptly in such a manner as to enable interested Members to become acquainted with them'. Footnote 5 clarifies the term 'regulations' so as to encompass 'laws, decrees or ordinances which are applicable generally'. Where an SPS measure constrains exports, or has the potential to constrain them, Art 5.8 entitles an exporting member to request from the member maintaining the measure an explanation of an SPS measure which is not based on the 'relevant international standards, guidelines or recommendations'.[15] Article 8 requires members to adopt the control, inspection and approval procedures set out in Annex C. This includes obligations regarding fees, information requirements, confidentiality and publication of a standard processing period for each procedure. It also includes an obligation to undertake and complete such procedures without undue delay and without discrimination in favour of domestic over imported products.

The ambit of these provisions has been the subject of exhaustive consideration by the appellate body in three decisions which will now be analysed in detail, before moving onto the recent panel decision in *EC–Biotech* which is dealt with in the next chapter, on the treatment of GMOs under the WTO agreements.

15 Or where such standards, recommendations or guidelines do not exist.

2.2.1 EC–Beef Hormones[16]

The relationship between Arts 3.1 and 3.3 was considered in detail by the WTO panel when it ruled on the case brought by Canada and US against the EC in respect of its ban on the sale of hormone-fed beef on the grounds of the potential carcinogenic effect of growth hormones in food. The ban applied equally to domestic beef as to imported beef. There was nothing in the relevant international standards to justify such a ban so the issue was raised of the extent to which pre-emption of such standards was permitted by the SPS Agreement. The EC chose not to justify the ban by reliance on Art 5.7 as it regarded the ban as definitive rather than merely provisional. The initial panel decision found against the EC. One of its grounds was that 'based on' in Arts 3.1 and 3.3 meant the same as 'conform to' in Art 3.2, thereby outlawing SPS measures that were more stringent than those adopted as international standards by the *Codex Alimentarius*.[17] The panel found that the EC was also in breach of Art 5.5 in permitting the use of anti-microbial agents, Carbadox and Olaquindox, in feed given to piglets, as both had carcinogenic potential. Given that the measure in question had been justified on the grounds of fears of the carcinogenic potential involved in the use of hormones to promote growth in beef, there was therefore an arbitrary and unjustifiable distinction between the measure and the tolerance of Carbadox and Olaquindox.

The panel's interpretation of Art 3 was reversed when the appellate body held that the SPS Agreement entitled a party to take health measures that adopt more stringent standards than the international standards set out in the *Codex* recommendations. In particular, 'based on' in Arts 3.1 and 3.3 did not mean the same as 'conform to' in Art 3.2.[18] The *Codex* recommendations were not binding norms under Art 3.1, and Art 3.3 was not to be viewed as an exception to Art 3.1, thereby imposing the burden of proof on the member relying on it to justify its adoption of standards higher than the international standards. The burden of proof was on the complainant to show a prima facie breach of either of Arts 3.1, 3.3 and 5.5 and only if this was established did the burden shift to the respondent. Article 3.3 was, however, worded so as to be explicitly subject to Arts 5.1–5.8 and consequently a member could adopt higher SPS standards only on the basis of a 'risk assessment'. Contrary

---

16 *EC–Beef Hormones. European Communities–Measures Concerning Meat and Meat Products (Hormones).* WT/ DS/48/R/CAN, WT/DS/26/R/US. Panel report 18 August 1997. WT/ DS/ 48/AB/R, WT/DS/26/AB/R. Appellate body report 16 January 1998. See also Goh, G and Ziegler, A, 'A real world where people live and work and die: Australian SPS measures after the WTO Appellate Body's decision in the Hormones Case' (1998) 32(5) JWT 271.

17 This body is the international commission set up by the Food and Agriculture Organisation of the United Nations (FAO) Conference and the World Health Assembly in 1961/62 to make recommendations on food safety standards.

18 The appellate body stressed that the burden of proof falls on the complainant to show a prima facie breach of the SPS Agreement.

to the view of the original panel, the words 'scientifically identifiable risk' did not implicitly prescribe a certain magnitude or threshold level of risk. Instead, the question was whether an SPS measure was sufficiently supported or reasonably warranted by the risk assessment.

However, the EC's scientific data did not constitute such a 'risk assessment' as it was not specifically geared to the carcinogenic risks of hormones when used to promote growth in livestock. Indeed, with a single exception,[19] the reports provided by the EC all concluded that the use of hormones for growth promotion in cattle was safe if good practice was followed. No assessment had been made of the risks of the possible failure of good veterinary practice in the US and Canada which formed another part of the EC's justification for the measure. Furthermore, the EC submitted no evidence in relation to the growth hormone melengestrol acetate (MGA), although this is perhaps understandable given that the US and Canada declined to submit any assessment of MGA on the ground that the material they were aware of was proprietary and confidential. Consequently, the measure still failed to conform to the SPS Agreement.

The appellate body, however, reversed the panel's finding that the measure contravened Art 5.5. The discrepancy between the measure and the EC's tolerance of anti-microbial agents in feed given to piglets, both of which had carcinogenic potential, meant that the measure displayed 'arbitrary or unjustifiable distinctions' in the levels of SPS protection that the EC considered to be appropriate in different situations. However, these distinctions did not result in 'discrimination or disguised restrictions on international trade'. The appellate body examined the legislative history of the measure and found that the intention behind it was a genuine desire to protect the health of consumers rather than a covert desire to protect beef producers within the EC.

The decision is of immense importance in that it justifies, at least in theory, the adoption of higher SPS standards than 'the relevant international standards' provided the correct 'risk assessment' is performed. The effect of the initial panel ruling would have been to make it very difficult, if not impossible, to impose such higher standards. However, in practice it may be very difficult to conduct a risk assessment as specific as that required by the appellate body. A risk assessment specifically geared to the carcinogenic effects of growth-producing hormones in food might well take some time to conduct and would mean the measure could only be justified once it had been shown that some human beings had developed cancer as a result of eating such beef. A risk assessment of MGA would be even more difficult to undertake, given

19 Dr Lucier identified a risk that between zero and one person in a million who eat 500 grams of meat, treated with oestrogens for growth promotion purposes in accordance with good practice, per day over their lifetimes would develop cancer. However, the panel pointed out that not only was a risk in this statistical range not a 'scientifically identified risk', the risk was caused by the *total* amount of oestrogens in treated meat, not by the small fraction thereof added for growth promotion purposes.

the refusal of the US and Canada to reveal material of which they were aware, on grounds of confidentiality.

One of the arguments put forward by the EC was that the measure was justified by the precautionary principle whereby potential hazards must be addressed before they occur. Lack of scientific knowledge as to the likelihood of the risk occurring should not be a bar to such preventive action, taking into account the adverse consequences that would occur were the risk to materialise. The fact that the precautionary principle had appeared not only in national environmental legislation, but also in international environmental agreements led to the conclusion that it now formed part of customary international law. The appellate body declined to rule on this point, merely observing that the principle was, in any event, reflected in Arts 3.3 and 5.7 of the agreement. However, the principle could not override the specific wording of Arts 5.1 and 5.2. The result is that in practice it will be very difficult to justify measures that ban the import of products that 'might' in future cause harm to the health or life of human beings, animals or plants, other than under Art 5.7. At the time of writing the EC has still failed to conform to the recommendations of the appellate body and on 12 July 1999 the US was authorised to impose trade sanctions against it.

The EU's response to the decision of the appellate body was to review the available scientific information and to seek new evidence on the risk to human health of hormone residues in meat products. In 1999, the Scientific Committee on Veterinary Measures relating to Public Health (SCVMPH) concluded that oestradiol 17â should be considered a carcinogen. For the other five hormones the SCVMPH concluded that the current state of knowledge did not make it possible to give a quantitative estimate of the risk to consumers. This led to the amendment of Directive 96/22 by Directive 2003/74, which was approved on 22 July 2003. The new directive confirmed the prohibition of substances having a hormonal action for growth promotion in farm animals and drastically reduces the circumstances under which oestradiol 17â might be administered to food producing animals for purposes other than growth promotion. As regards the other five hormones, the provisional prohibition would continue to apply while the EC sought more complete scientific information to clarify the present state of knowledge of these substances. The Commission would regularly review scientific information that may become available in the future. The EU maintained that the new directive brought it into compliance with its obligations under the SPS Agreement and called on the US and Canada to drop their sanctions on imports from the EU. However, the US and Canada maintained their sanctions and in November 2004 the EU initiated proceedings under the DSU against Canada and the US.[20]

20 *United States–Continued Suspension of Obligations in the EC–Hormones Dispute.* DS/320. Panel established 17 February 2005.

An additional response to the decision of the appellate body came on 2 February 2000 when the European Commission adopted a Communication on the use of the precautionary principle to inform all interested parties as to how the Commission intends to apply the principle both at EU and international level.[21] The Communication is an attempt to demonstrate that use of the principle is consistent with the EU's international agreements, including those under the WTO Agreement. It sets out in Annex III four components of risk assessment that are not too dissimilar to the elements of a risk assessment that is compliant with Art 5.1 in the light of *EC–Beef Hormones*. A possible point of departure is the statement that:

> When the available data are inadequate or non-conclusive, a prudent and cautious approach to environmental protection, health or safety could be to opt for the worst-case hypothesis. When such hypotheses are accumulated, this will lead to an exaggeration of the real risk but gives a certain assurance that it will not be underestimated.

When compared with the facts in *EC–Beef Hormones*, this statement would appear to justify the measure on the grounds of opting for the cumulative worst-case scenarios that there is a failure of good practice in the administration of growth hormones in the US and Canada and/or that further scientific evidence becomes available confirming the risks to health from administration of growth hormones even in accordance with good practice. However, such an analysis would suggest that justification for the measure should have been sought under Art 5.7.

The Communication states that measures based on the precautionary principle should be, *inter alia*:

> proportional to the chosen level of protection;
> non-discriminatory;
> consistent with similar measures already taken;
> based on an examination of the potential benefits and costs of action or lack or action (including, where appropriate and feasible, an economic cost/benefit analysis);
> subject to review in the light of new scientific data;
> capable of assigning responsibility for producing the scientific evidence necessary for a more comprehensive risk assessment.

The following points can be made about these general principles of application. First, the SPS measure in *EC–Beef Hormones* would probably fail to satisfy the requirement of consistency given the differential treatment of

---

21 *Communication from the Commission on the Precautionary Principle* Com (2000) 1 final.

Carbadox and Oliquandox.[22] Secondly, the criterion of comparing the costs of action and non-action focuses on 'the overall cost to the Community' and does not take into account the dis-benefits to a potential exporter outside the EC who is adversely effected by an EC measure that is justified by reference to the precautionary principle. Thirdly, the requirement of proportionality is elaborated as follows at 6.3.1.

> The risk reduction measure should not be limited to immediate risks where the proportionality of the action is easier to assess. It is in situations in which the adverse effects do not emerge until long after exposure that the cause-effect relationships are more difficult to prove scientifically and that – for this reason – the precautionary principle often has to be invoked. In this case the potential long term effects must be taken into account in evaluating the proportionality of measures in the form of rapid action to limit or eliminate a risk whose effects will not surface until ten or twenty years later or will affect future generations. This applies in particular to effects on the eco-system. Risks that are carried forward into the future cannot be eliminated or reduced except at the time of exposure, that is to say immediately.

At first glance, this appears to justify the measure at issue in *EC–Beef Hormones*. However, the problem with the appellate body's assessment of the scientific evidence before it in that case was not that the 'cause-effect relationship' was difficult to prove but that there was no evidence to suggest a threat to health if growth hormones were properly administered. The EC's concern was based on the carcinogenicity of hormones in general. From this it extrapolated the possibility that in future it might be established that they would be shown to pose a risk to health when used as growth promoters for beef cattle. A cost-benefit analysis that considered the welfare of citizens in the EC might suggest that the precautionary principle should be invoked, because no detriment would be suffered within the EC by lack of access to beef reared in this way. However, the cost-benefit analysis might yield very different results if it were to take into account the economic interests of parties outside the EC. Taking this into account, it is not surprising that, when the Communication was discussed by the SPS Committee on 15–16 March 2000, both developed and developing countries expressed reservations with the use of the precautionary principle on the ground that its use would lead to unpredictability as regards market access and would act as a brake on scientific research.

---

22 It was for this reason that the panel found that the measure was not in conformity with Art 5.5.

2.2.2 Australia–Salmon[23]

The dispute involved a challenge by Canada to Australia's 1975 regulation Q86A, covering the import of fresh, chilled or imported salmon. Canada argued that with salmon Australia took a very conservative approach to risk, but was much more relaxed as regards risks of the same disease agents affecting non-salmonid products. It pointed to the fact that there had been no reported case of a dead eviscerated fish resulting in an exotic disease introduction. In contrast, there were many documented introductions in the case of live fish, even in Australia. In a final report of 1996 Australia recommended retention of the present quarantine restrictions.

An initial complication was in identifying the SPS measure in question. Under the 1988 Conditions the Director of Quarantine allowed import of heat treated salmon products for human consumption. The panel proceeded on the basis that these constituted the relevant SPS measure. However, the appellate body held that the relevant restriction was the import prohibition in regulation Q86A. Heat treatment in the 1988 conditions applied only to smoked salmon whereas the product at issue was fresh, chilled or frozen salmon. Nonetheless, there was sufficient material to enable the appellate body to complete the analysis as regards the claims under Arts 5.1 and 5.5, but not as regards the claim under Art 5.6.

The first issue was whether this report constituted a valid 'risk assessment', as required by Art 5.1. This involved a three-tiered analysis. First, the member must identify the diseases it wants to prevent as well as the potential biological/economic consequences associated with their entry, establishment or spread. On the facts, Australia's 1996 report passed this first hurdle. Secondly, the member must evaluate the likelihood of the entry of these diseases, which meant the probability, rather than possibility, of the entry of the diseases which the measure aimed to prevent. Something more was needed that merely Evaluation might be done either quantitatively or qualitatively and there was no need to establish a certain magnitude or threshold level of degree of risk. The evaluation of risk had to be distinguished from the member's right to set its appropriate level of protection. The member might legitimately decide on a policy of 'zero risk', but would have to base its policy on a valid risk assessment. An evaluation based on 'theoretical uncertainty' or which merely conducted *some* form of evaluation of the likelihood of entry would not amount to a valid risk assessment. Thirdly, the likelihood of entry of the diseases in question must be evaluated according to the SPS measures which might be applied. Australia's 1996 report contained no substantive evaluation of the relative risk associated with the different options it set out. *Some* evaluation had been attempted but that was insufficient. Australia

---

23 *Australia–Salmon. Australia–Measures affecting the importation of salmon.* WT/DS18/R. Panel report 12 June 1998. WT/DS18/AB/R. Appellate body report 20 October 1998.

was, therefore, in breach of Art 5.5 and, by implication, also in breach of Art 2.2.

The second issue was whether the measure was consistent with Art 5.5, and, by implication, with Art 2.3. This issue, again, involved a three-tiered analysis. First, had the member adopted different appropriate levels of sanitary protection in several 'different situations'? This comparison did not require the disease and the biological and economic consequences to be the same for 'different' situations. Situations could be compared if they involved *either* a risk of entry, establishment or spread of the same or a similar disease *or* a risk of the same or similar 'associated potential biological and economic consequences'. For situations to be comparable it was enough to have in common a risk of entry, establishment or spread of *one* disease of concern, not *all* diseases. Secondly, did those levels of protection exhibit differences which were 'arbitrary or unjustifiable'? It was significant that Australia had applied more lenient sanitary measures when dealing with the import of herring used as bait and for live ornamental fin fish even though the risk of disease from these imports was at least as high, if not higher, than that associated with salmon imports. Thirdly, did the measure embodying these differences result in 'discrimination or disguised restrictions on international trade'? The measure also fell at this hurdle, taking into account the arbitrary differences in the level of protection applied to salmon imports as compared to that applied to imports of other fish that were susceptible to the same diseases at which the measure was directed. The unexplained failure of the 1996 report to recommend conditional importation of Canadian salmon, as recommended in the 1995 draft, suggested that this arbitrary difference in treatment was the result of covert protectionism. However, this factor does not seem to have been determinative of the appellate body's findings. Even had there been no suggestion of protectionist intent the measure would still have been in breach of Art 5.5 due to the arbitrary discrepancy between the ban on salmon imports and the tolerance of imports of other fish which posed at least an equal risk of the introduction of the diseases to which the measure was directed. In contrast, in *EC–Beef Hormones*, the finding of discrepant treatment between the measure and the comparator measures did not lead to such a finding in the absence of any evidence of protectionist intent behind the measure.

The third point of challenge by Canada came under Art 5.6 which involved another three-tiered analysis. First was there another SPS measure that was 'reasonably available, taking into account technical and economic feasibility'? There clearly was because the 1996 final report had set out four alternative options to an outright import ban. Secondly, could any of these four options have achieved Australia's appropriate level of sanitary protection? The appellate body found it impossible to rule on this point because the 1996 final report had not substantively evaluated the risks associated with the various quarantine options set out therein. The panel had mistakenly examined the alternative quarantine policy options by reference to the 1988 Conditions on heat-treatment, rather than by reference to the original 1975 regulation. This meant that there was no other factual element in the panel report that would allow the appellate body to examine the alternative quarantine policy options. Thirdly, would the alternative measure be significantly less trade restrictive than the current measure? Again, it was clear that this was the case as any of the four options canvassed in the 1996 final report would allow some imports, unlike the current SPS measure. Because of the impossibility of determining whether or not the second condition had been satisfied, the appellate body overturned the panel's finding that there had been a breach of Art 5.6. It did not, however, make any positive finding of consistency with Art 5.6.

Australia subsequently took steps to bring its measure into conformity with the SPS Agreement such as loosening the restrictions on the import of salmon as well as tightening the restrictions on the import of herring used as bait and live ornamental finfish.[24] In its compliance report in 2001,[25] the panel noted that in 1999 Australia had concluded an Import Risk Analysis which avoided the flaws identified in the 1996 final report. Key risk factors for each of the seven diseases were pointed out, such as the kind of control measures in case of disease establishment, the type of salmon with the highest prevalence, most infected tissues, survival rate and risk related to waste. For *each*, and not merely *some*, of these diseases the 1999 report identified and discussed a series of risk management measure that might be applied. The discussion of each risk management measure was made in the light of the effect a measure would have on the key risk factors previously identified in the report. However, the panel noted that there was no rational relationship between the 1999 report and the requirement that Canadian Salmon could be imported only it if were 'consumer ready'. Accordingly, the measure was still not based on a risk assessment as required by SPS Agreement, Art 5.1. For the same reason the measure failed to satisfy the requirements of Art 5.6.

2.2.3 Japan Varietals [26]

In 1950 Japan imposed an import ban on various fruits, as potential hosts of codling moth, which affected eight fruits from the US. In practice, the ban could be lifted if the fruits needed to be fumigated with methyl bromide, subject to Guidelines published by Japan in 1987 to assess the efficacy of this

---

24 However, no stricter controls had been imposed on the internal movement of dead Australian fish.

25 *Australia–Salmon. Australia–measures affecting the importation of salmon.* WT/DS18/RW. Article 21.5 panel report 18 February 2000.

26 *Japan–Varietals. Japan–Measures affecting agricultural products.* WT/DS76/R. Panel report 27 October 1998. WT/DS76/AB/R. Appellate body report 22 February 1999.

treatment. The US objected to the fact that the Guidelines, which constituted an SPS measure,[27] required separate quarantine approval for each new variety of the fruits subject to the measure. Japan justified this requirement by pointing to scientific studies which indicated that the efficacy of fumigation treatment *might* differ between varieties of the same fruit. However, the evidence before the panel showed that there was no evidence that such differences, which were not biologically pronounced, were due to varietal differences. Japan had made no attempt to determine whether varietal differences actually constituted a factor causing the differences in the test results. This determination could be made by conducting sorption tests on different varieties of a product.[28] The appellate body upheld the panel's decision that the measure was not in conformity with Art 2.2 or Art 5.1 due to the lack of a rational relationship between the measure and the available scientific information. In particular, Art 2.2 could not be limited to situations in which the scientific evidence was 'patently' insufficient.[29]

Alternatively, Japan tried to justify the measure by reference to Art 5.7. The appellate body found that this contained four cumulative requirements. First, there must be a situation where the relevant scientific information was insufficient. Secondly, the measure must be adopted on the basis of available pertinent information. Thirdly, a member might not maintain a provisional measure unless it sought to obtain the additional information necessary for a more objective assessment of risk. Fourthly, the member must review the measure accordingly within a reasonable period of time. Japan had failed to satisfy the third and fourth of these requirements.[30] Japan's failure to examine the appropriateness of its varietal testing requirement meant that it had not complied with the third of these requirements. Japan had also failed to comply with the fourth requirement, even though its obligation to review the measure had only come into existence on 1 January 1995 when the SPS Agreement came into force. The varietal testing requirement had first been applied in 1969, and, in relation to the US products in issue, in 1978. During this period, Japan had had ample opportunity to obtain further information on the relationship between varietal differences and quarantine efficacy.

27 The Guidelines were of general applicability and of a character similar to laws, decrees and ordinances which were explicitly referred to in the footnote to Annex B, para 1.
28 At paras 8.38–8.40.
29 Article 5.1 could be viewed as a specific application of the basic obligations set out in Art 2.2, but this did not mean that Art 2.2 was limited 'in favour' of Art 5.1.
30 No argument was offered as to whether the requirements of the first sentence had been satisfied, particularly as regards whether, in fact, there was an absence of sufficient scientific evidence regarding the relationship between varietal differences and the effectiveness of quarantine treatment.

Chapter 3

Genetically modified organisms and the WTO agreements

The conflict between environmental protection and the free trade principles of the WTO has recently come to a head in the context of GMOs. Traditionally, new varieties of plants have been developed by crossing two existing varieties to create a hybrid. This has used the natural process of sexual reproduction through pollination. In contrast, with GMOs the process by which desirable traits from one organism are transferred to another is that of recombinant DNA technology. This combines DNA molecules from different sources in the laboratory and are these are then artificially inserted into the plant. The DNA molecules may come from an unrelated plant or from another species altogether, such as an animal.

In *First the Seed*, Kloppenburg provides an illuminating account of the political and economic dynamics behind the advance of the biotechnology industry in the US.[1] In a series of landmark decisions in the 1980s, the US courts recognised that utility patents could be granted over new varieties of both plants and animals. The industry has also been successful in convincing public regulatory bodies of the doctrine of substantial equivalence between GM seeds and their conventional counterparts. This argument was accepted in 1985 by the Co-ordinated Framework for Regulation of Biotechnology, which held that no new laws should govern GM products. Instead they should be governed by existing laws on the release and consumption of seeds and foodstuffs. The principle was reaffirmed by the US Food and Drug Administration (FDA) in 1992. In 1993 the FDA approved Monsanto's sales of recombinant bovine growth hormone to the dairy industry, despite the fact that it would lead to no advantages in quality or lower consumer prices. The same applies for GM corn and soya. However, these have proved modestly useful for farmers, not so much from a cost perspective, but from the simplification of the spraying process. In 1998 the United States Department of Agriculture (USDA) tried to include GM foods when defining organic standards but backed down after public outcry.

---

1 Kloppenburg, J, *First the Seed*, 2nd edn, 2004, Madison, WI: University of Wisconsin Press.

Against this benign legal and regulatory background in the US, the bio-technology industry has become a major economic force. By 2004, 145 million acres worldwide had been planted with GM crops. GM crops are incorporated into 70 per cent of US processed food.[2] The first GM crop was Calgene's 'flavr savr' tomato which was released in 1994 but was a failure as its GM traits offered no advantages. In 1996, Monsanto released GM corn with Bt (bacillus thuringiensis) toxins incorporated as a pesticide. Then Round up Ready versions of soy, cotton and canola were released with tolerance to glysophate. In 1996, 2 million acres worldwide were planted with GM crops. By 2003, the figure was 167 million, 98 per cent of which occurred in five countries; the US (63 per cent), Argentina (21 per cent), Canada (6 per cent), China (4 per cent) and Brazil (4 per cent). Currently, four GM crops are grown commercially – soya, canola, cotton and corn. GM crops are currently engineered to express two traits – Bt action and glysophate resistance. By 2002, 32 per cent of corn in the US, 71 per cent of soya and 70 per cent of cotton was GM.[3] In Argentina the figure for soya is approaching 100 per cent.

The development of the biotechnology industry has, however, met with considerable public hostility, particularly in Europe. Public hostility to the use of GMO products is based on three objections. The first is the biodiversity objection that the use of GMO seeds in agriculture may lead to crossovers into existing plant varieties.[4] This is a particular concern for organic farmers who risk losing their organic accreditation in the event that any traces of GM material appear in their produce.

Additionally, the use of GMO seeds, due to their engineered tolerance to glysophates, encourages increased used of pesticides, with consequent adverse effects on plants and animals. The widespread use of Bt action in GM crops has led to fears that insects will develop resistance to the Bt toxins which are introduced indiscriminately in this way. Kloppenburg notes that:

'Bacillus thuringiensis has long been a useful tool for vegetable growers who have not wanted to use synthetic pesticides for the control of certain caterpillars. Insects did not develop resistance to this natural pesticide because it was used sparingly in widely dispersed fields, accounting for a relatively small total acreage. When the Bt toxin gene is incorporated into crop plants, however, the toxin is expressed in every cell of the plant and that plant makes the toxin available throughout an entire growing season.'[5]

2   Op. cit., Kloppenburg, fn 1, p 292.
3   Op. cit., Kloppenburg, fn 1, p 305.
4   This consideration can also be used as a ground of objection to the import of GM food products on the basis of the risks to biodiversity in the country of export due to possible crossovers into non-GM species.
5   Op. cit., Kloppenburg, fn 1, p 315.

Kloppenburg also points to the increased used of glysophates and the development of Roundup Ready resistant weeds since the introduction of GM varieties into the US in 1996.[6]

That there is some scientific basis to this objection may have been evidenced by the following. In 1999 a Cornell University study suggested that pollen from Bt corn could prove a threat to the Monarch butterfly.[7] In 2001, evidence came to light of GM cross-pollination not only with non-GM corn within the US, but also with corn grown in the mountains of Mexico.[8] In 2003, the results of a three-year programme of field trials of GM crops in the UK were published by the Royal Society. They revealed that the cultivation of GM oilseed rape and sugar beet were harmful to the environment. The results were more favourable as regards GM maize, although this had been compared to a conventional maize growing regime that used a herbicide so toxic it has since been banned in Europe. In 2004, the government gave approval for the commercial growing of GM maize, but Bayer Cropscience decided not to go ahead with planting.[9]

Secondly, there is a public health objection that food containing material from GM products may cause a long-term threat to human health. Currently, there is no scientific data that substantiates this risk, but objections are based on the precautionary principle in that, with any novel method of food production, it is impossible to rule out the possibility that long-term exposure to the product may result in health risks to consumers. There is considerable hostility to GM foods among the public in Europe that derives from a series of foods scares, such as the bovine spongiform encephalopathy (BSE) scare, that has sapped confidence in the pronouncements of food regulators. Distrust of GM food has been exacerbated by incidents of cross-contamination. The most notable of these occurred in 2000 when food grade corn was discovered to have been accidentally contaminated with Aventis' Starlink bt GM which had been approved only for use as an animal feed. Similar contamination has been found in Japan, Britain and Denmark.[10]

---

6 Op. cit., Kloppenburg, fn 1, p 316: 'it is now clear that farmers growing Roundup Ready soybeans are using two to five times more herbicide (in pounds applied per acre) than those using other weed management systems (Benbrook 1999: 2)'. Kloppenburg's reference is to Benbrook, C, *Evidence of the Magnitude and Consequences of the Roundup Ready Soybean Yield Drag from University-Based Varietal Trials in 1998*, AgBio Tech InfoNet Technical Paper no 1, 13 July 1999.

7 Losey, J, Rayor, S and Carter, M, 'Transgenic pollen harms monarch larvae' (1999) 399 *Nature* 214.

8 Quist, D and Chapela, I, 'Transgenic DNA introgressed into traditional maize landraces in Oaxaca, Mexico' (2001) 414(29) *Nature* 541.

9 Greenpeace UK, *Farmscale Trials*, 11 August 2006. www.greenpeace.org.uk/contentlookup.cfm?CFID=1437354&CFTOKEN=&SitekeyParam=D-I-B (accessed 12 March 2007).

10 Pollack, A, 'Bioengineered food found in European Corn', *The New York Times*, 7 November 2000.

Thirdly, there is the economic objection that the widespread use of GM seeds will make farmers dependent on a few monopoly producers, leading to what has been termed 'bio-serfdom'. As will be shown in the discussion of the TRIPS Agreement, the biotechnology industry has been determined to prevent farmers from continuing their existing practice of saving and re-using seed. It has done this by rigorous enforcement of the contracts it imposes on those purchasing its seeds, and also by taking patent infringement suits against farmers, such as Canada's Percy Schmeiser, who make use of GM seeds that have drifted onto their land.[11]

In the future, the biotechnology industry is more likely to secure its goal of extinguishing the farmer's privilege to save and re-use seed, by the incorporation of the so-called 'terminator gene' into its product to render it sterile. In 2006, Monsanto acquired the patent to this gene and, although it has not currently incorporated it into its products, this can only be a matter of time.

These objections are likely to be met in one of two ways. The first is by an outright ban on the use of GMO seeds in agriculture and on the import of food products that contain, or may contain, material from GMO sources. The second is a requirement that food products containing GMO material must be labelled as such. I shall now examine the treatment of GMOs in two contexts: the detailed framework for the treatment of GMOs under the Cartagena Protocol to the Convention on Biological Diversity 1992; and the regulation of GMOs within the EU. Against this background, I shall then consider to what extent restrictions on the use or marketing of such products is compatible with the WTO agreements, with particular reference to the recent decision of the WTO panel on this issue in *EC–Biotech*.[12]

3.1 The Cartagena Protocol

The Cartagena Protocol to the Convention on Biological Diversity 1992 provides a detailed framework for the treatment of GMOs. The protocol was concluded on 29 January 2000 and came into force on 11 September 2003. The protocol primarily deals with living modified organisms (LMOs), for example GMO seeds. Article 4 applies the protocol to 'transboundary movement, transit, handling and use of all living modified organisms that may have adverse effects on the conservation and sustainable use of biological diversity, taking into account risks to human health'. Article 7.1 provides for the application of an Advance Informed Agreement procedure (AIA) prior to the first intentional movement of an LMO for intentional release in a receiving country. A time framework is then provided within which the country

---

11 *Monsanto Canada Inc v Schmeiser* 2004 SCC 34.
12 *EC–Biotech. European Communities–Measures Affecting the Approval and Marketing of Biotech Products*. WT/DS291/R, WT/DS292/R, WT/DS293/R. Panel report 29 September 2006.

of import may make a decision as to whether to approve the transfer, with or without conditions, or to reject the proposed transfer. Article 10.4 requires reasons to be given for any decision other than an unconditional approval. In coming to a decision the importing party must consider a risk assessment, which can be carried out either by itself or by the exporter who may be required to bear the cost of such assessment. According to Art 15.1 this risk assessment shall evaluate 'the possible adverse effects of living modified organisms on the conservation and sustainable use of biological diversity, taking into account risks to human health'. Critically, parties are authorised to use a precautionary approach in coming to a decision. Article 10.6 provides that:

> Lack of scientific certainty due to insufficient relevant scientific information and knowledge regarding the extent of the potential adverse effects of a living modified organism on the conservation and sustainable use of biological diversity in the Party of import, taking into account risks to human health, shall not prevent the Party from taking a decision, as appropriate, with regard to the import of the living modified organism in question . . . in order to avoid or minimise such potential effects.

The AIA procedure does not apply to LMOs intended for direct use as food, or feed, or for processing. These 'commodity' LMOs currently amount to around 90 per cent of traded LMOs. Limited documentary requirements are provided in respect of these commodities with Art 18.2 requiring that they be accompanied by documentation that 'clearly identifies them as "may contain" living modified organisms and as not intended for intentional introduction into the environment'. Article 11 provides that a country that approves a commodity LMO shall list that approval on the Biosafety Clearing House. Article 11.4 provides that: 'A Party may take a decision on the import of living modified organisms intended for direct use as food or feed, or for processing, under its domestic regulatory framework that is consistent with the objective of this Protocol.' Once again, a party is authorised to adopt a precautionary approach in making such a decision, with Art 11.8 providing that:

> Lack of scientific certainty due to insufficient relevant scientific information and knowledge regarding the extent of potential adverse effects of a living modified organism on the conservation and sustainable use of biological diversity in the Party of import, taking also into account risks to human health, shall not prevent that Party from taking a decision, as appropriate, with regard to the import of that living modified organism intended for direct use as food or feed or for processing in order to avoid or minimize such potential adverse effects.

The protocol's specific authorisation of a precautionary approach, not only in Arts 10.6 and 11.8, but also in the Preamble and in Art 1, provides a striking point of dissimilarity between the protocol and the WTO agreements. Under the SPS Agreement the precautionary principle has no part to play in the analysis of the 'risk assessment' that is called for by Art 5.1 and appears only to find expression in Art 5.7. However, Art 5.7 provides for only a provisional determination in instances of scientific uncertainty whereas the protocol explicitly mandates a final decision to be made in such circumstances. Furthermore, Art 5.7 calls for the decision to be reviewed 'within a reasonable time'. Under the protocol, in contrast, there is no obligation for an importing party to review a decision in respect of commodity LMOs and, as regards LMOs covered by Art 4, it can only be required to review its decision if requested to do so by an exporting party who claims that circumstances have changed since the original decision.

The negotiators of the Biosafety Protocol also intended to address the issue of liability and redress for damage resulting from the transboundary movements of LMOs but were unable to agree as to the details of a liability regime under the protocol.[13] Accordingly, an enabling clause, Art 27, was included in the final text of the protocol, to mandate further negotiations on this issue. The initial meeting of the Conference of the parties established an Open-ended Ad Hoc Working Group of Legal and Technical Experts on Liability and Redress (the Ad Hoc Group) to fulfil this mandate. The Ad Hoc Group comprises representatives nominated by parties to the protocol, and is open to the participation as observers of any non-party state, as well as to international organisations, non-governmental organisations and industry. By decision BS-I/8 it resolved to undertake the following tasks, with the aim of completing its work in 2007: reviewing the information relating to liability and redress for damage resulting from transboundary movements of LMOs; analysing general issues relating to the potential and/or actual damage scenarios of concerns, and application of international rules and procedures on liability and redress to the damage scenarios; elaborating options for elements of rules and procedures on liability and redress, including the definition and nature of damage, valuation of damage to biodiversity and to human health, threshold of damage, causation, channelling of liability, the roles of importing and exporting parties, the standard of liability, mechanisms of financial security and the right to bring claims.

So far, there have been two meetings of the Ad Hoc Group, the first in Montreal in May 2005 and the second, also in Montreal, in February 2006. The second meeting led to the development of an indicative list of criteria for

---

13 The issue of tortious liability for adventitious contamination by GMOs arose in the Aventis Starlink incident in the US. The resulting claims were settled out of court. The issue of how liability for such an incident might arise under English tort law is considered by Lee, M and Burrell, R, 'Liability for the Escape of GM Seeds: Pursuing the "Victim"?' (2002) 65 MLR 517 and by Rodgers, C, 'Liability for the release of gmos into the environment: exploring the boundaries of nuisance' (2003) 62 CLJ 371.

the assessing the effectiveness of any rules and procedures referred to in Art 27 and these are contained in Annex I to document UNEP/CBD/BS/ COP-MOP/3/10. This document also contains different options relating to scope, damage and causation, which were developed by the Ad Hoc Group after its review of the differing view that emerged from its first meeting.

3.2 Regulation of GMOs within the EU

EC regulation of GMOs begins with Directive 90/222 'on the deliberate release into the environment of genetically modified organisms'. This contained the approval procedures for the assessment by the competent authority of the member state when a GMO was to be placed on the market for the first time. Once approved, member states would not be able to prohibit or restrict trade in or use of the product. However, Art 16 allowed member states to adopt provisional safeguard measures where there were 'justifiable reasons to consider a product constitutes a risk to human health or to the environment'.

Directive 2001/18, introduced under Treaty of Amsterdam, Art 95, replaced Directive 90/220 on 17 October 2002. The directive aimed at making the procedure for granting consent to the deliberate release and placing on the market of GMOs more efficient and more transparent. Consents would be limited to a period of 10 years which would be renewable. After being placed on the market, GMOs would be subject to a process of compulsory monitoring. Annex II contains the principles relevant to the environmental risk assessment that must be undertaken before GMOs are approved for release. This is a more extensive risk assessment procedure than that provided for in Directive 90/220 and extends to cumulative, long-term effects on human health and the environment, including biological diversity and non-agricultural eco-systems.[14]

The new directive also contains a procedure that allows for the release of GMOs to be modified, suspended or terminated where new information becomes available on the risks of such release. The Commission is obliged to consult the competent scientific committees on any question which may affect human health and/or the environment, and may also consult ethical committees. Every three years, it must publish a summary of the measures taken in the member states to implement the Directive, report on experience with GMOs placed on the market, as well as issuing an annual report on ethical issues.

The procedure for introduction of GMOs into the environment for experimental purposes involves approval by the competent national authority of the member state within whose territory the experimental release is to take

---

14 Consents granted before 17 October 2002 under Directive 90/220 for the placing on the market of a GMO as or in a product may be renewed before 17 October 2006, in accordance with the simplified procedure set out in Directive 2001/18, Art 17(2)–(9).

place, on the basis of an evaluation of the risks presented by the GMO for the environment and human health. The authorisation procedure is a purely national one and an approval by one member state will not affect other member states.[15]

In contrast, the approval procedure for authorising the placing on the market of GMOs, as such, or as a component in products involves all member states, as any such authorisation implies the free movement of the authorised products throughout the EU. The application is initially made by the 'notifier' to the competent national authority of a member state. If the application is rejected the 'notifier' may submit a fresh application to another member state. If it is approved, the other member states are then informed of the decision through the European Commission and will then examine the assessment report. If there are no objections at this stage, the competent national authority that gave the approval will authorise the product to be placed on the market throughout the EU. If objections are raised, there then follows a conciliation phase among the member states, the Commission and the 'notifier' to attempt a resolution of outstanding questions. If this is not possible, the Commission must then seek the opinion of the European Food Safety Authority (EFSA), following which the Commission will present a draft decision to the Regulatory Committee composed of representatives of the member states for an opinion. If the Committee gives a favourable opinion by qualified majority, the Commission adopts the decision.

If not, the draft decision is submitted to the Council of Ministers for adoption or rejection by qualified majority. If the Council does not act within three months, the Commission is required to adopt the decision.

Article 23 allows member states to prohibit an approved GMO on the basis of new or additional information made available since the date of approval where the member state had detailed grounds for considering the GMO constituted a risk to human health or the environment.[16] Article 21 allows member states to take provisional safeguard measures until a full assessment had been made at EC level which would result either in the modification of the marketing approval or the ending of the safeguard measure.[17]

Foods and food ingredients containing GMOs were subject to a further

---

15 However, other member states and the European Commission may make observations to be examined by the competent national authority.

16 It is also possible to argue for a derogation under EC Treaty, Art 95.5, but the conditions set out therein are likely to prove to difficult for a member state to satisfy. *Land Oberösterreich und Österreich v Commission* (Joined Cases T–366/03 and T–235/04), decision of the Court of First Instance (fourth chamber), 5 October 2005.

17 Provision for national safeguard measures also occurs in Directive 2002/53 concerning genetically modified seed varieties inscribed in the common catalogue of varieties. In 2005, Poland and Greece invoked these provisions (Art 16(2) and Art 18 respectively) to request a prohibition on the use of approved GM seeds contained in the common catalogue.

measure, Commission Regulation 258/97 concerning novel foods and novel food ingredients. The regulation was aimed at ensuring that foods and food ingredients did not present a danger for consumers, did not mislead them or were not nutritionally disadvantageous for them. It contained an evaluation procedure similar to that in Directive 220/90. The initial application was to the competent body of a member state and any eventual approval allowed the marketing of the food throughout the EU. There was, however, a simplified procedure which allowed a product containing GMOs to be placed on the market if it was 'substantially equivalent' to one that already existed. The regulation also laid down labelling requirements including the presence of GMOs, as well as the presence of materials giving rise to ethical concerns. The regulation also contained a national safeguard provision, Art 12, which was invoked by Italy in September 2000 as regards trade in and use of products deriving from four GM maize varieties.[18] Since 2003, approval of GMOs has taken place under Commission Regulation 1829/2003, which is discussed below.

Labelling was initially dealt with by Directive 90/220 which allowed the option of a 'may contain' form of labelling. This was replaced by Council Regulation 1139/98, which entered into force on 3 September 1998, requiring that a food or food ingredient, produced from GM soyabean or maize, must be labelled as such on the ingredient list of the foods label. The labelling requirements would not apply if the proportion of GM soya and maize, in the event of accidental contamination, did not exceed 1 per cent of the total proportion of the foodstuff. From 2003, labelling has fallen under Commission Regulation 1830/2003, which is discussed below.

Between 1998 and 2004 there was a *de facto* moratorium on EC approvals on new GMO products. This was due to the declaration in June 1999 by the 'Group of Five', Denmark, Italy, France, Greece and Luxembourg, that they would seek to prevent applications being approved at EC level until the EC adopted rules on labelling and traceability. During this period the Commission took no action against the provisional safeguard measures taken by Austria, France, Germany, Greece, Italy and Luxembourg. The moratorium and the safeguard measures were challenged in the WTO proceedings in *EC–Biotech*. The moratorium came to an end with the introduction of the stricter rules on labelling and traceability that had been demanded by the Group of Five. These rules are contained in two new regulations concerning GMOs.

First, there is Commission Regulation 1829/2003 on genetically modified food and feed which became legally binding across all member states on 18 April 2004. This covers authorisation procedures and labelling issues. The regulation requires labelling for all food and feed products derived from GM

---

18 With the introduction of Commission Regulation 1829/2003, Italy ceased to apply its safeguard measure.

sources, regardless of the presence of detectable novel genetic material in the final product and regardless of the quantity of intentionally used GM ingredient present. All food and feed that contain, consist of or are produced from GMOs will have to be labelled at the point of sale. The regulation includes two thresholds: a 0.9 per cent threshold for the accidental presence of approved GMOs in a non-GM source, and a 0.5 per cent threshold for those which have not yet been approved in the EU but which have received a favourable assessment from an EC Scientific Committee. In applying either threshold food manufacturers will need to be able to demonstrate due diligence. The intentional use of GM ingredients at any level will require a corresponding label. There is zero tolerance for any GM variety that is not approved and does not have a favourable assessment from an EC Committee. GMOs which fall outside these categories cannot be imported into the EU.

The regulation, which also covers products already on the market, provides for a single authorisation procedure, 'one door – one key', for all food and feed containing GMOs, including their deliberate release into the environment. A single risk assessment is performed and a single authorisation is granted for a GMO and all its uses. A GMO likely to be used as food and feed can only be authorised for both uses, so avoiding problems such as were experienced in 2000 in the US with Aventis Starlink maize where traces of a strain of GM maize, which was authorised only for animal feed, ended up in food destined for human consumption. The regulation abandons the simplified procedure, previously applied in Commission Regulation 258/1997, for approval of a product containing GMOs which was 'substantially equivalent' to one that already existed. The new procedure is based on a single scientific evaluation carried out by the EFSA in accordance with the risk assessment criteria contained in Annex II of Directive 2001/18. This is a point of departure from the approval procedure adopted in Directive 2001/18 whereby the initial notification is made to the competent national authority of a member state. Another point of departure is that the regulation does not contain a national safeguard provision such as Art 23 of Directive 2002/18.[19] Article 5.5 deals with authorisation of 'GMOs or food containing or consisting of GMOs' and concludes by stating that: 'In such case, Articles 13 to 24 of Directive 2001/18/EC shall not apply.'

Secondly, there is Commission Regulation 1830/2003 concerning the traceability and labelling of GMOs and the traceability of food and feed products produced from GMOs and amending Directive 2001/18/EC. This became

---

19 Article 34 of the regulation deals with emergency measures as follows:

> Where it is evident that products authorised by or in accordance with this Regulation are likely to constitute a serious risk to human health, animal health or the environment, or where, in the light of an opinion of the Authority issued under Article 10 or Article 22, the need to suspend or modify urgently an authorisation arises, measures shall be taken under the procedures provided for in Articles 53 and 54 of Regulation (EC) No 178/2002.

binding on all member states on 16 January 2004, and covers traceability and labelling of GMOs. The regulation creates a regime for tracing and identifying GMOs, and food and feed products derived from GMOs, at all stages of their placing on the market. In addition, it will enable products to be withdrawn from the market if any unexpected adverse effects were to arise. Business operators, when using or handling GM products, are required to transmit and retain information at each stage of the placing on the market. These rules are applicable within the EU and govern entry into the EU.

To complete the picture regarding the current regulatory background in the EU regarding GMOs, three other provisions must be mentioned. First, unintentional transboundary movements of GMOs and exports of GMOs to third countries fall under Parliament and Council Regulation 2003/1946. Secondly, contained used of genetically modified microorganisms falls under Directive 90/219, as amended by Directive 98/91. This regulates research and industrial work activities on organisms such as genetically modified viruses or bacteria, under conditions of containment, such as in a laboratory. Thirdly, there is the Environmental Liability Directive, Directive 2004/35, which member states were required to implement by 30 April 2007. It makes operators of activities listed in Annex III, including the transport, use, and release of GMOs, strictly liable in respect of remediation of environmental damage caused by their activities. The directive is discussed in Chapter 11.

3.3 EC–Biotech [20]

On 29 August 2003, three complainants, the US, Canada and Argentina, initiated consolidated WTO proceedings against the EC.[21] Their challenge was directed first at the moratorium on new GMO approvals between 1998 and 2003, secondly at EC product specific measures relating to such approval within the framework of the EC legislation that covered approvals at that time,[22] and thirdly at various prohibitions maintained by individual member states by virtue of national safeguard measures in that legislation.

After the initiation of the WTO dispute procedure in August 2004, the moratorium, which was one of the measures in dispute, came to an end on 19 May 2004 when the European Commission authorised the import of food products made from genetically modified Bt11 sweet maize. Since the ending of the moratorium, five GMO products and four GMOs for feed use have been authorised.[23] By 2006, farmers were cultivating approved GM crops

---

20 *EC–Biotech. European Communities–Measures Affecting the Approval and Marketing of Biotech Products.* WT/DS291/R, WT/DS292/R, WT/DS293/R. Panel report 29 September 2006.

21 Claims DS/291/03, DS/292/03 and DS/293/03, respectively.

22 Directive 90/222/EEC, Commission Regulation 258/97 and Directive 2001/18.

23 *Questions and Answers on the Regulation of GMOs in the EU*, Annexes 1b and 3, http://ec. europa.eu/food/food/biotechnology/gmfood/qanda_en.pdf (accessed 12 March 2007).

on 65,000 hectares in six member states, Portugal, Spain, Germany, France, Czech Republic and Slovakia.[24]

However, the continuance of national safeguard measures has been a continuing source of frustration to those who would like to see the cultivation of GM crops within the EU.[25] In 2003, following the introduction of the two new regulations on GMOs, the Commission requested a reconsideration of the prohibition on the use of approved GMOs by the eight member states that were relying on the national safeguard provisions. The Commission requested these member states to submit new information which it then passed on to EFSA for its opinion. In July 2004, EFSA concluded that the additional information did not invalidate the original risk assessments applying them.[26] The Commission proposed decisions requiring the member states to lift the prohibitions, but on 24 July 2005 the EU Council of the Environment rejected these proposals. The Commission then made a further reference to EFSA in respect of Austria's bans on MON 810 and T25.[27] In March 2006, EFSA concluded that the two products were unlikely to cause any adverse effects on human and animal health or on the environment. Accordingly, in October 2006, the Commission made a second attempt to secure the repeal of the two Austrian safeguard measures. However, on 18 December 2006, the Council on the Environment, by a qualified majority, again rejected the Commission's proposals. The reason for the rejection was because the two strains of GM maize had not been approved under Directive 2001/18, which contains harmonised environmental risk assessment criteria for GMOs which were absent from Directive 90/220, under which the approvals were originally granted.[28] The different agricultural structures and regional ecological characteristics in the EU also needed to be taken into account in a more systematic manner in the environmental risk assessment of GMOs. On 20 February 2007, the Environment Council also rejected the Commission's proposal that Hungary

---

24 Fletcher, A, *EU must wake up from 'GM food inertia'*, 1 March 2007, www.foodnavigator.com/news/ng.asp?id=74604-europabio-gm-biotech (accessed 12 March 2007).

25 An illuminating analysis of the current complexities of EU regulation of GMOs is provided by Ostrovsky, A, 'Up Against a Wall: Europe's Options for Regulating Biotechnology through Regulatory Anarchy' (2007) 13 ELJ 110.

26 Throughout this period the European Commission, on the one hand, was seeking the repeal of national safeguard measures whilst the EC, on the other hand, was arguing before the WTO panel that the measure involved no violations of the EC's obligations under the WTO agreements. The contrast between what was being said by EFSA and the Commission and the scientific evidence put forward before the WTO panel is summarised by Friends of the Earth Europe, Greenpeace, *Hidden Uncertainties What the European Commission doesn't want us to know about the risks of gmos*, April 2006, www.foeeurope.org/publications/2006/hidden_uncertainties.pdf (accessed 15 March 2007).

27 The other national safeguard measures have become irrelevant as the GM products in question are no longer being marketed.

28 The EFSA approvals were under Directive 90/220, rather than under Directive 2001/18.

be required to lift its ban on MON 810 maize which it had imposed under the national safeguard clause.

The interim final report of the panel in *EC–Biotech* came out in February 2006 and was shortly afterwards was leaked to the public. The final report of the panel award was eventually circulated on 29 September 2006. The EC has decided not to appeal the award. The complainants' challenge was threefold in nature. First, the measures were in breach of provisions of the SPS Agreement. Secondly, the measures were in breach of provisions of the GATT. Thirdly, the measures were in breach of provisions of the TBT Agreement. The panel found in favour of the complainants on the first of these grounds and, therefore, saw no need to make findings on the other two grounds.

The first issue was whether the SPS Agreement covered the three challenged measures. SPS Agreement, Annex A does not expressly address environmental protection, unlike TBT Agreement, Art 2.2, for example, which expressly refers to 'the environment'. However, Directives 90/220 and 2001/18 repeatedly listed as one of their purposes the protection of the environment. The EC argued that this showed that the measures should be dealt with under the TBT Agreement rather than the SPS Agreement. The panel, however, found that SPS Agreement, Annex A.1(a) and (b) covered measures applied to protect animal and plant life or health from certain risks. Thus, to the extent Directives 90/220 and 2001/18 were applied to protect animals and plants as part of their purpose of protecting the environment, they were not *a priori* excluded from the scope of application of the SPS Agreement.

The central purpose of the two directives was to protect human health and the environment when placing on the market GMOs either in themselves or in products, and to avoid adverse effects on human health and the environment which might arise from the deliberate release of GMOs. Although neither directive explicitly identified what potential risks for human health and the environment had to be assessed prior to a release of GMOs into the environment, they nevertheless identified the information required in an application for marketing approval. This encompassed the characteristics of the GMO, such as: toxic or allergenic effects; information on pathogenicity, communicability, host range, antibiotic resistance patterns, and the potential for excessive population increase in the environment or the competitive advantage of the GMOs in relation to the unmodified recipient or parental organism(s). Directive 2001/18 also addressed the methodology to be followed to perform an environmental risk assessment, which mentioned that potential adverse effects of GMOs may include, for instance, disease to humans including allergenic or toxic effects; disease to animals and plants including toxic, and where appropriate, allergenic effects, among others.

The panel found that a GMO could constitute a 'pest', which under the SPS Agreement includes weeds, provided it interacted in some way with plants or humans. The GMO did not have to be pathogenic or injurious, nor did the product subject to an SPS measure itself have to be the pest which gave rise to the risks at which the measure was directed. Accordingly, most of the purposes to which the directives were addressed fell within heading (a), which covers measures 'to protect animal or plant life or health within the territory of the Member from risks arising from the entry, establishment or spread of pests, diseases, disease-carrying organisms or disease-causing organisms'.

The panel also found that GMOs could constitute a 'feedstuff' and so fell within heading (b), which covers measures 'to protect human or animal life or health within the territory of the Member from risks arising from additives, contaminants, toxins or disease-causing organisms in foods, beverages or feedstuffs'. The term 'feedstuff' was wide enough to include a GM crop that had been grown for a different purpose, but was eaten by animals, including wild fauna, so becoming 'food' for that animal. The term 'additive' was also capable of encompassing GMOs which were still 'substances' notwithstanding that genes themselves contained and encoded instructions for the creation of various substances. To the extent a GM plant produced allergenic effects other than as a food, it would constitute a 'pest' and fall within heading (c), which covers measures 'to protect human life or health within the territory of the Member from risks arising from diseases carried by animals, plants or products thereof, or from the entry, establishment or spread of pests'. The risk of a GMO causing physical damage to property or economic damage, as well as damage to the environment other than damage to the life or health of living organisms would fall within heading (d), which covers measures 'to prevent or limit other damage within the territory of a Member from the entry, establishment or spread of pests'. Damage to biodiversity, however, implied damage to living organisms which would be more likely to fall under the types of risks referred to in headings (a) and (b).

Turning next to Commission Regulation 258/97, Art 3.1 stated that foods and food ingredients falling within the scope of the regulation must not: (1) present a danger for the consumer; (2) mislead the consumer; and (3) differ from foods or food ingredients which they are intended to replace to such an extent that their normal consumption would be nutritionally disadvantageous for the consumer. The first of these purposes fell within the ambit of heading (b) of Annex A.1 and so constituted an SPS measure. However, to the extent that the regulation sought to achieve the second and third of these purposes, it fell outside the definitions in Annex A.1, and therefore did not amount to an SPS measure. A measure incorporating different purposes could, therefore, fall within the scope of application of more than one WTO agreement, although it was unclear what happens when there is such an overlap. To the extent that a purpose fell under the SPS Agreement, that agreement would apply. To the extent that a purpose fell outside the SPS Agreement, it was likely that another agreement, probably the TBT Agreement or the GATT, would apply. The question of overlapping purposes is likely to be important in the context of labelling requirements which were not at issue in this dispute.

Having brought the three EC measures within the scope of the SPS Agreement the next step required analysis of whether these measures had violated any of the obligations set out thereunder. The EC moratorium was not a decision to reject all biotech applications, but rather to defer all approvals until certain conditions had been satisfied. The moratorium claims therefore did not fall within the scope of SPS Agreement, Arts 2.2, 2.3, 5.1, 5.6, 5.7 and 7. Article 5.1, for example, referred to 'requirements and procedures', but did not cover the way in which these were applied. Instead, the moratorium constituted a breach of Art 8 in that between 1998 and 2003 it had led to 'undue delays' in the granting of approval to new GMO products. These could not be justified by the lack of EC legislation on labelling and traceability. An expeditious decision was required and, if the science was still evolving, or the EC wanted to rely on the precautionary principle, then it still needed to make a decision, which it could base either on Art 5.1 or on Art 5.7.

In contrast, the national safeguard measures did fall to be considered under Arts 5.1 and 5.7. The panel, applying similar legal reasoning to that applied to this issue in the context of the EC moratorium, concluded that the purposes behind each of the nine safeguard measures fell within the definition of an SPS measure in Annex 1(a). The panel then examined Art 5.1 and ruled that the words 'as appropriate to the circumstances' did not mean that the risk assessment could be appropriate to the circumstances of the state applying the measure. Where there was little available scientific evidence these words might provide some flexibility as to how, but not whether, the definition of a 'risk assessment' in Annex A(4) had been satisfied. The measures here were not based on the original EC risk assessments, as supplemented by new material containing a divergent opinion. This was not the hypothetical situation contemplated by the appellate body in *EC–Beef Hormones*,[29] where the risk assessment itself contained divergent opinions. If the later reports were based on an earlier risk assessment, but disagreed with it, members must explain 'by reference to the existing assessment, how and why they assess risks differently, and to provide their revised or supplemental assessment of the risks'.[30] In approaching this task, the panel confined itself to examining reports written before the date of its establishment on 29 August 2003.

After a detailed examination of the evidence, the panel concluded that none of the scientific studies produced by the member states to justify their safeguard measures constituted a valid risk assessment as required by Art 5.1. There were various reasons for the failure of these scientific studies to amount

29 *EC–Beef Hormones. European Communities–Measures Concerning Meat and Meat Products (Hormones)*. WT/ DS/48/R/CAN, WT/DS/26/R/US. Panel report 18 August 1997. WT/ DS/ 48/AB/R, WT/DS/26/AB/R. Appellate body report 16 January 1998.
30 Paragraph 73058.

to a valid risk assessment capable of displacing the initial EC risk assessments on the products which had led to their approval for marketing within the EC.

First, and most commonly, there is the failure to evaluate the likelihood, ie the probability of a risk, as required by the decision of the appellate body in *Australia–Salmon*.[31] This can be seen with the Reasons Document on Bt-176 supplied by Austria and Germany, and the studies each refers to, as well as with Austria's Reasons Document on MON 810. Austria's prohibition on MON 810 maize was justified by reference to the need to protect environmentally sensitive areas from spillovers from GM crops. Austria relied on the Hopplicher study, but this contained no indication of the relative probability of the potential risks it identified, referring to possibilities of risks or the inability to determine probability as evidenced by findings such as 'contamination of natural gene pools through synthetic genes is incalculable in principle in predictive risk assessment'.[32]

A similar defect infected Austria's Reasons Document relating to its prohibition on Bt-176 maize stated that the possible risks were hard to assess and where not worth taking given the existence of adequate non-biotech maize products. It was also stated that the impact of the transfer of the *bla* gene to bacteria of humans and animals could not be fully evaluated. The Reasons Document also referred to two studies which examined the mechanism through which insects develop resistance to the Bt toxin. These studies focused on the development of resistance to Bt toxin due to the commercial production of transgenic Bt crops. The first study described a technique for estimating the likelihood that a particular population of insects would develop resistance to Bt toxin, focusing on insects feeding on Bt cotton. The second used genetic analysis to show that a single insect gene could confer resistance to several different strains of the Bt toxin, and examined the genetics underlying the evolution of resistance through feeding studies of insects on Bt toxins in dust form. The panel, however, found that: 'While the results of these studies may be of relevance to the assessment of the risks of the potential development of resistance to Bt-176 maize, neither study assesses the likelihood of this risk.'[33]

This was also the problem with study, by the Öko-Institut e.V., submitted by Germany to review the possible development of resistance to antibiotics due to the use of antibiotic resistance marker genes in transgenic plants. However, the study failed to evaluate the likelihood that the consumption of transgenic plants in general, much less of Bt-176 maize specifically, would

---

31 *Australia–Salmon. Australia–Measures affecting the importation of salmon.* WT/DS18/R. Panel report 12 June 1998. WT/DS18/AB/R. Appellate body report 20 October 1998.
32 Paragraph 73044.
33 Paragraph 73078.

lead to the spread of diseases due to the development of resistance to the relevant antibiotics. Although this study asserted a potential for adverse effects on human or animal health from the presence of antibiotic resistance marker genes (ARMG) in transgenic plants used as or in food/feed, it did not 'evaluate' that potential. It referred to possibilities, but did not determine likelihoods.[34]

Secondly, there is the lack of documentation referred to in connection with scientific studies mentioned in Austria's Reasons Document. Elsewhere, studies were referred to, but discounted as they had been written after the date at which the panel was established.

Thirdly, some of the studies were based on a different type of Bt strain to the one covered by the national safeguard measure in issue. Austria's Reasons Document relating to its prohibition on MON 810 showed that it had been concerned about the effects of the product on non-target organisms and the development of resistance in insects. The document referred to the possibilities of risks, but did not itself evaluate the potential for adverse health effects or the likelihood of the risk of establishment, entry or spread of a pest. Austria relied on three scientific studies. The first study by Losey, entitled 'Transgenic pollen harms monarch larvae' described results from a laboratory experiment in which monarch butterfly caterpillars were fed Bt maize pollen. However, the focus was on a variety of Bt maize other than MON 810 maize. While the study noted that results on larvae consumption and growth rates had potentially profound implications for the conservation of monarch butterflies, there was no attempt to evaluate these potential implications. Instead, the study noted that the experimental results pointed to possible environmental outcomes. The study argued that monarch butterfly caterpillars were at risk from the production of Bt maize, but stated that '[t]he large land area covered by corn in this region suggests that a substantial portion of available milkweeds may be within range of corn pollen deposition'. Therefore, the study did not, in itself, amount to a risk assessment.[35]

A similar failure can be seen with regards to the 2001 Biomolecular Engineering Committee report relied on by France, which was addressed to all herbicide tolerant rape varieties, not specifically to those which were genetically modified. The report did appear to provide some evaluation of the likelihood of entry, establishment or spread of one of the 'pests' of concern, that is of hybrids between herbicide tolerant oilseed rape and some wild plants. However, this was addressed with respect to all herbicide tolerant oilseed rape varieties and not specifically those which are genetically modified. Nor did the report provide any analysis of the associated potential biological and economic consequences of these hybrids, nor did it purport to evaluate the

34 Paragraph 73151.
35 Paragraph 73097.

likelihood of entry, establishment or spread of these hybrids according to the SPS measures which might be applied.[36]

Fourthly, the wrong type of test has been conducted. This can be seen with the Hillbeck study put forward by Austria as regards MON 810. This described a feeding study in which insects were fed a liquid diet containing Bt toxins, rather than being fed Bt plants directly and did not, therefore, evaluate the potential for adverse effects associated with the insects eating MON 810 maize plants. It also noted, in its conclusion, that 'trials investigating predation efficiency and predator performance under field conditions are necessary before conclusions regarding the potential ecological relevance of the results presented [. . .] can be drawn'.[37]

Fifthly, some of the reports which were done in laboratory conditions pointed out the need for further trials in the field. The Hillbeck study used a maize hybrid containing a gene from Bt, to provide information regarding the impact on non-maize eating insects of eating herbivorous insects raised on Bt maize and was thus aimed at evaluating non-target impacts of Bt crop cultivation. The study concluded that, in this experiment, differences in mortality existed for insect predators fed prey raised on Bt versus non-Bt maize, but noted that '[n]o conclusions can be drawn at this point as to how results from [. . .] laboratory trials might translate in the field'.[38] The Saxena study examined the potential for Bt toxin to be released into the soil from the roots of Bt maize. The study used a variety of Bt maize called NK4640Bt which differs from the variety which is subject to the German safeguard measure. While the study measured the toxin released into the soil surrounding the roots of maize plants, the authors note that they have 'no indication of how soil communities might be affected by Bt toxin in [. . .] the field' and that '[f]urther investigations will be necessary to shed light on what might happen underground'. Thus, this study neither purported to evaluate the potential consequences associated with the release of Bt exudates into the soil, nor provided information specifically related to the product at issue in this safeguard measure, Bt-176 maize.[39]

There remained the possibility that the safeguard measures might be justified by reference to Art 5.7. The panel agreed with the EC that this provision existed as an autonomous right and not by way of an exception. However, there was an implicit cross-reference between this provision and Art 5.1 which showed that scientific evidence would only be 'insufficient' if it did not allow the performance of a risk assessment as defined in Annex A(4). The panel rejected the EC's argument that there was a relationship between the 'sufficiency' of scientific evidence required for a risk assessment and the level of

---

36 Paragraph 73120.
37 Paragraph 73098.
38 Paragraph 73148.
39 Paragraph 73149.

SPS protection which a member sought to achieve. A member's protection might be relevant to the question of which risks a member decided to assess with a view to taking regulatory action, and were certainly relevant to the actions taken to achieve a member's chosen level of protection against risk.[40] Yet the protection goals chosen by a member had no relevance to the task of assessing the existence and magnitude of potential risks. The problem for the EC was that all the measures in question had already been subject to risk assessments when the products initially received approval. None of the evidence considered in the analysis of Art 5.1 could be said to have constituted an alternative risk assessment. There had, therefore, been a failure to satisfy the first requirement of Art 5.7, that there was 'insufficient' scientific evidence at the time the measure was introduced. Accordingly, there was no need to consider whether there had also been a failure to satisfy the other cumulative requirements of Art 5.7.

The panel also considered two other arguments. The first was the separate claim made by Argentina which was based on the provisions of Art 10 relating to the special and differential treatment to be afforded to developing nations. The panel held that there had been no violation of Art 10 and that the EC was not required to weigh the interests of Argentina, as a developing nation, over the interests of consumers in the EC. Secondly, there was the argument advanced by the EC account should be taken of the Convention on Biodiversity and the Cartagena Protocol, in the same way in which the appellate body had made use of CITES in *US–Shrimp/Turtle*.[41] However, the panel found that the convention could be disregarded as it had not been ratified by all parties to the dispute.[42] The panel also followed the lead of the appellate body in *EC–Beef Hormones*[43] in declining to express a view as to whether the precautionary principle had become established as a rule of general, or customary, international law. Finally, the panel's findings that the moratorium involved a breach of Art 8, and that the national safeguard measures involved a breach of SPS Agreement, Art 5.1, made it unnecessary for it to complete the analysis of whether there had also been breaches of the TBT agreement or of GATT, Arts III.4 and XI, as the complainants had argued.

40 Factors in risk assessment that affected the level of confidence of scientists conducting an evaluation would also bear on this issue.

41 *US–Shrimp Turtle. United States–Import Prohibition of Certain Shrimp and Shrimp Products.* WT/DS/58/R. Panel report 15 May 1998. WT/DS/58/AB/R. Appellate body report 12 October 1998.

42 Argentina and Canada had signed the convention, but not ratified it. The US had done neither.

43 *EC–Beef Hormones. European Communities–Measures Concerning Meat and Meat Products (Hormones).* WT/ DS/48/R/CAN, WT/DS/26/R/US. Panel report 18 August 1997. WT/ DS/ 48/AB/R, WT/DS/26/AB/R. Appellate body report 16 January 1998.

3.4 The aftermath of the decision

The recent decisions of the Environment Council to reject the Commission's proposals that Austria and Hungary be required to drop their safeguard measures pose a big problem for the EC. As matters stand, the continuance of the Austrian measures will place the EC in breach of the panel's recommendations in *EC–Biotech*. The next step would be for the US, Canada and Argentina to seek to impose trade sanctions against the EC for its failure to implement the findings of the panel. The critical issue that will arise when the panel comes to hear the compliance proceedings will be whether new scientific studies have been produced to justify the safeguard measures. The fact that EFSA has maintained its approval of the GM maize strains despite the submission of new evidence makes it unlikely that the EC will be able to convince a compliance panel that it has now conducted a valid risk assessment as required by Art 5.1.

It is also likely that the US and other exporters of GMOs will now turn their attention to the EU's rigorous regime of labelling and traceability requirements. This is likely to prove the biggest obstacle to the establishment of a market for GM foods in Europe, given the hostility of European consumers to such foods. It is likely that these requirements in a future challenge under the WTO agreements. One avenue of challenge would be under the GATT.[44] It is arguable that mandatory labelling requirements constitute a quantitative restriction on imports and, therefore, violate Art XI. From a complainant's viewpoint this would have the attraction of avoiding the threshold issue of whether or not the product subject to the labelling requirement was 'like' other products which were not subject to this requirement. The application of the Interpretative Note *ad* Art III would be critical to this issue.[45] In both the *Tuna Dolphin* awards the GATT panel found that the note covers only those measures that are applied to the product as such. In the second of these awards the panel noted that 'the import embargoes distinguished between tuna products according to harvesting practices and tuna import policies of the exporting countries' and that 'none of these practices, policies and methods could have any impact on the inherent character of tuna as a product'. However, in contrast, a labelling requirement

---

44 See Chang, S, 'GATTING a green trade barrier: eco-labelling and the WTO Agreement on Technical Barriers to Trade' (1997) 31(1) JWT 137; Zedalis, R, 'Labeling of Genetically Modified Foods – The Limits of GATT Rules' (2001) 35(2) JWT 301.

45 The note refers to:

> Any internal tax or other internal charge, or any law, regulation or requirement of the kind referred to in paragraph 1 which applies to an imported product and to the like domestic product and is collected or enforced in the case of the imported product at the time or point of importation, is nevertheless to be regarded as an internal tax or other internal charge, or a law, regulation or requirement of the kind referred to in paragraph 1, and is accordingly subject to the provisions of Article III.

based on the fact that a product contained GMO material does go to the 'inherent character' of the product, rather than to the way it is produced. The whole point of the labelling is to inform consumers as to what is contained in the product itself, rather than to give information as to how it has been produced.

Assuming, then, that Art XI did not apply, the next issue would be whether there had been a violation of either Art I or Art III.4 on the ground that GM products or products containing GM materials should be treated as 'like' their conventional equivalents. The complainant would rely heavily on the criteria of end-use substitutability for the two products under comparison. In contrast, the respondent would rely on the physical difference in DNA structure between the two products under comparison, although this criterion is rather weak when the labelled product contains only small traces of GMO material. Following the appellate body's findings in *EC–Asbestos*,[46] health risks associated with the product measure would inform consideration of these criteria. However, it would be difficult for the member imposing the labelling requirement to justify it on public health grounds, given the lack of scientific evidence as to the potential adverse impacts on human health that would be entailed by consumption of food containing GMO material.

Instead, the most promising avenue for justifying such a measure would be by reference to the criterion of consumer preferences. These preferences would be based on two considerations. First, there are fears as to the long-term safety of consumption of food containing GMO material. Secondly, there are concerns as to the potential hazards to biodiversity, through cross-pollination of GM crops. Although members could not rely on such considerations to prohibit such products, this does not mean that the same should apply to preferences exhibited by consumers. Consumers have a right to know what they are eating and that right to know should not be conditional on their conducting a risk assessment in accordance with SPS Agreement, Art 5.1. Consumers should be entitled to apply their own precautionary approach to what they eat, no matter how idiosyncratic that might be. There is also no reason to disregard consumer preferences when they are based on PPM criteria, such as concerns about the potential hazards to biodiversity involved in the cultivation of GMOs.

The extent to which consumer preferences, however 'unreasonable' from some scientific viewpoints, can inform the issue of 'likeness' will probably prove critical to any future labelling dispute. This is because a finding that a labelling requirement violated either Art I or Art III.4 would almost certainly dispose of the issue. It would be very difficult for the respondent member to rely on the exceptions in Art XX(b) or Art XX(g). The lack of any current

---

46 *EC–Asbestos. European Communities–Measures Affecting Asbestos and Products Containing Asbestos.* WT/DS/135/R. Panel report 19 September 2000. WT/DS/135/AB/R. Appellate body report 12 March 2001.

scientific evidence as to any public health risks involved in consuming products incorporating GMOs would preclude reliance on para (b). Objections based on the possible adverse impacts on biodiversity due to cultivation of GMOs might enable the respondent member to argue that its labelling requirement related to the 'conservation of exhaustible natural resources'. However, this would run into the old problem of whether reliance can be placed on the exceptions in Art XX when the measure is based on PPM criteria. Furthermore, it would be somewhat inconsistent to justify a measure on this ground when the member imposing the measure allowed the cultivation of GMOs within its territory.

Labelling requirements could also be challenged under the TBT Agreement. Mandatory labelling requirements would amount to a 'technical regulation', as defined in Annex 1, but under Art 1.5 would not fall under the TBT Agreement if they constituted an SPS measure. This would require a determination of the purposes behind the current EC labelling requirements. To the extent that they are directed at protection of public health they would fall under the SPS Agreement.[47] To the extent that they are directed at providing information to consumers, they would fall within the TBT Agreement. The next issue would be whether the technical regulation fell foul of Art 2.1 in that it accorded less favourable treatment to imported GMO food than to 'like products of national origin and to like products originating in any other country' which were not subject to the measure in question. At this point of the enquiry, the same issues would be raised as to the 'likeness' of GMO products and their conventional equivalents as were discussed earlier in relation to Art III.4.

Assuming a negative answer to the question of 'likeness' for the purposes of the analysis required under Art 2.1, the measure could still be challenged under Art 2.2 on the ground that it was 'more trade restrictive than necessary'. In doing so the panel would need to consider whether the aim of the measure was 'to fulfil a legitimate objective' which includes '. . . prevention of deceptive practices, protection of human health or safety; animal or plant life or health; or the environment'. In assessing risks in relation to a legitimate objective, the relevant elements of consideration would be '. . . available scientific and technical information, related processing technology or intended end-uses of products'. In the absence of any concrete evidence as to the existence of health risks involved in consumption of GMO food, a labelling measure could not be said to have the legitimate objective of 'protection of human health or safety'. However, the measure could be justified by reference to 'the prevention of deceptive practices', on the ground that consumers had

---

47 Such a measure would fall under the definition in Annex A.1, heading (b), as a measure applied 'to protect human . . . life, or health within the territory of the Member from risks arising from additives, contaminants, toxins or disease-causing organisms in foods, beverages of feedstuffs'.

a legitimate expectation of being able to decide for themselves whether or not to purchase food containing GMO produce. Finally, there is the issue of whether such a measure was 'more trade restrictive than necessary'. This might well lead to a finding that the EU's labelling requirements violate Art 2.2 on the grounds that the legitimate aim of the 'prevention of deceptive practices' could have been achieved through an alternative labelling measure that was less trade restrictive, such as the 'may contain' wording that was an option under Directive 90/220.

3.5 Conclusion

How well, then, has the emerging WTO law tackled the task of balancing the conflicting goals of free trade and environmental protection? To answer this question I propose to examine five particular areas of controversy: the over-lap of jurisdictional competence between the WTO agreements and MEAs; the overlap of jurisdictional competence between the WTO agreements them-selves; the ability of members to base environmental regulation on PPM criteria; the evidential threshold applicable to the justification of measures on grounds of health or environmental protection; the administrative obli-gations imposed on members in designing and implementing measures.

3.5.1 Jurisdictional overlap between the WTO agreements and MEAs

International environmental problems, of the sort addressed in the *Tuna Dolphin* and *US–Shrimp/Turtle* references, are most effectively addressed by multilateral agreements. A beneficial effect of the decisions in these refer-ences has been to spur the US into further efforts to negotiate multilateral agreements with the complainants, which might not have been made had the panels simply upheld the validity of the initial unilateral measures.[48] It is vital, therefore, that when a multilateral agreement is successfully concluded its provisions are given due weight when considering a dispute under one of the WTO agreements which involves a measure which is justified under that MEA. In this regard, the decision of the appellate body in *US–Shrimp/Turtle* is a positive development in that it gives clear encouragement to the practice of solving international environmental problems by multilateral agreement. The decision of the panel and the appellate body in the compliance proceed-ings confirms that unilateral measures may still be used provided there has been a good faith effort to negotiate such an agreement and that the measures are applied flexibly.

---

48 It is widely thought that the panel decision in *Tuna Dolphin 1* contributed towards the adoption of the Agreement on the Reduction of Dolphin Mortality in the Eastern Pacific Ocean 1992.

These decisions implicitly create a presumption that measures justified by reference to a MEA will be compliant with the WTO agreements in the context of a dispute between members, both of whom are party to that MEA. It is unlikely that a panel could go further than this without finding that the MEA had constituted a waiver of certain WTO obligations as between the parties to the MEA. In any event, the flexibility of the current situation might be regarded as desirable in that it reserves to panels the ability, by reference to the *chapeau*, to find against measures that are disproportionately trade restrictive given the objectives of the MEA. This capacity is likely to be particularly useful to prevent abuses by members of provisions, such as CITES, Art XIV.1, that permit parties to take stricter domestic measures than those mandated by the MEA in question.

However, there still remain uncertainties. First, the sea turtle species in *Shrimp/Turtle* were migratory and all appeared in US waters. This creates a factual nexus, albeit tenuous, between the measure and US jurisdiction. The appellate body declined to comment on what the position under Art XX(g) would have been in the absence of this nexus. There remains, therefore, the possibility that, in the absence of such a nexus, a measure that is either mandated, or justified, under the terms of an MEA will not be regarded as falling within Art XX(g). Secondly, there is the question of what effect a MEA will have on a non-party. The tolerance of unilateral measures in limited situations that emerges from the compliance proceedings in *Shrimp/Turtle* indicates that the existence of the MEA may be taken into account for the purposes of GATT, Art XX, even where the complainant is not a party to it. However, it must be recalled that in *Shrimp/Turtle* the measure, although not justified under the terms of CITES, was taken with a view to conserving a species protected under that treaty, and that the parties to the WTO disputes were also parties to CITES. In this situation it is relatively easy for to establish prima facie validity for the measure and then to pass on consider its validity under the *chapeau*. This would not be the case where the complainant had no connection at all with the MEA invoked, directly or indirectly, by the member imposing the measure. Accordingly, it is no surprise to find that the panel in *EC–Biotech* declined to take account of the provisions of the 2000 Cartagena Protocol on Biosafety, on the grounds that none of the three complainants were parties to this MEA. It is, however, possible that a MEA could achieve such a widespread level of international acceptance that it constitutes a *ius cogens* norm of international law and, thereby, becomes binding on non-parties. Given the reluctance of panels and the appellate body to rule on whether the precautionary principle has become part of customary international law, it is unlikely that such a finding will be made in any future dispute involving a non-party to a MEA.

3.5.2 Jurisdictional overlap between the WTO agreements

There is still some uncertainty as to the demarcation lines between the various WTO agreements. For example, in *EC–Asbestos* Canada initially based its challenge on three agreements, the GATT, the TBT Agreement and the SPS Agreement, although by the time of the hearing it had abandoned its claim under the SPS Agreement. The appellate body's decision was a useful reminder of the importance of Art III as regards import restrictions designed to protect public health. Its willingness to allow public health considerations to be taken into account in its analysis of the four criteria relevant to the issue of 'likeness' means that many such measures are capable of justification on the grounds that they do not involve a violation of the GATT at all. If the banned product is regarded as 'unlike' a substitute product, because of the health risks it brings with it, that will mean there is no violation of Art III.4 and no need to justify the measure under Art XX, where the burden of proof will fall on the respondent. However, given the expansive interpretation of SPS Agreement, Annex A in *EC–Biotech* it is likely that many public health measures will fall under that agreement rather than under the GATT.

This leads to the issue of whether a measure may need to be assessed under more than one agreement. In *EC–Biotech* the panel applied the principle of judicial economy to this issue. Having found that the measures were not in conformity with the SPS Agreement, there was no need to consider their conformity with either the GATT or the TBT Agreement. In doing so it followed the example of the appellate body in *Reformulated Gasoline* where its finding that the US measure involved a violation of the GATT meant that there was no need to consider the parallel claim of violation of the TBT Agreement. However, the position is different where the measure is found to be in conformity with the first agreement to be considered. Thus, in *EC–Asbestos*, the appellate body, having made such a finding with regard to the GATT, went on to make a partial consideration of the measure's conformity with the TBT Agreement. However, there remains the possibility of a measure that is found to be in conformity, then being found to be in violation of the TBT Agreement.

This scenario would be impossible where the measure is challenged under the SPS Agreement and the GATT. A finding of conformity with the SPS Agreement would then lead to the presumption that the measure fell within the scope of GATT, Art XX(b). The fact that the requirements of the *chapeau* find expression in provisions of the SPS Agreement effectively makes this presumption an irrebuttable one. Another area of potential overlap would be between the SPS Agreement and the TBT Agreement. At first sight, this would seem to be precluded by the TBT Agreement, Art 1.5 which excludes SPS measures from its scope. However, the panel in *EC–Biotech* acknowledged that a measure with multiple purposes, only some of which fell within the definition of an SPS measure in Annex A.1, might need to be considered under more than one agreement. This was the case as regards Commission Regulation 258/97, which was partly directed at providing information to prevent consumers being mislead. This was not a purpose that fell within the definition of an SPS measure. Therefore, had the panel found the regulation to have been in conformity with the SPS Agreement, it would then have had to reassess it under either the GATT or the TBT Agreement.

3.5.3 The ability of members to base environmental regulation on PPM criteria

The treatment of PPM criteria by GATT and WTO panels has resulted in a severe limitation on the development of policies to deal with the transnational nature of environmental damage. PPM criteria play no part in the analysis of 'likeness' that determines whether or not there has been an initial violation of the GATT under Art I or Art III, or whether a measure is a non-discriminatory administration of quantitative restrictions under Art XI. As regards Art XX(g), the decision of the appellate body in *US–Shrimp/Turtle* can be seen as giving some limited recognition to PPM criteria. However, as has already been observed in connection with the relationship of the WTO agreements to MEAs, this decision is, potentially, quite limited by two factors. First, the PPM in question, the mode of harvesting shrimp, was directed at the goal of preserving a species listed in CITES, Annex I, an international treaty with a substantial number of signatories, including the parties to the reference. Secondly, the migratory nature of sea turtles and their appearance in US territorial waters meant that there was sufficient nexus between the US and the measure. In the absence of this nexus the position is unclear. The two GATT panels in *US–Tuna Dolphin* gave different answers to this question and in *US–Shrimp/Turtle* the appellate body refrained from comment on the point.

In the absence of these special factors, it is likely that PPMs will still be regarded as insufficient criteria to justify the invocation of Art XX(b) or Art XX(g). This makes it very difficult for members in the developed world to deal with the problem of 'the race to the bottom' whereby investment relocates to countries in the developing world which do not apply the same rigorous environmental and safety regulations as apply in the developed world.[49] For example, the EU, on animal welfare grounds, might decide to prohibit battery farming within member states. It would, however, be unable to prevent the import of battery farmed eggs from outside the EU which would be able to undercut the price of eggs produced within the EU. For the purposes of the GATT, EU eggs and non-EU eggs would still be eggs, and

---

49 This also gives rise to the issues of foreign direct liability which are considered elsewhere in this book.

therefore 'like products', no matter how they were produced. A similar analysis would apply to 'eco-taxes' that attempted to compensate for the advantages available to the importers of products made under a less demanding environmental regime.

The following justifications appear on the WTO's website for the difference in treatment between product and process requirements.[50] Process requirements are said to be more subjective than product ones. Arguments of sovereignty militate against process requirements as an example of one member imposing its standards on another. Politically and economically it is preferable for each member to determine which standards it applies within its jurisdiction. This political autonomy should also bring environmental benefits in that each member would then be able to tailor the standards they apply within their territory to the particular conditions prevailing therein. There is strength behind all these arguments. Yet there is also validity in the counter-arguments that members that impose high domestic environmental standards should not be put at a competitive disadvantage thereby. There is also the question of environmental 'spillovers' whereby the means of production causes environmental damage in the member imposing the PPM restriction. The restriction is now directed at protecting the environment importing member, so weakening one of the main objections to PPMs, that they involve the extra-territorial application of national production standards. This issue is likely to become increasingly important as new MEAs are concluded to deal with the problem of global warming. For example, imported goods might be taxed by reference to the carbon used in their production. Such developments are likely to lead to a reappraisal of the status of PPMs under the WTO agreements.

3.5.4 The evidential threshold applicable to the justification of measures on grounds of health or environmental protection

One of the principal objections to the use of PPM criteria is that they involve an interference with the sovereignty of the exporting member who is expected to conform with standards applicable in the territory of the member imposing the measure. The other side of this argument is that, for measures taking effect within their own territory, members should be free to adopt whatever standards of public health and environmental protection they deem appropriate. The appellate body has accepted these arguments. In *Australia–Salmon* it stated that a member could, if it saw fit, adopt a policy of zero-risk as regards a particular SPS problem, whilst in *EC–Asbestos* it states that Art XX(b) entitled France to adopt a policy that sought a 'halt' to the spread of

---

50 www.wto.org/english/tratop_e/envir_e/cte03_e.htr (accessed 19 March 2007).

asbestos-related diseases. Where international SPS standards exist, the decision in *EC–Beef Hormones* affirms the right of members to adopt more rigorous standards.

The appellate body has also sought to be accommodating as regards the type of scientific evidence upon which a member is entitled to base a measure aimed at public health protection. In *EC–Asbestos* it stressed that a member was not obliged to follow the 'preponderant' scientific evidence and could, instead, rely on a divergent, but qualified and respected, scientific opinion. A similar approach had been taken in *EC–Beef Hormones* as regards the scientific evidence on which a member may rely when performing a 'risk assessment' as required under SPS Agreement, Art 5.1. Not only can a member rely on a qualified, respected minority scientific opinion,[51] there is also no need for that opinion to establish a particular magnitude or threshold of risk.

However, the appellate body then went on to hold that Art 5.1 requires a 'rational relationship' between the measure and the risk at which it is directed. This in turn requires that there be some threshold for evaluating the potential of the risk. In *Australia–Salmon* the appellate body held that a risk assessment must evaluate the likelihood, that is to say the probability of a risk. This requirement is critical to the findings in *EC–Beef Hormones* and *EC–Biotech* that the measures in question were not based on an adequate risk assessment. The risk assessment required must be quite specific. In *EC–Beef Hormones* the EC attempted to justify its measure by reference to the established scientific data that the growth hormones in question were carcinogenic when directly ingested by humans. However, they failed to produce any evidence to show that there was a health risk in eating meat which had been reared with the aid of such hormones. Indeed, the scientific evidence clearly stated that such meat posed no risk to human health, if good practice was followed. Nor had the EC provided any evidence as to the risks that good practice would not be followed by beef farmers in Canada and the US. In *EC–Biotech* the same problem comes up. The initial scientific assessments of the products at EC level found them to be safe. Although the member states produced copious scientific reports, all these managed to do was to suggest that the cultivation of GMOs 'might' lead to future biodiversity risks. This was not enough to cross the threshold set in *Australia–Salmon* that there must be an evaluation of the likelihood of the risk materialising. The science must deal with probabilities, not possibilities. Even when the science relied on by the EC appeared to surmount that threshold, it was still not specific enough. The findings either related to a different type of GMO, or derived from laboratory tests, rather than field trials.

The decisions raise a serious problem for legislators in WTO members that seek to respond to public anxieties on health matters. From Thalidomide to

---

51 This is particularly so 'where the risk involved is life-threatening in character and is perceived to constitute a clear and imminent threat to public health', para 194.

the BSE crisis, the history of scientific innovation over the last century is littered with instances of the unexpected materialisation of risks in products that were widely believed to be safe at the time of their introduction. This has led to widespread distrust of scientific assurances as to the safety of new products and production processes. Where there is evidence that a risk 'might' eventuate, a WTO member will have to weigh up the possible hazards of this so far unquantifiable risk against the drawbacks of doing without the product. With hormone-fed beef, the 'possible' risk identified by Dr Lucier was that a small number of people within the EC would develop cancer as a result of eating meat that had been treated with growth hormones. With the cultivation of GMOs the risk is of cross-pollination and irreversible damage to biodiversity and to organic farmers. As against this, where is the drawback of going without these products, when equivalents can readily be produced by conventional means? This argument was put forward by Austria in *EC–Biotech* as regards its safeguard measures in relation to GM maize, but was rejected by the panel. What has been left out of this balancing process are the economic interests of those foreign producers of hormone-reared beef and GMOs which are injured as a result of the measure designed to safeguard the public of the importing member from a risk that 'might' materialise.

One way out of this dilemma would be by invoking the precautionary principle, but neither the appellate body in *EC–Beef Hormones* nor the panel in *EC–Biotech* has accepted that this principle modifies the provisions of the SPS Agreement. In any event, the precautionary principle itself might require the application of a threshold as regards the likelihood of risk. Another possible way out of this dilemma would be by way of reliance on Art 5.7, which allows for the adoption of a provisional measure 'in cases where relevant scientific evidence is insufficient'. The problem here, though, is in determining whether the case is one in which there is 'insufficient' scientific evidence. The panel in *EC–Biotech* found that there was an essential cross-reference between this requirement and the risk assessment provisions in Art 5.1. Given that the EC had, on the basis of scientific evidence, approved the GMOs in question, that constituted a 'risk assessment' under Art 5.1 which prevented the EC from justifying the national safeguard measures under Art 5.7 on the basis that the scientific evidence was 'insufficient'. Critically, the panel rejected the EC's argument that a risk assessment that identified possible, rather than probable risks, could constitute a valid risk assessment if those possible risks were risks of very substantial, long-term environmental harm. Nor was any leeway allowed due to the fact that the risks involved the introduction of a completely new means of food production. It is, therefore, likely that had the EC in *EC–Beef Hormones* tried to rely on Art 5.7, the appellate body would still have found against it, given the scientific reports that the consumption of meat from hormone-reared animals was safe, provided the hormones were administered in accordance with good practice. Although the appellate body in that case stated that the precautionary principle was expressed through

Art 5.7, this must be doubted given the linkage identified by the panel in *EC–Biotech* between this provision and Art 5.1.

3.5.5 The administrative obligations imposed on members in designing and implementing measures

One of the great successes of the WTO has been in rooting out bad administrative practices. This can be evidenced in the lack of transparency in *Japan–Varietals*, the incomplete risk analysis in the 1996 final report in *Australia–Salmon*, and the requirement of the US in *US–Shrimp/Turtle* that importing countries adopt identical shrimp harvesting measures as the US. This latter requirement seems particularly objectionable in that it could be viewed as an example of the world's most powerful state laying down the law to developing countries. The follow-up to these decisions does not reveal any obvious environmental detriment. In *Australia–Salmon* the compliance report shows that in 1999 Australia did manage to conduct a proper risk assessment. In *US–Shrimp/Turtle* the US made serious efforts to conclude a multilateral agreements with the complainants as well as introducing a degree of flexibility into the application of its guidelines. These decisions are likely to have the beneficial effect of forcing legislators to get it right first time, to take care to be even handed and flexible in drawing up and implementing the measure, to make use of the best available scientific procedures to conduct a proper risk assessment.

However, on the debit side of the ledger, there is the issue, highlighted in *US–Reformulated Gasoline*, as to whether the panel and the appellate body gave sufficient consideration to the administrative difficulties in applying measures in such a way as to comply with the requirements of the *chapeau*. The follow-up to the decision of the appellate body is more controversial. Claims have been made that the effect of the revised EPA Guidelines has been to lead to a degradation of air quality in the north eastern US as well as to divert EPA funds into the costly business of monitoring data from foreign refineries. To some extent these criticisms can be met by the point that it is reasonable to expect the richest nation in the world to comply with demanding administrative requirements. The hard cases will arise in future disputes as to the standard of administrative good practice that is required for the purposes of the *chapeau* as regards measures implemented by a member in the developing world. The danger is that in setting too exigent a standard, legislators in such countries may be deterred from using trade measures to promote domestic health and environmental goals. Again, it remains to be seen how satisfactory the WTO agreements prove as a framework for dealing with this balancing process.

Chapter 4

The WTO side agreements (2). GATS, TRIMS and TRIPS

Apart from the TBT and SPS Agreements, which were considered in Chapter 2, in the context of environmental protection measures which amounted to restrictions on trade, the WTO Agreement contains three other side agreements which are relevant to the capacity of members to introduce measures to protect the environment. These are the General Agreement on Trade and Services (GATS), the Agreement on Trade-Related Investment Measures (TRIMs) and the Agreement on Trade-Related Aspects of Intellectual Property Rights (TRIPS).

4.1 GATS

GATS came into effect on 1 January 1995 as one of the new agreements established under the Uruguay Round. GATS has received comparatively little attention in the trade/environment debate, reflecting, perhaps, an assumption that services are environmentally clean. This may be the case as regards professional services, such as accountancy and legal practice, but it is nonetheless the case that many service industries will have substantial environmental impacts. Transportation services, for example, will impact on a nation's infrastructure, its road networks, as well as generating air and noise pollution and use of hazardous substances for vehicle operation and maintenance which will need to be disposed of. Water services, including sewage, will have an impact on pollution from waste disposal sites, and energy use in waste and water treatment.[1] Health services, too, will entail the use and disposal of hazardous material.

Unlike most other WTO agreements, not all members are bound by all the obligations of GATS. The agreement contains a core of obligations that are of general obligation, most favoured nation treatment in Art II and

---

1 A detailed analysis of the potential impact of GATS on water services is contained in a paper produced jointly by the Centre for International Environmental Law (CIEL) and the World Wildlife Fund (WWF). Ostrovksy, Speed and Tuerk, 'GATS, Water and the Environment. Implications of the General Agreement on Trade in Services on water resources', www.ciel.org/Publications/GATS_WaterEnv_Nov03.pdf (accessed 19 April 2007).

transparency obligations in Art III. GATS then provides for additional obligations that will apply only when a member has explicitly agreed to do so in respect of a particular service sector. GATS, Art XIX mandates members to conduct negotiations on 'specific commitments'. These negotiations were launched in March 2000 and contain a sub-part, the 'Market Access Phase' which aims to increase the scope and depth of commitments by members to the market access principles in Art XVI and the national treatment principles in Art XVII.[2] Each member has a 'schedule of commitments' involving a list of service sectors and sub-sectors, against each of which it will indicate that, as regards the market access and national treatment obligations: it is 'unbound'; it is 'bound'; it is 'bound' subject to conditions or limitations. The third option gives members the opinion of entering specific commitments on a limited basis, for instance, by preserving certain existing regulations that are inconsistent with the market access and national treatment obligations. However, once a commitment has been made, the member is locked in and can withdraw only by granting concessions in other sectors. A member which has indicated limitations designed to enhance environmental protection in particular service sectors cannot, therefore, introduce new, inconsistent, legislation to deal with these problems in the light of a subsequent change in circumstances. In addition, the WTO has established a working party to elaborate principles relating to domestic regulation affecting services as mandated by Art VI. 4.[3]

The Doha Ministerial Declaration adopted on 14 November 2001 established deadlines for the submission of requests by members for specific commitments by June 2002 and offers for the same by March 2003.[4] These deadlines were extended, but at the time of the suspension of the Doha Round in August 2006 the deadlines they still had not been met.[5] Paragraph 31(iii) mandates negotiations on 'the reduction or, as appropriate, elimination of tariff and non-tariff barriers to environmental goods and services'.

Article I.1 provides that GATS 'applies to measures by Members affecting trade in services'. A 'trade in services' is defined by Art I. 2 as the supply of a service in the following four modes. The first mode is that of cross-border trade where the service is supplied 'from the territory of one Member into the territory of any other Member'. The second mode involves consumption abroad, involving the supply of services 'in the territory of one Member to the service consumer of any other Member'. The third mode is that of commercial presence, which involves the supply of a service 'by a service supplier of one Member through commercial presence in the territory of any other Member'. The fourth mode is that of the presence of natural persons where

2   The methods of negotiation were set out in the Negotiating Guidelines in March 2001.
3   WTO Negotiating Guidelines, para 7 expresses the aim that this process be completed before the conclusion of the market access phase of the negotiations.
4   Paragraph 15.
5   Negotiations resumed in February 2007.

there is the supply of a service 'by a service supplier of one Member, through presence of natural persons of a Member in the territory of any other Member'.

Services are defined in Art I. 4(b) as including 'any service in any sector except services supplied in the exercise of governmental authority'. Article I.3(c) then provides that ' "a service supplied in the exercise of governmental authority" means any service which is supplied neither on a commercial basis, nor in competition with one or more service suppliers'. Article I.3 defines 'measures by Members' as those taken by central, regional or local governments and authorities, and by non-governmental bodies in the exercise of powers delegated by central, regional or local governments or authorities. In addition, each member is required to take 'such reasonable measures as may be available to it to ensure their observance by regional and local governments and authorities and non-governmental bodies within its territory'.

Article I has a very wide scope in that it covers not only regulation of services, but also measures 'affecting' a service and may therefore cover regulation of production, sale or trade in goods. GATS has the capacity to cover foreign investment through the third mode of service supply, that of commercial presence, referred to in Art I.2. Inevitably, this will lead to overlap between GATS and GATT. The appellate body in *EC–Bananas III*[6] held that no measures are excluded *a priori* from the coverage of GATS and that the agreements may both operate simultaneously. They also confirmed that 'affecting' means 'has an effect'. Therefore regulation of a product is capable of falling within the ambit of GATS if that regulation has an effect on a foreign service supplier in connection with its use or disposal of the product.

Article I covers all services in any sector, save for services supplied in the exercise of government authority. The negotiations on requests and offers for specific sectoral commitments under GATS have been based on a classification document drawn up by the GATT Secretariat during the Uruguay Round which lists sectors and sub-sectors covered by GATS.[7] During the negotiations following the Doha Round, some members have pressed to revise the list to include services 'incidental to manufacturing, such as drilling' and services relating to pure manufacturing such as 'manufacture on a fee or contract basis'.[8] The current GATS classification lists four environmental services – sewage, refuse disposal, sanitation and similar, and 'other' environmental services. The EC has proposed the inclusion of water services which raised the general question of whether public services will necessarily be exempt from GATS by reason of the exclusion in Art I.3 of services

6   *EC–Bananas III. European Communities–Regime for the Importation, Sale and Distribution of Bananas.* WT/DS27/AB/R. Appellate body report 9 September 1997.
7   WTO Scheduling Guidelines 2001, attachment 8.
8   US Energy Services Proposal WTO 2000 and European Energy Services Proposal WTO 2001, respectively.

supplied 'neither on a commercial basis nor in competition with one or more service suppliers'.

GATS imposes only two general obligations on members: most favoured nation treatment, under Art II.1, and transparency, under Art III. However, where specific commitments have been undertaken in particular service sectors, three additional obligations apply.

4.1.1 Article VI. Domestic regulation

The first additional set of obligations are to be found in Art VI which deals with domestic regulation. The Preamble to GATS contains a recognition of:

> ... the right of Members to regulate, and to introduce new regulations, on the supply of services within their territories in order to meet national policy objectives and, given asymmetries existing with respect to the degree of development of services regulations in different countries, the particular need of developing countries to exercise this right ...

Notwithstanding this, Art VI has the capacity to effect a very large degree of restriction on the ability of members to regulate services.

Article VI.1 sets out the general principle that members 'shall ensure that all measures of general application affecting trade in services are administered in a reasonable, objective and impartial manner'. Article VI.2 then goes on to require members:

> ... to maintain or institute as soon as practicable judicial, arbitral or administrative tribunals or procedures which provide, at the request of an affected service supplier, for the prompt review of, and where justified, appropriate remedies for, administrative decisions affecting trade in services. Where such procedures are not independent of the agency entrusted with the administrative decision concerned, the Member shall ensure that the procedures in fact provide for an objective and impartial review.

Administrative fairness with regard to timely decisions when authorisation for the supply of service is provided for under Art VI.3, which requires the competent authorities of a member to inform the applicant of their decision within a reasonable period of time after the submission of an application considered complete under domestic laws and regulations. It also provides that: 'At the request of the applicant, the competent authorities of the Member shall provide, without undue delay, information concerning the status of the application.'

Article VI.4 provides, as follows, for the developments of disciplines relating to regulatory standards.

With a view to ensuring that measures relating to qualification requirements and procedures, technical standards and licensing requirements do
not constitute unnecessary barriers to trade in services, the Council for
Trade in Services shall, through appropriate bodies it may establish,
develop any necessary disciplines.

These disciplines shall aim to ensure that such requirements satisfy, *inter
alia*, the following three requirements. First they must be 'based on objective
and transparent criteria, such as competence and the ability to supply the
service'. Secondly, they must not be 'more burdensome than necessary to
ensure the quality of the service'. Thirdly, in the case of licensing procedures,
they must not in themselves amount to a restriction on the supply of the
service. Article VI.5 provides that pending the entry into force of such disciplines, members:

> . . . shall not apply licensing and qualification requirements and technical
> standards that nullify or impair such specific commitments in a manner
> which: (i) does not comply with the criteria outlined in sub-paragraphs
> 4(a), (b) or (c); and (ii) could not reasonably have been expected of that
> Member at the time the specific commitments in those sectors were made.

In determining a member's compliance with this obligation, 'account shall
be taken of international standards of relevant international organizations[9]
applied by that Member'. Where specific commitments have been undertaken
regarding professional services, Art VI.6 requires each member to provide
'for adequate procedures to verify the competence of professionals of any
other Member'.

A Working Party on Domestic Regulation (WPDR) has been established
as the forum for the development of the disciplines under Art VI.4. These
negotiations have given rise to various concerns as to the eventual ambit of
these disciplines. Of the three GATS obligations applicable when specific
commitments have been undertaken, Art VI.4 has by far the greatest potential for restricting the regulatory capacity of members in that it will affect all
domestic regulation across the board, and will not be restricted to regulation
that violates the market access and most favoured nation provisions of GATS
that also apply when specific commitments have been undertaken.

The first concern regarding the future ambit of Art VI. 4 has been whether
any resulting disciplines will apply to all service sectors, or whether they will
be limited to service sectors in which members have made specific commitments. Article VI.4 simply mandates the development of 'any necessary disciplines'. The WTO's 1999 Note on 'Domestic Regulation' argues that such

---

9 The term 'relevant international organizations' refers to international bodies whose membership is open to the relevant bodies of at least all members of the WTO.

disciplines should apply generally in all sectors. This issue, however, appears to have been resolved by heading B of the Consolidated Working Paper of the WPDR in July 2006, which recommends that these disciplines should apply only to sectors in which specific commitments have been undertaken.[10] Secondly, the wide scope of the negotiating mandate is evidenced by its reference to a 'measure relating to . . .'. This makes it likely that any regulation that has an effect on services will fall within the scope of the Art VI.4 disciplines. The EC, for example, has expressed the view that regulations 'include controls on land use, building regulations and technical requirements, building permits and inspections . . . environmental regulations'.[11]

Thirdly, Australia has proposed that domestic regulation be subject to a 'necessity' test whereby any domestic regulation adopted to meet a legitimate policy objective should be the least trade restrictive possible.[12] This begs the question of what constitutes a 'legitimate' policy objective. Earlier proposals suggested the provision of a list of such objectives, with the EC arguing in favour of the inclusion of 'protection of the environment', while other members have argued that this is implicit in the term 'quality of services'.[13] However, agreement has not been forthcoming and the consolidated working paper of July 2006 contains general references to 'national policy objectives' and 'legitimate policy objectives'. Further, the wording 'least trade restrictive' recalls the restrictive interpretation of the word 'necessary' in GATT, Art XX(b). The EC, on the other hand, has called for a 'proportionality' test, but one which does not involve an assessment of the validity or rationale of the policy objective behind the domestic regulation.[14]

Fourthly, the US has also proposed that the new disciplines under Art VI.4 include an expanded transparency obligation, based on TBT Agreement, Art 2.9, whereby draft regulations would be made available to other members for comments. Further, the proposal would oblige the regulating member to discuss the comments on request and to take these written comments and the results of discussions with other members into account in framing the regulation.[15] Fuchs and Tuerk have commented:

> In practice, the US proposal might enable influential WTO Members to more easily exert pressure on their weaker counterparts, obliging them to

10 JOB(06)/225.
11 WTO 2001, EC, Proposal on Construction and Related Engineering Services, para 10.
12 WTO 2000, Australia Domestic Regulation Sept 2000 Communication: WTO 2000 Australia, Construction and Engineering Services Proposal, para 7; WTO 2001 Australia Engineering Services Proposal, para 6.
13 WTO 2001, EC, Domestic Regulation Informal Communication, p 3.
14 WTO 2001, EC, Domestic Regulation: Necessity and Transparency, para 17.
15 WTO 2000, US Transparency Submission to WPDR, para 11. The transparency proposals contained in heading E of the consolidated Working Party of July 2006 have turned out to be more limited than those proposed by the US.

amend draft legislation and regulations. It is likely that such practices will, to a greater extent, serve the interests of those WTO Members who have the administrative resources to keep abreast of law making processes in other Member states.[16]

Fifthly, concern has been expressed as to the effect of transparency obligations on environmental impact assessments and sustainable impact assessments, in the light of proposals that licensing and qualification requirements be 'as simple as possible' or 'strictly necessary for the purpose of licensing'.[17]

4.1.2 Article XVI. Market access

The second obligation relates to market access through the four modes of supply identified in Art I. This is covered by Art XVI, para 1 of which provides that 'each Member shall accord services and service suppliers of any other Member treatment no less favourable than that provided for under the terms, limitations and conditions agreed and specified in its Schedule'.

Article XVI.2 then provides the following list of measures which a member 'shall not maintain or adopt either on the basis of a regional subdivision or on the basis of its entire territory, unless otherwise specified in its Schedule . . .'. First, there are 'limitations on the number of service suppliers whether in the form of numerical quotas, monopolies, exclusive service suppliers or the requirements of an economic needs test . . .'. Secondly, there are 'limitations on the total value of service transactions or assets in the form of numerical quotas or the requirement of an economic needs test . . .'. Thirdly, there are 'limitations on the total number of service operations or on the total quantity of service output expressed in terms of designated numerical units in the form of quotas or the requirement of an economic needs test . . .'. This is subject to a footnote to the effect that it does not cover measures of a member which limit inputs for the supply of services. This limitation, however, does not apply as regards the limitations specified in the second category of measures. Fourthly, there are:

> . . . limitations on the total number of natural persons that may be employed in a particular service sector or that a service supplier may employ and who are necessary for, and directly related to, the supply of a specific service in the form of numerical quotas or the requirement of an economic needs test . . .

---

16 Fuchs and Tuerk, 'The General Agreement on Trade in Services (GATS) and future GATS-Negotiations – Implications for Environmental Policy Makers', on behalf of the Federal Environmental Agency, November 2001, www.ciel.org/Publications/GATS_Implications_Nov02.pdf, p 46 (accessed 19 April 2007).
17 Op. cit., CIEL-WWF Paper, fn 1, pp 39–40.

Fifthly, there are 'measures which restrict or require specific types of legal entity or joint venture through which a service supplier may supply a service . . .'. Sixthly, there are 'limitations on the participation of foreign capital in terms of maximum percentage limit on foreign shareholding or the total value of individual or aggregate foreign investment'.

These provisions clearly have a significant potential impact on environmental regulation, given that limitations on the use of natural resources in areas such as forestry, mining and tourism are frequently used as a principal tool of conserving those resources. Quantitative restrictions on outputs or inputs would fall under the first three categories listed in para 2. However, limitations based on the number of service operations in the third category are subject to the footnote that this does not cover measures of a member which limit inputs for the supply of services, whereas limitations based on the total value of service transactions are not. The joint paper by CIEL and the WWF[18] notes that, '. . . from an environmental and water management perspective, there is no reason for treating these two policies differently'. The paper also notes that most of the sub-paragraphs of Art XVI.2 specify a *form* of prohibited measure. The natural reading of these sub-paragraphs is such that a measure would have to have both the effect *and* the form specified for it to be in breach of Art XVI.2. However, an alternative reading is possible whereby Art XVI.2 would be violated whenever a measure had the effect, but not the form, specified. Such an interpretation would greatly widen the ambit of this provision.[19]

4.1.3 Article XVII. National treatment

The third obligation, provided under Art XVII, is that of national treatment whereby 'each Member shall accord to services and service suppliers of any other Member, in respect of all measures affecting the supply of services, treatment no less favourable than that it accords to its own like services and service suppliers'.[20] Paragraph 2 provides that this requirement may be met 'by according to services and service suppliers of any other Member, either formally identical treatment or formally different treatment to that it accords to its own like services and service suppliers'. Paragraph 3 then provides that: 'Formally identical or formally different treatment shall be considered to be less favourable if it modifies the conditions of competition in favour of services or service suppliers of the Member compared to like services or service suppliers of any other Member.'

18 Op. cit., fn 1, p 33.
19 Op. cit., fn 1, p 34.
20 Specific commitments assumed under this Article shall not be construed to require any member to compensate for any inherent competitive disadvantages which result from the foreign character of the relevant services or service suppliers.

The problem that this provision poses for environmental regulators is that apparently even-handed regulation may be regarded as *de facto* discrimination between 'like' service providers. For example, distinctions based on the nature of the technology used by a service provider, the size of a company, the nature and location of its assets, may all fall foul of this provision.[21] If control of the service provider is out of the host country, then the host country may seek to impose higher standards to ensure domestic regulation is truly enforceable.[22] Furthermore, long-standing environmental regulation in a particular market may give a *de facto* advantage to domestic providers who have had longer to adapt to it than new foreign entrants. Another example of potential discrimination is the practice of some members of requiring electricity companies to buy a certain percentage of 'green' electricity which may involve a *de facto* advantage to local suppliers. As regards tourism, the EC has proposed in its mode three requests that it will not target exceptions and limitations which are targetted at protecting areas of particular historic and artistic interest, but no such undertaking has been made as regards exceptions and limitations which are targetted at protecting the environment.[23] As regards distribution, Switzerland has stated that: 'Health, safety, urban planning and the environment are amongst the reasons often adduced by Members in order to enact rules affecting the supply of a distribution service. Although such rules are legitimate, they can at times be more restrictive than is truly necessary.'[24]

4.1.4 General exceptions

Article XIV[25] provides for general exceptions as follows:

> Subject to the requirement that such measures are not applied in a manner which would constitute a means of arbitrary or unjustifiable discrimination between countries where like conditions prevail, or a disguised restriction on trade in services, nothing in this Agreement shall be construed to prevent the adoption or enforcement by any Member of measures:
>
> . . .

---

21 In *EC–Bananas III*, the appellate body approved the finding of the panel at 7.322 that entities providing like services should be regarded as 'like service suppliers' which uses only the service as the comparator and does not take into account the characteristics of different service providers.

22 There may also be legitimate policy reasons in some sectors for favouring nationals as opposed to foreigners. The Ciel-WWF joint paper, op. cit., fn 1, p 43, give examples of such measures in the context of water management, namely, restricting ownership of land on which there are springs to local people or giving them preferential access to water use.

23 WTO 2000, EC Tourism Services Proposal, para 10.

24 WTO 2001, Switzerland, GATS 2000, para 10.

25 Article XIV *bis* contains further security exceptions.

(b) necessary to protect human, animal or plant life or health . . .

Of particular significance, is the fact that Art XIV contains only one exception that would potentially apply to environmental regulation affecting services, unlike the position under GATT, Art XX which contains the additional exceptions in heading (g) 'relating to the conservation of exhaustible natural resources'. Not only does the wording in Art XX(g) cover a wider range of environmental measures than those covered by sub-heading (b), but the wording 'relating to' has been subject to a less restrictive interpretation than the word 'necessary' that is found in heading (b). It is still uncertain whether restrictions on services based on legitimate grounds of environmental protection might entail violations of provisions of GATS. In the light of this it is essential that environmental protection is adequately covered by the exceptions in Art XIV. Unfortunately, this is not the case given that Art XIV does not include an exception of the sort included in GATT, Art XX (g) and, instead, is limited to the exception provided in Art XX (b).

4.2 TRIMS

TRIMs is the one WTO agreement that expressly addresses investment. However, under Art 1 its scope is limited to 'investment measures related to trade in goods only'. Such measures are subject to the 'national treatment' provision contained in GATT, Art III.4, and to the prohibition on quantitative restrictions on imports contained in GATT, Art XI, subject to the usual exceptions contained in the GATT. TRIMS contains an illustrative list of measures that will violate these obligations.[26] As regards Art III.4 these are measures that require:

(a) the purchase or use by an enterprise of products of domestic origin or from any domestic source, whether specified in terms of particular products, in terms of volume or value of products, or in terms of a proportion of volume or value of its local production; or
(b) that an enterprise's purchases or use of imported products be limited to an amount related to the volume or value of local products that it exports.

As regards Art XI, these are measures which restrict:

(a) the importation by an enterprise of products used in or related to its local production, generally or to an amount related to the volume or value of local production that it exports;

26 These types of measure are known as 'performance requirements' and are generally prohibited under the bilateral and multilateral investment treaties, which are discussed in Chapters 6 and 7.

(b) the importation by an enterprise of products used in or related to its local production by restricting its access to foreign exchange to an amount related to the foreign exchange inflows attributable to the enterprise; or

(c) the exportation or sale for export by an enterprise of products, whether specified in terms of particular products, in terms of volume or value of products, or in terms of a proportion of volume or value of its local production.

4.3 The TRIPS Agreement. The impact of IP rights on environmental protection

A major innovation of the Uruguay Round that led to the establishment of the WTO was the conclusion of the TRIPS Agreement which aimed to secure the enforcement of minimum standards of protection of IP rights amongst members. TRIPS came into force on 1 January 1995. Developing countries, and economies in transition from central planning, most of which had previously not protected IP rights under their national laws, were given until 1 January 2000 to comply with its obligations to introduce laws giving a minimum standard of protection for various IP rights, such as patents, trademarks, copyright, and geographical indicators.[27] Least developed countries were given a further period of compliance until January 2006 which has been extended to 1 July 2013.[28]

TRIPS lays down both the minimum substantive standards of protection and the procedures and remedies to enable effective enforcement of all the main areas of IP rights such as patents, copyright. The protection of IP rights is subject to both national treatment and most favoured nation provisions.[29] The WTO sees TRIPS as having struck an appropriate balance in protecting IP between the short-term interests in maximising access and the long-term interests in promoting creativity and innovation.[30] This is reflected in Art 7, 'Objectives', which recognises that the protection of IP should contribute to the promotion of technological innovation and to the transfer and dissemination of technology, to the mutual advantage of users and producers of

27 Article 65, paras 2 and 3. The deadline in respect of pharmaceutical patents was 1 January 2005 for developing country Members. For least-developed country members this deadline was originally 1 January 2006, but this has been extended to 1 January 2016.

28 Article 66.1. However, during this transition period such members are bound by the obligations contained in Arts 3 (national treatment), 4 (most favoured nation) and 5 (Multilateral Agreements on Acquisition or Maintenance of Protection). As regards the patenting of pharmaceuticals, the deadline was originally 1 January 2006, but this has been extended to 1 January 2016.

29 Articles 3 and 4 respectively. Article 5 provides that these obligations do not apply to 'procedures provided in multilateral agreements concluded under the auspices of WIPO [the World Intellectual Property Organisation] relating to the acquisition or maintenance of intellectual property rights'.

30 www.wto.org/english/tratop_e/trips_e/intel2_e.htm (accessed 19 April 2007).

technological knowledge and in a manner conducive to social and economic welfare and to a balance of rights and obligations.

Article 27.1 sets out the basic rule of patentability whereby patents are to be available for any invention, whether a product or process, in all fields of technology without discrimination, where those inventions meet the standard substantive criteria for patentability – namely, that it is new, it involves an inventive step, and it is capable of industrial application. The interpretative note states that these last terms equate with the terms 'non-obvious' and 'useful' respectively, which derive from US patent law. Members must also make the grant of a patent dependent on adequate disclosure of the invention and may require information on the best mode for carrying it out.[31] On its website relating to TRIPS, the WTO states that:

> Disclosure is a key part of the social contract that the grant of a patent constitutes since it makes publicly available important technical information which may be of use to others in advancing technology in the area, even during the patent term, and ensures that, after the expiry of the patent term, the invention truly falls into the public domain because others have the necessary information to carry it out.[32]

The ambit of Art 27.1 is likely to come under increased scrutiny now that developing countries have become required to introduce legislation to provide protection for pharmaceutical products. One such country is India, which has become the world's principal supplier of generic copies of pharmaceuticals. India's Patent Act 2005 is intended to secure compliance with India's TRIPS obligation while at the same time providing the maximum permissible leeway for its generic producers. One such provision is s 3(d), which forbids the patenting of derivative forms of known substances (for example, salts, polymorphs, metabolites and isomers) unless they are substantially more effective than the known substance. This is an attempt to prevent the practice of 'evergreening' by which patents are sought for minor improvements to old drugs. In 2006, the Patent Controller in Chennai relied on this provision to refuse Novartis' application for a patent for its drug 'Gleevec' which is used to treat myeloid leukaemia. Novartis has brought proceedings before the Chennai High Court to declare that s 3(d) is inconsistent with India's obligations under TRIPS, because Art 27.1 refers only to the need for an 'inventive

---

31 Article 29.1 provides that:

> Members shall require that an applicant for a patent shall disclose the invention in a manner sufficiently clear and complete for the invention to be carried out by a person skilled in the art and may require the applicant to indicate the best mode for carrying out the invention known to the inventor at the filing date or, where priority is claimed, at the priority date of the application.

32 Op. cit., fn 4.

step' without any further requirement that this step makes the new product 'substantially more effective' than the old product on which it is based. The court heard the case in February 2007, but at the time of writing no judgment has been delivered.

Article 28.1 specifies the minimum rights that must be conferred by a patent under TRIPS. These are those rights common to most national patent laws, principally the right of the patent owner to prevent unauthorised persons from using the patented process and making, using, offering for sale, or importing the patented product or a product obtained directly by the patented process. Under TRIPS, the available term of protection must expire no earlier than 20 years from the date of filing the patent application. There is no obligation to issue an extension to this term to compensate for regulatory delays in marketing new pharmaceuticals. It is important to realise that TRIPS deals with the *minimum* level of protection that members are required to afford to IP rights. It is does not preclude individual members agreeing to provide a higher level of protection. This is frequently provided for in so-called 'TRIPS plus' provisions in bilateral investment treaties between a developed member and a developing member. One consequence of such agreements is that this increased level of protection for IP rights must also be afforded 'immediately and unconditionally to the nationals of all other Members' by reason of the 'most favoured nation' provisions contained in Art 4.

Article 27 provides for three exceptions to the basic rule on patentability. First, there are inventions the prevention of whose commercial exploitation is necessary to protect *ordre public* or morality, including to protect animal or plant life or health or to avoid serious prejudice to the environment.[33] This is subject to the proviso that 'such exclusion is not made merely because the exploitation is prohibited by their law'. Secondly, there are diagnostic, therapeutic and surgical methods for the treatment of humans or animals.[34] Thirdly, there are certain plant and animal inventions. Article 27.3(b) contains an exception as regards the patentability of plants and animals, but this does not extend to 'micro-organisms and essentially biological processes for the production of plants or animals other than non-biological and microbiological processes'. The provision then goes on to deal with plant varieties and stipulates that these must be protected either by patenting or 'an effective *sui generis* system or by any combination thereof' regime. Article 27.3(b) then concludes by stating that 'the provisions of this subparagraph shall be reviewed four years after the date of entry into force of the WTO Agreement'.

Article 27.3 represents a compromise that reflects the different approaches of the various patenting regimes of members as to whether plants and

33 Article 27(2).
34 Article 27(3)(a).

animals are capable of being patented. US law is extremely wide in this respect and allows a utility patent to be granted over both plants and living organisms, including animals. In contrast, European Patent Convention 1973, Art 53 states that plants and animals are not patentable,[35] whilst Canada, in 2002, rejected the patenting of higher life forms.[36] It is uncertain how GM seeds fall to be treated under Art 27.3. The plant itself can clearly be excluded from patenting, but the patent may cover the genes and cells within the plant that give it distinguishing traits, such as resistance to Roundup. The issue then arises as to whether use of the seed or the plant constitutes a violation of the patent over those genes and cells. In 2004, by a 5:4 majority, the Canadian Supreme Court in *Monsanto Canada Inc. v Schmeiser*[37] held that unauthorised use of the seed and the plant would constitute and infringement of the patent over the genes and cells within it, notwithstanding that the plant itself was not patentable. However, there is much to be said for the view of the minority that:

> Allowing gene and cell claims to extend patent protection to plants would render this provision of TRIPS meaningless. To find that possession of plants, as the embodiment of a gene or cell claim, constitute a 'use' of that claim would have the same effect as patenting the plant.[38]

Patenting is clearly one option for protection of plant varieties under Art 27(3), but protection is also possible through an effective *sui generis* system. TRIPS gives no indications as to what might constitute such a system. One obvious *sui generis* regime that would be an alternative to patenting, as a means of plant breeder protection would be one of the two regimes set up by the International Union for the Protection of New Varieties of Plant (UPOV). The latest version, UPOV 1991, entered into force in 1998, after which its predecessor, UPOV 1978, became closed to new accessions. There are significant differences between the two versions, which will be discussed later. However, given that UPOV 1978 was the version in force when TRIPS was implemented on 1 January 1995, it must be the case that a member that decides to stay with the 1978 regime, as Norway opted to do in 2005, will be compliant with its obligations under Art 27.3(b) of TRIPS. Nor does this provision preclude the adoption of a form of plant breeder protection that is

---

35 This position has subsequently been modified by Art 3(2) of Directive 98/44/EC on the legal protection of biotechnological interventions, provides that biological material isolated from its natural environment or produced by a technical process 'may be the subject of an invention even if it previously occurred in nature'.

36 *Harvard College v Canada (Commissioner of Patents)* [2002] 4 SCR 45, 2002 SCC 76 (known as the *Harvard Mouse* case).

37 *Monsanto Canada Inc. v Schmeiser* 2004 SCC 34

38 Paragraph 167.

based on neither version of UPOV, so long as it is 'effective'. However, many developing members have found that it is economically and politically impossible to develop an alternative plant breeder protection regime to suit their national priorities. This is because their need for foreign investment leads them to conclude bilateral investment agreements with developed members who have insisted on the inclusion of 'TRIPS plus' provisions obliging the developing member to accede to UPOV 1991 or to accept the patentability of plants.

Protection of IP rights does not directly impact on environmental protection. If a patent is granted on GM soya, TRIPS obliges other members to protect the IP rights of the patent holder. It does not oblige them to allow the product to be used or sold. Such issues fall to be adjudicated under the SPS Agreement. However, three issues reveal a potential conflict between the provisions of the TRIPS Agreement and environmental protection in a wide sense. First, there is the impact of IP rights on traditional farmers' rights, such as the right to save, use and exchange seed. Concerns have also been expressed that granting IP rights over plants promotes genetic uniformity by encouraging global rather than local production of seeds, leading to a reduction in biodiversity, with a limited number of homogenous strains being increasingly vulnerable to disease. Secondly, there is the question of how traditional knowledge should be treated. Thirdly, there is the tension between the interests of holders of pharmaceutical patents who need to be given an economic incentive for research and development into new drugs, and the needs of those who cannot afford patented drugs and must rely on cheaper generic versions.

4.3.1 Farmers' rights

The development of the biotechnology industry in the last 30 years has set up a conflict between the holders of IP rights of plants and seeds, and farmers who have traditionally enjoyed the free right of harvesting and re-using seed from their crops. There have been three avenues by which plant breeders might obtain protection in new varieties which they develop. Two of these are legal, the third is scientific.

The first avenue of protection is through legislation directed specifically at plant breeders' rights. The international regime for protecting plant breeders' rights is that provided by UPOV. The current version of the regime is UPOV 1991 which came into effect in 1998 following which it became impossible to accede the earlier version, UPOV 1978, although many countries have continued with this regime and have chosen not to 'upgrade' to the 1991 version. With regard to protected plant species, the breeder's prior authorisation is required for production of the variety for commercial purposes, offering of the variety for sale and marketing of the reproductive, propagating material of the variety. To be protected a variety must be: novel, distinct, stable and uniform.[39] Both versions of UPOV allow the use of protected varieties as an initial source of variation for the creation of new varieties which may then be marketed without the need to obtain the authorisation of the initial breeder. UPOV 1991 provides that if the new variety is essentially the same as the protected variety, the owner of the protected variety enjoys the same rights over the variant.

A major change effected in UPOV 1991 is the downgrading of the farmer's right to save seed to an 'optional exception' to the rights of the plant breeder. UPOV 1978 allows farmers to use their harvested material from a protected variety for any purpose. In contrast UPOV 1991 provides that it is for national governments to decide whether farmers should be allowed, within reasonable limits, and safeguarding the legitimate interests of the rights holder, to reuse the harvest of protected varieties on their own land holdings without the authorisation of the rights holder. Not only does UPOV 1991 weaken the rights of farmers to reuse saved seed, it also prevents farmers from exchanging or selling such material. In addition, UPOV 1991, unlike its predecessor, allows for double protection through patenting as well as through plant breeders' rights.[40] The negotiation of bilateral agreements which include 'TRIPS plus' provisions, which often mandate accession to UPOV 1991, has led to many developing countries legislating to prohibit the use of saved seed, other than that grown on the farmer's own land, so outlawing the practice of seed exchange between farmers. However, the position may be modified by International Undertaking on Plant Genetic Resources, Art 9.3 which came into effect in June 2004. This recognises the farmer's right to 'save, use, exchange and sell farmed saved seeds', but includes the proviso 'subject to national legislation'. The treaty makes it clear that responsibility for realising these rights lies with national governments.

The second avenue of protecting new plant varieties is that of patenting. This avenue has proved more appealing to US biotechnology corporations. In 1980, the US Supreme Court in *Diamond v Chakrabarty*[41] held that all plant breeding products were potentially patentable under the regime for general utility patents. A living organism was held to be patentable as falling within the definition in 35 USC, s 101 of 'any new and useful process, machine, manufacture, or composition of matter, or any new and useful improvement thereof'. In 1985, the US Board of Patent Appeals in *ex p Hibberd*[42] held that

---

39 In contrast, UPOV 1978 used the term 'homogenous'.
40 There are two other important differences between UPOV 1978 and UPOV 1991. First, UPOV 1991 obliges all parties to bring all plant species within the scope of plant breeders' rights protection within 10 years of accession. Secondly, UPOV 1991 increases the minimum periods of protection to 20 years for plants and 25 years for trees and vines from the periods of 15 and 18 years respectively under UPOV 1978.
41 *Diamond v Chakrabarty* 447 US 303 (1980).
42 *ex p Hibberd* 227 USPQ (BNA) 443 (1985).

a utility patent could be applied for in respect of a plant notwithstanding that it might also be protected under existing legislation protecting the rights of plant breeders.[43] This resulted in the existence of two parallel systems of plant breeder protection in the US, first by way of patenting, secondly by way of existing legislation protecting the rights of plant breeders. The principal piece of legislation is the Plant Variety Protection Act 1970 (PVPA), which introduced a measure of patent-like protection to developers of novel, sexually reproduced (that is to say by seed) plants.[44] Provided the criteria of novelty, uniformity and stability were satisfied, the breeder acquired the right to exclude others from using the variety for 17 years, although protected varieties could still be used for research, and farmers could continue their traditional practice of saving, reusing and reselling seed. However, in 1994 the PVPA was amended in accordance with the provisions of UPOV 1991 which restricts farmers' rights over the seed of protected varieties.[45] In the event of a conflict between these two legal avenues of protection, the protection afforded by patenting will prevail. This was confirmed in 2001 by the Supreme Court in *JEM AG Supply v Pioneer Hi-Bred International*,[46] where it held that the scope of a utility patent over a patent on hybrid corn seed was not restricted by the farmers' rights exception in the PVPA 1970.

Utility patents have the advantages of lower fees and allow protection of not just the whole plant but also of its separate components, DNA sequences, genes, cells, as well as methods of acquiring, and techniques of studying and developing, genetic material.[47] This permits the licensing of those components. There is no exemption for research. Research *with* the seed would be fair use but not research *on* the seed. This, together with the patenting of processes in the development of biotechnology, has put licensing obstacles to conducting research, the so-called 'tragedy of the anti-commons'. The granting of a utility patent also clearly restricts the farmer's right to replant, in that purchase of a patented seed would give the farmer only the right to use the seed, but not to make the product.

However, as Kloppenburg notes, the biotech industry has seen large investments yield very few marketable products, and these are easily copied –

---

43 In 1987 the Patent and Trademark Office ruled that animals, too, could be patented.
44 There is also the Plant Patent Act 1930 which covered only asexually propagated species – those involving budding, grafting and cutting.
45 In 1995, the Supreme Court, in *Asgrow Seed v Winterboer* 513 US 179 (1995) held that the PVPA exception covered only farmers who saved seeds to replant on their own land, and did not create a right to sell such seeds to third parties.
46 *AG Supply v Pioneer Hi-Bred International* 534 US 124 (2001), p 127.
47 Patenting does, however, have two disadvantages over reliance on plant breeders' rights legislation. First, the applicant must satisfy the requirement of 'non-obviousness'. Secondly, enough information must be provided 'to enable any person skilled in the art . . . to make or use the same' as required by 35 USC, s 112. This would be satisfied by the deposit of a sample organism at an approved repository with unrestricted access.

by seed saving.[48] The industry's response to this problem has been twofold. First, the industry has been aggressive in its enforcement of its patent rights. These rights are pursued through the technology use agreements Monsanto signs with farmers. These prohibit replanting and limits Monsanto's liability for losses associated with the technology. They require the use only of Roundup and allow Monsanto free access to the farmers' fields. In countries which have not taken the US lead and permitted the patenting of plants and higher life forms, the issue arises as to how the patenting of genes and plant cells mandates protection by restrictions on the use of the seed and the resultant plant. Where farmers have chosen to use GM seed the issue will not arise as they will be subject to strict contractual obligations regarding its use under their licenses with the patent holder. However, the issue is a live one when a third party makes use of such seed. In 2004, this issue came before the Supreme Court of Canada in *Monsanto Canada Inc. v Schmeiser*.[49]

Mr Schmeiser farms canola commercially in Saskatchewan in a conventional, non-organic, manner. In 1996, five neighbouring canola farmers planted Roundup Ready Canola. Seeds from their land drifted onto Mr Schmeiser's 370-acre field. In spring 1997, Mr Schmeiser planted seeds he had saved from this field. When he sprayed a three-acre patch with Roundup he found that approximately 60 per cent of the plants survived, indicating that the plants contained Monsanto's patented gene and cell. In the autumn of 1997, he harvested the canola from this three-acre patch, but did not sell it. Instead, he kept it separate, and stored it over the winter. The following spring he took this harvest to a seed treatment plant where it was treated for use as seed. It was then planted in nine of his fields. Trials showed that 95 to 98 per cent of this 1998 crop was 'Roundup Ready' canola.

Monsanto proceeded against Mr Schmeiser for unauthorised use of their patent which was not on the plant itself, but rather, on their invention of chimeric genes that confer tolerance to glyphosate herbicides such as Roundup, and on cells containing those genes. The trial judge concluded that Mr Schmeiser had infringed Monsanto's patent by planting canola seed saved from his 1997 crop, which he knew or ought to have known was Roundup tolerant. By a 5:4 majority the Supreme Court of Canada upheld this finding. The majority held that Monsanto's patent was valid, as it made no claim as regards the genetically modified plant itself, but was limited to the genes and the modified cells that made up the plant. Mr Schmeiser had infringed the patent by 'using' the patented cell and gene, by saving and planting the seed, and then by harvesting and selling plants that contained the patented cells and genes. Infringement was established where a defendant's commercial or business activity involving a thing, of which a patented

48 Kloppenburg, J, *First the Seed*, 2nd edn, 2004, Madison, WI: University of Wisconsin Press, pp 298–301.
49 2004 SCC 34.

part was a component, necessarily involved use of the patented part. It therefore, did not require use of the gene or cell in isolation. The issue of infringement was unaffected by the fact that the patented characteristic was of no benefit to Mr Schmeiser who did not use Roundup herbicide as an aid to cultivation. However, this factor was significant in denying Monsanto the remedy they had claimed, which was an account of profits, rather than an award of damages. Mr Schmeiser's profits were precisely what they would have been had he planted and harvested ordinary canola. Therefore, Monsanto's victory against Mr Schmeiser proved something of a pyrrhic one. Not only were they awarded no account of profits but no award of costs was made against Mr Schmeiser.

The minority, taking into account previous rulings of Canadian courts that higher life forms were unpatentable, adopted a purposive construction and concluded that the gene claims and the plant cell patents did not grant exclusive rights over the plant and all of its offspring. Patents must be interpreted from the point of view of the person skilled in the art who must also be taken to know the law. Such a person could not reasonably have expected that patent protection for genes and plant cells would extend to unpatentable plants and their offspring. Against this background, there had been no 'use' of the subject matter of the invention. Mr Schmeiser, as user, was entitled to rely on the reasonable expectation that plants, as unpatentable subject matter, fell outside the scope of patent protection and his cultivation of plants containing the patented gene and cell did not, therefore, infringe Monsanto's patent.

Apart from these two legal avenues of protection, there is a third, scientific, avenue by which the biotechnology industry has sought to protect its patent rights. This has been through its search for a 'terminator gene' which renders seed sterile. In 1998, the Genetic Use Restriction Technology (GURT) was patented, by which seed could be made sterile – the so-called 'Terminator Technology'. This may prove a more effective method of combatting farmer plantback than the use of litigation, particularly in countries with weak IP laws. In 2004, Monsanto stopped selling Roundup Ready soya seed to Argentina because of the fact that half the acreage was being sown with saved seed.[50] In 2006, Monsanto, which in 1999 made a public statement that it did not intend to use this technology, acquired the rights to the GURT patent.

In 2000, the parties to the Convention on Biological Diversity 1992 (CBD) agreed to a moratorium on field trials and commercial release of GURT seeds. In March 2006, at the eighth Conference of the Parties, an attempt was made by Canada, Australia and New Zealand to modify this position to allow a 'case-by-case' risk assessment of the technology. It has been argued that the 'terminator gene' will protect biodiversity by allowing the used of

---

50 Op. cit., fn 48, p 320.

gm seeds without the risk of crossover. There is strong interest in using the 'terminator gene' for GM trees where the problem of crossover is more acute, as tree pollen can travel 2,000 kilometres, whereas pollen from field plants can travel only a few kilometres. Although the proposal was rejected, it is likely that it will be resurrected for the ninth Conference of the Parties, scheduled to take place in Germany in 2008.

Public plant breeding institutes provide an alternative means of developing new plant varieties to that being undertaken by the biotechnology industry. The most important international collection of germplasm is that held in the gene banks of the Consultative Group on International Agricultural Research (CGIAR). This was initially collected under a regime of common heritage. The FAO has produced an International Undertaking on Plant Genetic Resources and in 1994 it initiated negotiations to harmonise this with the provisions of the CBD. One problem was that CBD, Art 15.3 did not cover *ex situ* collections of genetic resources outside the country of origin and acquired prior to the adoption of the CBD. This would exclude the CGIAR collections from the access provisions of Art 15. It was, therefore, agreed to bring much of the germplasm held by the CGIAR into the public domain under the trusteeship of the FAO. Access would be 'facilitated' rather than 'free', in that access would be open to other adherents of the FAO Undertaking who had also agreed to provide the sharing of benefits envisaged by the CBD. The terms of the agreements signed between the FAO and CGIAR Centres stipulate that the germplasm within the in-trust collections will be made available without restriction to researchers around the world, on the understanding that no IP protection can be applied to the material. Seed samples are thus made available by the individual Centres under a standard Material Transfer Agreement which precludes the claiming of IP rights over germplasm 'in the form received'.[51] The FAO International Undertaking also establishes a mechanism for sharing the benefits of the commercialisation of germplasm, although the level, form and manner of payment are still to be defined. In November 2001, the Treaty became available for signature and on 29 June 2004 the treaty obtained the necessary 40 ratifications to come into force, including that of the US.

4.3.2 Traditional knowledge

In the US patents have been granted over products derived from traditional knowledge, such as neem, basmati rice and the Andean root crop, Maca. These patents utilise traditional knowledge, but because this is oral it is not regarded as 'prior art' and therefore the applicant is able to satisfy the

---

51 It is likely that there would be no breach of this provision if such germplasm were patented after subsequent modification by the recipient.

steps of novelty and inventiveness.[52] The genetic resources of the developing world are, therefore, supplied free as 'common heritage'. They are then modified in the developed world which then sells back to the developing world the patented commodity that has been developed on the back of its unacknowledged and unremunerated prior knowledge.[53] Another adverse consequence of patenting of processes derived from traditional knowledge is the increased demand made on the product as a result of its commercialisation. For example, the granting of a US patent on a fungicidal process derived from the neem tree has resulted in neem seeds being bought up by the pesticide manufacturer that uses the neem patent, and pricing them out of the reach of ordinary Indians.

One possible means of addressing these issues is the CBD which has 190 parties and came into force in December 1993. Article 1 describes the object-ives of the CBD as:

> ... the conservation of biological diversity, the sustainable use of its components and the fair and equitable sharing of the benefits arising out of the utilization of genetic resources, including by appropriate access to genetic resources and by appropriate transfer of relevant technologies, taking into account all rights over those resources and to technologies, and by appropriate funding.

Article 3 defines genetic resources as 'genetic material of actual or poten-tial value of plant, animal, microbial or other origin, containing functional units of heredity'.

The reference in Art 1 to 'all rights' over genetic resources and technologies would include any IP rights, but not any rights over traditional knowledge, as the CBD neither creates nor recognises any such rights. The CBD deals with traditional knowledge in Art 8(j), which provides:

> Subject to its national legislation, respect, preserve and maintain knowl-edge, innovations and practices of indigenous and local communities embodying traditional lifestyles relevant for the conservation and sus-tainable use of biological diversity and promote their wider application with the approval and involvement of the holders of such knowledge, innovations and practices and encourage the equitable sharing of the

---

52 In 2000, the European Patent Office, however, denied a patent on the basis that the claim of novelty had been destroyed on the basis of clearly demonstrated prior public use. The deci-sion was upheld on appeal on 8 March 2005. For further details see, Bullard, L, 'Freeing the Free Tree A briefing paper on the first legal defeat of a biopiracy patent: the neem case', March 2005, www.twnside.org.sg/title2/FTAs/Intellectual_Property/IP_and_other_Topics/FreeingtheFreeTree-Linda_Bullard.doc (accessed 14 March 2007).
53 A detailed analysis of this issue is provided by Dutfield, G, *Intellectual Property Rights. Trade & Biodiversity*, 2000, London: Earthscan Publications Ltd.

benefits arising from the utilization of such knowledge, innovations and practices . . .

The provision is limited first by the reference to national legislation and secondly by the hortatory language by which the parties are to 'encourage' the equitable sharing of benefits arising from the use of traditional knowledge. The reference to 'respect, preserve and maintain knowledge, innovations and practices of indigenous and local communities' does not create any rights in those communities over such knowledge, innovations and practices.

Although the CBD creates no rights in the holders of traditional knowledge, it does provides a route whereby national governments can control access to such knowledge before it becomes transformed into IP rights owned by companies in the developed world. Article 15, which is titled, 'access to genetic resources', starts by recognising, 'the sovereign rights of States over their natural resources, the authority to determine access to genetic resources rests with the national governments and is subject to national legislation'.[54] Where access to such rights is granted it is to be 'on mutually agreed terms and subject to the provisions of this Article'[55] and is to be 'subject to prior informed consent of the Contracting Party providing such resources, unless otherwise determined by that Party'.[56] For the purposes of the CBD, the references in Art 15 to the provision of genetic resources by a contracting party is limited to two situations.[57] The first is where the contracting party which provides the genetic resources is the country of origin of the resource. The second is where the contracting party has acquired the resource in accordance with the CBD.

Each contracting party is required to endeavour 'to create conditions to facilitate access to genetic resources for environmentally sound uses by other Contracting Parties and not to impose restrictions that run counter to the objectives of this Convention'[58] and 'to develop and carry out scientific research based on genetic resources provided by other Contracting Parties with the full participation of, and where possible in, such Contracting Parties'.[59] Article 15 concludes with a requirement that each contracting party:

54 Paragraph 1.
55 Paragraph 4.
56 Paragraph 5.
57 Paragraph 3. The same also applies to references to genetic resources that appear in Arts 16 and 19. Article 15.3 has the effect of excluding all *ex situ* collections of genetic resources outside the country of origin and acquired prior to the adoption of the Convention, such as the CGIAR gene banks. This problem has been addressed by the conclusion of facilitated access agreements between the FAO and the CGIAR centres.
58 Paragraph 2.
59 Paragraph 6.

... shall take legislative, administrative or policy measures, as appropriate, and in accordance with Articles 16 and 19 and, where necessary, through the financial mechanism established by Articles 20 and 21 with the aim of sharing in a fair and equitable way the results of research and development and the benefits arising from the commercial and other utilization of genetic resources with the Contracting Party providing such resources. Such sharing shall be upon mutually agreed terms.[60]

The effect of Art 15, therefore, is to sanction the commercialisation of biodiversity through bilateral agreements such as that concluded in 1992 between Costa Rica and Merck.[61] Costa Rica's National Biodiversity Institute (INBio) gave Merck exclusive access to biological materials collected by it in return for an upfront payment of $1,000,000. One problem for developing countries which are rich in genetic materials is the method by such materials should be priced. Upfront payments may be too low and royalties may be difficult to negotiate given the imbalance of legal resources. Agreements may only work if a clear association of a crop material with a people or community can be established. The requirement of 'prior informed consent' is also likely to be a difficult concept to apply. For instance, whose consent should be obtained, and will such persons have enough knowledge for that consent to be informed?

In contrast to the treatment afforded to holders of traditional knowledge, once that knowledge has been appropriated and turned into IP rights in genetic resources and technology, the CBD treats those rights in an altogether different way. Article 16 is full of references that afford recognition to such rights, sitting alongside various hortatory references as to how those rights should be used in ways that are supportive of the CBD. Article 16 deals with the transfer of 'technologies that are relevant to the conservation and sustainable use of biological diversity or make use of genetic resources and do not cause significant damage to the environment'. Paragraph 2 provides for access to and transfer of technology to developing countries 'under fair and most favourable terms, including on concessional and preferential terms where mutually agreed'. However, it then subjects such transfers to IP rights as follows: 'In the case of technology subject to patents and other IP rights, such access and transfer shall be provided on terms which recognize and are consistent with the adequate and effective protection of intellectual property

---

60 Paragraph 7.
61 A similar agreement was concluded in 2003 by the South African San Council to give the nomadic San people a share of the profits realised from the commercialisation of the Hoodia plant which they had used from time immemorial to stave off hunger. Diaz, CL, 'Intellectual Property and Biological Resources. An overview of key issues and current debates', Wuppertal Institute for Climate, Environment and Energy, 2005, pp 18–20, www.wupperinst.org/ globalisierung/pdf_global/intellectual_property.pdf (accessed 7 March 2007).

rights.' The paragraph ends by stating that its application is to be consistent with paras 3, 4 and 5.

Article 16.3 requires the contracting parties to take 'legislative, administrative or policy measures, as appropriate' to ensure developing countries which provide genetic resources are provided access to and transfer of technology which makes use of those resources. This includes technology protected by patents and other IP rights 'where necessary'. This falls short of creating a right to traditional knowledge but appears to create a right of access to the products of that knowledge. However, the paragraph dilutes any such right by the following qualifications. Apart from the wording 'where necessary', there is the fact that the transfer of technology is to be 'on mutually agreed terms', through the provisions of Arts 20 and 21 and, most importantly, is to be 'in accordance with international law and consistent with paras 4[62] and 5 below'. Paragraph 5 contains a recognition that 'patents and other intellectual property rights may have an influence on the implementation of this Convention' and obliges the contracting parties to 'co-operate in this regard subject to national legislation and international law in order to ensure that such rights are supportive of and do not run counter to its objectives'.

The reference to international law brings in the obligations owed by contracting parties under the WTO agreements, including TRIPS. Article 22, 'Relationship with Other International Conventions' also provides in para 1 that:

> The provisions of this Convention shall not affect the rights and obligations of any Contracting Party deriving from any existing international agreement, except where the exercise of those rights and obligations would cause a serious damage or threat to biological diversity.

This provision, however, does not affect the TRIPS agreement because it was not 'an existing international agreement' at the time the CBD came into force in December 1993.

Article 19 deals with the handling of biotechnology and distribution of its benefit. Each contracting party is required to:

> ... take legislative, administrative or policy measures, as appropriate, to provide for the effective participation in biotechnological research activities by those Contracting Parties, especially developing countries, which

---

62 Each contracting party shall take legislative, administrative or policy measures, as appropriate, with the aim that the private sector facilitates access to, joint development and transfer of technology referred to in para 1 above for the benefit of both governmental institutions and the private sector of developing countries and in this regard shall abide by the obligations included in paras 1, 2 and 3 above.

provide the genetic resources for such research, and where feasible in such Contracting Parties:[63]

and to:

... take all practicable measures to promote and advance priority access on a fair and equitable basis by Contracting Parties, especially developing countries, to the results and benefits arising from biotechnologies based upon genetic resources provided by those Contracting Parties. Such access shall be on mutually agreed terms.[64]

The parties must also:

... consider the need for and modalities of a protocol setting out appropriate procedures, including, in particular, advance informed agreement, in the field of the safe transfer, handling and use of any living modified organism resulting from biotechnology that may have adverse effect on the conservation and sustainable use of biological diversity.[65]

There has been much discussion, both within the CBD and within the Council for TRIPS as to the relationship between the two agreements.[66] Within the WTO, this began with the review of Art 27.3 (b) that began in 1999. The scope of this has been expanded by para 19 of the 2001 Doha Ministerial Declaration, which states:

We instruct the Council for TRIPS, in pursuing its work programme including under the review of Article 27.3(b), the review of the implementation of the TRIPS Agreement under Article 71.1 and the work foreseen pursuant to para 12 of this declaration, to examine, inter alia, the relationship between the TRIPS Agreement and the Convention on Biological Diversity, the protection of traditional knowledge and

---

63 Paragraph 1.
64 Paragraph 2.
65 Paragraph 3. Paragraph 4 then provides:

> Each Contracting Party shall, directly or by requiring any natural or legal person under its jurisdiction providing the organisms referred to in paragraph 3 above, provide any available information about the use and safety regulations required by that Contracting Party in handling such organisms, as well as any available information on the potential adverse impact of the specific organisms concerned to the Contracting Party into which those organisms are to be introduced.

66 A good survey of developments up to February 2005 is provided by Diaz, CL, 'Intellectual Property and Biological Resources. An overview of key issues and current debates', Wuppertal Institute for Climate, Environment and Energy, 2005, pp 24–42, www.wupperinst.org/globalisierung/pdf_global/intellectual_property.pdf (accessed 7 March 2007).

folklore, and other relevant new developments raised by members pursuant to Article 71.1. In undertaking this work, the TRIPS Council shall be guided by the objectives and principles set out in Articles 7 and 8 of the TRIPS Agreement and shall take fully into account the development dimension.

There are currently four basic positions that WTO members have been taken on this issue.[67] The first proposal is that the CBD's obligations on disclosure should become part of the conditions for obtaining a patent under TRIPS. This would require an amendment to TRIPS whereby patent applicants had to disclose: the country of origin of genetic resources and traditional knowledge used in the inventions; evidence that they received 'prior informed consent' as required by the CBD and; evidence of 'fair and equitable' benefit sharing as required by the CBD. This proposal is supported by a group of members, represented by Brazil and India, and including Bolivia, Colombia, Cuba, the Dominican Republic, Ecuador, Peru, Thailand, and supported by the African group and some other developing countries. The second proposal is that TRIPS be amended to require disclosure through the World Intellectual Property Organisation (WIPO). Switzerland has proposed amending the regulations of WIPO's Patent Co-operation Treaty (and, by reference, WIPO's Patent Law Treaty) so that domestic laws may ask inventors to disclose the source of genetic resources and traditional knowledge when they apply for patents. Failure to meet the requirement could hold up a patent being granted or, when done with fraudulent intent, could entail a granted patent being invalidated. The third proposal, put forward by the EU, is that there should be examination of the viability of a system that requires all patent applicants to disclose the source or origin of genetic material, but with the legal consequences for non-compliance falling outside the scope of patent law. Fourthly, the US has proposed that the CBD's objectives on access to genetic resources, and on benefit sharing, could best be achieved through national legislation and contractual arrangements based on the legislation, which could include commitments on disclosing of any commercial application of genetic resources or traditional knowledge.

4.3.3 Pharmaceuticals

The global regime for the protection of IP established by TRIPS has important public health implications for developing countries. Most of their citizens

67 WTO, 'TRIPS: Reviews, article 27.3(B) and related issues. Background and the current situation', www.wto.org/english/tratop_e/trips_e/art27_3b_background_e.htm (accessed 7 March 2007). These issues are dealt with in greater depth in the note by the CTE Secretariat, *The relationship between the TRIPS Agreement and the Convention on Biological Diversity – Summary of issues raised and points made*, 8 February 2006, IP/C/W/368/Rev.1, www.wto.org/english/tratop_e/trips_e/ipcw368_e.pdf (accessed 7 March 2007).

will be too poor to afford drugs manufactured in the developed world, yet, particularly with conditions such as AIDS, access to such drugs is literally a matter of life and death. A solution to the problem has been found through recourse to generic copies of patented drugs. Before the establishment of TRIPS the patent holder could do nothing to prevent such authorised copying in the absence of legislation allowing for the patenting of pharmaceuticals in either the country making the generic copies or the country importing them.[68]

This, however, will cease to be the case when the obligations in TRIPS come to have universal application. TRIPS sets out the following timetable for the application of its substantive standards to the protection of pharmaceuticals. Developing countries had until 1 January 2005 to introduce the appropriate patent legislation. The deadline for least developed countries was originally set at 1 January 2006, but on 27 June 2002, the Council for TRIPS, pursuant to the instruction in the Doha Declaration on the TRIPS Agreement and Public Health, extended this deadline until 1 January 2016. At the expiry of these deadlines, both developing and least developed countries will be required to give effect not only to new patent applications, but also to patents still under protection at the end of the respective transition periods.

TRIPS also establishes a 'mailbox' system which allows for the filing of applications for patents for pharmaceutical product inventions after 1 January 1995. These applications must then be examined by the member in question at the end of the transitional deadline applicable to it. If found to be patentable by reference to their filing (or priority) date, a patent would have to be granted for the remainder of the patent term counted from the date of filing. If a pharmaceutical product that was the subject of a 'mailbox' application obtained marketing approval prior to the decision on the grant of a patent, an exclusive marketing right of up to five years must be granted, subject to certain conditions.

By 1 January 2016, then, all members will be subject to the obligations set out in TRIPS as regards the protection of patents in pharmaceuticals. More importantly, this has already been the case since 1 January 2005 as regards developing countries, such as India, one of the major manufacturers of generic copies of patented drugs. Such members will now have to operate within the constraints of TRIPS. Art 8 authorises members, in formulating or amending their rules and regulations, to adopt measures necessary to protect public health and nutrition. This would appear to give members the option of using a range of public policy measures outside the field of IP to address issues of access to and prices of drugs, such as price or reimbursement controls. However, it is subject to the proviso that 'such measures are consistent

---

68 An extensive analysis of the public health issues raised by TRIPS can be found in Matthews, D, *Globalising Intellectual Property Rights*, 2002, London: Routledge.

with the provisions of the Agreement'. In determining the extent to which the member can justify an abrogation of the rights of the patent holder to obtain affordable access to a pharmaceutical, reference must be made to two provisions of TRIPS, Arts 30 and 31.

Article 30 allows limited exceptions to be made by members provided that such exceptions do not unreasonably conflict with a normal exploitation of the patent and do not unreasonably prejudice the legitimate interests of the patent owner, taking account of the legitimate interests of third parties. For example, a member might allow generic producers to conduct research on a pharmaceutical while it was still under patent, without the authorisation of the patent holder, so as to enable them to obtain regulatory approval to market their generic version as soon as the patent expired.[69] In *Canada–Patent Protection for Pharmaceutical Products*, the panel held that a Canadian law to this effect fell within the exception created by Art 30, although the exception did not justify the authorisation of the generic producer to manufacturer stocks of its copy in readiness for marketing at the expiry of the patent.[70]

Article 31 allows for compulsory licensing for the use[71] of the subject matter of a patent, by either a government or third parties authorised by the government, where this is permitted under the law of a member. TRIPS does not specify the grounds on which this can be done, but it does set out various conditions which have to be satisfied, so as to protect the legitimate interests of the patent owner. Paragraph (a) requires that authorisation of such use be considered on its individual merits. Paragraph (b) requires the proposed user to have made efforts, prior to use, to obtain authorisation from the right holder on reasonable commercial terms and conditions and that such efforts have not been successful within a reasonable period of time.

This requirement may be waived in two situations. First, where there is a case of a national emergency or other circumstances of extreme urgency; secondly, in cases of public non-commercial use. The use authorised must be non-exclusive, and its scope and duration is to be limited to the purpose for which it was authorised. The authorisation is liable to termination 'if and when the circumstances which led to it cease to exist and are unlikely to recur. The competent authority shall have the authority to review, upon motivated request, the continued existence of these circumstances . . .'.[72] Paragraph (h) requires the right holder to be paid 'adequate remuneration in the circumstances of each case, taking into account the economic value of the authorisation'. Members may also use compulsory licensing under Art 31 to take action against anti-competitive practices.[73] Where a practice has been deter-

---

69 This type of provision is sometimes referred to as a 'Bolar' provision.
70 *Canada–Patent Protection for Pharmaceutical Products*. WT/DS114/R. 17 March 2000.
71 Other than use authorised by Art 30.
72 Paragraph (g).
73 Paragraph (k).

mined after due process of law to be anti-competitive, compulsory licences need not comply with the provisions in paras (b) and (k).

The condition that has posed particular problems for generic manufacturers wishing to export copies of on-patent pharmaceuticals, is that contained in para (f). This requires such use to be authorised 'predominantly for the supply of the domestic market of the Member authorizing such use'. This causes problems for countries which need access to cheaper generic copies of on-patent pharmaceuticals. It is likely that they will lack the capacity to manufacture such copies themselves. They will therefore need to import copies from a country, such as India, where there is an established generic pharmaceutical industry. However, if, as is the case with India, that country is now subject to the provisions of TRIPS protecting pharmaceutical patents, export of generic copies of on-patent pharmaceuticals will only be permitted in accordance with the provisions of Art 31. However, the exporting member may have difficulty in establishing that the licence is 'predominantly' for the supply of its domestic market.

The public health implications of TRIPS were addressed in a separate declaration on TRIPS and Public Health at Doha on 14 November 2001. Paragraph 4 affirmed that TRIPS 'can and should be interpreted and implemented in a manner supportive of WTO members' right to protect public health and, in particular, to promote access to medicines for all'. Paragraph 5 then stated that: 'Each member has the right to grant compulsory licences and the freedom to determine the grounds upon which such licences are granted.' Following on from this, para 6 mandated the Council for TRIPS to find an expeditious solution to the problem Art 31(f) causes to members 'with insufficient or no manufacturing capacities in the pharmaceutical sector . . . in making effective use of compulsory licensing . . .'. The result was the Waiver Decision of 30 August 2003 that dispensed with Art 31(f), subject to various conditions to protect patent holders from abuse of compulsory licensing. The WTO General Council on 6 December 2005 approved the making permanent of these changes, the first amendment of a core WTO agreement. This will now be formally built into the TRIPS Agreement, through a new Art 31 *bis*, when two-thirds of the WTO's members have ratified the change. They have set themselves until 1 December 2007 to do this. The waiver remains in force until then. There is, however, nothing to prevent 'TRIPS plus' agreements being negotiated which contain terms restricting a member's rights to rely on the provisions of Art 31 *bis*.[74]

The amendment itself is in three parts. Five paragraphs come under an additional article, Art 31 *bis*. Paragraph 1 allows pharmaceutical products made under compulsory licences to be exported to countries lacking

74 For a detailed discussion of this issue, see Morin, JF, 'Tripping up TRIPS debates. IP and health in bilateral agreements' (2006) 1(1/2) Int J Intellectual Property Management 37, pp 37–53, www.inderscience.com/storage/f867591011123412.pdf (accessed 7 March 2007).

production capacity. The scope of the waiver does not require that the compulsory licence is required for dealing with any specific diseases.[75] Paragraph 2 requires 'adequate remuneration pursuant to art. 31(h)' to be paid in that member 'taking into account the economic value to the importing Member of the use that has been authorised in the exporting Member'. The other paragraphs deal with avoiding double remuneration to the patent owner, regional trade agreements involving least-developed countries, 'non-violation' and retaining all existing flexibilities under the TRIPS Agreement.

A further seven paragraphs are included in a new Annex to TRIPS. These set out terms for using the system, and cover such issues as definitions, notification, avoiding the pharmaceuticals being diverted to the wrong markets, developing regional systems to allow economies of scale, and annual reviews in the TRIPS Council. An 'appendix' to the Annex deals with assessing lack of manufacturing capability in the importing country.

The Annex to TRIPS starts by defining 'pharmaceutical product',[76] 'eligible importing Member'[77] and 'exporting Member'.[78] It then specifies the conditions for obtaining the compulsory license under Art 31 *bis* (1). The eligible importing member must notify the Council for TRIPS, specifying the names and expected quantities of the product(s) needed, confirming that it has insufficient or no manufacturing capacities in the pharmaceutical sector for the product(s) in question[79] and that where a pharmaceutical product is patented in its territory, it has granted, or intends to grant, a compulsory licence in accordance with Arts 31 and 31 *bis* of TRIPS and the provisions of its Annex.

The compulsory licence issued by the exporting member is subject to the following conditions. Only the amount necessary to meet the needs of the eligible importing member(s) may be manufactured under the licence and the entirety of this production shall be exported to the member(s) which has notified its needs to the Council for TRIPS. Products produced under the

---

75 The US had initially taken this position in the para 6 negotiations.

76 '. . . any patented product, or product manufactured through a patented process, of the pharmaceutical sector needed to address the public health problems as recognized in paragraph 1 of the Declaration on the TRIPS Agreement and Public Health (WT/MIN(01)/DEC/2). It is understood that active ingredients necessary for its manufacture and diagnostic kits needed for its use would be included'.

77 '. . . any least-developed country Member, and any other Member that has made a notification to the Council for TRIPS of its intention to use the system set out in Article 31 *bis* and this Annex ("system") as an importer, it being understood that a Member may notify at any time that it will use the system in whole or in a limited way, for example only in the case of a national emergency or other circumstances of extreme urgency or in cases of public noncommercial use'.

78 '. . . a Member using the system to produce pharmaceutical products for, and export them to, an eligible importing Member'.

79 The appendix to the TRIPS Annex provides a presumption that least-developed country members have insufficient or no manufacturing capacities in the pharmaceutical sector.

licence must be clearly identified as being produced under the system through specific labelling or marking. Before shipment begins, the licensee must post on a website the quantities being supplied to each destination and the distinguishing features of the product(s). The exporting member must notify the Council for TRIPS of the grant of the licence, including the conditions attached to it. An eligible importing member must take reasonable measures within its means, proportionate to its administrative capacities and to the risk of trade diversion to prevent re-exportation of the products that have actually been imported into their territories under the system. All members must ensure the availability of effective legal means to prevent the importation into, and sale in, their territories of products produced under the system and diverted to their markets inconsistently with its provisions.

The WTO website for TRIPS notes that members may need to change their own laws in give effect to the amendment. So far, Norway, Canada and India have informed the WTO that their laws are complete, while the Republic of Korea and the EU have said their new laws are on the verge of coming into force. A group of developed countries are listed as announcing that they will not use the system to import. The following other countries have announced separately that if they use the system as importers it would only be for emergencies or extremely urgent situations: Hong Kong China, Israel, Korea, Kuwait, Macao China, Mexico, Qatar, Singapore, Chinese Taipei, Turkey and the United Arab Emirates.

The General Council chair, Amina Mohamed, Kenya's ambassador, has issued a statement to reassure those who feared that the decision might be abused and undermine patent protection.[80] It describes members' 'shared understanding' on how the decision is to be interpreted and implemented and states that: the decision will be used in good faith in order to deal with public health problems and not for industrial or commercial policy objectives; issues such as preventing the medicines getting into the wrong hands are important; in general special packaging and/or special colouring or shaping should not have a significant impact on the price of pharmaceuticals.

Apart from having recourse to compulsory licensing under Art 31(f), a member can address the issue of securing affordable on-patent pharmaceuticals by purchasing them through parallel importation. The manufacturer of the pharmaceutical may have patented the drug in two members and have decided to sell it at a lower price in the territory of member A than in that of member B. Parallel importation occurs where member C imports the drug at the lower price from a supplier in member A. Whether or not this involves an infringement of the rights of the patent holder in member A depends on whether its rights have become exhausted once that particular batch of drugs have been offered for sale in member A. Article 6 of TRIPS deals with this by

80 www.wto.org/english/news_e/news05_e/trips_319_e.htm (accessed 19 April 2007).

stating that 'nothing in this Agreement shall be used to address the issue of the exhaustion of intellectual property rights'. However, this is subject to the provisions of national treatment and most favoured nation provisions contained in Arts 3 and 4 respectively.

Chapter 5

Trade and the environment within the EC

The consolidated EC Treaty[1] contains three fundamental provisions relating to the free movement of goods within the internal market of the EU.[2] These provisions, with different numbering, were included in the initial Treaty of Rome 1957 which established the European Common Market.[3] Article 28 (formerly Art 30) prohibits, as between member states, quantitative restrictions on imports or 'measures having equivalent effect'. These words bring in 'indistinctly applicable' measures where an even-handed measure has the effect of restricting imports. Article 29 (formerly Art 34) contains a similar prohibition regarding quantitative restrictions on export. It has, however, been interpreted so that it applies only to distinctly applicable measures. Article 30 then provides that these two provisions:

> . . . shall not preclude prohibitions or restrictions on imports, exports or goods in transit justified on grounds of public morality, public policy or public security; the protection of health and life of humans, animals or plants; the protection of national treasures possessing artistic, historic or archaeological value; or the protection of industrial and commercial property.

There then follows the important proviso that: 'Such prohibitions or restrictions shall not, however, constitute a means of arbitrary discrimination or a disguised restriction on trade between Member states.' The grounds listed in Art 30 are exhaustive and apply equally to distinctly and indistinctly applicable measures.

---

1   This is based on the EC Treaty of Amsterdam, which came into effect on 1 May 1999, as amended by the Treaty of Nice which came into effect on 1 February 2003.
2   Two other important provisions relating to the establishment of the internal market are Art 25, which prohibits customs duties and charges of equivalent effect, and Art 90 on internal taxation.
3   Throughout this chapter the new numbering will be used, except where direct quotation is made from cases using the old numbering.

There is also a separate ground on which indistinctly applicable measures may be justified, which is based on the 'rule of reason' enunciated by the European Court of Justice (ECJ) in *Cassis de Dijon*.[4] In the absence of harmonisation at EC level, obstacles to free trade due to disparities between national laws are permitted if applied without discrimination to both domestic and imported products and are necessary, and proportionate, for the effectiveness of various mandatory requirements. These initially covered 'the effectiveness of fiscal supervision, the protection of public health, the fairness of commercial transactions and the defence of the consumer'. Since 1988, the ECJ has also recognised environmental protection as a mandatory requirement.[5] Environmental protection may, therefore, justify an indistinctly applicable measure whereas a distinctly applicable measure can be justified only under the narrower ground of 'the protection of health and life of humans, animals or plants' under Art 30. Where it is sought to justify a measure under either Art 30 or the rule of reason, a threefold test is applied by the ECJ. The measure must be necessary. It must be proportionate to the objective pursued. The measure must be the least restrictive of the internal market.[6]

The architecture of the EC Treaty of Amsterdam as regards trade and the environment would, so far, appear to be somewhat simpler than that under the WTO. There are no 'most favoured nation' and 'national treatment' provisions as appear in GATT, Arts I and III, nor is there a separate provision on quantitative restrictions, such as GATT, Art XI. Furthermore, there are no separate side agreements such as the SPS and TBT Agreements.[7]

However, there is an even more important difference between the treatment of trade and the environment under WTO agreements and its treatment within the EU and that is the capacity of EC legislation to introduce harmonised environmental standards that apply throughout the EC. EC Treaty, Art 2 lists the various tasks of the EC which include the promotion of 'a harmonious, balanced and sustainable development of economic activities' as well as 'a high level of protection and improvement of the quality of the environment'. Article 3 then lists the activities of the EC which include, in para (1) 'a policy in the sphere of the environment'. The importance of this policy is reinforced by Art 6 which provides that: 'Environmental protection requirements must be integrated into the definition and implementation of the Community policies and activities referred to in Article 3, in particular with a view to promoting sustainable development.' Article 152.1 then provides that:

---

4   *Cassis de Dijon* (Case 120/78) [1979] ECR 649.
5   *Danish Bottles* (Case 302/86) [1988] ECR 4607.
6   Whether or not other member states have adopted less restrictive measures is not relevant to this enquiry.
7   See, generally, as regards trade and the environment within the EC, Scott, J, *EC Environmental Law*, 1998, London and New York, NY: Longman; Kramer, L, *EC Environmental Law*, 6th edn, 2006, London: Sweet & Maxwell; Wiers, J, *Trade and the Environment in the EC and the WTO. A legal analysis*, 2002, Groningen: Europa Law Publishing.

'A high level of human health protection shall be ensured in the definition and implementation of all Community policies and activities.'

The EC's policy on the environment is set out in title XIX 'Environment', which comprises Arts 174–176.[8] Article 175 provides the legislative basis for EC legislation over environmental matters. The Environmental Liability Directive, Directive 2004/35, is an example of harmonised environmental legislation introduced through Art 175. Legislation, which may be by way of either regulations or directives, is enacted through the co-decision process set out in Art 251. Environmental legislation may also be introduced, on the same basis, under Art 95 which deals with harmonisation measures which are directed at the establishment and functioning of the internal market.[9] The EC's legislation on the introduction of GMOs is an example of harmonised environmental legislation that has been principally introduced through Art 95.[10] The EC also has a limited legislative competence in the field of public health under Art 152.[11]

Harmonised environmental legislation raises the question of the extent to which member states may introduce stricter protective measures than those contained in the harmonised EC legislation. This will depend on the character of the harmonised legislation. If it is 'exhaustive' in nature this will preclude divergent national measures, subject to any provisions in the harmonised legislation permitting national safeguard measures. Where legislation is introduced under Art 175, national safeguard measures may be introduced or maintained under Art 176. Such measures must be notified to the Commission and must be compatible with the EC Treaty. On the other hand, where legislation is introduced under Art 95 a more rigorous regime is applied with national safeguard measures being subject to the approval of the Commission. Different criteria inform the Commission's decision, depending on whether the member state is seeking to maintain an existing national measure under

8   Articles 174–176 replace Arts 130 R, S and T, which were inserted into the Treaty of Rome in 1986 through the Single European Act which came into effect on 1 July 1987. Before this, EC legislation on the environment was introduced under either Art 94 (formerly Art 100), which dealt with the harmonisation of national laws to further the internal market or Art 308 (formerly Art 235), which dealt with the EC's general and residual powers.

9   Article 95 replaces Art 100A, which was inserted into the Treaty of Rome in 1986 through the Single European Act.

10 Harmonised measures on public health may be introduced in two areas through the co-decision procedure set out in Art 251. The first is through measures setting high standards of quality and safety of organs and substances of human origin, blood and blood derivatives, but any such measures shall not prevent any member state from maintaining or introducing more stringent protective measures. Secondly, 'by way of derogation from Article 37, measures in the veterinary and phytosanitary fields which have as their direct objective the protection of public health'.

11 The limited nature of that competence was affirmed in a case involving a prohibition on tobacco advertising, *Germany v European Parliament and Council* (Case C–376/98) [2001] ECR I–8419.

Art 95.4, or whether it is seeking to introduce a divergent national measure under Art 95.5. If the Commission approves a national derogation under either of these heads Art 95.7 requires it immediately to consider whether to propose an adaptation of the harmonised measure.

5.1 Quantitative restrictions on imports and exports. Articles 28 and 29

In assessing the compatibility of a member state's environmental measures with the Treaty provisions relating to the free movement of goods within the internal market, it must first be established that there has been a breach of either Art 28 or Art 29. The burden of proof at this stage falls on the party that wishes to challenge such a measure.

Article 28 states that: 'Quantitative restrictions on imports and all measures having equivalent effect shall, without prejudice to the following provisions, be prohibited between Member states.' Article 29 contains a similarly worded provision as regards exports. The various terms of these provisions merit detailed analysis.

First, there is the reference to 'measures'. These must be taken by member states, as well as by public bodies such as local and regional governments, administrative or judicial bodies. Non-binding measures are covered, such as the establishment of a government sponsored body to promote the sales of nationally produced goods.[12] Governmental inactivity can also constitute a 'measure' as was the case when the French Government failed to take swift action against a blockade by local farmers directed at Spanish strawberries.[13] Although the articles do not deal with private bodies, their activities will be covered when national legislation grants them regulatory and disciplinary powers which prevent the free movement of goods.[14]

Secondly, there is the reference to the 'quantitative restrictions on imports'. This covers any measure which amounts to total or partial restraint on imports, whether these be direct, indirect, parallel imports and re-imports, as well as goods in transit. Any type of 'goods' may be the subject of an import restriction, so long as they have an economic value. That value, however, need not be a positive one. For example, waste for disposal, as opposed to waste for recovery, has a negative value, but in *Walloon Waste*[15] restrictions on the import of such waste were covered by Art 28 in that they formed the subject of a commercial transaction by which payment was made for the disposal of such waste.

Thirdly, there is the reference to 'measures having equivalent effect'. In

---

12 *Commission v Ireland* (Case 249/81) [1982] ECR 4005.
13 *Commission v France* (Case C–265/95) [1997] ECR I–6959.
14 *R v Royal Pharmaceutical Society of Great Britain* (Cases 266–267/87) [1989] ECR 1295.
15 *Commission v Belgium (Walloon Waste)* (Case C–2/90) [1992] ECR I–4431.

Procureur du Roi v Dassonville,[16] it was held that Art 30 applied to 'all trading rules enacted by Member states which are capable of hindering, directly, or indirectly, actually or potentially, intra-community trade' even if that hindrance is slight. This means that discriminatory intent is not required to trigger a violation of the articles. It will be enough if a facially neutral measure has the effect of adversely impacting imports more than domestic products, or even the potential for such an effect. In this respect, the rule is not subject to a *de minimis* exception.[17] This means that regulatory measures which are not directly related to the sale of a product may nonetheless fall within Art 28 if their effect is to restrict imports. The *Dassonville* formula applies a principle of mutual product recognition whereby a product legally sold in one member state must be allowed to be sold in all other member states, subject to justification under either Art 30 or the rule of reason.[18]

However, a measure which has no potential effect on trade between member states will fall outside Arts 28 and 29. In *Peralta*,[19] the master of an Italian vessel was fined pursuant to Italian legislation which imposed on an absolute prohibition of oil from any vessel into Italian territorial waters. The fine was challenged, unsuccessfully on a variety of grounds. One argument was that the Italian legislation violated Art 28 because it required Italian vessels to carry costly equipment which made imports of chemical products into Italy more expensive, so creating an obstacle to trade. The ECJ[20] rejected the argument, as follows:

> ... it is sufficient to observe that legislation like the legislation in question makes no distinction according to the origin of the substances transported, its purpose is not to regulate trade in goods with other Member states and the restrictive effects which it might have on the free movement of goods are too uncertain and indirect for the obligation which it lays down to be regarded as being of a nature to hinder trade between Member states.[21]

16 *Procureur du Roi v Dassonville* (Case 8/74) [1974] ECR 837.
17 *Bluhme (Danish Bees)* (Case C–67/97) [1998] ECR I–8033. See, also, *Preussenelektra* (Case C–379/98) [2001] ECR I–2099.
18 The principle of mutual recognition was also introduced in *Cassis de Dijon*, under the reference to mandatory requirements.
19 *Peralta* (Case C–379/92) [1994] ECR I–3453.
20 Paragraph 24.
21 See, also, *Krantz v Ontranger der Directe Belastingen* (Case C–69/88) [1990] ECR I–583, where a similar analysis was applied to national legislation which authorised the collector of direct taxes to seize goods, other than stocks, which are found on the premises of a taxpayer even if those goods are from, and are the property of, a supplier established in another member state, and also, *CMC Motorradcenter v Pelin Baskiciogullari* (Case C–93/92) [1993] ECR I–5009, in relation to a German sales law requirement on pre-contractual disclosure of information.

A further limitation on the width of the *Dassonville* formula came in *Keck v Mithouard*.[22] The ECJ distinguished between 'measures regulating certain selling arrangements' (that is to say where, when and how the product was sold) and 'product-related' rules (that is to say rules about the size, content, packaging, labelling, etc of the product). The former would fall beyond Art 28 provided that: (i) they applied both to imported and domestic products; and (ii) they affected imported and domestic products in the same manner, in law and fact. The ECJ, therefore, held that Art 28 did not cover a French restriction on the sale of certain categories of goods at a loss, even though it entailed a restriction of the volume of sale of these products, including imports. The ECJ recognised that its decision had the effect of overruling its previous decisions. It did not specify which decisions were being overruled, but must have been referring to its previous findings that Art 28 covered restrictions on advertising[23] and on Sunday trading.[24] Paragraph 17 of *Keck* makes it clear that the restriction on selling arrangements must apply equally to domestic and non-domestic sellers and must affect them in the same manner, in law, and in fact.

Whilst *Keck* was seen as clarifying and limiting the scope of Art 28, its ambit was not as wide as was originally perceived. First, there is the question of what is meant by 'certain selling arrangements'. This could refer to static arrangements, such as restrictions on hours of opening and the premises from which goods can be sold. Alternatively, it could also cover dynamic arrangements, such as the ways in which goods are marketed. Subsequent cases, particularly those relating to advertising, have applied *Keck* to these dynamic forms of selling arrangements. In *Leclerc Siplec*,[25] the ECJ held that a French restriction on advertising did not fall within Art 28 and rejected the opinion of Advocate General Jacobs that Art 28 should apply whenever a measure entails a substantial restriction on market access, there being a presumption to this effect whenever the measure was directed at the product itself.[26] However, a selling arrangement that is bound up with the definition of the product itself will fall within Art 28. In *Familiapress*,[27] the ECJ held that there had been a violation of Art 28 by an Austrian law preventing the offering of prizes by periodicals for crossword competitions as this would have entailed a German magazines which offered such prizes having to alter the form of its periodical for the Austrian market. Similarly, in *Bluhme* restrictions as to the types of bees that could be kept on the island of Lso were held to fall within Art 28 as they were concerned with the intrinsic nature of the product, the bees.

22   *Keck v Mithouard* (Cases C–267 and C–268/91) [1993] ECR I–6097.
23   *Keck v Mithouard* (Cases C–267 and C–268/91) [1993] ECR I–6097; *Aragonesa de Publicidad* (Joined Cases C–1/90 and C–176/90) [1991] ECR I–4151.
24   *Torfaen* (Case C–145/88) [1989] ECR 3851.
25   *Leclerc Siplec* (Case C–412/98) [1995] ECR I–179.
26   Both, however, reached the same conclusion.
27   *Familiapress* (C–368/95) [1997] ECR I–3689.

Secondly, there is the requirement in para 16 of the judgment in *Keck* that the measure must not have a differential impact, in law or in fact, as between domestic traders and importers. The Court referred to this requirement in *De Agostini*,[28] which was concerned with a Swedish ban on advertising aimed at children under 12, and also on advertising of skincare requirements. In applying this test, the ECJ appears to have adopted the methodology of the 'substantial restriction on market access' test it rejected in *Leclerc Siplec*. Similarly, in *Wettbewerb*,[29] Art 28 was held to cover an Austrian restriction on sales by travelling butchers who did not have a permanent establishment in the region, in that it would have the effect of disadvantaged importers who would be required to set up a permanent establishment in the region.

Thirdly, in *Alpine Investments*,[30] it was held that *Keck* could not justify a restriction on the provision of services, in breach of Art 49 (formerly Art 59), where the restriction, although even-handed, was not confined to sales within the national territory. The measure in question was a Dutch restriction on cold calling of potential investors in the futures market which applied without distinction to any company within the Netherlands. The ECJ stated that:

> A prohibition such as that at issue is imposed by the Member State in which the provider of services is established and affects not only offers made by him to addressees who are established in that State or move there in order to receive services but also offers made to potential recipients in another Member State.[31]

The position is different with regard to Art 29. In *Groenveld*,[32] a Dutch prohibition on stocking, preparing or processing horsemeat fell outside the scope of Art 29 in that it did not have as its 'specific object or effect' the restriction of patterns of exports. Therefore, it is only 'distinctly applicable' restrictions on exports that fall within Art 29. Restrictions on how goods are produced within a member state, provided they apply equally to goods for the domestic market and goods for the export market, will fall outside Art 29 as 'indistinctly applicable' measures. This can be seen in *Oebel*,[33] where a German restriction on night work at bakeries was held not to violate Art 29. The measure 'applied objectively to the production of goods of a certain kind without drawing a distinction depending on whether such goods are intended for the national market or for export'. The same reasoning also

---

28 *De Agostini* (Joined Cases C–34/95, C–35/95 and C–36/95) [1997] ECR I–3843, para 44.
29 *Wettbewerb* (Case C–254/98) [2000] ECR I–0151.
30 *Alpine Investments* (Case C–384/93) [1995] ECR I–1141.
31 Paragraph 38. The Court rejected the view that there should be convergence between Art 28 and Art 49 in the light of *Keck*.
32 *Groenveld* (Case C–15/79) [1979] ECR 3409.
33 *Oebel* (Case 155/80) [1981] ECR 1993.

applied as regards the potential effect of the measure on imports. However, where such a restriction applies only to goods that are to be exported Art 29 will apply.[34]

Violations of Arts 28 and 29 may be challenged in a variety of ways. Under Art 226, the Commission may bring proceedings before the ECJ against the member state imposing the measure, under Art 227, another member state can initiate such proceedings.[35] Alternatively, as these provisions have direct effect, they may be invoked directly before a national court. This would enable a person affected by the measure to argue that it was invalid because it involved a violation of one of these articles. If the position under EC law is unclear the national court may then refer the matter to the ECJ under Art 234.

Violations of Arts 28 and 29 are also capable of giving rise to a right to damages against the member state in question, irrespective of whether the provision in question had direct effect.[36] This right is subject to the three conditions. First, the rule must have been intended to confer rights on the individuals making the claim. This is satisfied as regards Arts 28 and 29. Although the articles impose a prohibition on member states, they also create rights for individuals which the national courts must protect.[37] Secondly, the breach must be sufficiently serious.[38] In determining this, the ECJ has identified the following factors that are to be considered:

> ... the clarity and precision of the rule breached, the measure of discretion left by that rule to the national or Community authorities, whether the infringement and the damage caused was intentional or involuntary, whether any error of law was excusable or inexcusable, the fact that the position taken by a Community institution may have contributed towards the omission, and the adoption or retention of national measures or practices contrary to Community law.[39]

Thirdly, there must exist a direct causal link between the breach of the member state obligation and the subject matter of the claim. This is essentially a matter for the national court to determine. These conditions were all

---

34 *Bouhelier* (Case 53/76) [1977] ECR 197. However, in *Jongeneel Kaas v Netherlands* (Case 53/76) [1984] ECR 483, Art 29 was held not to cover quality control rules on cheese that applied to domestic production but not to imports, because the rules covered all domestic production, and not just production for export.
35 Political considerations have meant that Art 227 has rarely been used.
36 This right to damages derives from *Francovich* (Cases C–6 and C–9/90) [1991] ECR I–5357.
37 *Pigs Marketing Board v Redmond* (Case 83/78) [1978] ECR 2347, paras 66 and 67.
38 This requirement was introduced in *Brasserie du Pêcheur* and *Factortame* (Cases C–46/93 and C–48/93) [1996] ECR I–1029.
39 See para 56.

satisfied in *Hedley Lomas* as regards a breach of Art 29.[40] The member state is then required to make reparation in accordance with its domestic law on liability for the consequences of the loss and damage caused. However, its domestic law on this issue must not be less favourable than that relating to similar domestic claims, nor must it make it impossible or excessively difficult in practice to obtain such reparation.

5.2 Harmonisation and national measures. The general principles

In *Gourmetterie Van den Burg (Red Grouse)*,[41] the ECJ held that where there has been exhaustive harmonisation by the EC, divergent national measures may no longer be justified by reference either to Art 30 or to the rule of reason set out in *Cassis de Dijon*, unless the harmonising EC legislation expressly permits national derogations. Furthermore, the position is different where the harmonised measures have been introduced under one of the two bases for introducing EC legislation relating to the environment. The first is under Art 95 relating to harmonisation directed at the establishment and functioning of the internal market. National safeguard measures will now be dealt with under paras 4 and 5 depending on whether a member state seeks to maintain an existing measure or whether it seeks to introduce a new national measure. The second is under Art 175 relating to the EC's environment policy, as set out in Art 175. The validity of divergent national measures will then fall to be determined under Art 176. However, the general principles regarding national measures will still be relevant where the EC measure is introduced on another basis such as Art 37, relating to agriculture, or under Art 152, relating to public health. The general principles will be considered first, before moving to an analysis of the principles applicable where the harmonised legislation is based on either Art 95 or Art 175.

Where there has been harmonisation, and the EC legislation provides no express right for member states to maintain or introduce divergent national measures, one must first ascertain whether the measure actually lies in the same area occupied by the harmonised legislation. For example, in *R v London Boroughs Transport Association ex p Freight Transport Association*,[42] a ban was imposed in London on lorry traffic night, subject to a scheme of individual licensing for heavy goods vehicles on condition that they were fitted with an air-brake silencer. The Court of Appeal found that this area

---

40 *R v Ministry of Agriculture, Fisheries and Food ex pHedley Lomas (Ireland) Ltd* (Case C–5/94) [1996] ECR I–2553.
41 *Gourmetterie Van den Burg (Red Grouse)* (Case C–169/89) [1990] ECR I–2143.
42 *R v London Boroughs Transport Association ex parte Freight Transport Association* [1991] 1 WLR 828, noted by Weatherill, S, 'Regulating the Internal Market: Result Orientation in the House of Lords' (1992) 17 EL Rev 299.

had been exclusively harmonised by the directive. The House of Lords, however, overrruled this decision, finding that the directive did not cover the area at all, in that it was directed to the removal of obstacles to trade caused by technical requirements and did not cover measures aimed at noise reduction. Similarly, in *Motte*,[43] where the directive contained a positive list of permissible food colourant additives, it was held that the harmonisation effected did not extend to controlling the use of a permitted colourant for a specific food. This matter remained within the discretion of the member state.

If the measure does fall within the area of harmonised legislation, then one must determine whether that legislation is exhaustive in its nature. This requires a careful examination of the terms of the relevant legislation. The presence of a right of pre-emption in the legislation, or the fact that the legislation sets out minimum rather than maximum standards, are both strong indicators of the non-exhaustive character of the harmonised measure. However, this is not always the case. In *Gourmetterie Van den Burg (Red Grouse)*,[44] the issue was whether the Wild Birds Directive had effected exhaustive harmonisation, so precluding the Netherlands from banning the import of a species that was hunted and sold lawfully in another member state and was not protected by the directive. Article 14 of the directive permitted member states to take more stringent measures, but the ECJ held that its scope was limited to birds that were either protected by the directive, or were migratory, or occurred within the territory of the member state imposing the measure. None of these conditions was satisfied as regards the red grouse.

Two cases on animal welfare, *Compassion in World Farming*[45] and *Hedley Lomas*,[46] show the fact that harmonisation sets out minimum standards does not preclude a finding that it is exhaustive in nature. Both cases involved directives based on Art 37 (formerly Art 43) which provides the general base for agricultural legislation. In *Compassion in World Farming*, the UK refused to restrict the export of calves for rearing in veal crates, the use of which it had banned domestically. The case tested the UK Government's assertion that such a measure would have been in violation of Art 29. The relevant directive, Directive 91/629, established requirements for newly built or rebuilt holdings to ensure the well being of calves, subject to a lengthy period of implementation which delayed many important provisions until 2007. The health of calves was clearly within the scope of the directive, which sought to balance animal protection with the operation of the internal market in calves. The ECJ held that the directive was exhaustive in character, even though it

---

43 *Motte* (Case C–247/84) [1985] ECR 3887.
44 *Gourmetterie Van den Burg (Red Grouse)* (Case C–169/89) [1990] ECR I–2143.
45 *R v Minister of Agriculture, Fisheries and Food ex p Compassion in World Farming Ltd* (Case C–1/96) [1998] ECR I–1251.
46 *R v Ministry of Agriculture, Fisheries and Food ex p Hedley Lomas (Ireland) Ltd* (Case C–5/94) [1996] ECR I–2553.

provided for minimum standards, which fell below those set out in the European Convention on the Protection of Animals kept for farming purposes, and contained long transitional periods. Article 11.2 allowed member states to maintain or apply stricter measures within their territories and was, therefore, an indication that the directive was exhaustive in respect of any other measure. The ECJ also rejected the argument propounded by Advocate General Leger that there could be no harmonisation until the expiry of the transitional periods, because these periods were themselves exhaustively laid down by the directive.[47]

In *Hedley Lomas*, the UK refused to grant export licences for veal calves destined for slaughter in Spain, which did not stun animals before slaughter as required by Directive 74/1577. The measure violated Art 29 and could not be justified under Art 30 as it concerned a harmonised subject area, even though there was no harmonisation of the monitoring procedure or penalties for violating the directive. Rather than taking unilateral action against another member state, the UK should have filed a complaint with the Commission about Spain's conduct, or proceeded against Spain directly, under Art 227.

5.2.1 Article 95. Internal market harmonisation

Environmental legislation may be introduced under Art 95 where it relates to harmonisation of the internal market. Paragraph 1 provides for the introduction of such legislation through the provisions on qualified majority voting contained in Art 251.[48] Where the Commission proposes to introduce harmonised legislation under Art 95, it is required, by para 3, to take as a base 'a high level of protection, taking account in particular of any new development based on scientific facts' where its proposals concerning 'health, safety, environmental protection and consumer protection'. Paragraph 10 provides that such harmonisation measures 'shall, in appropriate cases, include a safeguard clause authorising the Member states to take, for one or more of the non-economic reasons referred to in Article 30, provisional measures subject to a Community control procedure'.

Paragraph 8 deals with the situation where a member state raises a specific

---

47 The previous, somewhat similar, case of *Holdijk* (Joined Cases 141/81 to 143/81) [1982] ECR 1299 was distinguished on the grounds that the measure there was applied within the territory of the member state and that the case had been decided before the adoption of the directive.

48 The same procedure is used for legislation introduced under Art 175. Before the Treaty of Amsterdam there used to be an important procedural difference between the two legislative bases. Harmonised measures could be introduced under Art 95 through the co-decision process by qualified majority voting whereas measures introduced under Art 175 required only the consultation of the European Parliament and needed the approval of all member states.

problem on public health in a field which has been the subject of prior harmonisation measures. In such a situation it is required to bring it to the attention of the Commission which must then immediately examine whether to propose appropriate measures to the Council. The Commission and any member state are authorised under para 9 to refer allegations of improper use by another member state of the powers provided for in Art 95 directly before the ECJ.

Article 95 deals with divergent national measures in two ways, depending on whether a member state is seeking to maintain existing measures, or whether it is seeking to introduce divergent measures, after the introduction of harmonised measures under this article. In both situations the member state must notify the Commission. Having received notification under these two headings from a member state, the Commission, under para 6, must, within six months, approve or reject the national provisions involved. In doing so, it must verify 'whether or not they are a means of arbitrary discrimination or a disguised restriction on trade between Member states and whether or not they shall constitute an obstacle to the functioning of the internal market'. During this process the member state, having made its notification, has no right to be heard by the Commission, as the procedure is initiated by the member state rather than by an EC institution.[49] A failure of the Commission to make a decision within the six-month period specified in para 6 is to be regarded as approval. However: 'When justified by the complexity of the matter and in the absence of danger for human health, the Commission may notify the Member State concerned that the period referred to in this paragraph may be extended for a further period of up to six months.' In the event that the Commission grants approval, para 7 requires it immediately to examine whether to propose an adaptation to the harmonised measure. This provides an impetus for the upward harmonisation of environmental protection standards contained in harmonised measures based on Art 95.

Where a member state seeks to maintain national legislation after the adoption of a harmonisation measure, the matter is governed by para 4. There are two grounds on which the member state can seek to maintain such a measure. The first is where it deems it necessary to maintain such provisions on grounds of major needs referred to in Art 30.[50] The second is by reference to major needs relating to the protection of the environment or the working environment. The member state must notify the Commission of

---

49 *Denmark v Commission* (Case C–3/00) [2003] ECR I–2643 as regards a notification under para 4. The position is the same as regards a notification under para 5. *Land Oberösterreich und Österreich v Commission* (Joined Cases T–366/03 and T–235/04), judgment of the Court of First Instance (fourth chamber), 5 October 2005.

50 This replaces the previous reference in Art 100A.4 to the *applying* of national measures, which had led to uncertainty as to whether this was limited to maintaining existing measures or covered the introduction of new measures.

such provisions as well as the grounds for maintaining them. The member state may maintain its measure unless and until the Commission rejects its notification.

The application of para 4 was considered by the ECJ in *Denmark v Commission*.[51] The case arose out of the Commission's rejection of a notification by Denmark in respect of an existing prohibition on the use of sulphites and nitrites/nitrates in food that was more stringent than the harmonised measure introduced under Art 95. The Court held that the Commission should not have made its decision by reference to the possibility of amending the harmonisation measure, nor should it have dismissed the technological need for a measure, as opposed to an assessment of the health effects of a given substance, as a relevant criterion in undertaking the analysis mandated by Art 30. The Commission had also wrongly found that a member state which sought to *maintain* a divergent measure under Art 95.4 must prove that this is justified by a problem specific to that member state or by new scientific evidence – the two criteria applicable to the *introduction* of divergent measures.[52] Despite these errors, the Commission had validly rejected the application as regards sulphites on the basis of the major need to protect public health, one of the conditions referred to in Art 95.5. That being so, the Commission was not further required to consider whether the divergent measures satisfied the three other conditions set out in para 6.[53]

Where a member state seeks to introduce new measures imposing stricter standards than those contained in the harmonised EC legislation, the matter falls under para 5. This provides different grounds for notification to those which are specified in para 4. The national measure must be 'based on new scientific evidence relating to the protection of the environment or the working environment on grounds of a problem specific to that Member State arising after the adoption of the harmonisation measure'. As with para 4, the member state introducing such measures must notify the Commission of the envisaged provisions as well as the grounds for introducing them.

Paragraph 5 was in issue in *Land Oberösterreich und Österreich v Commission*.[54] In March 2003, Austria notified the Commission of a draft law of the Province of Upper Austria that sought to make the province a GM-free zone. The notification was intended to secure, on the basis of Art 95.5, a derogation from Directive 2001/18. The Commission referred the matter to the EFSA, which concluded that the information supplied by Austria did not contain

51 *Denmark v Commission* (Case C–3/00) [2003] ECR I–2643.
52 However, if such factors existed, they could be highly relevant in guiding the Commission in its decision.
53 As regards nitrates, however, the Commission's decision was vitiated by its failure to take sufficient account of a 1995 opinion which criticised the conditions of use for nitrites under that directive.
54 *Land Oberösterreich und Österreich v Commission* (Joined Cases T–366/03 and T–235/04), judgment of the Court of First Instance (fourth chamber), 5 October 2005.

any new scientific evidence which could justify banning GMOs in Upper Austria. Accordingly, the Commission adopted Decision 2003/653/EC of 2 September 2003 to the effect that the divergent measure could not be justified under Art 95.5 because there was no new scientific evidence to show that a specific problem in the Upper Austria had arisen following the adoption of Directive 2001/18 which made it necessary to introduce the notified measure.[55]

The Court of First Instance (fourth chamber) held that the Commission was not obliged to give a right of hearing to the member state which had made a notification under Art 95.5.[56] As to the substance of the dispute, the Commission had rejected Austria's arguments that there was a specific problem which applied to Austria due to the small size of farms in the Province. This, however, was a common characteristic to be found in all member states. Moreover, EFSA had concluded that the scientific evidence disclosed 'no new or uniquely local scientific information on the environmental or human health impacts of existing or future GM crops or animals' nor had it shown that Upper Austria had 'unusual or unique ecosystems that required separate risk assessments from those conducted for Austria as a whole or for other similar areas of Europe'. Austria had failed to put forward evidence to rebut these findings and had been unable to state whether the presence of GMOs had even been recorded in Upper Austria. As the requirements in Art 95.5 were cumulative, it was sufficient for the rejection of the request for derogation that only one of those conditions had been satisfied. Austria had also argued that the Commission should have taken into account the fact that the notified measure was a measure of preventive action within the meaning of Art 174.2, justified by the precautionary principle. However, this argument was irrelevant to a notification under Art 95.5. At the time of writing the case has been appealed to the ECJ.

5.2.2 Article 175. Environmental harmonisation

Article 175.1 provides the legislative basis, in accordance with the co-decision procedure under Art 251, to introduce action to achieve the objectives of the Community's policy on the environment.[57] These are set out in para 1 of Art 174, as follows:

---

55   This was also the basis for the Commission's decision in *Commission v Germany* (Case C–512/99) [2003] ECR I–845, where the Commission's decision was upheld by the ECJ.
56   The ECJ had already decided in *Denmark v Commission* (Case C–3/00) [2003] ECR I–2643 that no right to be heard existed as regards Art 95.4.
57   Article 175.2 provides that unanimity is required for legislation on the following: provisions primarily of a fiscal nature; measures affecting town and country planning, quantitative management of water resources or affecting, directly or indirectly, the availability of those resources, land use, with the exception of waste management; measures significantly affecting a member state's choice between different energy sources and the general structure of its energy supply.

- preserving, protecting and improving the quality of the environment,
- protecting human health,
- prudent and rational utilisation of natural resources,
- promoting measures at international level to deal with regional or worldwide environmental problems.

Paragraph 2 then sets out the principles of EC policy on the environment. The EC is required to 'aim at a high level of protection taking into account the diversity of situations in the various regions of the Community.' EC policy is to be based on the precautionary principle, the need for preventive action, the rectification of environmental damage at source, as a priority, and the principle that the polluter should pay. Environmental harmonisation measures must include, where appropriate, 'a safeguard clause allowing Member states to take provisional measures, for non-economic environmental reasons, subject to a Community inspection procedure'.

Paragraph 3 then requires the EC's environmental policy to be prepared taking into account the following factors:

- available scientific and technical data,
- environmental conditions in the various regions of the EC,
- the potential benefits and costs of action or lack of action,
- the economic and social development of the EC as a whole and the balanced development of its regions.[58]

The implementation of para 4 requires the member states to finance and implement the EC's environmental policy, without prejudice to certain matters of an EC nature. However, para 5 provides for temporary derogations and/or financial support from the Cohesion Fund set up pursuant to Art 161, should a measure adopted under para 1 involve disproportionate costs for the public authorities of a member state. This provision is without prejudice to the polluter pays principle.

Finally, Art 176 allows member states to maintain or introduce more stringent protective measures than the harmonised measures adopted under Art 175, provided the Commission is notified and the measure is compatible with the Treaty. This brings in Arts 28 and 29, as well as the justifications under Art 30 and the rule of reason. These issues will be determined by the ECJ. In contrast, the equivalent provisions in Art 95 require a determination by the Commission, in accordance with the criteria specified in paras 4, 5 and 6. In *Dusseldorp*,[59] it was argued that Art 176 could not be invoked when EC

58 Co-operation by the EC and member states with third countries and competent international organisations is required under para 4.
59 *Dusseldorp* (Case C–203/96) [1998] ECR I–4075.

legislation had wholly regulated the area in question, as was the case with the waste regulation in question which contained an exhaustive list of grounds on which objection could be made to shipments of waste. Both the Advocate General and the ECJ were of the view that Art 176 applied within the limits of the Treaty. This view is justified by the clear wording of the article which must displace the general rule set out in *Gourmetterie Van den Burg (Red Grouse)* [60] that exhaustive harmonisation precludes reliance on Art 30 or the rule of reason. [61]

It is also important to note that the principles set out in Art 174 inform EC policy, but do not form a basis for challenging divergent national legislation on the environment. [62] In *Peralta*, Italian legislation on marine pollution which went beyond the requirements in MARPOL, the International Maritime Organisation's international convention on marine pollution, was challenged on the ground that it was, thereby, not in conformity with Art 174. The ECJ ruled that it could neither rule on a treaty to which the EC was not a party, nor interpret Art 174 in the light of its requirements, and stated that:

> ... [Article 130r] is confined to defining the general objectives of the Community in the matter of the environment. Responsibility for deciding what action is to be taken is conferred on the Council by [Article 130s]. Moreover, Article [130t] states that the protective measures adopted pursuant to [Article 130s] are not to prevent any Member State from maintaining or introducing more stringent protective measures compatible with the Treaty. [63]

The compatibility of EC legislation with Art 175 came under review for the first time in *Safety Hi-Tech*. [64] The Italian court referred a challenge by Hi-Tech to the validity of Art 5 of Commission Regulation 3093/94 on Substances that Deplete the Ozone layer due to its potential incompatibility with Arts 28 and 174 of the EC Treaty. The challenge had been been made by Hi-Tech to the prohibition under the regulation on the use and marketing of HCFCs (hydrochlorofluorocarbons) for firefighting. The ECJ recognised that there was a need to strike a balance between the objectives and principles mentioned in Art 174 and the complexity of implementing them. In the light

---

60   *Gourmetterie Van den Burg (Red Grouse)* (Case C–169/89) [1990] ECR I-2143.
61   However, the ECJ then went on to find that the Dutch national safeguard measure was in breach of Art 29 and could not be justified by either Art 30 or the rule of reason.
62   Occasionally, as in *Walloon Waste* the ECJ will refer to the principles set out in Art 174 in its analysis of whether the measure can be justified by reference to the rule of reason.
63   *Peralta* (Case C–379/92) [1994] ECR I–3453, para 57.
64   *Safety Hi-Tech* (Case C–284/95) [1998] ECR I–4301.

of this any review must be limited to deciding whether the adoption of the regulation had involved a manifest error of appraisal regarding the conditions for applying Art 174. It was argued that the regulation only took into account the ozone depletion potential of HCFCs and failed to take into account two other environmental protection criteria, global warming potential and atmospheric lifetime factors. Such an analysis would have shown that HCFCs were less harmful than permitted substances such as halons. However, when dealing with a specific environmental problem, the EC legislature was not also required to adopt measures relating to the environment as a whole. Article 174.1, fourth heading, conferred on the Council legislative competence in relation solely to certain specified aspects of the environment, provided this contributed to the preservation, protection and improvement of the quality of the environment. A failure by the EC to ban the use of other substances, even if assumed to be illegal, could not in itself affect the validity of the prohibition on the use of HCFCs. Hi-Tech also referred to the authorisation of the use of halons, which display a much higher ozone depletion potential than HCFCs, thereby representing a greater threat to the ozone layer. This, it argued, amounted to a failure by the regulation to ensure a high level of environmental protection as required by Art 174.2. However, this requirement did not require the EC to aim for the highest level of environmental protection that was technically possible. It was enough to aim for a high level of protection and this had been achieved as the regulation went further than required by the EC's international obligations under the Montreal Protocol, and also contained provision for member states to adopt stricter measures.

Hi-tech also argued that the Regulation had failed to take account of the available scientific and technical data, as required by Art 174.3, in that the alternative substances permitted for firefighting were more damaging than HCFCs. The ECJ rejected this argument on two grounds. First, the regulation itself provided for the periodic review of ozone depleting substances which would authorise the Commission in the light of changing scientific knowledge to amend the permitted uses of HCFCs. Secondly, the case-file in the proceedings before the Italian court showed that, when the regulation was adopted, there were, from the scientific point of view, alternatives to the use of HCFCs, involving recourse to products less harmful to the ozone layer, such as water, powder and inert gases. Having found that the regulation was validly introduced under Art 175, the ECJ concluded that it was compatible with Art 28 by reference to the rule of reason. A comparison of HCFCs with other similar substances showed that the measure was clearly necessary for the protection of the environment and its restrictions were found to be proportionate.

5.3 The two justifications for violating Arts 28 and 29

Provided the measure is not in a field that is covered by exhaustive EC harmonisation, there are two grounds of justification which will take it out of the ambit of Arts 28 and 29. The first is provided by Art 30 (formerly Art 36) of the EC Treaty. The second derives from the decision of the ECJ in *Cassis du Dijon* whereby the 'rule of reason' provides that a measure will not violate Art 28 or Art 29 if it is directed to a 'mandatory requirement of the Community'. In both cases the burden of proof lies on the member state that seeks to justify a measure that violates either Art 28 or Art 29.

5.3.1 Article 30

The first sentence of Art 30 states:

> The provisions of Articles 28 and 29 shall not preclude prohibitions or restrictions on imports, exports or goods in transit justified on grounds of public morality, public policy or public security; the protection of health and life of humans, animals or plants; the protection of national treasures possessing artistic, historic or archaeological value; or the protection of industrial and commercial property.

This provides an exhaustive list of the grounds which will prevent a measure from violating Arts 28 or 29. The ground that is relevant to environmental protection is that of 'the protection of health and life of humans, animals or plants', but this will not cover environmental protection measures where there is no threat to health or life. Thus in *Walloon Waste*,[65] a measure prohibiting import of non-dangerous waste for disposal within Wallonia could not be justified under Art 30. The threat to life and health, however, need not be imminent. In *Danish Bees*,[66] the exception was held to cover the potential extinction of a distinct sub-species of brown bee on the island of Lso as result of cross-breeding. In *Preussenelektra*,[67] measures to promote the use of renewable electricity came under this heading because of their contribution to the reduction of global warming, which would avert a future risk to health and life. Public health measures fall under both Art 30 and the rule of reason. However, in *Aragonesa*, it was held that they need only be justified under Art 30.[68]

---

65   *Commission v Belgium (Walloon Waste)* (Case C–2/90) [1992] ECR I–4431.
66   *Bluhme (Danish Bees)* (Case C–67/97) [1998] ECR I–8033.
67   *Preussenelektra* (Case C–379/98) [2001] ECR I–2099.
68   *Aragonesa de Publicidad* (Joined Cases C–1/90 and C–176/90) [1991] ECR I–4151.

The aim behind the measure is a significant factor in determining the applicability of the exceptions listed in Art 30. In *Dusseldorp*,[69] a Dutch measure requiring reprocessing of oil filters at a Dutch plant was motivated by economic considerations and could not therefore be justified on grounds of environmental protection. In *Preussenelektra*, the Advocate General was of the view that the measure could not be justified with reference to grounds of security. The measure pursued environmental objectives and security of supply was only a side effect. Similarly, in *Compassion in World Farming*,[70] the ground of public morality could not be relied on as a justification for a possible ban on the export of veal calves in crates because it was subsidiary to the main ground, the health of animals, which could not be relied because of EC harmonisation in this field.

The second sentence then continues, in language similar to that used in the *chapeau* to GATT, Art XX, 'Such prohibitions or restrictions shall not, however, constitute a means of arbitrary discrimination or a disguised restriction on trade between Member states'. This sentence has been interpreted as being subject to the same threefold test applied in *Cassis du Dijon* to measures justified under the rule of reason. First, is the measure 'necessary'? This entails an analysis on cause and effect in determining whether the measure will achieve its aim. Secondly, is it proportionate? This requires a balancing of the intensity of the measure's restriction on trade with the degree of protection it can achieve. Thirdly, are there alternative means of achieving the aims of the measure which are less restrictive of trade?

5.3.2 The 'rule of reason' and mandatory requirements

The concept of mandatory requirements was set out as follows in *Cassis du Dijon*:

> Obstacles to movement within the community resulting from disparities between the national law relating to the marketing of the products in question must be accepted in so far as those provisions may be recognised as being necessary in order to satisfy mandatory requirements relating in particular to the effectiveness of fiscal supervision, the protection of public health, the fairness of commercial transactions and the defence of the consumer.[71]

This concept differs from Art 30 in two respects. First, it does not provide an exception to Arts 28 and 29, but provides that, where a mandatory

---

69   *Dusseldorp* (Case C–203/96) [1998] ECR I–4075.
70   *R v Minister of Agriculture, Fisheries and Food ex p Compassion in World Farming Ltd* (Case C–1/96) [1998] ECR I–1251.
71   *Cassis de Dijon* (Case 120/78) [1979] ECR 649, para 8.

requirement exists, the measure never falls within their ambit, provided that it is necessary and proportionate. Secondly, the list of mandatory requirements is not closed and is capable of extension as circumstances change. Protection of the environment was added in *Danish Bottles*,[72] in the light of the recognition of EC policy in this area following the changes in the Single European Act. However, it is subject to the same proportionality test that is present in the second sentence of Art 30.

5.3.3 Proportionality

The proportionality test has been applied in very few environmental cases, many of which have been decided without reference to it. The test was, however, applied in *Danish Bottles*.[73] In 1981 the Danish Government introduced a mandatory requirement that beer and soft drinks be marketed in returnable containers of an approved type, which excluded metal cans. In 1984, it gave an allowance to each producer to use up to 3,000 hectolitres each year in returnable but non-approved containers. There was some partial relaxation for importers who merely wished to test the Danish market. The ECJ held that there was a breach of Art 28 as regards the restriction relating to non-approved returnables, but not as regards the deposit and return arrangements. Environmental protection was recognised as a mandatory requirement under the rule of reason, but although the deposit and return scheme was necessary to achieve this aim, the same was not true of the approved container requirement. The approved container measure would protect the environment by guaranteeing a maximum degree of re-use. This protection could not be achieved by alternative means. As Scott points out, the limited quantity of imported drinks sold in Denmark meant the additional degree of environmental protection was in practice marginal.[74]

In *Germany-Crayfish*,[75] a German law prohibited the import of live crayfish for commercial purposes. Its aim was to protect native species from diseases and from loss of biological distinctiveness by cross-breeding with non-indigenous sub-species. The ECJ found that the measure was disproportionate in that other less restrictive measures could have achieved its aim, such as health checks on imports and regulation of the marketing of crayfish on German territory. The decision has been criticised as placing a very high burden of proof on the member state on this issue. The import ban may have been the only means of guaranteeing zero risk to native species.

---

72   *Danish Bottles* (Case 302/86) [1988] ECR 4607.
73   *Danish Bottles* (Case 302/86) [1988] ECR 4607.
74   Scott, J, *EC Environmental Law*, 1998, London and New York, NY: Longman, p 70.
75   *Germany-Crayfish* (Case C–131/93) [1994] ECR I–3303.

In contrast, in *Bluhme (Danish Bees)*,[76] the ECJ demonstrated a greater sympathy for the practicalities involved in protecting biodiversity. A Danish law prohibited the keeping of bees on the island of Lso other than those of a particular sub-species of brown bee. The aim was to prevent the distinct sub-species being lost by cross-breeding. The ECJ found that Art 28 was engaged as the measure went beyond a restriction on selling arrangements of the kind seen in *Keck* in that it affected the character of the product. Nor could the impact of the regulation on trade be said to be too uncertain or indirect. The aim of the measure in protecting biodiversity fell under the heading in Art 30 of protecting the life of the animals within the sub-species. In this case, there was dispute as to whether the measure was 'distinctly applicable', hence the reliance by the ECJ on Art 30 rather than on the rule of reason. However, it may be questioned whether the threat of the loss of the Lso brown bee as a distinct sub-species could be regarded as a threat to its life or health.

In *Aragonesa*,[77] a regional prohibition in Spain on advertising of alcoholic drinks with a strength of more than 23 degrees was held to be proportionate to the aim behind the measure, the campaign against alcoholism. Nor did it constitute a means of arbitrary discrimination or a disguised restriction on trade between Member States, since it did not distinguish between products according to their origin. This conclusion was not affected by the fact that the region in question produced more beverages having an alcoholic strength of less than 23 degrees than beverages with a higher alcohol content.

The threefold test involves a balancing of the grounds of justification with their effects on the internal market. Generally, the ECJ will defer to the level of protection chosen by national legislatures. In *Brandsma*,[78] German legislation that prohibited the marketing of pesticides without prior authorisation, even though the product might lawfully be sold elsewhere in the EC, was held to be justified by Art 30, subject to the proviso that account must be taken of tests and analyses carried in another member state where they are or may become available. In *Sandoz*,[79] however, the ECJ held that proportionality required a Member State to authorise the marketing of foodstuffs to which vitamins had been added when this addition met a real need, especially a technical or nutritional one.

In *Aher-Wagen*,[80] the ECJ upheld German legislation providing that aircraft registered in another member state could be registered in Germany only if they complied with stricter noise standards as regards noise emissions from aircraft than those set out in Directive 80/51 (which provided for

76 *Bluhme (Danish Bees)* (Case C–67/97) [1998] ECR I–8033.
77 *Aragonesa de Publicidad* (Joined Cases C–1/90 and C–176/90) [1991] ECR I–4151.
78 *Brandsma* (Case C–293/94) [1996] ECR I–3159.
79 *Sandoz* (Case C–174/82) [1983] ECR 2445.
80 *Aher-Wagen* (Case C–389/96) [1998] ECR I–4473.

minimum harmonisation in this area). The measure was found to be proportionate in that limiting noise emissions from aircraft was the most effective way of limiting the noise pollution they generate. The German measure allowed a limited exemption for aircraft already registered in Germany before the directive. These aircraft were subject to stricter standards when they underwent technical modifications or were temporarily withdrawn from service. The exemption allowed the German authorities to determine the number of such aircraft and to know that in time their number would reduce when they were replaced by new aircraft. The policy would be undermined by extending the exemption to aircraft already registered in other member states as they were not subject to the stricter standards applicable to the German aircraft covered by the exemption.

A similar analysis, based on the practicalities of securing compliance with the aims of the measure, was applied to a national restriction in *Preussenelektra*.[81] The Advocate General had taken the view that the limitation of a German measure, requiring electricity generators and distributors to purchase a given percentage of electricity from renewable sources, to German renewables was disproportionate. However, the ECJ disagreed, holding that the nature of electricity was such that it was difficult to determine its source once it had entered the transmission and distribution system. The Commission took the view in its Proposal for Directive 2000/C311 E/22 on promotion of renewable electricity that a system of certificates of origin for renewable electricity, capable of being subject to mutual recognition, was needed to make the trade work. Although not stated expressly, this reason meant that the differentiation between domestic and imported renewables was not disproportionate. The measure was, therefore, compatible with Art 30.

However, this balancing act is very difficult in the absence of scientific certainty as to the causal relation between a substance and its ill effects and the intensity of the risks. The burden of proof lies on the importing state. With protection of human life and health, states have been allowed to err on the side of caution. A risk is serious even if it attaches only to a small number of vulnerable or sensitive consumers.[82] A cautious approach to public health can also be seen in the unsuccessful UK challenge, in 1996, to Commission Decision 96/239, under the former Art 173.[83] The decision prohibited beef and veal exports from the UK to Member and non-Member States, due to the BSE crisis. It was held that the Commission's decision had been based on the protection of public health and the transmissibility of BSE to humans was now seen as the most likely explanation of the new variant Creutzfeldt-Jakob disease. Despite imperfect knowledge of the disease, the Commission

---

81   *Preussenelektra* (Case C–379/98) [2001] ECR I–2099.
82   *Melkunie BV* (Case C–97/83) [1984] ECR 2367, para 19.
83   *Commission v UK* (Case C–180/96) [1996] ECR I–3993.

could take into account its fatal consequences and the fact that exposure to BSE was the likeliest explanation. A minimum evidence of scientific uncertainty, though, is required. In *Germany Beer*,[84] Germany's rules on beer additives were held to violate Art 28, but were not covered by Art 30 because Germany had failed to adduce evidence to counter the claims of the EC's Scientific Committee for Food, as well as of the *Codex Alimentarius*, that these presented no risk to public health.

Where animal health has been at stake, the ECJ seems to have been more willing to find the national measure to be disproportionate. In *Monsees*,[85] the ECJ found to be disproportionate an Austrian measure that restricted the transport by road of animals for slaughter by requiring such transport to be carried out only as far as the nearest suitable abattoir within national territory and with a maximum journey time of six hours and distance of 130 kilometres. These conditions would have made international transit by road of animals for slaughter almost impossible in Austria. Less restrictive alternative measures for protecting the health of animals were available, as shown by the provisions contained in Directive 95/29.

5.4 Distinctly and indistinctly applicable measures

Justification under the rule of reason is available only in respect of indistinctly applicable measures. Distinctly applicable measures can be justified only by reference to Art 30 which has a more narrowly defined list of exhaustive exceptions – measures necessary to protect the life of humans, animals or plants – but contains no reference to environmental protection per se. An unsuccessful attempt was made to add such a reference prior to the conclusion of the Treaty of Amsterdam. The classification of an environmental protection measure is therefore critical in determining the basis for its justification. A particular problem arises with measures which distinguish on the basis of the origin of the goods. Such distinctly applicable measures should only be justified by reference to Art 30.

However, the ECJ has been reluctant to follow its own logic when environmental protection is at stake. It has either found ways of reclassifying a distinctly applicable measure as an indistinctly applicable one, or else it has given a judgment without dealing with the issue at all and leaving it unclear whether the measure has been justified under Art 30 or the rule of reason. The most notorious example of judicial creativity on this issue can be seen in *Walloon Waste*.[86] What was at issue was the justification of a prohibition of the deposit in Wallonia of waste from outside that region. The measure

---

84 *Germany-Beer* (Case C–178/84) [1987] ECR 1227.
85 *Monsees* (Case C–350/97) [1999] ECR I–2921.
86 *Commission v Belgium (Walloon Waste)* (Case C–2/90) [1992] ECR I–4431.

clearly distinguished between Walloon and non-Walloon waste and should, therefore, have been regarded as distinctly applicable in the light of the court's previous decision in *Du Pont de Nemours*,[87] that a distinction on regional rather than national grounds would still render a measure distinctly applicable. Hazardous waste would clearly have fallen within the public health exception in Art 30, but justification on this ground was not possible as the measure was not in conformity with Directive 84/631 which constituted an exhaustive harmonisation measure in this field. Disposal of non-hazardous waste was not, however, covered by the directive. The ECJ found that the accumulation of waste, even before it could constitute a danger to health, did, however, constitute a threat to the environment.

However, to apply this mandatory ground of justification, the Court needed to get round the fact that the measure was clearly distinctly applicable. This it did by reference to Art 174.2 which required rectification of environmental damage at source. This meant waste should be disposed of as close as possible to its point of transaction so as to minimise transit, which was in conformity with the principles recognised by the Basel Convention 1989. There were, therefore, two different types of goods: Walloon waste and non-Walloon waste. The connection of waste with the place of production meant the prohibition was not discriminatory. The decision has been criticised on the grounds that the ECJ was essentially applying an analysis of the merits of justification to the logical prior, and distinct, process of classification of the measure as distinct or indistinct. A similar distinction was, however, argued for Advocate General Fennelly in *Danish Bees* to the effect that the measure was not distinctly applicable as the Lso sub-species of bee was a different type of product to other sub-species.[88] The ECJ, however, made its decision solely by reference to justification under Art 30.

In *Aher-Wagen*,[89] the ECJ justified the measure by reference to the cumulative effect of health and the environment, but never specified whether it was relying on Art 30 or the rule of reason. The measure required aircraft to satisfy noise emission standards before being registered in Germany, but was distinctly applicable in that it granted an exception to German aircraft that had already been registered at the time of the measure. In *Dusseldorp*,[90] the Dutch Government banned the export of oil filters and gave a local processor the exclusive right to process them. Exports would be permitted only if the importing state applied standards higher than the Dutch ones. Again, the measure was clearly distinctly applicable, but the court did not simply rely on this to find that the measure could not be justified under the rule of reason.

---

87   *Du Pont de Nemours* (Case C–21/88) [1990] ECR I–889.
88   *Bluhme (Danish Bees)* (Case C–67/97) [1998] ECR I–8033.
89   *Aher-Wagen* (Case C–389/96) [1998] ECR I–4473.
90   *Dusseldorp* (Case C–203/96) [1998] ECR I–4075.

Rather, it stated that the ground of protection of the environment could not be relied on when the measure had been introduced for economic grounds to allow the Dutch operator to have a constant supply of material so as to be able to operate profitably.

In *Preussenelektra*,[91] the measure under scrutiny was German legislation which required German electricity networks to buy a set percentage of supplies from German renewable energy sources. Advocate General Jacobs argued that the *Walloon Waste* analysis of this issue was flawed in that determining whether a measure was 'distinctly' applicable was a preliminary, neutral step whose purpose was to indicate which ground of justification could be relied upon. He then identified two reasons why the ECJ should adopt a more flexible approach to mandatory application of the ground of environmental protection. First, there was the heightened awareness of the environment in the Amsterdam Treaties, particularly in Art 6 EC. Although there may be no immediate threat to the health or life of humans, animals and plant, as protected under Art 30, environmental harm poses a mores substantial, longer-term threat to the whole eco-system. Secondly, national measures were inherently liable to be distinctly applicable in that they differentiate on the basis of the nature and origin of the harm, although the current measure seemed disproportionate in its exclusion of foreign suppliers of renewable electricity.

Unfortunately, the ECJ declined this invitation to clarify this issue. It found that the measure could be justified in that it aimed to reduce greenhouse gasses which was a priority objective of the EC as manifest by its signing up to both the UN Framework Convention of Climate Change 1993 and the 1997 Kyoto Protocol. The integration of environmental protection into the definition and implementation of other EC policies was mandated by Art 6 as well as the preamble to Directive 96/92, which stated that this ground authorised Member States to give priority to renewable electricity under Arts 8.3 and 11.3. The ECJ did not explicitly state the ground on which the measure could be justified, but its statement that 'the measure aimed to protect the health and life of humans, animals and plants' points to justification on the ground of Art 30.

5.5 Extra territoriality

One of the controversies within the WTO is the extent to which PPMs can be relied on to justify restrictions on the imports of goods. Such restrictions involve an extra-territorial objection to the way in which the product is manufactured. The treatment of this issue under the EC Treaty is not entirely clear. First, extra-territorial measures may be justified by the terms of a piece of EC

---

91 *Preussenelektra* (Case C–379/98) [2001] ECR I–2099.

legislation. *Gourmetterie Van den Burg (Red Grouse)*[92] is one such case. A Dutch game store had been offering for sale red grouse imported from the UK where it had been lawfully hunted in accordance with both UK and EC law. The Wild Birds Directive, Directive 79/409 regulated the powers of Member States to conserve wild birds and the ECJ held that it effected exhaustive harmonisation in this area, so precluding reliance on Art 30. Therefore, the powers of Member States to protect species occurring outside their territory were limited to situations covered by the directive. This applied only to birds which, unlike the red grouse, were endangered, migratory or occurring within the territory of the regulating Member State.

In contrast, in *Festen*,[93] a Dutch law to forbid the marketing of birds occurring outside the territory of Member States was held to be justifiable under Art 30 because the Wild Birds Directive aimed to protect biodiversity by prohibiting the import of wild sub-species that were not indigenous to the EC. The terms of the directive, therefore, sanctioned extra-territorial application of national law for species protected by the directive. Another example of when extra-territorial legislation may be justified by reference to the terms of EC legislation can be seen in the Commission's decision that a German ban on the import of *corallum rubrum* was justified under Art 30. *Corallum rubrum* is a species of coral, used in the making of jewellery, that occurs in the Mediterranean and whose existence is under threat. Although not protected under either EC legislation or that of the exporting country, Italy, Germany convinced the Commission that it could rely on Regulation 3636/82 which implements, within the EC, the CITES Convention on trade with endangered species. Article 15.1(c) permits Member States to take environmental measures for 'the conservation of a species or a population of a species in the country of origin', although such measures must comply with the Treaty, in particular Art 30.

The above decisions were all made by reference to the terms of EC legislation which covered the field. Apart from this, the ECJ has shown a distinct unwillingness to sanction extra-territorial national measures. In *Hedley Lomas*,[94] the ECJ held that the UK restriction on exports of veal to Spain constituted a breach of Art 29, notwithstanding Spain's failure to stun animals before slaughter as required by Directive 74/1577. The UK was not entitled to take unilateral action to force Spain to comply with its obligations under the Directive. Nor could the UK rely on Art 30 as the case involved exhaustive harmonisation by the relevant directive. However, even where this is not the case, the ECJ has shown a distinct unwillingness to justify extra-territorial

---

92   *Gourmetterie Van den Burg (Red Grouse)* (Case C–169/89) [1990] ECR I–2143.
93   *Festen* (Case C–202/94) [1996] ECR I–355.
94   *R v Ministry of Agriculture, Fisheries and Food ex p Hedley Lomas (Ireland) Ltd* (Case C–5/94) [1996] ECR I–2553.

measures under Art 30. In both *Inter Huiles*[95] and *Dusseldorp*,[96] it held that Art 30 could not be relied on to justify a 'local grab' measure preventing the export of waste products for recycling, because the recycling could have been done just as effectively, on environmental grounds, in other Member States. The decisions, however, leave open the possibility that the measure could have been justified had environmental standards in other Member States been lower than that in the member state applying the measure. Similarly, in *Alpine Investments*,[97] it held that the interests of foreign consumers, who might be affected by cold calling from the Netherlands, was not a matter for the Dutch authorities. However, the measure could be justified were it established that cold calling was having an adverse affect on the financial reputation of the Netherlands. This suggests that extra-territorial measures may be justified when they prevent adverse 'spillovers' into the territory of the Member State which imposes the measure. The *corallum rubrum* decision also suggests that justification may be possible where the measure seeks to protect something which can be regarded as part of the common heritage of the EC.

Even if measures which aim to protect the environment of another Member State are potentially within the scope of either Art 30 or the rule of reason, the concepts of necessity and proportionality might defeat reliance on either of the two grounds of justification. If the measures failed to have an impact on the production processes in the other Member State it is likely they would not be regarded as 'necessary' and even if the measure were marginally beneficial it might still not be regarded as 'proportionate'.

5.6 MEAs and the EC

Article 281 (formerly Art 210) gives the EC legal personality. Article 300 (formerly Art 228) deals with the EC's capacity to enter contractual relations with other persons and organisations, with para 7 providing that such agreements 'shall be binding on the institutions of the Community and on Member States'. This gives rise to two issues relating to the interface of trade and the environment within the EC.

The first is the extent to which the WTO agreements form part of the internal law of the EC. This question first arose in the context of the GATT. In *International Fruit Co v Produktschap voor Groenten en fruit*,[98] the ECJ held that its provisions did not have direct effect. This was because of the flexibility of the GATT, with its possibilities of derogation and the power of members to withdraw unilaterally from their obligations thereunder. In *Portugal v*

---

95 *Inter Huiles* (Case C–172/82) [1983] ECR 555.
96 *Dusseldorp* (Case C–203/96) [1998] ECR I–4075.
97 *Alpine Investments* (Case C–384/93) [1995] ECR I–1141.
98 *International Fruit Co v Produktschap voor Groenten en fruit* (Cases C–21–24/72) [1972] ECR 1219.

Council,[99] the ECJ took a similar view of the effect of the obligations under-taken by the EC under the WTO agreements, notwithstanding the more binding nature of these obligations. A general principle has, therefore, been established that the legality of an EC measure cannot be reviewed, either by individuals or Member States, in the light of the EC's obligations under the WTO agreements.[100] This principle of non-reviewability applies even follow-ing the adoption of a report by a WTO appellate body about the incompati-bility of EC law with obligations under the WTO agreements.[101] There are, however, two exceptions to this rule. First, where the EC intended to imple-ment a particular obligation assumed in the context of the WTO.[102] Secondly, where the EC measure refers expressly to the precise provisions of the WTO agreements.[103]

The position has been complicated recently by the decision of the ECJ in the *Biret* cases.[104] These arose out of the proceedings under the SPS Agreement in *EC–Beef Hormones*. A French company sought compensation, under Art 288,[105] for the damage which it claimed to have suffered as a result of the EC's prohibition on the import into the EC from the US of beef from animals that had been treated with growth hormones. The Court of First Instance dismissed the claim as it fell outside the two exceptions set out above. The case was then appealed to the ECJ which criticised the failure of the Court of First Instance to address the argument that the legal effects of the DSB decision of 13 February 1998 vis-à-vis the EC called into question the ECJ's finding that the WTO rules did not have direct effect. However, the ECJ pointed out that the DSB decision had given the EC a period of 15 months to comply with the award and it was not until that period had expired that a claim under Art 288 could arise in respect of the EC's failure to comply. The problem for the claimants was, by that time, they had become bankrupt and all their losses had accrued before the expiry of this period. The decision creates a limited third exception to the ECJ's previous decisions that the EC's obligations under the WTO agreements do not have direct effect. However, as confirmed in *Van Parys*,[106] the general rule remains that

---

99 *Portugal v Council* (Case C–149/96) [1999] ECR I–8395.
100 The Commission, however, may challenge Member States in respect of their non-compliance with the EC's obligations under the WTO agreements.
101 *Van Parys* (Case C–377/02), judgment of the European Court of Justice, 1 March 2005.
102 *Fediol v Commission* (Case 70/87) [1989] ECR 1781.
103 *Nakajima v Council* (Case C–69/89) [1991] ECR I–2069.
104 *Biret International SA v Council of the EU* (Case C–93/02 P) [2003] ECR I–10497. *Etablissements Biret & Cie SA v Council of the EU* (Case C–94/02 P) [2003] ECR I–10565.
105 Paragraph 2 provides, 'In the case of non-contractual liability, the Community shall, in accordance with the general principles common to the laws of the Member States, make good any damage caused by its institutions or by its servants in the performance of their duties'.
106 Op. cit., fn 100.

that neither Member States nor individuals can seek to review the legality of EC legislation by reference to the EC's undertakings under the WTO agreements, even where the EC fails to comply with the recommendations of the appellate body.[107]

The second issue is whether Member States retain any power to conclude autonomous MEAs with other Member and non-Member States. This raises, in a different context, the issue of harmonisation. If the EC has 'occupied the field' by concluding an international agreement with the same subject matter, it will then become necessary to determine the legislative base on which the EC's agreement was adopted. If it was under Art 133, pursuant to the common commercial policy, there will be no room for further measures in the same field by Member States. On the other hand, if it was adopted under Art 175, national measures, which impose stricter standards than those contained in the MEA concluded by the EC, will be permitted under Art 176. However, if the MEA concluded by a Member State prohibited the import of goods from a third-party state, a problem would arise if those goods entered the through a Member State which was not a party to the MEA in question. Once the goods had entered the EC they would be regarded as a product in free circulation and assimilated to domestic production. Therefore, any attempt to prevent their entry into the territory of the member that had concluded the MEA would amount to a breach of Art 28.

Whether the conclusion of an international agreement falls within Art 133 or Art 175 has proved to be a very controversial and complex issue. The ECJ has provided little guidance, and its conclusions have not always been easy to justify. In the past it has ruled that the conclusion of the Cartagena Protocol was an environmental agreement,[108] and that the Energy Star Agreement with the US was a trade measure.[109] More recently, it held that the conclusion of the Rotterdam Convention was both a trade and environmental measure and, therefore, the implementing legislation, Regulation 304/2003, should have been introduced on a dual basis.[110]

5.7 Conclusion

The tension between free trade and environmental protection is played out in the EC against a rather different background than that provided by the GATT. The principles of free movement of goods that are secured principally by Arts 28 and 29 are not directed at discrimination and involve no threshold

---

107 For further analysis of this issue, see Koutrakos, P, *EU International Relations Law*, 2006, Oxford: Hart Publishing, pp 288–95.
108 Opinion 2/00 [2001] ECR I–9713.
109 *Commission v Council* (Case C–281) [2002] ECR I–12049.
110 *Commission v Council* (Case C–178/03) [2006] ECR I–107, case noted by Koutrakos, P, (2007) 44 CMLR 171. The Court, however, allowed the regulation to remain in force for long enough to allow for its reintroduction on this basis.

requirement of 'likeness' as is the case with GATT, Arts I and III. Instead, Arts 28 and 29 are directed at all obstacles to the free movement of goods, whether discriminatory or not, subject to the threshold limitations of *Keck*, and, as regards Art 29, of *Groenveld*. As such their scope is far wider than the 'most favoured nation treatment' and 'national treatment' provisions of GATT. However, the creation of the WTO Agreement has led to an important shift from the anti-discrimination principles of GATT to an obstacle-based approach similar to that adopted in the EC. This new approach manifests itself in the new side agreements such as the SPS Agreement and the TBT Agreement whose role in the trade/environment debate is now coming to overshadow that of the GATT.

There are two constraints on this obstacle based approach to securing free trade. The first is Art 30. This refers to 'the protection of health and life of humans, animals or plants' and, as is the case with GATT, Art XX(b), has a rather limited application to environmental protection. The second is through the 'rule of reason' set out by the ECJ in *Cassis de Dijon* which allows restrictions on the free movement of goods to be justified by reference to the mandatory requirements of the EC. Since 1988, in *Danish Bottles* the ECJ has recognised that protection of the environment as a mandatory requirement. 'Protection of the environment' is rather wider than the wording of Art XX(g) 'relating to the conservation of natural resources', although there is probably no real difference between the concepts given the expansive interpretation that Art XX(g) has been given by the appellate body in *US–Reformulated Gasoline* and *US–Shrimp/Turtle*. Reliance on the two grounds of justification requires a Member State to show that its trade restriction is necessary, is proportionate, and that there is no alternative measure for achieving its aim that is less restrictive of trade. The language may be different, but the underlying concepts are very similar to those expressed in the *chapeau* to Art XX.

The Court has faced similar problems in dealing with these exceptions as have come up in disputes under GATT 1947 and the WTO agreements. For example, the question of the threshold of scientific certainty required to justify a measure comes up in *Germany–Beer*, whilst the question of whether the availability of alternative restrictive measures that are less trade-restrictive comes up in *Germany–Crayfish*. Essentially, the trade/environment issue before the ECJ has been treated in a similar fashion to the way in which it has been dealt with by panels and the appellate body applying the WTO agreements. The jurisprudence of the ECJ does, however, have one distinctive feature. It has had to deal with the problem raised by 'distinctly applicable' measure. These can be justified only by reference to the more limited criteria set out in Art 30. Rather than tackle this issue head on, the ECJ has got round the problem through judicial creativity, some would say disingenuousness, as in the *Walloon Waste* case or through a studied ambiguity as to which ground of justification it is actually applying, as in *Preussenelektra*.

However, there is a significant difference between the EC's approach to the balancing of trade and environment concerns when compared with the balance struck under the WTO agreements. Within the EC, unlike the WTO, environmental protection does not have a merely 'negative' character, as an exception to a set of free trade obligations. Instead, environmental protection, along with the establishment of the internal market, is one of the fundamental objectives of the EC. Unlike the WTO, the EC possesses a legislative capacity to raise environmental standards through its legislative capacity, under either Art 95 or Art 175. This has led to the introduction of a considerable amount of harmonisation in this area, which has had the overall effect of raising environmental standards in the EC. This 'positive' approach, though, is only possible among a group of Member States who share a relatively high level of economic development and could not readily be transposed into a global context, due to the huge differences in development between different nations.

Harmonisation also raises new problems which do not occur within the WTO, principally the internal problem of determining the extent to which harmonisation allows individual Member States to apply stricter national standards in the harmonised area. Most environmental harmonisation will be based on either Art 95 or Art 175. The ability of Member States to introduce higher standards differs markedly depending on the legislative base on which the harmonised measure was introduced. Where harmonisation is based on Art 95 the Commission's approval is required, subject to the cumulative criteria set out in paras 5 and 6. However, far more leeway is allowed to national safeguard measures when the harmonised measure is introduced under Art 176. The Commission's consent is no longer required. Instead, it must be notified of the measure which must be in accordance with the provisions of the EC Treaty. Furthermore, Art 175 specifies wide-ranging environmental criteria for the introduction of harmonised legislation under Art 175, such as the precautionary principle and the polluter pays principle. However, the Court of First Instance in *Land Oberösterreich und Österreich v Commission* has made it clear that these principles do not inform the Commission's approval of a new national safeguard measure that derogates from harmonised legislation introduced under Art 95. So much then for the EC's arguments before WTO panels in *EC–Beef Hormones* and *EC–Biotech* that the precautionary principles has become established as a norm of customary international law.

To add another twist to this issue, national safeguard measures may also be justified by reference to derogation provisions in the harmonised legislation itself. This was the case with the national prohibitions on the introduction of GMOs in *EC–Biotech*. EC harmonisation in this area has been described as a system of 'regulatory anarchy'. This seems apt in the light of the Commission's recent failures to compel Austria and Hungary to abandon their prohibitions on the use of specific GMOs which have repeatedly been approved as safe for use within the EC. The price of diversity, reflecting strongly held public feeling on this issue, is that the EC will be unable to comply with the binding recommendations of the panel in *EC–Biotech*. Future litigation on this issue under the WTO agreements seems inevitable. Moreover, such litigation may well have internal consequences within the EC. Decisions such as *Portugal v Council* and *Van Parys* make it clear that EC legislation is not subject to review either by Member States or by individuals on the grounds of its non-conformity with the EC's obligations under the WTO agreements. However, the ECJ's finding in *Biret* that non-compliance with the binding recommendations of a DSB panel can impose a non-contractual liability on the EC under Art 288, means that the EC's external commitments may now seep back into its internal structure. Future claimants may not be so obliging as to become bankrupt before this liability comes into existence, at the end of the compliance period.

Chapter 6

Investor protection and environmental regulation (1). Customary international law and the European Convention on Human Rights

Environmental regulation does not impact solely on trade. It can also have a substantial impact on investment. For example, a foreign investor that is operating a factory will suffer adverse economic consequences as a result of the host state's introducing stiffer emission controls. The foreign investor, along with its domestic competitors, will simply have to absorb the extra costs and pass them on to its customers, unless the measure can be challenged through the local courts by way of judicial review. However, there is one additional route of challenge that is available to the foreign investor, but not to domestic operators. That is to persuade its home state to take proceedings against the host state for a failure to accord the foreign investor the minimum treatment to which aliens are entitled under customary international law.[1]

However, save where there has been a taking of its property by the host state, recourse to customary international law is unlikely to produce any useful result for the foreign investor, even if its home state can be persuaded to take on its case. For a start, there is by no means universal agreement among states that such an obligation actually exists. The existence of a minimum standard of treatment, which can be breached even if the treatment of the alien has been in accordance with the laws of the host state, has been propounded throughout the twentieth century by the developed, capitalist, states, most notably the US. The 1920s produced a series of claims between Mexico and the US arising out of the treatment of US nationals following the Mexican revolution. The claims involved mistreatment to the person of the alien in a time of civil disorder, most notably the *Neer* claim in 1926.[2] This involved the murder of a US citizen who was the superintendent of a mine in Mexico, on his way home form work. The claim arose out of the failure of the Mexican authorities to make any serious investigation into the offence. The General Claims Commission concluded that, for there to have been a breach

---

1 That is, the law derived from a consistent practice of states accompanied by the conviction of states that the practice set is required by law.
2 *Neer* (1926) 4 UNRIAA 60.

of customary international law, there would have had to be convincing evidence 'either (1) that the authorities administering the Mexican law acted in an outrageous way, in bad faith, in wilful neglect of their duties, or in a pronounced degree of improper damage, or (2) that Mexican law rendered it impossible for them properly to fulfil their task'.

At about the same time, the Permanent Court of International Justice in the *Chorzow Factory* case considered the application of this minimum standard to the protection of the property, rather than the person of the alien. The case involved an expropriation by Poland of a German owned factory, which was unlawful as it involved the breach of a treaty between the two nations. The court held that all expropriations of an alien's property, whether lawful or not, required compensation. The court then established how compensation should be assessed where the expropriation had been unlawful.

However, controversy attended the issue of whether there was any norm of customary international law that prescribed the measure of compensation that should be awarded to a foreign investor in the event of a lawful expropriation of its property. Most Latin American states argued that the state's obligation to the alien was that of 'national treatment', to afford it the same treatment under its law as that afforded to its own nationals.[3] Therefore, the alien would have to be content with the same measure of compensation as that afforded to nationals whose property had also been subject to expropriation. In contrast, the US propounded the view that customary international law required the payment to the foreign investor in such circumstances of 'prompt, adequate, and effective' compensation, irrespective of its entitlement under the national law of the expropriating state. This view came to be known as the 'Hull formula' after the US Secretary of State, Cordell Hull who had expounded it in 1938 in a series of exchanges with Mexico regarding claims by US nationals whose property had been taken in the Mexican revolution.

After the Second World War, the argument of the Latin American states was eagerly taken up by developing countries, in the wake of the wave of nationalisations of investments that occurred first in the communist takeover of Eastern Europe and then in the decolonialisation of Africa and Asia. As will be shown later in this chapter, the existence, or otherwise, of a minimum standard of treatment under international law has important implications for assessing the compensation to which a foreign investor is entitled in the event of an expropriation. Under the 'national treatment' standard, it would have to accept the compensation offered to domestic investors who had also suffered a taking of their property. In contrast, the 'minimum standard of

---

3   This was the view advocated by the late nineteenth-century Argentinian international jurist Carlos Calvo who gave his name to the 'Calvo clause', which gives exclusive jurisdiction over disputes over foreign investment contracts to national tribunals.

treatment' would allow for the compensation due to the foreign investor to be assessed at a higher rate.

In the light of this divergence of views between the developed, capital-exporting, states and the developing states, the minimum standard for the treatment of aliens has not developed into a rule capable of protecting their economic interests, save in the extreme instance where there is a state taking of their property. However, the principles set out in *Neer* may also be capable of encompassing instances of administrative impropriety and judicial abuse which adversely affect the property of a foreign investor, as evidenced by the following statement of the International Court of Justice in *Elettronica Sicula SpA (ELSI) United States v Italy*:

> Arbitrariness is not so much something opposed to a rule of law, as something opposed to the rule of law . . . It is wilful disregard of due process of law, an act which shocks, or at least surprises a sense of judicial propriety.[4]

It is not surprising then that protection of foreign investors through traditional state-to-state proceedings alleging violations of customary international law has proved something of a dead end. Over the last 40 years, however, a new development, the BIT, has privatised the international protection of investors.[5] These treaties give investors of one party a direct right of action, through arbitration, against the government of the other country in the event of a violation of various provisions designed to protect investors, which extend beyond the prohibition on expropriation under international law. In contrast to the position under customary international law, most BITs will permit the investor to commence proceedings, even though it is not in a position to show that it has exhausted local remedies against the respondent state. More than 2000 of these BITs have now been concluded. The UK is currently party to 84 BITs, the US to 37. Common to nearly all these BITs are variants of the following provisions: 'national treatment' and 'most favoured nation treatment' provisions which extend the GATT disciplines on trade into the field of investment; provisions entitling the investor to fair and equitable treatment in accordance with international law; provisions entitling the

---

4   *Elettronica Sicula SpA (ELSI) United States v Italy* (1989) ICJ 15, p 76. Similar reasoning was expressed by the tribunal in *Amco v Indonesia* (1983) 23 ILM 354, (1988) 27 ILM 1281, (1986) 1 ICSID Reports 509, to justify an award of damages on the basis of a denial of justice arising out of procedural defects in the process by which the foreign investor's licences to operate in Indonesia were revoked. This development is roundly criticised by Sornarajah, M, *The International Law on Foreign Investment*, 2nd edn, 2004, Cambridge: Cambridge University Press, pp 157–8.

5   The first BIT was signed on 26 November 1959 between West Germany and Pakistan, coming into force on 28 November 1962.

investor to compensation in the event of expropriation.[6] These last two provisions require a reference back to customary international law and it is through the awards made by tribunals constituted pursuant to BITs that the case law on the norms of customary international law has developed in recent years. However, the prevalence of BITs does not necessarily mean that their provisions can be used as evidence of the development of new norms of customary international law. Sornarajah has argued that, despite their outward similarity, 'there is so much divergence in the standards in bilateral treaties that it is premature to conclude that they give rise to any significant rule of international law . . . These treaties are best seen as creating *lex specialis* between the parties rather than as creating customary principles of international law'.[7]

Until recently, no BITs had been concluded between developed states. However, two major developed states, Canada and the US are parties to NAFTA, along with Mexico. NAFTA came into force on 1 January 1994 and contains extensive provisions on investor protection in Chapter Eleven.[8] At the time, NAFTA was the only major multilateral agreement on investment of general application to all investment sectors.[9] Its provisions now form the basis of the Central American Free Trade Agreement 2004 (CAFTA)[10] and the 2004 US-Australia and US-Singapore Free Trade Agreements. Although individual states have been prepared to conclude BITs to encourage inward investment, there has been a general unwillingness, particularly among developing countries, to sign up to a multi-lateral treaty containing the usual provisions to be found in BITs. In 1998, the OECD drafted a Multilateral Agreement on Investment (MAI) which attempted just such an undertaking, but the attempt was dropped in October 1998 following opposition to

6 The interaction between BITs and the development of customary international law on expropriation is analysed by Guzman, A, 'Explaining The Popularity of Bilateral Investment Treaties: Why LDCs Sign Treaties That Hurt Them', 26 August 1997, www.jeanmonnetprogram.org/papers/97/97–12-II.html, VII B (accessed 15 March 2007).

7 Sornarajah, M, *The International Law on Foreign Investment*, 2nd edn, 2004, Cambridge: Cambridge University Press, p 206. Guzman, op. cit., fn 6, takes the same view, claiming that, 'BITs, therefore, rather than representing the codification of customary law, are actually a derogation from it . . . the existence of BITs should be taken as evidence that there is no customary law guaranteeing prompt, adequate and effective compensation'. Sornarajah, however, recognises the role that BITs can play in elucidating the principles of existing norms of customary international law, stating, at p 224: 'There is little doubt that bilateral investment treaties contribute to the development of a concept of property in international law.'

8 The wording of Chapter Eleven is largely derived from the US Model BIT of 1986.

9 In contrast, the Energy Charter Treaty 1994, to which the US is not a party, deals only with rights of investors in a designated economic sector.

10 Negotiations are also currently in progress with regard to the drafting of the Free Trade Agreement of the Americas which would expand the NAFTA model to include states in Central and Southern America as well as the Caribbean.

some of its provisions from France and Canada.[11] Since then, there have been attempts to introduce some measure of investment protection into the WTO under the aegis of the GATS. In the Doha Round, which started in 2001 and was suspended from August 2006 to February 2007, members were mandated to negotiate with each other to extend the sectors which they would subject to the voluntary provisions of GATS. In addition, a Working Party on Domestic Regulation has been examining the scope of GATS, Art VI. These developments are covered in Chapter 4.

6.1 Customary international law on expropriation

Under customary international law a state is entitled to take proceedings against another state in respect of mistreatment there of one of its nationals.[12] As regards the property of a foreign investor, the relevant rule of customary international law is that which entitles an alien to compensation in the event that its property is nationalised or expropriated.[13] Where the expropriated property is owned by a corporation, as opposed to a natural person, the International Court of Justice held, in the *Barcelona Traction*[14] case, that the state with which that corporation has a close permanent connection will have title to bring proceedings against the expropriating state. The place of incorporation will be a strong indicator of this necessary connection. Individual shareholders, however, do not generally have any separate right of protection under international law and must rely on the protection afforded to the company. A state may not bring a claim on behalf of one of its nationals unless that person has exhausted its local remedies in the respondent state.[15] Proceedings may not be brought directly by the investor, but must be brought by the investor's home state, unless the investor is able to rely on investor-state arbitration provisions contained in a BIT.

---

11 For an analysis of the MAI, see Baughen, S, 'Investor Rights and Environmental Obligations. Reconciling the Irreconcilable?' (2001) 13 JEL 199, pp 215–18.
12 The injury to the national will be regarded as a wrong to its state of nationality. *Mavrommatis Palestinian Concessions Case (Jurisdiction)* (1924) PCIJ, Ser A, No 2.
13 See, further, Dolzer, R, 'Indirect Expropriations: New Developments', NYU Colloquium on Regulatory Expropriations in International Law, 26/27 April 2002, p 64. Appleton, B, 'Regulatory Takings: The International Law Perspective', NYU Colloquium on Regulatory Expropriations in International Law, 26/27 April 2002, p 35; Waelde, T and Kolo, A, 'Environmental Regulation, Investment Protection and "Regulatory Taking" in International Law' (2001) 50 ICLQ 811; Wagner, J, 'International Investment, Expropriation and Environmental Protection' (1999) 29 Golden Gate UL Rev 465.
14 *Barcelona Traction* (1970) ICJ Reports 3, (1970) 9 ILM 227.
15 Brownlie, *Principles of Public International Law*, 6th edn, 2003, Oxford: Oxford University Press, pp 472–81.

6.1.1 Defining expropriation

Until the early 1970s the major problems arising under customary international law were concerned with the measure of compensation due in the event of nationalisation of property. Since then, outright nationalisations have become much rarer. Instead the question has arisen as to whether the effect of regulations on an investment could constitute an expropriation. In the absence of authority from the International Court of Justice on this issue, reference must, instead, be made to decisions of tribunals that have made awards under BITs which purport to apply customary international law on expropriation. In particular, some useful guidance as to what state conduct short of nationalisation can amount to expropriation can be derived from the awards of the Iran-US claims tribunals.[16]

The awards show that expropriation includes indirect or 'creeping' expropriation which strips the investor's property of value without any formal transfer of title to the state or to a third party. For example, in *Tippetts*, the Iran-United States Claims tribunal held that the expropriation occurred when the Iranian Government appointed a new manager of the partnership which the claimant had established with an Iranian engineering firm prior to the Iranian revolution.[17] The tribunal reasoned as follows:

> A deprivation or taking of property may occur under international law through interference by a state in the use of that property or with the enjoyment of its benefits, even where legal title to the property is not affected. While assumption of control over property by a government does not automatically and immediately justify a conclusion that the property has been taken by the government, thus requiring compensation under international law, such a conclusion is warranted whenever events demonstrate that the owner was deprived of fundamental rights of ownership and it appears that this deprivation is not merely ephemeral. The intent of the government is less important than the effects of the measures

16 Aldritch, G, 'What Constitutes a Compensable Taking of Property? The Decisions of the Iran – United States Claims Tribunal' (1994) 88 Am J Int'l L 585. Caution should, however, be exercised, in dealing with these awards given the rather wider remit of the tribunals to deal with other measures affecting property rights. Aldritch, who was one of the arbitrators on the Claims Tribunal, expresses the view that some of the decisions made a finding on this basis so as to avoid the application of the full compensation standard that would be applicable to all takings of property rights under the Treaty of Amity 1955 between the US and Iran.

17 Many of the awards involved nominally temporary appointments of supervisors and managers for companies by the government of Iran. However, by the late 1983, when the first claims came to be heard, it had become clear that such interference had become permanent.

on the owner, and the form of the measures of control or interference is less important than the reality of their impact.[18]

This passage, which has been much quoted in subsequent literature on creeping expropriation, suggests that the principal factual enquiry required of a tribunal is one which assesses the extent to which a government measure has led to permanent impairment of rights of ownership over particular property. This involves an effects-based analysis of the measure on the investment. It is possible that a level of government interference which would not ordinarily be sufficiently severe to constitute an expropriation, might be regarded as expropriatory if the interference involves a breach of a stabilisation clause in the contract between the foreign investor and the host government. In *Revere Copper & Brass, Inc v Overseas Private Invest Corp*, the majority arbitrators held that when Jamaica repudiated its contract, Revere's future decisions as regards its investment were turned into gambles, the antithesis of the rational decision making that lies at the heart of any control. They stated:

> We regard these principles as particularly applicable where the question is, as here, whether actions taken by a government contrary to and damaging to the economic interests of aliens are in conflict with undertakings and assurances given in good faith to such aliens as an inducement to their making the investments affected by the action.[19]

The dissenting arbitrator, Francis Bergan, however, noted that the tax rise imposed on Jamaica in breach of the stabilisation clause was not confiscatory, either under international law or under US domestic takings law.

The *Tippetts* analysis raises the question of what weight the intent behind a measure should play in determining whether or not there has been an expropriation. Although the most important factor is the effect of the measure on the investment, governmental intent is not altogether discounted in the analysis. It is merely 'less important' than the effect of the measure. However, does governmental intent have *any* role to play in a determination of whether or not there has been an expropriation? A negative answer was given by the tribunal in *Phillips*, where it stated not only that it 'need not determine the intent of the Government of Iran', but also that 'a government's liability to compensate for expropriation of alien property does not depend on proof that the expropriation was intentional'.[20] In contrast, the tribunal in

---

18 *Tippetts, Abbett, McCarthy, Stratton v TAMS-AFFA Consulting Eng'rs of Iran* 6 Iran-US Cl Trib Rep 219 (1984), pp 225–6.
19 *Revere Copper & Brass, Inc v Overseas Private Invest Corp* (1980) 56 ILR 258, (1978) 17 ILM 1321, p 1331.
20 *Phillips Petroleum Co Iran v Islamic Republic of Iran* 21 Iran-Us Cl Trib Rep 79 (1989), p 115.

Sea-Land Sev, Inc v Iran (*Sea-Lands*) referred to the need to establish 'deliberate governmental interference' with the conduct of Sea-Lands' operations.[21]

The role of intent needs to be analysed in two distinct contexts. First, there is the causative issue which involves a determination of what link needs to be established between government action and the destruction of an alien's fundamental rights in a piece of property. At the very least, the adverse effects sustained by an investment must follow from the acts of governments or agencies whose actions can be attributed to the government. Losses sustained as a result of a failure to act on the part of government bodies should therefore, not be capable of giving rise to a claim for expropriation. This was the case in *Sea-Lands*, where the tribunal found that the government of Iran was not obliged to pay compensation in respect of losses sustained consequent upon the deterioration in the situation at the port of Bandar Abbas consequent upon inactivity on its part. A similar finding was later made in *Olguin v Paraguay*, where the tribunal found that the failure on part of Paraguayan authorities to monitor activities of financial institutions, one of which, La Mercantil, had collapsed owing substantial sums to a Peruvian investor, Mr Olguin, did not constitute an expropriation. The tribunal observed that:

> For an expropriation to occur, there must be actions that can be considered reasonably appropriate for producing the effect of depriving the affected party of the property it owns, in such a way that whoever performs those actions will acquire, directly or indirectly, control, or at least (*sic*) the fruits of the expropriated property. Expropriation therefore requires a teleologically driven action for it to occur; omissions, however egregious they may be, are not sufficient for it to take place.[22]

This formulation, though, goes beyond merely ruling that omissions cannot found an expropriation claim in extending such a rule to government actions.[23] The concept of a 'teleologically driven action' is essentially a means of distinguishing those who are directly affected by a measure from those who are merely indirectly affected thereby. The question it requires a tribunal

21 *Sea-Land Sev, Inc v Iran* 6 Iran-US Cl Trib Rep 149 (1984), p 166.
22 *Olguin v Paraguay* (ICSID Case No Arb/98/5), 26 July 2001, para 84.
23 There may, however, be situations in which a specific failure to act on the part of a state entity is capable of constituting an expropriation. This was the analysis adopted in *CME v Czech Republic*, Uncitral arbitration, partial award, 13 September 2001, in respect of a failure of the Czech Media Council to take proceedings against a Czech company in respect of a violation of the terms of its licence to broadcast television which occurred when it terminated its contract with the company managing the television station. The omission, though, was a natural follow-on from previous actions by the Media Council in altering the terms of the licence agreement so as to weaken the position of the ousted contractual party and formed part of a course of conduct very specifically directed at that party. This was not a case, as in *Olguin* or *Sea-Lands*, of generalised failures by governmental bodies that led to incidental losses on the part of the investor.

to ask is: 'At whom was this government action directed?' Thus, if a government expropriates X and that has the indirect effect of putting one of X's suppliers out of business, an expropriation claims would be generated only as regards the losses sustained by X, but not the supplier.[24] The reference to a transfer of benefit to the government in question is more problematic. If the benefit of X's property has been transferred that will clearly show that the measure was directed at X. However, the measure may still be shown to have been directed at X without any transfer of benefit. The tribunal in *Tippetts* explicitly rejected an argument that a transfer of benefit is a requirement for a finding of expropriation, and, for this reason, preferred the term 'deprivation' to 'taking'.[25]

The second context in which intent needs to be considered is in determining whether a state is relieved of its obligation to compensate for an expropriation if the measure in question was motivated by concerns of public welfare. Brownlie notes that:

> Jurists supporting the compensation rule recognise the existence of exceptions, the most widely accepted of which are as follows: . . . as a legitimate exercise of police power, including measures of defence against internal threats; . . . loss caused indirectly by health and planning legislation and the concomitant restrictions on the use of property.[26]

The latter exception is probably not a true exception given that most restrictions on the use of property are unlikely to have economic consequences that are sufficiently severe as to constitute an expropriation in the first place. The former exception, however, is more problematic. Under customary international law the police powers exception[27] has a very limited ambit. The exception would cover forfeiture for crime, bona fide general

---

24 This position approximates to that pertaining under NAFTA, Chapter Eleven as a result of the interpretation given by the tribunal in *Methanex v USA*, award on jurisdiction, 28 August 2002, to the phrase in Art 1101 'a measure relating to an investor'.

25 However, *Lauder v Czech Republic*, Uncitral arbitration, final award, 3 September 2001, seems at odds with *Tippetts* on this point. The claim arose out of the same facts as those in *CME v Czech Republic*, but with the suit being brought by an investor, rather than the company, under a different BIT. The tribunal found that the loss of the investment in the company operating a Czech television station was simply the consequence of a contractual dispute between two private parties. The tribunal found that there was no evidence of any state action amounting to expropriation, and stressed the absence of any transfer of any benefits from the investor to the Czech Republic.

26 Brownlie, *Principles of Public International Law*, 6th edn, 2003, Oxford: Oxford University Press, pp 511–12, fn 11.

27 The term appears to bear a wider meaning under US takings law. In *Hawaii Housing Authority v Midkiff* 467 US 229 (1984), p 240, the Supreme Court held that '[t]he public use requirement [of the Takings Clause] is . . . coterminous with the scope of a sovereign's police powers'.

taxation or measures necessary for the maintenance of public order, provided the state action in question is not discriminatory and is not designed to cause the alien to abandon the property to the state or to sell it at a distress price.[28] The limited nature of this latter category is illustrated by *Tecnicas Medioambientales Tecmed SA v United Mexican States (Tecmed)*.[29] The tribunal awarded compensation under a BIT between Mexico and Spain,[30] in respect of a refusal by a Mexican state agency, INE, to renew a licence to operate the Las Viboras landfill site. Having once been used as for landfill, the site had no alternative economic use. INE's decision was made in response to considerable local opposition based on the proximity of the site to the town of Hermosillo.[31] However, for the police powers exception to come into play, the local opposition would have had to be so pronounced as to result in a state of emergency, which, on the facts, was not the case. The tribunal stated that the situation in Hermosillo was not comparable to that pertaining in *Elettronica Sicula SpA (ELSI) (US v Italy)*, which arose out of a temporary requisition in 1968, by the Mayor of Palermo, of a factory which was being shut down by the US company which owned it. Due to the high level of unemployment in Sicily at the time, the facts potentially fell within the police powers exception. However, the International Court of Justice never ruled on this point, and instead rejected the claim on the ground that the requisition had not impeded the orderly disposal of the investor's assets.[32]

Expropriations outside the scope of a state's police powers will entail an obligation to compensate notwithstanding the public interest considerations behind the state's action, nor the fact that such action is lawful.[33] In *Cia del Desarollo de Santa Elena SA v Republic of Costa Rica*,[34] US interests acquired a beach property in 1970 with a view to development for tourism. By a decree of 5 May 1978, Costa Rica took the property for inclusion as part of a national park. The award dealt primarily with the quantum of compensation

---

28 *Too v Greater Modesto Insurance Associates* 23 Iran-US Cl Trib Rep 378 (1989), pp 387–8, in which the seizure by the US Internal Revenue Service of a liquor licence owned by an Iranian national in California to satisfy over $70,000 of overdue taxes was held to fall within the scope of the state's police powers.

29 *Tecnicas Medioambientales Tecmed SA v United Mexican States (Tecmed)* (ICSID Case No ARB (AF)/00/2) (Spain/Mexico BIT), award, 29 May 2003.

30 Article V referred to 'nationalisation, expropriation or measures of similar effect'.

31 After the site's location had been approved new regulations were introduced which would have prevented the siting of a waste disposal sites so close to a town the size of Hermosillo. Under Mexican law, INE could not take such factors into account but could consider only the manner in which the site had been operated.

32 *Elettronica Sicula SpA (ELSI) (US v Italy)* (1989) ICJ 15, 20 July 1989.

33 *Chorzow Factory. FR Germany v Poland* (1928) PCIJ Ser A, No 17 *(Chorzow Factory)* makes it clear that even a lawful expropriation entails an obligation to compensate, although a higher quantum of compensation may be awarded where the expropriation is unlawful.

34 *Cia del Desarollo de Santa Elena SA v Republic of Costa Rica* (ICSID Case No ARB/96/1), award, 17 February 2000.

to be awarded in respect of the expropriation but the tribunal also found that the purpose of protection of the environment that motivated the taking did not absolve Costa Rica from its obligation to compensate, as follows:

> ... The purpose of protecting the environment for which the Property was taken does not alter the legal character of the taking for which adequate compensation must be paid. The international source of the obligation to protect the environment makes no difference.[35]

The tribunal then went on to state that:

> Expropriatory environmental measures – no matter how laudable and beneficial to society as a whole – are, in this respect similar to any other expropriatory measures that a state may take in order to implement its policies: where property is expropriated, even for environmental purposes, whether domestic or international, the state's obligation to pay compensation remains.[36]

A slightly different approach was taken in *Tecnicas Medioambientales Tecmed SA v United Mexican States (Tecmed)*,[37] in which the tribunal stated that the concept of proportionality adopted in jurisprudence of the ECHR in relation to claims under Art 1 of the First Protocol of the European Convention on Human Rights could play a useful role in determining whether there had been a compensable expropriation. An agency of the Mexican Government, INE, refused to renew a licence to operate a landfill site by taking into account local opposition based on the site's proximity to the town of Hermosillo. However, under Mexican law, INE was only entitled to make its decision by reference to the manner of the site's operation. Although there had been some breaches of the terms of the license, these were not substantial and were easily remedied and, accordingly, the refusal to renew the licence

---

35 Paragraph 71. See, also, *Phelps Dodge Corp v Islamic Republic of Iran* 10 Iran-US Cl Trib Rep 121 (1986), p 130 where the tribunal held that the financial, economic and social motivations behind a law, pursuant to which a transfer of management had been effected, did not relieve the government of Iran of its obligation to compensate in respect of the expropriation.

36 Paragraph 72. For criticisms of the decision, see Sornarajah, M, *The International Law on Foreign Investment*, 2nd edn, 2004, Cambridge: Cambridge University Press, pp 385–6. A similar finding was made in *SPP (Middle East) v Arab Republic of Egypt*, ICSID award, 20 May 1992 (1992) 32 ILM 937. In its award of damages, the tribunal, having rejected the discounted cash flow approach as too speculative, observed, at paras 190–1, that, in any event, damages awarded under this method could not take account of profits that would have been made after 1979, after which further development of the site would have become illegal under the Convention Concerning the Protection of the World Cultural and Natural Heritage 1972 (UNESCO World Heritage Convention).

37 *Tecnicas Medioambientales Tecmed SA v United Mexican States (Tecmed)* (ICSID Case No ARB (AF)/00/2) (Spain/Mexico BIT), award, 29 May 2003.

here was a disproportionate response. However, under the ECHR jurisprudence discussed below, a deprivation of possessions, which equates to an expropriation under customary international law, will rarely, if at all, be proportionate in the absence of compensation. In contrast, a measure which affects a control of use will often be 'proportionate in the absence of compensation, but such claims would not constitute expropriations under customary international law, because of the absence of the requisite severity of impact on the investment'. It must, therefore, be doubted, whether the concept has any role to play in developing the jurisprudence of customary international law as to what state conduct constitutes and expropriation.

6.1.2 What property can be subject to an expropriation?

For there to be a recovery for expropriation, there must be a taking of property. For this purpose, goodwill or market access have not been regarded as capable of amounting to property. For example, in the *Oscar Chinn* case,[38] the Belgium Government, with a view to maintaining viable shipping on the river Congo, gave a subsidy to Union Nationale des Transports (UNATRA) and directed it to charge nominal freight rates. The effect was to close down the business of Mr Chinn, who was UNATRA's sole competitor. However, this was held not to amount to an expropriation, because: 'The Court . . . is unable to see in his original position – which was characterised by the possession of customers and the possibility of making a profit – anything in the nature of a genuine vested right.'[39] A similar position was adopted in *Sea-Land Sev Inc v Iran*[40] in relation to a claim that there had been an expropriation by virtue of Sea-Lands' loss of its acquired right to use and benefit from port facilities in Bandar Abbas due to the inactivity of the Iranian Government after the 1980 revolution, which had led to disruption in the functioning of the port.

A somewhat different position appears to have been taken by the tribunal in *CME v Czech Republic*.[41] The investor claimed in respect of losses it had sustained as a result of contractual breaches by its Czech partner in the running of the Czech television station, TV Nova. The investor argued that these had been facilitated by a variation in the terms of the contract that had been entered into in 1996 to forestall threatened administrative proceedings by the Czech Media Council. The Czech Republic, relying on *Oscar Chinn*, argued that:

> . . . what CME says it has lost is not property, nor even rights under the initial or amended contracts. What CME says it has lost is the measure

---

38 *Oscar Chinn (UK v Belgium)* (1934) PCIJ, Ser A/B, No 63, 12 December.
39 At p 88.
40 *Sea-Land Sev Inc v Iran* 6 Iran-US Cl Trib Rep 149 (1984), p 166.
41 *CME v Czech Republic*, Uncitral arbitration, partial award, 13 September 2001.

by which the business advantage to it of the initial agreement exceeds that of the amended agreement. That is not a property right. The law recognises and upholds rights created by contract, but there is no legal concept of a separate property right to the maintenance of a particular balance of commercial power.

The point was not really addressed by the tribunal when it found that there had been an expropriation. However, it is possible to distinguish the two cases. *CME* was a case where state action altered the terms of an existing contract which then allowed one party to use its new powers under the renegotiation to oppress the other. Oscar *Chinn*, on the other hand, was a case where state action induced customers who might have been expected to contract with Chinn in the future to contract instead with UNATRA due to its more favourable rates. Therefore, it is an instance of state interference with contractual expectations rather than with vested contractual rights,[42] which are capable of forming the basis of an expropriation claim under customary international law.

However, where a state breaks a contract it has made with a foreign investor, that breach will not in itself amount to an expropriation. Something more is needed to take the matter out of the sphere of an ordinary breach of contract, through which recourse must be had through the courts in accordance with the system of law specified by the contract. For a breach of contract to constitute a violation of customary international law, by its transformation into an expropriation, there must be an attempt by the state party to use its superior powers to escape its contractual liabilities, for instance, by legislation that annuls the contract.[43]

6.1.3 Causation

Next, one must consider the requisite causal link that has to be established between the loss of property and the actions or inactions of the state. Most expropriation claims will involve some form of action by the state entity, whether at national or local level, or an administrative body. However, there

---

42 A similar finding was made in *SPP (Middle East) v Arab Republic of Egypt*, ICSID award, 20 May 1992 (1993) 32 ILM 933, where a claim for expropriation succeeded in respect of losses sustained by the claimant under a contract to develop a site near the Pyramids for tourism when the Egyptian government introduced legislation precluding further development on the site.

43 *Phillips Petroleum Co Iran v Islamic Republic of Iran* 21 Iran-US CTR 79 (1989) is an example of where the conduct of the state in relation to its contract with the investor crossed this line and amounted to an expropriation. In contrast, *SGS v Philippines* (Arb/02/6), decision on jurisdiction, 29 January 2004, is an example of where a breach of contract by the state was not regarded as an expropriation. A similar finding was made in a NAFTA claim under Art 1110 in *Waste Management v Mexico* (Arb (AF)/00/3), award, 30 April 2004.

may be occasions when the loss suffered would have occurred in any event. One such case is *Elettronica Sicula SpA (ELSI) (US v Italy)*.[44] In 1968, the Mayor of Palermo requisitioned a factory owned by an Italian subsidiary of a US corporation which had decided to close it down. The requisition lasted six months and was ultimately adjudged by the Italian courts to have been unlawful. The assets of the Italian company were eventually disposed of and the US, on behalf of the parent company, claimed that the assets were disposed of at an undervalue because the requisition had prevented an orderly disposal of the subsidiary's assets. The International Court of Justice (ICJ), though, rejected the claim, finding that the loss which was sustained by the Italian corporation was due to the US parent's decision to cease funding it, and that the six-month requisition had not, in fact, prevented an orderly, and more profitable, disposal of assets.[45]

6.1.4 Assessing the quantum of an expropriation claim

There has been no uniform practice of states as to the measure of compensation to be awarded for expropriations. The developed capitalist states of the West have espoused the 'Hull formula' propounded in 1938 by Secretary of State Cordell Hull in connection with claims against Mexico arising out of the requisitioning of property of US citizens. This requires 'prompt, adequate and effective' compensation. However, this formula has not received universal acceptance and some Latin American states have argued that no compensation is payable at all. An intermediate position appears in the General Assembly Resolution 1803 of 1962 on Permanent Sovereignty over Natural Resources, para 4 of which reads:

> Nationalisation, expropriation or requisitioning shall be based on grounds or reasons of public utility, security or the national interest which are recognised as overriding purely individual or private interests, both domestic and foreign. In such cases the owner shall be paid appropriate compensation, in accordance with the rules in force in the State taking such measure in the exercise of its sovereignty and in accordance with international law. In any case where the question of compensation gives rise to a controversy, the national jurisdiction of the State taking such measures shall be exhausted. However, upon agreement by sovereign States and other parties concerned, settlement of the dispute should be made through arbitration or international adjudication.

44 *Elettronica Sicula SpA (ELSI) United States v Italy* (1989) ICJ 15, 20 July 1989.
45 For this reason, the tribunal saw no need to rule on whether the requisition and the conduct of the local authorities in tolerating a worker's occupation of the factory amounted to a 'taking' or 'espropriazoni' under the Friendship, Commerce and Navigation Treaty 1948 between the US and Italy, Art V.

The reference here is to 'appropriate' compensation in accordance with the rules both of the expropriating state and of international law.

Similar wording has been subsequently adopted in UN Charter of Economic Rights and Duties of States of 12 December 1974, Art 2(c), which was opposed by Belgium, Denmark, Germany, Luxembourg, the UK and the US. OECD Draft Convention on Protection of Foreign Property 1967, Art 21, on the other hand, contains the following wording, 'No one shall be deprived of his property except on payment of just compensation, for reasons of public utility or social interest, and in the cases and according to the forms established by law'. The reference to 'just' compensation reappears in the Restatement (Third) of Foreign Relations Law of the United States 1986, 712(1), which stipulates that under international law there is state responsibility for injury resulting from 'a taking by the state of the property of a national of another state that (a) is not for a public purpose, or (b) is discriminatory, or (c) is not accompanied by provision for just compensation'. The commentary explains that a state is responsible 'when it subjects alien property to taxation, regulation, or other action that is confiscatory or that prevents, unreasonably interferes with, or unduly delays, effective enjoyment of an alien's property or its removal from the state's territory'.

Statements from the judgment of the Permanent Court of International Justice in the *Chorzow Factory* case has been used to justify the application of a standard of 'full' compensation (that is to say the 'Hull Formula') to all expropriations.[46] However, neither the decision nor the statements relied on can bear such an interpretation. The case involved the expropriation by Poland of a German-owned factory in Upper Silesia (which had been transferred to Poland under the Treaty of Versailles 1919). The most significant factor in the subsequent assessment of damages was the Permanent Court of International Justice's (PCIJ's) initial finding in 1926 that the expropriation had been unlawful under the terms of a 1922 Treaty between Poland and Germany which related to Upper Silesia.[47] More specifically, Art 6 set out what Poland could and could not do by way of expropriation in the transferred territory, and the expropriation of this factory fell outside the expropriations permitted thereunder.

After the failure of negotiations between the two states as to restitution of the factory, the PCIJ considered the issue of the damages available to Germany. The PCIJ noted that this was not a lawful expropriation for which 'fair' compensation was required. It would still have been unlawful even if compensation had been offered. Therefore, the compensation payable would not necessarily be limited to the value of the undertaking at the date of its dispossession, together with interest to the date of payment. Such a limitation would apply only if the expropriation were lawful and the only wrongful act

46 *Chorzow Factory. FR Germany v Poland* (1928) PCIJ, Ser A, No 17.
47 *Chorzow Factory (1)* (1926) PCIJ, Ser A, No 7.

by Poland had been a failure to pay the 'just' price for the factory. As for illegal expropriations:

> reparation must as far as possible wipe out all consequences of the illegal act and re-establish the situation which would in all probability, have existed if the act had not been committed. Restitution, in kind, or if this is not possible, payment of a sum corresponding to the value which a restitution in kind would bear.

The decision makes it clear that the legality of the expropriation will have an important effect on the amount of compensation that can be claimed.[48] In particular, a claim for future profits that would have been earned by the foreign investor, had there been no expropriation, can only be awarded under the restitutionary measure applicable for illegal expropriations. There are two possible valuation methods which would take into account the *lucrum cessans* of lost profits. The first is the 'going concern' method, which values all the assets of the company, including intangibles such as goodwill, existing contracts, future commercial prospects, and deducts from these, on a similar basis, its liabilities. The second is the 'discounted cash flow' method which Chapter IV 6(i) of The World Bank's Guidelines for Foreign Direct Investment[49] recommends where the company expropriated is a going concern.[50] The Guidelines define 'discounted cash flow value', in Chapter IV (6), as:

> ... the cash receipts realistically expected from the enterprise in each future year of its economic life as reasonably projected minus that year's expected cash expenditure, after discounting this net cash flow for each year by a factor which reflects the time value of money, expected inflation, and the risk associated with such cash flow under realistic circumstances. Such discount rate may be measured by examining the rate of return available in the same market on alternative investments of comparable risk on the basis of their present value.

On the other hand, the compensation for lawful takings would not include any amount for future profits, as such, and would be limited to 'just

---

48 The tribunal in *Amoco International Finance Corp v Iran* 15 Iran-US Cl Trib Rep 189 (1987), (1988) 27 ILM 1314 thought that the following factors would point towards the unlawfulness of the expropriation: the absence of any compensation; the fact that the taking was made without proper legislative authority; the absence of a public purpose behind the expropriation, as where there is an intent to discriminate against nationals of a particular country. On the facts, however, the tribunal found that the expropriation was lawful.

49 http://ita.law.ca/documents/WorldBank.pdf (accessed 1 March 2007).

50 However, if the investment has not had time to establish a business record at the time of the expropriation the discounted cash flow method will be rejected as being too speculative, as in *SPP (Middle East) v Arab Republic of Egypt* (1992) 32 ILM 937, and also in *Metalclad v Mexico* (ICSID Case No ARB(AF)/97/1), 30 August 2000, a claim under NAFTA, Chapter Eleven.

compensation'. One possible way of calculating this would be by reference to the net book value of the company, taking account the paper value of its assets at the date of the expropriation.[51] However, in its partial award the Iran-US Claims Tribunal in *Amoco International Finance Corp v Iran*,[52] while applying the distinction between lawful and unlawful takings, rejected this as the measure of valuation for a lawful expropriation. Although such an expropriation would not give rise to an award of future profits, the general profitability of the company needed to be considered in assessing its value as at the date of its expropriation.

There have been no subsequent decisions of either the PCIJ or the International Court of Justice on this point. As regards state practice, all the claims arising out of nationalisations since 1945 have involved the acceptance payment of less than full compensation, usually on a lump-sum basis to be distributed pro rata among the expropriated investors of the state making the claim. Further support for the proposition that the 'Hull formula' has not become part of customary international law can be derived from the fact that, in domestic proceedings in which this issue has arisen, both the Supreme Court in the US[53] and the House of Lords have taken the view that there was no agreed international law standard of compensation.[54]

In contrast, earlier arbitral awards involving expropriations have allowed compensation in respect of loss of future profits, although these have involved submission to national law, and some have involved unlawful takings.[55] The decisions of the Iran-US Claims Tribunal, set up to deal with losses suffered by nationals of both nations following the Iranian revolution in 1979, have

51 This seems to have been the most common method of valuation applied in 174 nationalisations in the 1970s according to a 1981 study by the United Nations Commission on Transnational Corporations: Sunshine RB, 'Terms of Compensation in Developing Countries' Nationalisation Settlements'.

52 *Amoco International Finance Corp v Iran* 15 Iran-US Cl Trib Rep 189 (1987), (1988) 27 ILM 1314.

53 *Sabbatino v Banco Nacional de Cuba* 376 US 378 (1964). The US Court of Appeals, second circuit, subsequently reviewed this issue in *Banco Nacional de Cuba v Chase Manhattan Bank* 658 F 2d 875 (1981), noting that the consensus of nations may well be towards the 'appropriate compensation' standard, although '. . . this would not exclude the possibility that in some cases full compensation would be appropriate'.

54 *Williams and Humbert v W&H Trademarks* [1986] AC 386. The issue has come up under European Convention on Human Rights, First Protocol, Art 1 in *Lithgow v United Kingdom* (1986) 8 EHRR 329 and *James v United Kingdom* (1986) 8 EHRR 123. However, both involved claims by national, rather than foreign, investors and throw no light on the customary international law standard as the ECHR held that First Protocol, Art 1 did not oblige the application of customary international law to the treatment of a state's own nationals. These could, legitimately, be awarded a measure of compensation that was lower than that mandated by customary international law.

55 See cases such as *Delagoa Bay Rly*, Whiteman, 3 Damages 1694 (1900) and the *Schufeldt Claim*, Whiteman, 3 Damages 1652 (1930). For a more detailed analysis of these claims, see Sornarajah, op. cit., fn 4, pp 457–61.

largely followed this lead and found that 'full compensation' was required, albeit subject to various qualifications which frequently lead to a substantial reduction in the amount of damages awarded.[56] The US arbitrators advocated the application of the 'Hull Formula' whilst, unsurprisingly, their Iranian counterparts argued in favour of the much lower compensation norms asserted by developing nations. The European arbitrators tended to apply the norm of full compensation, but were willing to reduce the amount of compensation due to special factors. Accordingly, many awards represent a compromise on this issue. The question of compensation is complicated by the fact that the issue of valuation came up not only in the context of the applicable standard of customary international value, but also in the light of the Treaty of Amity between Iran and the US which required the payment of the 'full equivalent' of the property taken.

In *American International Group, Inc v Iran*,[57] the claimant argued that its compensation for the taking of its equity interest in an insurance company should be valued as a going concern, including a sum for loss of profits. The tribunal agreed, but applied a discount to take account of factors such as the economic and political changes in Iran after the 1979 revolution that would affect the future profitability of the company. In *Sedco Inc v NIOC*,[58] the tribunal approached the issue of valuation from the premise that the Hull formula had become the norm under customary international law by the time of the Second World War. It then considered whether there had been any subsequent alteration in this norm. Neither the widespread acceptance of lump sum settlements for nationalisations nor valuation provisions in BITs could be regarded as *opinio juris*. However, Resolution 1803 had effected a change in the position and now reflected customary international law as regards formal, systemic, industry-wide nationalisations. One-off takings directed at foreign investors, though, were still subject to 'full' compensation. Awards based on 'full compensation' were made in a number of other claims,[59] but the amount of compensation awarded was subject to reduction due to the effect of the change socio-economic circumstances in Iran on the future viability of the investment.[60]

---

56 A detailed analysis the issue of valuation under customary international law, with particular reference to the awards of the Iran-US Claims Tribunal, is provided by Amerasinghe, C, 'Issues of Compensation for the Taking of Alien Property in the Light of Recent Cases and Practice' (1992) 41 ICLQ 22.

57 *American International Group, Inc v Iran* 4 Iran-US Cl Trib Rep 96 (1983).

58 *Sedco Inc v NIOC* 10 Iran-US Cl Trib Rep 181 (1986).

59 In *Starrett Housing Corp v Iran* 16 Iran-US CTR 112 (1987), the taking of a housing project that was nearing completion was valued using the 'discounted cash flow' method.

60 For this reason, in *Phelps Dodge Corp v Iran* 10 Iran-US CTR 157 (1986), the investor was awarded only the amount of its original investment, while in *Sola Tiles Inc v Iran* 12 Iran-US Cl Trib Rep 3 (1987), the investor received only one-sixth of its claim due to the fact that the market for high quality tiles, of the sort which it had manufactured, had collapsed after the revolution.

The distinction made in *Chorzow Factory*, as to the different measures of compensation applicable to lawful and to unlawful expropriations, was taken up by the tribunal in *Amoco International Finance Corp v Iran*.[61] Amoco claimed in respect of its half share in Kharg Island Chemical Co (Khemco). The Iranian Government effectively took control of Khemco's operations in July 1979 and although from that time on Amoco lost its right of management in Khemco, the actual expropriation did not occur until December 1980 with the government's formal annulment of its rights in Khemco. The tribunal first found that the expropriation had been lawful. It had been made pursuant to Iranian legislative authority, albeit by this time Amoco had already lost its practical rights of control over its investment for some time. Indeed, when it came to valuation, the tribunal fixed on July 1979 as the appropriate date for assessing the value of the taken investment. Although no compensation had been paid, the formal expropriation in December 1980 contained a procedure for obtaining 'adequate compensation'. Nor was the expropriation rendered unlawful by the fact that it involved a breach of a stabilisation clause in the agreement between Amoco and NPC which established Khemco. Finally, the tribunal rejected as unsubstantiated the allegation that the expropriation had been discriminatory in that it was aimed at harming American interests rather than being for a public purpose.

Having established that it was dealing with a lawful expropriation, the tribunal held that under *Chorzow Factory* compensation should be on the basis of the 'just price of what was expropriated'. However, future profits could be awarded only for unlawful expropriations. For this reason, the tribunal rejected the discounted cash flow method which Amoco had argued for. The tribunal also rejected the net book value on which Iran had relied, as this would exclude from valuation such intangibles as contractual rights, goodwill, future prospects. The tribunal also found that market value was of no use as a measure of valuation when there was no market for the expropriated asset, or for goods identical to, or comparable to it. This was likely to be the case with transactions 'of such a magnitude that they are relatively rare, always individualised, and prompted by special circumstances and motives, like transactions relating to large corporations, the share of which are not traded on stock exchanges'.[62]

Instead, the taking of the claimant's interest in Khemco should be valued as a 'going concern'. This would encompass:

> . . . not only the physical and financial assets of the undertaking but also the intangible assets of the undertaking which contributed to its earning power, such as contractual rights (supply and delivery contracts, patent licences, and so on), as well as goodwill and commercial prospects.

---

61 *Amoco International Finance Corp v Iran* 15 Iran-US Cl Trib Rep 189 (1987), (1988) 27 ILM 1314.
62 Paragraph 219.

> Although those assets are closely limited to the profitability of the
> concern, they cannot and must not be confused with the financial capital-
> isation of the revenues which might be generated by such a concern after
> the transfer of property resulting from the expropriation (*lucrum
> cessans*).[63]

In finding the going concern value, these elements had to be considered
an organic totality whose value exceeded that of its component parts.[64] The
tribunal, having rejected both the net book value, and the discounted cash
flow methods advocated by the parties, ordered the claimant to provided
data on those elements it had identified as being relevant to the assessment of the value of the enterprises as a going concern, as of 31 July 1979,
which was the date at which the claimant lost *de facto* control of its
investment.

Judge Brower concurred with the result but his separate opinion was critical of the majority's treatment of future profits when valuing a lawful
expropriation. He analysed the scheme of valuation set out in the *Chorzow
Factory* case, as follows.[65] With a lawful expropriation the claimant was
entitled to damages that equalled the value of the undertaking it had lost,
including any potential profits, as of the date of the taking, together with any
consequential loss. With an unlawful taking, the claimant was entitled to
the higher of the following two alternatives. First, the measure of damages
applicable to a lawful expropriation. Secondly, the value of the undertaking,
including lost future profits, as shown by its probable performance subsequent to the date of the loss and prior to the date of the award, based on
the actual post-taking experiences.

6.2 The European Convention on Human Rights.
Article 1 of the First Protocol

The European Convention on Human Rights was signed in Rome on
4 November 1950. It was ratified by the UK in 1951. Since 1966, individual
UK citizens have been allowed to petition the European Court of Human
Rights (ECHR) in Strasbourg directly. The Human Rights Act 1998, most of
which came into force on 2 October 2000, now implements the Convention
directly into the law of the UK, so allowing violations of the Convention to
be challenged before the courts of the UK. Initially, the Convention contained no provisions on the right to property but in 1952 the First Protocol
was added, with Art 1 providing that:

---

63 Paragraph 264.
64 Paragraph 265.
65 Paragraph 18.

Every natural or legal person is entitled to the peaceful enjoyment of his possessions. No one shall be deprived of his possessions except in the public interest and subject to the conditions provided for by law and by the general principles of international law.

The preceding provisions shall not, however, in any way impair the right of a State to enforce such laws as it deems necessary to control the use of property in accordance with the general interest or to secure the payment of taxes or other contributions or penalties.

In *Sporrong and Lonnroth v Sweden*, the ECHR analysed Art 1 as comprising three distinct rules.[66] The first, general, rule is found in the opening sentence and sets out the principle of peaceful enjoyment of property. The second rule, in the next sentence, covers deprivation of possessions. The third rule, which is contained in the second paragraph, recognises the right of states to control the use of property in the general interest. The applicability of the second and third rules must be considered before determining whether there has been compliance with the first rule.

The general principles to be applied in determining whether or not there has been a violation of Art 1 were set out in *James v United Kingdom*.[67] The case arose out of the compulsory enfranchisement of leasehold dwelling houses forming part of the Duke of Westminster's estate affected under the Leasehold Reform Act 1967. First, the deprivation must be in the 'public interest'. In deciding this issue, national authorities enjoy a margin of appreciation because their direct knowledge of their society and its needs make them better placed in principle to assess this than the international judge. This judgement will be respected unless it is 'manifestly without reasonable foundation', which was not the case with Parliament's belief as to the social injustice to be remedied by the 1967 Act. The position was not altered by the fact that Parliament had chosen to achieve this goal by transferring property from one private individual to another. Not surprisingly, it has proved very difficult to mount a successful challenge to a measure on this ground. Secondly, there must exist a reasonable relationship of proportionality between the means employed and the aim sought to be realised. A 'fair balance' must be struck between the demands of the general interests of the community and the requirements of the protection of the individual's fundamental rights. The balance would not be fair if the applicant had to bear 'an individual and excessive burden'. There was, though, no need to apply a test of strict necessity. The availability of alternative solutions to the legislative solution actually adopted would provide only one factor, among others, to be used in determining the reasonableness of the means in achieving

---

66 *Sporrong and Lonnroth v Sweden* (1982) 5 EHHR 35, p 50, para 61.
67 *James v United Kingdom* (1986) 8 EHRR 123.

the legitimate aim being pursued.[68] Taking of property without payment reasonably related to its value would normally constitute a disproportionate interference. Where the applicant was a national, legitimate public interest objectives might call for less than reimbursement of full market value. This was the case with the Leasehold Reform Act 1967 whereby compensation was calculated by reference to site value alone and took no account of the value of the buildings. The reference to the general principles of international law in Art 1 would, though, preserve the compensation norms applicable thereunder as regards claims made by non-nationals.

6.2.1 'Deprivation of possessions' claims

A 'deprivation of possessions' without some compensation will, therefore, fail to satisfy the test of proportionality. In contrast, where the claim falls under the head of control of use,[69] rather than deprivation of possessions, public interest considerations will frequently determine that the measure was 'proportionate' notwithstanding the absence of any compensation.[70] The measure in question will still have to be lawful and in the public interest and will satisfy these criteria provided it has been made lawfully and is for a valid social or economic purpose. In deciding this, account must be taken of the wide 'margin of appreciation' that is ceded to local regulatory and legislative bodies.[71] The fact that the aim behind the measure could have been achieved in a less severe manner does not, of itself, render the measure disproportionate. Nor will the severity with which the measure affects an individual necessarily indicate that an absence of compensation is disproportionate. Thus, in *Pinnacle v United Kingdom*,[72] the fact that the measure was based on the

---

68 Paragraph 50.
69 Such claims are somewhat akin to 'partial takings' cases arising under the Fifth Amendment of the US constitution. However, the decisions of the Supreme Court in *Nollan v California Coastal Commission* 483 US 825, 107 SCt 3141 (1987) and *Dolan v City of Tigard* 114 SCt 2309 (1994) show that the margin of appreciation ceded to the state may be narrower in such cases.
70 See, further, Mountfield, H, 'Regulatory Expropriations in Europe. The Approach of the European Court of Human Rights' NYU Colloquium on Regulatory Expropriations in International Law 26/27, p 136; Anderson, D, 'Compensation for Interference with Property' (1999) 6 EHRLR 549, pp 543–8; Geradin, D, 'Free Trade and Environmental Protection in an Integrated Market: A Survey of the Case Law of the United States Supreme Court and the European Court of Justice' (1993) 2 J Trans'l L & Pol 141.
71 See, also, *Hatton v United Kingdom* [2003] ECHR 338, where the ECHR, overruling the Chamber Decision, held that the adverse affect on the applicants' sleep of a decision to increase the volume of night flights into Heathrow did not amount to a violation of Art 8. The government was entitled to give greater weight to the economic interests of the country than to the interests of the small number of individuals living underneath the flight path whose sleep would be disrupted thereby.
72 *Pinnacle Meat Processors Co v United Kingdom* (1998) 27 Eur HR Rep CD 217.

most urgent and compelling need to protect public health was fatal to the applicant's control of use claim.

It will therefore be critical to assess whether the claim is made in respect of a 'deprivation' or of a 'control of use'. This will involve a determination of the threshold issue of whether there has been a 'possession'. The goodwill of a professional practice was held to constitute a 'possession' in *Karni v Sweden*.[73] Economic interests connected with the running of the restaurant were classified in similar fashion in *Tre Traktorer v Sweden*, where the tribunal held that:

> ... the maintenance of the licence was one of the principal conditions for the carrying on of the applicant company's business and [that] its withdrawal had adverse effects on the goodwill and value of the goodwill and value of the restaurant.

In contrast, a stream of anticipated future income has been held not to constitute a 'possession'. This follows from the decision in *Pinnacle Meat Processors Co v United Kingdom*.[74] The applicant's business was de-boning cattle heads and selling the extract to manufacturers of processed meat. From 1989 onwards their business had become increasingly regulated due to concern about BSE. Against this background, they had invested heavily in specialised plant and equipment for this business. In 1996, the applicants were affected by legislation which prevented the sale of, *inter alia*, material extracted from cattle heads for animal or human consumption. At a stroke, the applicants' business was effectively wiped out. They received compensation of 65 per cent of the value of their unsold stock, but received nothing for the loss of goodwill or for their specialised equipment. As regards the goodwill, or 'the present value of the future income stream which the company can be expected to derive', although this might be an element in valuing a professional practice, future income, per se, would constitute a 'possession' only once it had been earned or an enforceable claim to it had come into existence. As regards the specialised plant and equipment, at least some of this remained useable for other meat operations, thereby ensuring the claim remained one for 'control of use' rather than for 'deprivation of possessions'. This finding meant that there could be no 'deprivation' claim in respect of the applicants' expectations of making future income from de-boning cattle heads. Although this expectation was totally wiped out, it did not constitute a 'possession'.[75]

---

73 *Karni v Sweden* (1988) 55 DR 157, p 165. The claim, however, fell under the 'control of use' heading, rather than that of 'deprivation of possessions'.

74 *Pinnacle Meat Processors Co v United Kingdom* (1998) 27 Eur HR Rep CD 217.

75 In contrast, the applicant's specialised de-boning equipment was a possession, but because it retained some residual value, the claim was one for 'control of use'. This failed as the compelling health problems to which the measure was addressed meant that it was proportionate even in the absence of compensation.

The dividing line between 'possessions' and mere anticipation of a future stream of income is a fine one as can be illustrated by *Adams v Scottish Ministers*.[76] This involved an application for judicial review of the Protection of Wild Mammals (Scotland) Act 2002, which was passed by the Scottish Parliament. The Act made it a criminal offence to engage in mounted fox-hunting with dogs or to allow land to be used for this purpose. One of the petitioners was Mr Adams, the self-employed manager of the Duke of Buccleuch's Hunt. Mr Adams did not own land on which hunting took place, nor did he own dogs which would be used for hunting. However, Mr Adams argued that the legislation would deprive him of his livelihood which would in turn lead to the loss of his licence over his current house which was tied to his work. The Lord Nimmo Smith in the Outer House of the Court of Session held that Mr Adams' economic interest in acting as a self-employed manager of foxhounds did constitute a 'possession', stating that the issue was not so much one of 'loss of profits, or loss of goodwill, as the loss simply of an opportunity to make a living by pursuing a particular activity'.[77] This analysis would appear to apply with equal force to the business of de-boning cattle heads in *Pinnacle*, and the judgment fails to make clear the basis on which the two cases are to be distinguished. Two possible distinctions can be suggested. First, Mr Adams' means of making a living was more specialised than that of the applicants in *Pinnacle*. Secondly, Mr Adams' livelihood also involved a tied house in which he lived.[78]

Having identified a 'possession', the applicant must next establish a 'deprivation' thereof. This will require a finding that the measure in question has completely denuded the possession of any economic value. A mere reduction in value will not constitute a 'deprivation'. For this reason, Mr Adams' claim for deprivation of his 'possessions', namely his livelihood and the tied house that went with it, failed because, 'it is by no means certain that he will cease to be employed, or in any event will be unable to continue to earn his living by using skills which he uses at present'.[79]

This restrictive approach to the definition of 'deprivation' follows a series of similar decisions by the ECHR. In *Tre Traktorer v Sweden*, it was held[80] that removal of a restaurant's licence to serve alcohol did not amount to a deprivation of the economic interests involved in the restaurants. There was no deprivation of these possessions as the company was left with some economic interests represented by the leasing of the premises and the property contained therein, which it eventually sold. In *Pinnacle v United Kingdom*,

---

76 *Adams v Scottish Ministers* [2003] SC 171, Ct of Session (Outer House).
77 Paragraph 129.
78 At para 129 Lord Nimmo Smith noted that as the house formed part of Mr Adams' emoluments 'it may be regarded as a tangible demonstration that this possession is a current asset'.
79 Paragraph 130.
80 *Tre Traktorer v Sweden* (1991) 13 EHRR 309, para 53.

there was no deprivation of the applicants' specialised de-boning equipment because it still retained some residual value, albeit a much reduced one. So too in *Fredin v Sweden*[81] and *Pine Valley v Ireland*,[82] there was no 'deprivation' of land whose value had been substantially, but not totally, eroded as a result of restrictions as to its use. All the above claims fell, instead, to be considered under the 'control of use' heading.

These decisions show just how hard it is for a claim to fall within the heading of 'deprivation of possessions'. A 'possession' has first to be identified and then it must been shown that the measure has totally stripped it of value rather than merely effecting a substantial reduction in its value. The problem is that in many instances what has been destroyed is not a 'possession' at all, but rather the ability to make future profits out from a particular pattern of trading. The physical possessions with which that future trading is to be accomplished will certainly amount to possessions, but so long as they have some residual value there will have no 'deprivation' or *de facto* expropriation. The claim will have to be brought under the 'control of use' heading instead where no presumption exists that the availability of compensation is generally required if the measure is to be regarded as 'proportionate'. What will have been totally destroyed will be a future income stream from a particular trade or employment and if that cannot be classified as a 'possession' there can be no question of a claim under Art 1 of the First Protocol in respect of its loss.

6.2.2 'Control of use' claims

If the claim cannot be brought within the rule relating to 'deprivation of possessions', it will generally have to be brought within the rule relating to 'control of use'[83] or, in exceptional cases, under the first sentence of Art 1 which refers to the entitlement to the peaceful enjoyment of possessions.[84] Such claims are somewhat akin to 'partial takings' cases arising under the Fifth Amendment of the US constitution. The success of any claim for compensation, therefore, is bound up with the requirement that the measure be proportionate, taking into account the balance between the public interest behind the measure and its effect on particular individuals. The measure in question will still have to be lawful and in the public interest and will satisfy

---

81 *Fredin v Sweden* (1991) 13 EHRR 784.
82 *Pine Valley Developments Ltd & Ors v Ireland* (1992) 14 EHRR 319.
83 However, the decisions of the Supreme Court in *Nollan v California Coastal Commission* 483 US 825, 107 SCt 3141 (1987) and *Dolan v City of Tigard* 114 SCt 2309 (1994) show that the 'margin of appreciation' ceded to the state may be narrower in 'partial takings' cases than is the case in 'control of use' cases under First Protocol, Art 1.
84 The claim in *Sporrong and Lonnroth v Sweden* fell under this heading, with the court applying the same principles as would govern a 'control of use' heading.

these criteria provided it has not been made *ultra vires* and is for a valid social or economic purpose. In deciding this, account must be taken of the wide 'margin of appreciation' that is ceded to local regulatory and legislative bodies. The fact that the aim behind the measure could have been achieved in a less severe manner does not, of itself, render the measure disproportionate. In *Tre Traktorer*, although the removal of the restaurant's licence was severe, it was not disproportionate, given the discrepancies in the applicant's book keeping concerning sales of alcohol which were very significant in relation to its total turnover. It did not matter that under the relevant Swedish law less severe measures could have been taken in relation to the restaurant in respect of these infractions.[85] Nor will the severity with which the measure affects an individual necessary indicate that an absence of compensation is disproportionate. Thus, in *Pinnacle*, the fact that the measure was based on the most urgent and compelling need to protect public health was fatal to the applicants' 'control of use' claim. The same was true in *Adams* of legislation based on 'the general interest in the prevention of cruelty to animals'.[86] In contrast, in *Chassagnou v France*,[87] a French law which obliged small landowners to allow hunting to take place on their land was held to place a disproportionate burden on those landowners who had ethical objections to hunting. Such landowners would not benefit from the provisions of the legislation that would have allowed them to hunt over the land of others.

Another factor which bears on the issue of proportionality is that of the reasonable expectations of the applicants as regards regulations that would restrict their ability to use their possessions in a particular manner. *Fredin v Sweden*[88] involved the issue of legitimate expectations as to land use in the context of planning legislation. In 1963, the applicants were granted a permit to extract gravel from their land. The following year legislation was enacted regulating the extraction of gravel. The applicants initially planned to use the land by granting a licence to Jehander, who had a near monopoly on gravel extraction in the area. However, in 1979, the applicants terminated the licence and decided to carry on this business themselves. By this time the 1964 law regulating gravel extraction had been subject to an amendment in 1973 which provided for the potential revocation of existing permits after a 10-year period starting on 1 July 1973. Against this background the applicants, in 1980, obtained permission to build a quay for use in their gravel

---

85 Paragraph 55.
86 There was also a failure to establish that the ban on hunting had led to any direct diminution in the value of the land used for this purpose. As regards the hounds, which were regarded as a form of specialised equipment, no averment had been made as to their value, nor was it inevitable that they would be put down after the ban came into effect.
87 *Chassagnou v France* [1999] ECHR 22.
88 *Fredin v Sweden* (1991) 13 EHRR 784.

business.[89] However, the permit specifically stated that it involved no assurance that the applicants would also be allowed to continue to extract gravel after the expiry of the 10-year period in July 1983. In the end a three-year close-down period was granted which was subsequently extended by a further 11 months. The applicants' 'deprivation' claim failed because the parcel of land from which gravel was extracted had been separated from the applicant's other adjoining properties for the sole purpose of serving the gravel business. The effects of the revocation, therefore, had to be assessed in the light of how the applicants' properties as a whole were affected. As these were not affected by the measure there was no 'deprivation'.[90]

It was also held to be significant that over the years the gravel exploitation business had become increasingly regulated and restricted. The major investment here was the construction of the quay in 1980/81. At this time the 1973 amendment to the 1964 Act was already in place and the authorities in giving permission made it quite clear that this was not varying the permission as regards the application of the 10-year rule. However, the original licence to Jehander to extract gravel was in 1963 before the 1964 Act. The initial restrictions on gravel extraction would not have been sufficiently onerous to constitute a taking. Subsequent extension of the regulations presumably must be reasonably anticipated over a period of time even if this leads ultimately to the land being completely unusable for the purpose of gravel extraction. The substantial period of notice given to the applicants before they finally had to cease gravel extraction, together with the cautionary wording appended to the grant of permission in 1980 to build a quay, probably tipped the scales as regards the assessment of the proportionality of the restriction. Similarly, in *Pine Valley Developments Ltd & Ors v Ireland*,[91] reference was made to the usual business risks that an applicant has to accept. One of these was the risk that when land is acquired it might prove impossible to obtain the planning permission necessary for a particular commercial use.[92]

---

89 So, too, in *Pinnacle* the investment in the specialised de-boning equipment had been made at a time when the BSE crisis had already led to substantial regulation of the applicants' business. The making of such an investment would have to be made against this background, with the risk of future extensions to the regulatory regime.

90 In addition, the applicants still retained ownership of the land that was affected, as well as its gravel resources. It must, however, be doubtful that either of these assets retained any real value once the applicants were no longer allowed to extract gravel.

91 *Pine Valley Developments Ltd & Ors v Ireland* (1992) 14 EHRR 319.

92 The case involved an apparently valid outline permission which the courts subsequently held to have been a nullity. It must be doubted whether this should also constitute one of the usual business risks accepted by a property developer. See, also, *Katte Klische v Italy* (1995) 19 EHRR 368.

Chapter 7

Investor protection and environmental regulation (2). NAFTA, Chapter Eleven

NAFTA is an extremely wide-ranging agreement between Mexico, Canada and the US which came into force on 1 January 1994. It contains 22 chapters covering topics such: as trade (Chapter Three); emergency action (Chapter Eight); government procurement (Chapter Ten); investment (Chapter Eleven); cross-border services (Chapter Twelve); financial services (Chapter Fourteen); competition policy (Chapter Fifteen); IP (Chapter Seventeen); publication, notification and administration of laws (Chapter Eighteen).

In many respects NAFTA is one of the most environmentally sensitive trade and investment agreement. The preamble commits the parties to attain the trade goals of the agreement 'in a manner consistent with environmental protection and conservation', while also including in NAFTA's goals that of promoting sustainable development and strengthening development and enforcement of laws and regulations. Chapter Seven deals with SPS measures, and Chapter Nine deals with technical standards, in terms very similar to those subsequently used in the SPS and TBT Agreements of the WTO. Chapter Eleven which protects the rights of investors contains two provisions in Art 1114 that endeavour to set these rights in the context of the protection of the environment.[1]

The relationship between NAFTA and the parties' rights and obligations

---

1 Article 1114: Environmental Measures

   1. Nothing in this Chapter shall be construed to prevent a Party from adopting, maintaining or enforcing any measure otherwise consistent with this Chapter that it considers appropriate to ensure that investment activity in its territory is undertaken in a manner sensitive to environmental concerns.

   2. The Parties recognize that it is inappropriate to encourage investment by relaxing domestic health, safety or environmental measures. Accordingly, a Party should not waive or otherwise derogate from, or offer to waive or otherwise derogate from, such measures as an encouragement for the establishment, acquisition, expansion or retention in its territory of an investment of an investor. If a Party considers that another Party has offered such an encouragement, it may request consultations with the other Party and the two Parties shall consult with a view to avoiding any such encouragement.

to each other under what was then the 1947 GATT is dealt with as follows. Article 103 reaffirms the parties' existing rights and obligations to each other under GATT whilst providing for the primacy of NAFTA in the event of inconsistency between the provisions of the two agreements. Article 2101, General Exceptions, then specifically incorporates GATT, Art XX and its interpretative notes into NAFTA for the purposes of Part Two (Trade in Goods), except to the extent that a provision of that part applies to services or investment, and Part Three (Technical Barriers to Trade), except to the extent that a provision of that part applies to services. Furthermore, Art 104 provides for the primacy of the CITES Convention 1973, the Montreal Convention 1987 in the event of any inconsistency between the specific trade obligations set out therein and the provisions of NAFTA. A similar provision exists as regards the Basel Convention 1989 'upon its entry into force for Canada, Mexico and the US'.[2]

In addition, NAFTA contains a side agreement, the North American Agreement on Environmental Co-operation (NAAEC), which is directed towards fostering environmental cooperation amongst the parties. One of the principal aims of the NAAEC is the promotion of effective enforcement by the parties of their domestic environmental legislation, through the Committee on Environmental Co-operation (CEC). Accordingly, the NAAEC provides, under Arts 14 and 15, a means by which anyone living in any of the three NAFTA parties may complain about a failure of enforcement of the environmental legislation in force in any those countries. The process involves the submission of a claim to the CEC. After reviewing the submission, the CEC may investigate the matter and publish a factual record of its findings, subject to approval by the CEC Council.[3]

In the event of a breach by a NAFTA party of any of the agreement's provisions, Chapter Twenty provides for provides for state-to-state arbitration. The agreement also contains a more limited provision for investor-state arbitration under Arts 1116 and 1117, but this right relates only to allegations of breaches of part A of Chapter Eleven.[4] Suit is by way of arbitration subject to the provisions of the New York Convention 1975, so making an

---

2 The primacy afforded to these MEAs is subject to the qualification that 'where a Party has a choice among equally effective and reasonably available means of complying with such obligations, the Party chooses the means that is least inconsistent with the other provisions of this Agreement'.

3 For criticisms of how this procedure has worked in practice, see Kibel, P, 'Awkward Evolution: Citizen Enforcement at the North American Environmental Law Commission' (2002) 32(7) Environmental Law Reporter 10769, especially pp 10780–1083.

4 Investor-State arbitration under Arts 1116 and 1117 is also available in respect of breaches of Art 1503.2 (State Enterprises) and Art 1502.3(a) (Monopolies and State Enterprises) 'where the monopoly has acted in a manner inconsistent with the Party's obligations under Section A and that the enterprise has incurred loss or damage by reason of, or arising out of, that breach'.

award readily enforceable. Arbitration is by way of three private law mechanisms, the International Centre for Settlement of Investment Disputes (ICSID), the ICSID Additional Facility, and the United Nations Centre for Trade Law (UNCITRAL).[5] Article 1131 provides that tribunals 'shall decide the issues in dispute in accordance with this Agreement and applicable rules of international law'.

An investor may claim in respect of its own losses under Art 1116. It may also claim under Art 1117 in respect of losses sustained by an enterprise that is owned or controlled directly by the investor. Article 1121 departs from the rule of customary international law requiring exhaustion of local remedies, by requiring the investor to choose between local remedies and Chapter Eleven arbitration.[6] The rule of exhaustion of local remedies has, however, been held to remain applicable to claims under Art 1105 which are based on violations of international law.[7]

Chapter Eleven grants the following substantive protections to investors of another party. Foreign investors are entitled to the benefit of 'national treatment' under Art 1102 and to the application of 'most favoured nation' principles under Art 1103. Article 1105 entitles foreign investors to the minimum treatment to which they are entitled under international law, 'including fair and equitable treatment and full protection and security'. Performance requirements, as regards both foreign and domestic investors are outlawed under Art 1106, subject to some limited exceptions.

However, the provision which has, perhaps, caused most controversy is Art 1110, which not only entitles foreign investors to compensation in the event of their investment being nationalised or expropriated, but also extends this protection to measures 'tantamount to nationalisation or expropriation'. The fact that the US was one of the three NAFTA parties led to fears that Art 1110 would be interpreted in the light of US domestic law on expropriation. Unlike Mexico and Canada, US jurisprudence recognises that regulations that restrict the economic use of property may, in certain circumstances, qualify as compensable 'takings'.

US takings law derives from the Fifth Amendment to the Constitution. This provides 'nor shall private property be taken for public use, without just compensation' and is made applicable to the states of the US by the Fourteenth Amendment. There are two categories of taking which may attract compensation. The first is physical taking of property for which the landowner must be compensated. In *Pennsylvania Coal Co v Mahon*,[8] in 1922, the Supreme

---

5 Article 1130.
6 Save as regards claims for 'injunctive, declaratory or other extraordinary relief, not involving the payment of damages'.
7 *Loewen v US*, award on merits, 26 June 2003.
8 *Pennsylvania Coal Co v Mahon* 260 US 393 (1922). The case involved the denial of permission to mine coal to protect buildings from subsidence.

Court held that this rule would also apply to a regulation whose effect was to strip land of any economic use. A second category which deals with regulations which adversely impact on the economic use of property, but fall short of stripping it of all economic use, so-called 'partial takings'. The Supreme Court has avoided setting hard and fast rules for determining when compensation will be awarded in such circumstances. The issue will have to be determined on a case-by-case basis and will involve an ad hoc balancing of various factors, such as the severity of the regulation's impact on the property owner, the legitimate expectations of the property owner as to land use and the nature of the regulation itself.[9] There has been concern that the peculiarly US jurisprudence on 'partial takings' will infect the construction of Art 1110.

The first Chapter Eleven suit, *Ethyl v Canada*,[10] was brought against Canada in September 1996, with a panel being established in late 1997. The claimant was the Ethyl Corporation, which is the sole manufacturer of the gasoline additive MMT. It claimed $251 million compensation from the Federal Canadian Government in respect of its ban on the import and transport of MMT within Canada. Although the use of MMT was not banned, the trade ban effectively prevented Ethyl from using it as a gasoline additive in Canada. The ban under bill C–29 formed part of the Canadian federal government's 'clean air agenda' and was motivated partly by public health considerations and partly by a desire to meet the concern of Canadian auto manufacturers that new limits on car emissions would not be achievable if MMT were permitted as a fuel additive. The ban may also partly have been motivated by a desire to promote Ethanol as a fuel additive which would assist Canadian farmers.

Ethyl challenged bill C–29 under NAFTA, Chapter Eleven on three grounds. First, it argued that the measure contravened the national treatment provisions of NAFTA in that it effectively prevented the sale of foreign made MMT in Canada. A counter-argument was raised by the Canadian Motor Vehicles Association (CMVA) that the measure did not favour domestic production of MMT as there was none and that the national treatment provisions were not breached merely because the domestic ethanol industry might receive an incidental benefit as a result of the measure. Secondly, it argued that the measure imposed a performance requirement on Ethyl to buy Canadian MMT. To trade in MMT and comply with the regulation Ethyl would have to buy Canadian made MMT which would entail it having to build blending plants in each Canadian province. Thirdly, it argued that the measure

---

9   These were the factors referred to in *Penn Central Transport Co v New York City* 438 US 104 (1978), in which the Supreme Court held that a denial of permission to build a 55-storey block on top of Grand Central Station, which had been designated as a landmark under New York State's Landmarks Preservation Act 1965, did not amount to a compensable partial taking.

10   *Ethyl v Canada*, award on jurisdiction, 24 June 1998.

amounted to 'expropriation' or was a measure 'tantamount to expropriation' in that it prevented Ethyl from carrying on its business in Canada.

The way in which Ethyl argued its case gave rise to the following concerns. First, that a purely economic analysis of 'likeness' would be adopted in interpreting Art 1102 and that no account would be taken of legitimate policy grounds for distinguishing on environmental grounds between domestic and foreign investors that were operating in a comparable economic sector. Secondly, that a wide 'effects' based interpretation would be applied to the definition of what constituted a 'performance requirement' under Art 1106. Thirdly, that the phrase 'tantamount to expropriation' in Art 1110 would be interpreted in line with US jurisprudence on 'partial takings', so as to give rise to a right to compensation to an investor that was adversely affected by a measure, in circumstances in which those effects were insufficiently substantial to amount to give rise to a claim for expropriation by the state of the foreign investor.

These issues were, however, to be left unresolved, for in July 1998 the Canadian federal government settled the claim by paying Ethyl $19.3 million, withdrawing the measure and declaring MMT to be safe.[11] The settlement was prompted by Ethyl's success in challenging the measure under the Canadian Agreement on Internal Trade (AIT), which promotes free trade between the provinces. The AIT panel found that although there was a legitimate objective behind the measure as required by Art 404, the measure unduly impaired access of goods. In particular, Art 404(c) required the adoption of the least trade restrictive measures necessary to meet a legitimate objective in restricting movements of goods between the provinces. Alternative measures existed, such as tradeable permits or a direct prohibition on the use of MMT, which would have been less restrictive of inter-state trade. The AIT decision gave a powerful impetus to settle the NAFTA dispute given that similar reasoning may well have been adopted by the NAFTA panel in deciding that the measure amounted to a violation of either Art 1102 or Art 1110 and was not justified by Art 1114(1) in that it was not 'otherwise consistent' with the treaty. In addition, the mixed objectives of the measure might have made it difficult to justify on the grounds of being 'sensitive to environmental concerns' as it could be argued that the measure was in truth sensitive to the concerns of Canadian car manufacturers. A total ban might have been easier to justify on health and safety grounds, although similar problems might have arisen with the nature of the risk assessment used to justify such a ban.[12]

11 The tribunal did, however, issue an award on jurisdiction on 24 June 1998 in which it ruled that Chapter Eleven did not require that the losses claimed by the investor had to have been incurred in the jurisdiction of the NAFTA party that had imposed the measure.

12 This issue was at the heart of the appellate body's award as to the application of the SPS Agreement in *EC–Beef Hormones. European Communities–Measures Concerning Meat and Meat Products (Hormones)*. WT/DS/48/R/CAN, WT/DS/26/R/US. Panel report 18 August 1997. WT/DS/48/AB/R, WT/DS/26/AB/R. Appellate body report 16 January 1998.

Since the settlement of *Ethyl v Canada*, there have been a plethora of Chapter Eleven suits brought against each of the NAFTA parties.[13] As will be seen, most of the anxieties expressed at the time of that first suit as to the impact of Chapter Eleven suits on environmental regulation have proved to be unfounded. Only one claim under Art 1110, that in *Metalclad v Mexico*, has succeeded to date. Investors have tended to have more success with claims based on Arts 1102 and 1105. However, before considering the way in which tribunals have dealt with the substantive provisions of Chapter Eleven, it is first necessary to consider some preliminary issues of definition. As will be shown, these will have an important impact on how the substantive issues are treated. Indeed, it can be argued, that the potential of Chapter Eleven to inhibit environmental regulation by the NAFTA parties is to be found not so much in the substantive provisions of Chapter Eleven but rather in the preliminary issues which inform them.

7.1 Threshold issues of definition

It is first necessary to address the threshold questions of how Chapter Eleven defines the key concepts of 'measure', 'investor' and 'investment'. It is just as important to analyse the interests that are capable of protection under Chapter Eleven as it is to define nature of the protection Chapter Eleven offers to investors and investments. The starting place for this enquiry is Art 1101 which defines the scope of Chapter Eleven, as follows:

1. This Chapter applies to measures adopted or maintained by a Party relating to:

    (a) investors of another Party;
    (b) investments of investors of another Party in the territory of the Party existing at the date of entry into force of this Agreement as well as to investments made or acquired thereafter by such investors . . .

Article 201 defines 'measures' so as to include 'any law, regulation, procedure, requirement or practice'. This covers not only measures of the central government, but also those of state and local governments, as in *Metalclad v Mexico*.[14] It also covers acts of civil servants which adversely impact on foreign investors, as in *Pope & Talbot v Canada*.[15] The definition has even proved wide

---

13   All the documents in all the Chapter Eleven suits can be accessed at www.naftaclaims.com (accessed 21 March 2007). The site is operated by Todd Weiler, an attorney who was involved in the early Chapter Eleven suits.
14   *Metalclad v Mexico*, final award, 2 September 2000.
15   *Pope & Talbot v Canada*, final merits award, 10 April 2001.

enough to include judicial proceedings both as regards procedure[16] and matters of substantive law.[17] It should be noted that although Art 1101 refers to 'adopting or maintaining' a measure, Art 1110 uses the narrower words 'take a measure'. Consequently, Art 1110 applies only to measures introduced after NAFTA came into force on 1 January 1994.

The 'measure' must also be one 'relating to' investors and investments of another party. What causal nexus between the measure and investors and investments is mandated by these words? The issue came up for consideration at a preliminary hearing in *Methanex v USA*.[18] Methanex is a Canadian enterprise that produces, transports and markets methanol which is one of the components needed to make methyl tertiary-butyl ether (MTBE). Concerns had arisen in California about leakage of MTBE from gasoline storage facilities into the water supply. Consequently, Governor Gray Davis issued an executive order providing for its removal from gasoline sold in California no later than by 31 December 2002, a deadline subsequently extended to 31 July 2003. Methanex initiated Chapter Eleven proceedings claiming that the measure constituted a breach of Arts 1105 and 1110.

At a preliminary hearing on jurisdiction the tribunal held that the measure could not be said to 'relate' to methanol in that it related only to MTBE, which Methanex did not manufacture.[19] The words 'relating to' signified something more than the mere *effect* of a measure on an investor or investment and required a legally significant connection between them.[20] The measure would, however, 'relate' to methanol were Methanex able to substantiate the allegations made in their amended claim that Governor Davis had introduced the measure with the intent of benefitting the US ethanol industry and penalising foreign producers of methanol and MTBE. On this basis the measure would 'relate' to a foreign producer for, in the absence of Californian producers of methanol, methanol could be regarded as a foreign product in California. Methanex, however, was unable to adduce evidence substantiating its allegations against Governor Davis and the tribunal reiterated its finding that the measure did not relate to MTBE in its final award on 3 August 2005.

The next threshold issue involves an analysis of the concepts of 'investors' and 'investments' of another party. Article 1139 defines 'investment' as including '(a) an enterprise', defined in Art 201 as 'any entity constituted or organized under applicable law, whether or not for profit, and whether privately-owned or governmentally-owned, including any corporation, trust,

---

16 *Loewen v USA*, award on merits, 26 June 2003.
17 *Mondev v USA*, final award, 11 October 2002.
18 *Methanex v USA*, award on jurisdiction, 28 August 2002. Final award, 3 August 2005.
19 In contrast, in *Ethyl v Canada*, the first Chapter Eleven suit to be brought, the measure, impacted directly on a product manufactured by the investor.
20 Paragraph 147.

partnership, sole proprietorship, joint venture or other association'.[21] Article 1139 continues with its definition of 'investment' to include:

(b) an equity security of an enterprise;
(c) a debt security of an enterprise;
(d) a loan to an enterprise;
(e) an interest in an enterprise that entitles the owner to share in income or profits of the enterprise;
(f) an interest in an enterprise that entitles the owner to share in the assets of that enterprise on dissolution, other than a debt security or a loan excluded from subparagraph (c) or (d);
(g) real estate or other property, tangible or intangible, acquired in the expectation or used for the purpose of economic benefit or other business purposes;
(h) interests arising from the commitment of capital or other resources in the territory of a Party to economic activity in such territory.

The wording of this final heading is particularly open-ended and capable of encompassing expectations of future trading profits in another NAFTA party. As will be discussed later, this raises important questions relating to the boundary between Chapter Eleven and other NAFTA provisions, such as those on trade in Chapter Three, and provision of cross-border services in Chapter Twelve, breaches of which can only be adjudicated under the state-to-state arbitration procedures set out in Chapter Twenty.

'Investment of an investor of a Party' is defined as 'an investment owned or controlled directly or indirectly by an investor of such Party'.[22] The wording here is again very wide, particularly in its use of the word 'indirectly', and is designed to prevent an investor from being disadvantaged by the doctrine of separate corporate personality.[23] Chapter Eleven provides two avenues by which investors may proceed. First, there is Art 1116 which provides for claims in respect of losses sustained by the investor as a result of the effect of a measure. In *GAMI v Mexico*,[24] the tribunal held that a minority shareholder

---

21   'Enterprise of a Party' is defined as 'an enterprise constituted or organized under the laws of, or principally carrying on its business in the territory of, a Party'. 'Person' is defined as a 'natural person or an enterprise' and 'person of a Party' as 'a national, or an enterprise of a Party'.
22   'Investor of a Party' is defined as 'a Party or state enterprise thereof, or a national or an enterprise of such Party, that seeks to make, is making or has made an investment'.
23   NAFTA, however, says nothing about the obligations of investors. Investors, therefore, would still be able to rely on the doctrine of separate corporate personality when defending a tort claim arising out of the actions or omissions of one of their subsidiaries.
24   *GAMI v Mexico*, final award, 15 November 2004. The position was unaffected by the fact that the Mexican company had sought remedies in the Mexican courts in respect of the expropriation. However, the shareholder's claim under Art 1110 failed for want of the necessary proof as to the extent to which the value of its holding had been diminished due to the expropriation.

in a Mexican company, which had suffered an expropriation of five of its sugar mills, could proceed under Art 1116 in respect of the loss sustained to the value of its shareholding as a result. Secondly, there is Art 1117, which provides for claims in respect of the loss suffered by the investment itself. The reference to 'indirect' control of an investment in Art 1139 means that many claims may be brought under either heading, for losses sustained by the investment will also result in loss being sustained by the investor who controls that investment, either directly or indirectly.[25] Claims may still be brought even though the investment has completely failed as of the date proceedings are instituted, as was the case in *Mondev v USA*.[26] However, for a claim to fall within Chapter Eleven, there must be continuous foreign ownership of the investment, not only up to the date at which proceedings are commenced, but continuing also through to the date of the hearing.[27]

Article 1139 then identifies what is *not* meant by 'investment'. Sub-heading (i) identifies claims to money that arise *solely* from one of two sources. First, 'commercial contracts for the sale of goods or services by a national or enterprise in the territory of a Party to an enterprise in the territory of another Party'. Secondly, 'the extension of credit in connection with a commercial transaction, such as trade financing, other than a loan covered by subparagraph (d)'. Sub-heading (j) excludes 'any other claims to money, that do not involve the kinds of interests set out in subparagraphs (a) through (h)'. However, the significance of the word 'solely' in exception (i) should be noted. As will shortly be shown in the analysis of the award in *SD Myers v Canada*, it is quite possible for claims which appear to fall within another NAFTA chapter, such as claims related to goods under Chapter Three, or relating to services under Chapter Twelve, to give rise to a parallel claim under Chapter Eleven.

These definitional issues were to play a significant part in the award in *SD Myers v Canada*.[28] In the early 1990s, SD Myers Incorporated (SDMI), a company based in Ohio, sought to import polychlorinated biphenyls (PCBs) from Canada to the US for processing in its Ohio facility. To this end, SDMI's shareholders set up a Canadian company, Myers (Canada), to assist in the obtaining and processing of orders for reprocessing Canadian PCBs at SDMI's plant in Talmadge, Ohio. At the time, Canadian law favoured the domestic treatment and disposal of PCBs, but the 1990 PCB Waste Export regulations did allow for exports to the US if the US EPA gave prior approval. The US Toxic Substance Control Act 1976 prohibited imports of PCBs,

---

25 See *Pope & Talbot v Canada* and *Mondev v USA*. In both cases the tribunal held that the claim had been properly brought under Art 1116 in respect of the investor's losses sustained as a result of the effects of a measure on its wholly owned subsidiary.

26 *Mondev v USA*, final award, 11 October 2002.

27 *Loewen v USA*, award on merits, 26 July 2003.

28 *SD Myers v Canada*, award on merits, 13 November 2000, (2001) 40 ILM 1408.

with very narrow exceptions. In October 1995, the EPA exercised its enforcement discretion to allow SDMI and nine other companies to import PCBs into the US for processing and disposal. In 1996, the EPA moved to make this informal policy a federal regulation and issued final Import for Disposal Rules that opened the US border to PCB imports for processing and disposal.

In November 1995, Canada issued an interim order banning exports of PCBs and stated that it sought time to review the contradictory legal situation in the US and review its international obligations under the Basel Convention 1989 concerning PCB trade. This Convention encourages countries not to engage in trade in toxic waste with non-parties; to ensure PCBs are disposed of in an environmentally friendly manner; and to develop a viable, long-term strategy to dispose of such waste at home. Furthermore, Canada also had doubts as to the conformity of the EPA's enforcement discretion with US law. Notwithstanding this, there were compelling environmental reasons against the measure, not least the fact that SDMI's Ohio site was closer to the Canadian PCB waste locations by the Great Lakes than its main Canadian competitor. An adverse side effect of the measure was the likelihood that some Canadian PCB owners, denied access to the cheaper US option, would not have used the Canadian facilities, but, would, instead, have chosen to hang on to the waste.

After making its assessment, Canada introduced new regulations on 4 February 1997 and Myers imported seven shipments of Canadian PCB waste into the US. On 20 July 1997, a US federal court found that the EPA's new Import Disposal Rule violated the Toxic Substance Control Act and the US border was thereafter permanently closed to further PCB trade. On 30 October 1998, SDMI claimed $20 million from Canada to cover lost profits during the 16-month period during which the EPA's tolerance of imports of PCBs had coincided with Canada's embargo on their export, alleging violations of Arts 1102, 1105, 1106 and 1110.

Canada challenged SDMI's right to proceed under Art 1116 in respect of losses it had sustained as an investor. Myers (Canada) was undoubtedly an 'enterprise', but its shares were not owned by SDMI, but, rather, by four members of the Myers family. Therefore, Canada argued, SDMI could not be an 'investor' in Myers Canada. In its initial, merits award, the tribunal reviewed the evidence of Dana Myers as to the corporate structure adopted by the Myers family in respect of its businesses and concluded that it did 'not accept that an otherwise meritorious claim should fail solely by reason of the corporate structure adopted by a claimant in order to organise the way in which it conducts its business affairs'. The tribunal's view was reinforced by the use of the word 'indirectly' in Art 1139.[29] The tribunal also identified,

---

29 Paragraph 229. Article 1139 refers to 'an investment owned or controlled directly or indirectly by an investor of such Party'.

without ruling on the point, various other grounds on which SDMI could have contended that it had an investment in Canada, namely, that it and Myers Canada were in a joint venture; Myers Canada was a branch of SDMI; it had lent money to Myers Canada; and its market share in Canada was an investment.

The tribunal reiterated these findings in its subsequent award on damages. It concluded that Myers (Canada) was an integral part of SDMI's business plan. All contracts actually carried out saw customers billed in its name.[30] Although Myers (Canada) did not destroy PCBs, which was done by SDMI over the border, SDMI planned to increase the involvement of Myers (Canada), for example by draining PCB contaminated materials prior to shipment, arranging cross-border transportation and dealing with any associated paperwork and permits that might be required. Chapter Eleven covered not just the current operation of an entity, but also extended to its expansion. What needed to be assessed was the overall damage to the economic success of the investor arising from the measure. Chapter Eleven required the loss to be linked causally to the interference with an investment located in a host state. It did not impose any additional requirement that all of the investor's losses must be felt in the host state to be recoverable.[31] This finding made it unnecessary to refer to other contentions advanced by SDMI such as that it had goodwill in Canada which was capable of being recognised as an intangible asset under Canadian law.[32] Canada subsequently initiated proceedings for judicial review before its Federal Court in which it challenged the tribunal's findings both on this issue and on the issue of whether SDMI could be regarded as an investor. However, on 14 January 2004, Judge Kelen upheld the award and found that the tribunal's approach to these issues had been fully justified by the wording the relevant provisions of Chapter Eleven.

This 'overall economic success' analysis effectively conflates the interests of SDMI, the investor, and those of Myers (Canada), the investment. Although the tribunal did not find there to have been an expropriation under Art 1110, this approach did enable it to award substantial damages to SDMI for breach of the 'national treatment' provisions of Art 1102 and the 'fair and equitable treatment' provisions of Art 1105.[33] The evidence of the clear protectionist

---

30 Paragraph 113.
31 This point was also raised by Canada before the tribunal in the preliminary hearing on jurisdiction in *Ethyl Corp v Canada*, the very first Chapter Eleven arbitration to be initiated. In its award on jurisdiction of 24 June 1998, the tribunal held that this was an issue relating to assessment of damages and was not a reason to exclude the claim. A finding to similar effect was made in relation to Canada's argument that the claim should be excluded because of its overlap with Chapter Three.
32 Paragraph 232.
33 Damages were calculated on a tortious basis. A complicated methodology was adopted to ascertain the effect of the temporary export ban on SDMI's business, which assumed a success rate of 44 per cent on its quotations for PCB disposal.

intent of the lead minister behind the measure, in aiming to protect Canadian remediators of PCBs from the competition posed by SDMI, meant that it was no surprise that the tribunal should find that the measure violated this provision.

However, the tribunal's liberal approach to this issue was to have a significant affect in the way in which it assessed the resultant losses suffered by SDMI as a result of the impact of the measure on its investment, Myers (Canada). Thus, SDMI was able to recover in respect of losses that had principally been suffered by itself rather than by its investment, Myers (Canada). The aggregation of the two entities makes it logical to compare the activities of the single economic entity with those of other Canadian processors of PCB waste and to allow recovery for loss of profits on potential processing contracts during the period of the export ban. Indeed, the wide definition of 'investment' in Art 1139 would have allowed SDMI to recover for profits lost as a result of being denied access to the Canadian market for PCB remediation even Myers (Canada) had never existed. 'Market access' would probably constitute an investment under heading (h) of Art 1139, which refers to 'interests arising from the commitment of capital or other resources in the territory of a Party to economic activity in such territory'.

A similar approach to this threshold question was adopted by the tribunal in *Pope & Talbot v USA*, where it held that the investor's access to the Canadian market could constitute a property right for the purpose of a claim under Art 1110. The tribunal in its final award in *Methanex v USA*[34] referred with approval to this finding and went on to state that. 'Certainly, the restrictive notion of property as a material "thing" is obsolete and has ceded its place to a contemporary conception which includes managerial control over components of a process that is wealth producing.' Items such as goodwill and market share might form part of the valuation of an enterprise in a comprehensive taking. However, the tribunal went on to add that 'it is difficult to see how they might stand alone, in a case like the one before the tribunal'.

In contrast, under customary international law, it is unlikely that commercial expectations[35] can constitute property for the purposes of an expropriation claim. Denial of market access entails a restriction on a specific use of real or personal property. In *SD Myers v Canada*, the investor was unable to use its remediation facilities to process Canadian PCB waste. A conventional property analysis, of the type applied in *Oscar Chinn*,[36] would view those facilities as the property, rather than any specific way of employing them. Once market access is treated a distinct category of property, though, it becomes far easier to categorise regulatory interference as amounting to an

---

34   *Methanex v USA*, final award, 3 August 2005. Part D, Chapter IV, para 17.
35   As opposed to vested contractual rights of the sort considered in *CME v Czech Republic*.
36   *Oscar Chinn (UK v Belgium)* (1934) PCIJ, Ser A/B, No 63, 12 December.

expropriation. For example, had the export ban in *SD Myers v Canada* been of a permanent nature (assuming the US had not prohibited imports in 1997), the only conventional taking would have been of Myers (Canada)'s broking business, whose value would have been comparatively small. There would have been no taking as regards SDMI as it could still use its US facilities to carry on a profitable business of PCB remediation in the US and elsewhere. However, once market access is recognised as amounting to a type of property in its own right, the way would have been open to a finding of a total taking of SDMI's property, namely its access to the Canadian market for PCB remediation.

Another significant issue in the tribunal's award was its treatment of Canada's argument that SDMI's claim could not fall under Chapter Eleven because it fell either under Chapter Three, which dealt with trade restrictions or under Chapter Twelve, which dealt with the provision of cross-border ser-vices. The claim, therefore, could only be brought under the state-to-state arbitration provisions of Chapter Twenty rather than through the investor-to-state provisions of Chapter Eleven. The tribunal rejected these arguments by applying the 'cumulative principle' which meant that 'in a given situation a government or private entity might have different rights under different trade provisions that generally complement, rather than diminish, each other'.[37]

This part of the decision, coupled with the expansive approach to the definition of investor and investment, makes it likely that measures which adversely affect trade expectations will suffice to form the basis of a Chapter Eleven claim, including one for expropriation, notwithstanding the fact that such a claim would also justify state-to-state proceedings under NAFTA, Chapter Three. Most claims based on a trade restriction, of the sort seen in the WTO jurisprudence, would be capable of sustaining a claim under Chapter Eleven. For the reasons set out later in this chapter, it is likely that compensation would be required wherever a measure fell within Art 1110, notwithstanding that, had the matter been pursued through state-to-state arbitration under NAFTA, Chapter Three, the same measure would have fallen within one of the exceptions provided by GATT, Art XX. Once there is a finding of an expropriation under Art 1110, an obligation to compensate comes into play, irrespective of the policy measures behind the measure that can inform the analysis of whether there has been a breach of other provisions of Chapter Eleven, such as Arts 1102 and 1105. Furthermore, the tribunal's reasoning would suggest that where a foreign branch of an investment is expropriated, compensation would go beyond the loss to the branch, but would extend to the loss sustained overall by the economic activities of the parent company. The only limitation, at the threshold stage, would be

---

37 Award on damages, para 131.

whether the measure was one 'relating to' the investment. The preliminary decision of the tribunal in *Methanex v USA* would screen out claims where the investor is indirectly affected by a measure, unless there was evidence of discriminatory intent towards the investor.[38]

7.2 Articles 1102 and 1103 – National treatment and most-favoured-nation principles

Article 1102 applies 'national treatment' principles so as to require each party to accord to investors of another party, or investments of investors of another party 'treatment no less favourable than that it accords, in like circumstances, to its own investors with respect to the establishment, acquisition, expansion, management, conduct, operation and sale or other disposition of investments'. Article 1103, in similar fashion, applies 'most favoured nation' principles to investors or investments of investors of another party, or non-party. These principles apply both prospectively and retrospectively to 'measures adopted or maintained by a Party'. The privileged position of foreign investors is boosted by Art 1104 which requires each party 'to accord to investors of another Party and investments of investors of another Party the better of the treatment required by Articles 1102 and 1103 . . .'

A crucial issue under these provisions is how the 'like circumstances' comparison is to be made. Under Art 1102, the comparison will be between the treatment accorded a foreign investment 'in like circumstances' to domestic investors; under Art 1103, with investors of any other state, not just those of a NAFTA party. In *SD Myers v Canada*, the tribunal had to assess the closure of the US-Canadian border to the export of PCBs under the 'national treatment' provisions of Art 1102. In doing so, it construed the word 'like' by reference to the construction of the term by WTO panels:

> The assessment of 'like circumstances' must also take into account circumstances that would justify governmental regulations that treat them [foreign investors] differently in order to protect the public interest. The concept of 'like circumstances' invites an examination of whether a non-national investor complaining of less favourable treatment is in the same 'sector' as the national investor. The Tribunal takes the view that the word 'sector' has a wide connotation that includes the concepts of 'economic sector' and 'business sector'.[39]

It was therefore clear that Myers were in 'like circumstances' with Canadian operators such as Chem-Security and Cintec:

---

38 Such discriminatory intent was clearly found to have been present in *SD Myers v Canada*.
39 Paragraph 250.

They were all engaged in providing PCB waste remediation services. SDMI was in a position to attract customers that might otherwise have gone to the Canadian operators because it could offer more favourable prices and because it had extensive experience and credibility. It was precisely because SDMI was in a position to take business away from its Canadian competitors that Chem-Security and Cintec lobbied the Minister of the Environment to ban exports when the US authorities opened the border.[40]

This analysis follows naturally from the prior aggregation of the business interests of SDMI and Myers (Canada) made by the tribunal in its analysis of what constituted the requisite 'investment'. However, had the tribunal regarded the investment as being exclusively limited to Myers (Canada), quite a different point of comparison would be needed.

Having identified the relevant domestic comparators to the investment, the next step was to identify whether the measure affected the investment differently from those comparators. The tribunal held that two factors had to be taken into account in determining whether a measure violated the 'national treatment' provisions of Art 1102. Was the practical effect of the measure such as to create a disproportionate benefit for nationals over non-nationals? Did the measure, on its face, appear to favour its nationals over non-nationals who were protected by NAFTA? The tribunal stressed that protectionist *intent* was important, but not decisive, in that 'treatment' suggests that practical impact is also required for there to be a breach of Art 1102. The tribunal determined these issues by reference to findings it had made earlier in the award as to the reasons behind the introduction of the measure. It had found that Canada's policy behind the ban on the export of PCBs was protectionist in that it was motivated by the desire and intent:

> ... to protect and promote the market share of enterprises that would carry out the destruction of PCBs in Canada and that were owned by Canadian Nationals. Other factors were considered, particularly at the bureaucratic level, but the protectionist intent of the lead minister in this manner was reflected in decision-making at every stage that led to the ban.

The lead minister's protectionist intent was evidenced by her statement in July 1995, at a meeting of senior officials of two Canadian operators of hazardous waste facilities, that Canada's policy was that PCB waste should

---

40   Paragraph 251.

be disposed of 'in Canada by Canadians',[41] which reiterated what she had said a month earlier in the House of Commons.[42]

Although the facts of the case disclosed no environmental justification for Canada's actions, the tribunal was at pains to stress that valid public interest considerations, such as environmental protection, formed part of the material that had to be considered when analysing the concept of 'likeness'. The tribunal started by acknowledging that the case law on 'likeness' under the GATT, as applied by the WTO panels and the appellate body, emphasised that the interpretation of 'like' must depend on all the circumstances of each case, with close attention being paid to the legal context in which that word appears.[43] The tribunal then noted that:

> In the GATT context, a *prima facie* finding of discrimination in 'like' cases often takes place within the overall GATT framework, which includes Article XX (General Exceptions). A finding of 'likeness' does not dispose of the case. It may set the stage for an inquiry into whether the different treatment of situations found to be 'like' is justified by legitimate public policy measures that are pursued in a reasonable manner.[44]

The legal context of Art 1102 included the various provisions of the NAFTA, its companion agreement the NAAEC and principles that are affirmed by the NAAEC (including those of the Rio Declaration). From this context there emerged the following principles:

- states have the right to establish high levels of environmental protection. They are not obliged to compromise their standards merely to satisfy the political or economic interests of other states;
- states should avoid creating distortions to trade;
- environmental protection and economic development can and should be mutually supportive.[45]

The tribunal then reiterated the place that environmental considerations would play in the analysis of 'likeness' under Art 1102, stating that such assessment:

---

41 Paragraphs 168–9.
42 Although Canada argued that the EPA's enforcement discretion was not lawful, as ultimately confirmed in US litigation in 1997, the tribunal (para 191) made no determination on this issue because Canada had acted on the basis of the law as it then appeared to exist.
43 Paragraph 244.
44 Paragraph 246.
45 Paragraph 247.

must also take into account circumstances that would justify governmental regulations that treat them differently in order to protect the public interest. The concept of 'like circumstances' invites an examination of whether a non-national investor complaining of less favourable treatment is in the same 'sector' as the national investor. The Tribunal takes the view that the word 'sector' has a wide connotation that includes the concepts of 'economic sector' and 'business sector'.[46]

One policy consideration which might have justified Canada's actions was the legitimate, indirect objective of keeping the Canadian industry strong so as to assure a continued disposal capacity. In reasoning that bore the clear imprint of WTO jurisprudence on GATT, Art XX, the tribunal rejected this alternative a justification for the measure on the grounds that:

> . . . where a state can achieve its chosen level of environmental protection through a variety of equally effective and reasonable means, it is obliged to adopt the alternative that is most consistent with open trade. This corollary also is consistent with the language and the case law arising out of the WTO family of agreements.[47]

Canada could have achieved its legitimate aim of maintaining its ability to process PCBs within Canada in the future either by sourcing all government requirements or by granting subsidies to Canadian remediators. These methods would have been less violative of NAFTA than the border closure.[48]

Dr Schwarz, the arbitrator appointed on behalf of SDMI, in his separate opinion went on to observe that although Art 1102 was not made subject to the equivalent of Art XX, read in its proper context the phrase 'like circumstances' in many cases did require the same kind of analysis as under Art XX. That legal context included the provisions of NAFTA, the NAAEC, and those principles, including those of the Rio Declaration, that are affirmed by the NAAEC.[49] One of the relevant provisions of NAFTA was Art 1114 which Dr Schwarz viewed:

> . . . as acknowledging and reminding interpreters of Chapter 11 (Investment) that the parties take both the environment and open trade very seriously an that means should be found to reconcile those two objectives and, if possible, to make them mutually supportive.[50]

---

46   Paragraph 250.
47   Paragraph 221.
48   Paragraph 195.
49   Paragraphs 129–130.
50   Paragraph 118.

Furthermore, all three NAFTA parties belong to the OECD. In 1993, it issued a clarification of 'like circumstances' as referred to in its Declaration on Investment 1976, as follows: 'The Committee also agreed that more general considerations, such as the policy objectives of member countries in various fields could be taken into account.'[51]

Accordingly, SDMI and its Canadian competitors could have been viewed as being in 'different circumstances' if the fact of exporting the waste into the US reasonably required differential treatment from the point of view of environmental protection:[52]

> The Canadian authorities could, for example, have acted promptly to ensure that all PCBs imported into the US were disposed or recycled rather than being put in landfills. The latter approach might have led to some seepage of waste back into the Canadian ecosystem.[53]

However, the facts disclosed no such environmental justification for the measure.

The ambit of Art 1102, and the relevance of the GATT jurisprudence on Art III to its interpretation, came up again for consideration in the final award in *Methanex v US*.[54] The parties argued for two different comparators to methanol, the product affected by the Californian measure. The US referred to US producers of methanol, whereas Methanex referred to the US ethanol industry. The tribunal upheld the US contention, regarding it as perverse 'to ignore identical comparators if they were available and to use comparators that were less "like", as it would be perverse to refuse to find and to apply less "like" comparators when no identical comparators existed'.[55] Forty-seven per cent of methanol producers in the US were domestic and were affected by the Californian measure in exactly the same way as Methanex.

The tribunal also rejected Methanex's argument that Art 1102 should be construed in the light of the GATT jurisprudence under Art III, so as to show that methanol and ethanol were in 'like circumstances' with each other because they both produced oxygenates used in manufacturing reformulated gasoline and were both competing directly for customers in the oxygenate market. The drafters of NAFTA had to be taken as having been fully conversant with the GATT whose provisions they had incorporated into Chapter Three which covers 'National Treatment and Market Access for Goods' and applies

---

51 This approach to the 'likeness' analysis can be seen in the subsequent findings of the appellate body in *EC–Asbestos* to the effect that public health issues regarding a product could form part of the material determining whether there had been a violation of GATT, Art III.4.

52 Paragraph 140.

53 Paragraph 141.

54 *Methanex v USA*, final award, 3 August 2005. Part IV – Chapter B.

55 Paragraph 17.

to 'any like, directly competitive or substitutable goods, as the case may be'. This wording had not been used in Art 1102, which referred, instead, to 'like circumstances'. In any event, even if the GATT jurisprudence applied, it would not assist Methanex who produced methanol as a feedstock for MTBE rather than as a gasoline additive in its own right. The tribunal took the view that ethanol and methanol products could not be said to in a competitive relationship with each other, stating that:

> Aside from the federal prohibition of the use of methanol as an oxygen-ate, methanol has been tried as a fuel in only limited experiments, but would require, if it were to be used, significant and expensive retro-adjustments in gasoline engines . . . Insofar as there is a binary choice, it is between MTBE and other lawful and practicable oxygenates.[56]

7.3 Treatment in accordance with international law – Article 1105

Article 1105.1 provides that: 'Each Party shall accord to investments of inves-tors of another Party treatment in accordance with international law, includ-ing fair and equitable treatment and full protection and security.' Its aim is to provide a remedy for foreign investors in respect of measures which are non-discriminatory, but nonetheless fall below the standards required under inter-national law.[57] Unlike Arts 1102 and 1103, the standard applied is an absolute one, and does not involve a comparison between the treatment afforded to the investor and the treatment afforded to its domestic competitors. The tribunal in *SD Myers v Canada* noted that the provision created 'a floor below which treatment of foreign investors must not fall, even if a government were not acting in a discriminatory manner'.[58] However, something more was required than an ordinary error of government for which the remedy was through internal political and legal processes. That additional factor would be present when an investor had been treated:

> . . . in such an unjust or arbitrary manner that the treatment rises to the level that is unacceptable from the international perspective. That determination must be made in the light of the high measure of defer-ence that international law generally extends to the right of domestic authorities to regulate matters within their own borders.[59]

---

56 Paragraph 28.
57 Article 1105.1 claims are not limited to claims for damages sustained by investments of investors. Therefore, claims for damages under it may be made by investors. The point was argued, and then conceded, by Canada in *Pope & Talbot v Canada*.
58 Paragraph 260.
59 Paragraph 263.

Various problems have arisen with the interpretation of Art 1105. First, there is the question of what is meant by the reference to 'international law'. Although it is clear that customary international law prescribes a minimum standard of treatment of aliens, the content of that norm is not easy to identify. Secondly, there is the question of whether the reference to 'international law' is limited to customary international law or whether it includes conventional international law. On this basis, breaches of other provisions in Chapter Eleven, or even in other provisions of NAFTA outside the investor-state provisions of Chapter Eleven, might in themselves provide evidence of a breach of Art 1105. Thirdly, there is the question of whether the reference to 'fair and equitable treatment' imposes additional obligations to those imposed under international law.

7.3.1 Initial interpretations of Art 1105

In three early awards, tribunals gave expansive answers to these questions. First, in *SD Myers v Canada*, the majority of the tribunal found that a breach of Art 1102 was capable of evidencing a breach of Art 1105 without any independent analysis of the facts. Having stated that the phrases 'fair and equitable treatment' and 'full protection and security' had to be read in conjunction with the phrase 'treatment in accordance with international law',[60] the majority found that 'the fact that a host Party has breached a rule of international law that is specifically designed to protect investors will tend to weigh heavily in favour of finding a breach of Art 1105'.[61] The rule in question was the 'national treatment' standard contained in Art 1102. The majority, therefore, interpreted the reference to 'international law' as including conventional international law.

Secondly, in *Pope & Talbot v Canada*, the tribunal interpreted the reference to 'fair and equitable treatment' as being additive to the reference to 'international law'. Whilst acknowledging that the language of Art 1105 suggested an inclusive interpretation, the tribunal adopted an additive interpretation by referring to the origin of the language of Art 1105.[62] This had grown out of the provisions of BITs negotiated by the US and other industrialised countries, in particular the Model BIT of 1987 whose equivalent provision to Art 1105 had clearly expressed the 'fair and equitable' requirements as being additional to the reference to international law. There was no evidence that the NAFTA parties had intended to reject the additive character of these BITs when they had drafted Art 1105.

Furthermore, if non-NAFTA parties were entitled to 'fair and equitable' treatment as an independent right under their BITs and NAFTA parties

---

60   Paragraph 262.
61   Paragraph 264.
62   Paragraphs 110–11.

were limited only to such treatment where it was mandated by international law, the disadvantaged NAFTA party could simply obtain such a right by turning to the national treatment provisions of Art 1102 and the most favoured nation provisions of Art 1103. This mandates a comparison of the treatment afforded to the investor with that afforded to the treatment of investors of another party, or a non-party, which are 'in like circumstances'. For example, a Mexican investor taking Chapter Eleven proceedings against the US could rely on provisions such as Art II.3[63] of the US-Albania BIT, which accords investors wider protection than that accorded under NAFTA.[64]

Applying these principles to the claim, the tribunal found, in part, for the investor. The claim had been put in two ways. First, there was the principal claim that Canada's implementation of the quota system under the US-Canadian Agreement on Trade in Softwood Lumber constituted a violation of Art 1105. The tribunal rejected this claim. Secondly, there was a subsidiary claim, arising out of the 'verification dispute'. After the investor initiated Chapter Eleven proceedings, it became subject to increasing harassment from Canada's Softwood Lumber Division (SLD). It was required to produce voluminous documentation in relation to a review of first decided to review the investor's claim that its investment had not received its due quota allocation and then asked for an explanation of an apparent discrepancy between its sale figures and the lumber it produced in previous years. The investor then turned that matter over to the lawyer who was dealing with its Chapter Eleven claim. The lawyer wrote to the SLD questioning its authority to conduct a verification review and to insist on production of records in Canada. In response, the SLD raised the possibility that non-co-operation could lead to the investor not being awarded any additional quota when future allocations came to be made under the agreement. The tribunal found that Canada's conduct during the 'verification review' had amounted to a breach of Art 1105.

The third award was that in *Metalclad v Mexico*, which is discussed in detail in the section on Art 1110. In brief, the claim arose out of a US investor which had acquired a Mexican waste disposal corporation, Coterin, which was trying to obtain licences to operate a landfill site. Representatives of the

---

63 Paragraph (a) contains an entitlement to 'fair and equitable treatment' that is additive to and not subsumed in the treatment to which the investor is entitled under international law. Paragraph (b) also provides that: 'Neither Party shall in any way impair by unreasonable and discriminatory measures the management, conduct, operation and sale or other disposition of covered investments.'

64 This was the finding made by the ICSID tribunal in its award on jurisdiction in *Maffezini v Spain* (ARB/97/7), 25 January 2000. The claim was made under a BIT between Spain and Argentina and the investor was able to rely on a more provision in the Spain–Chile BIT that was more favourable to investors, subject to the proviso that the third-party treaty must relate to the same subject matter as the basic treaty.

Mexican federal government gave assurances that Coterin would be able to operate its site and that obtaining any local permits would be a mere formality. However, due to substantial local opposition to the landfill site, the local and state authorities refused permits and obtained injunctions to prevent work being carried out on the site. The tribunal took the conventional international law approach of the tribunal in *SD Myers v Canada* a step further by reading into Art 1105 the transparency obligations imposed by NAFTA, generally by Art 102.1, more concretely by Chapter Eighteen.

As a result, Mexico was subject to an obligation under Art 1105 to ensure that there should be no room for doubt or uncertainty as to the legal requirements affecting investors.[65] Once the authorities of the central government became aware of any scope for misunderstanding or confusion, they came under a duty to ensure the correct position was promptly determined and clearly stated. The tribunal referred to the lack of a transparent and predictable framework for Metalclad's business planning and investment.[66] In coming to this conclusion, the tribunal, having heard conflicting evidence as to Mexican law, concluded that the municipality had exceeded its authority in refusing the permit. Its authority extended only to matters relating to the safe operation of the site, whereas its decision had been based on the wider issue of whether the site should be operating in the first place, an issue which fell to be decided by the federal government. The manner in which the municipality had reached its decision was also administratively flawed.

The award was then subject to judicial review in British Columbia. Justice Tysoe held that the tribunal had made decisions on matters beyond the scope of the submission to arbitration by deciding upon matters outside its remit. This was because the Chapter Eleven investor-state arbitration procedure was limited to claims which alleged breaches of an obligation under Section A of Chapter Eleven and of two articles contained in Chapter Fifteen. A Chapter Eleven claim could not, therefore, be decided by reference to the provisions of Chapter Eighteen. The transparency objectives referred to in Art 102.1 were implemented only through Chapter Eighteen and were not expressed in Chapter Eleven.[67] The tribunal had not simply interpreted Art 1105 as including a minimum standard of transparency. It had misstated the applicable law to include transparency obligations and it then made its decision on the basis of the concept of transparency.

---

65   Paragraph 76. This requirement probably goes beyond what is required under Chapter Eighteen.
66   Paragraph 99.
67   Paragraphs 70–1.

7.3.2 The Free Trade Commission's interpretation of Art 1105

These three awards caused a great deal of unease among the NAFTA state parties. In response to the way in which Art 1105 had been interpreted in these awards, the following interpretation was issued on 31 July 2001 by the Free Trade Commission.[68] It made the following three statements as to how Art 1105 was to be interpreted. First, it '. . . prescribes the customary international law minimum standard of treatment of aliens as the minimum standard of treatment to be afforded to investments of investors of another party'. This involves a clear rejection of the reference to conventional international law which was made by the tribunal in *SD Myers v Canada*. Secondly, 'The concepts of "fair and equitable treatment" and "full protection and security" do not require treatment in addition to or beyond that which is required by customary international law minimum standard of treatment of aliens'. This involves a clear rejection of the additive interpretation of these terms which the *Pope & Talbot* tribunal had adopted. Thirdly, 'A determination that there has been a breach of another provision of the NAFTA, or of a separate international agreement, does not establish that there has been a breach of Article 1105 (1)'. This involves a clear rejection of the approach of the tribunals in both *SD Myers v Canada* and *Metalclad v Mexico*.

7.3.3 Subsequent interpretations of Art 1105

Subsequent decisions have followed the letter of this interpretation, but not the spirit. Ironically, the first tribunal to consider the Interpretation was that in *Pope & Talbot* when it came to assess damages for the breach of Art 1105. Given the interpretation's clear rejection of the tribunal's previous, additive, interpretation of the relationship between the different elements of the article, this issue clearly needed revisiting. Although the use of the words 'shall be binding' in Art 1131.2 showed that interpretations were mandatory and not merely prospective in effect, it was legitimate to consider the question of whether the interpretation was in fact an amendment, which should therefore have been made pursuant to the provisions of Art 2202. The tribunal requested sight of any *travaux preparatoires* to Art 1105. Canada initially denied that any existed, but in the end provided 1,500 pages containing 40 preliminary drafts in none of which did the qualification 'customary' appear when reference was made to international law. The tribunal concluded that the NAFTA negotiators could, therefore, be assumed to have been aware of the fact that

68   This is the body established pursuant to Art 2001, 'comprising cabinet-level representatives of the Parties or their designees' whose tasks include the resolution of disputes regarding the interpretation or application of NAFTA.

'customary' international law is not the only source of international law, as is made clear by Statute of the International Court of Justice, Art 38.1.[69]

However, the tribunal found that there was no need to stray further into these contentious waters, because its initial award was still justified under the interpretation. Customary international law was not static and had evolved since the *Neer* case in the 1920s. It had evolved through state practice as evidenced by international agreements. The range of actions subject to international concern had broadened since *Neer*.[70] The OECD Draft Convention on Protection of Foreign Property 1967 showed that customary international law required a state to afford to foreigners as good treatment as it afforded to its own nationals. The 'fair and equitable treatment' requirement was central to BITs concluded since 1967. Their number now exceeded 1,800 and the practice of states was now represented by those treaties. The tribunal was, however, content to rely on the following statement of the International Court of Justice in *Elettronica Sicula SpA (ELSI) United States v Italy*:

> Arbitrariness is not so much something opposed to a rule of law, as something opposed to the rule of law ... It is wilful disregard of due process of law, an act which shocks, or at least surprises a sense of judicial propriety.[71]

This, too, showed that the current norm of customary international law now went beyond *Neer*. However, even applying *Neer*, Canada would still have violated the standards of *customary* international law through its assertions of non-existent policy reasons for forcing the investor to comply with very burdensome demands for documentation, refusals to provide the investor with information it had been promised, threats to reduce or even terminate the investor's export quotas, serious factual misrepresentations to the Minister regarding the investor, the suggestion of criminal investigation of the investor.

This approach was subsequently adopted by the tribunal in *Mondev v USA*.[72] The tribunal took the view that the key question was what was the con-

---

69   This directs the court to apply:

   a.   international conventions, whether general or particular, establishing rules expressly recognised by the contesting states;
   b.   international custom, as evidence of a general practice accepted as law;
   c.   the general principles of law recognised by civilized nations;
   d.   subject to the provisions of Article 59, judicial decisions and the teachings of the most highly qualified publicists of the various nations, as subsidiary means for the determination of rules of law.

   Heading (a) would cover other provisions of NAFTA.

70   *Neer* (1926) 4 UNRIAA 60.
71   *Elettronica Sicula SpA (ELSI) United States v Italy* (1989) ICJ 15, p 76.
72   *Mondev v USA*, award, 11 October 2002.

tent of customary international law providing for fair and equitable treatment and full protection and security in investment treaties? Canada again relied on the *Neer* case and again the tribunal refused to give such a limited content to the reference to international law in Art 1105. It gave three reasons for doing so. First, the case had not been concerned with a foreign investment, but rather with the physical security of the alien. Secondly, the substantive and procedural rights of individuals under international law had evolved since 1927. Thirdly, since 1927 there had emerged a body of concordant practice in over 2,000 bilateral and regional investment treaties. The Free Trade Commission (FTC) interpretation made it clear that the standard of treatment under Art 1105, including fair and equitable treatment, was to be found by reference to *existing* elements of the customary international law standard and were not intended to add to it. However, the content of the minimum standard necessarily evolved over time and could not be limited to its content in the 1920s.

The result of these decisions is that in practical terms we are back where we started from with 'fair and equitable treatment'. Instead of being additive to the reference to international law, as found by the tribunal in *Pope & Talbot v Canada*, the fact that the phrase has been so widely incorporated into BITs means that it has served to expand the content of the customary international law norm on the minimum treatment of aliens, from the egregious bad behaviour by a state towards the alien that was contemplated in *Neer*.[73] Nonetheless, this somewhat more expansive view of customary international law poses no real threat to the ability of legislators and administrators to make policy choices based on grounds of environmental protection, even though they may have some adverse impact on a foreign investor. In the substantive dispute in *Pope & Talbot v Canada*, the tribunal did, after all, find that none of the complaints about Canada's implementation of the quota system under the US-Canadian Agreement on Trade in Softwood Lumber constituted a violation of Art 1105. As regards the BC adjustment, and the Super Fee, which formed part of this complaint, the tribunal observed that:

> The choice made to resolve the BC stumpage dispute through the Super Fee undoubtedly required certain exporters to pay a price for a benefit accorded by BC to all producers in that province. Therefore, Canada might have chosen another approach to settlement, one that shared the burden more equitably across the range of BC producers that received

---

73   The reference to the recent burgeoning of the BIT is, however, something of a double-edged sword. It could plausibly be argued that it is the limited nature of customary international law that has led parties to conclude BITs. Therefore, it is difficult to see how the fact that individual states have sought over the last 20 or so years to improve the protection afforded to their investors, over that available under customary international law in state-to-state proceedings, can be taken as evidence of a new norm of customary international law.

the benefits of the stumpage reductions. However, it is not the place of this Tribunal to substitute its judgment on the choice of solutions for Canada's, unless that choice can be found to be a denial of fair and equitable treatment. Given the large number of BC producers affected by the settlement as well as the hierarchical treatment of shipment levels under the SLA itself, the Tribunal cannot conclude that Canada's decision to apportion the costs as it did was a denial of fair and equitable treatment to this Investment.

Subsequent Art 1105 claims, such as *Mondev v US*, have arisen out of judicial proceedings in one of the NAFTA parties. In *Loewen v US*,[74] the tribunal came very near to finding a breach of Art 1105 by the US arising from the way in which a a Canadian national had been treated in civil proceedings in Mississippi against a local litigant. The whole trial and its resultant verdict were 'clearly improper and discreditable' and could not be squared with minimum standards of international law and fair and equitable treatment. However, the tribunal found that there had been no violation of Art 1105. There would be no violation of customary international law where the claimant still had the opportunity to appeal against the decision within the US legal system. Article 1121 did not waive the duty to pursue local remedies in relation to a breach of customary international law constituted by a judicial act. Rather than appealing against the verdict, Loewen had entered into a settlement agreement and failed to supply any evidence as to its reasons for doing so. While it may have been reasonable for Loewen to do so, it could not be said that this was the only course of action reasonably open to it.[75]

The 'clearly improper and discreditable' test used by the tribunals in these two awards, offers some scope for arguing that a lack of administrative and judicial transparency, of the sort found in *Metalclad v Mexico*, might constitute a violation of Art 1105 by reference, not to other NAFTA provisions, but rather to the norms of customary international law regarding the minimum treatment to be afforded to aliens. However, it is important to realise that tribunals have consistently stressed that NAFTA is not to be regarded as a court of appeal from decisions of municipal legal systems. The issue arose in *Azinian, Davitian and Baca v Mexican*,[76] where a claim was made by US shareholders in a Mexican company, Desona, in respect of judicial decisions

---

74 Award on merits, 26 July 2003.
75 The tribunal found that Loewen had three options: to appeal against the decision, despite the risk of execution of its assets; to seek protection under Chapter Eleven of the Bankruptcy Code which would have resulted in a stay of execution against its assets; or to file a petition for *certiorari* and seek a stay of execution in the US Supreme Court.
76 *Azinian, Davitian and Baca v Mexico* (ICSID Case No ARB (AF)/97/2) (NAFTA), award, 1 November 1999.

annulling its concession contract for waste collection and disposal in the city of Nuacalpan de Juarez. The tribunal held that the fundamental problem with their claim was that 'they are victims of a breach of the Concession Contract. NAFTA does not, however, allow investors to seek international arbitration for mere contractual breaches'.[77] The claim as to the contract's invalidity had been upheld by three levels of Mexican courts. The claimant had neither contended nor proved that the Mexican legal standards for the annulment of concessions violated Mexico's Chapter Eleven obligations, nor that Mexican law on this point was expropriatory.[78]

7.4 Performance requirements – Article 1106

Article 1106.1 prohibits a party from imposing various performance requirements, or enforcing any commitment or undertaking, in connection with the establishment, acquisition, expansion, management, conduct or operation of an investment of an investor of a party or of a non-party in its territory. The requirements include the imposition of an undertaking to 'export a given level or percentage of goods or services',[79] or 'to achieve a given level or percentage of domestic content'[80] or 'to purchase, use or accord a preference to goods produced or services provided in its territory, or to purchase goods or services from persons in its territory'[81] or 'to transfer technology, a production process or other proprietary knowledge to a person in its territory . . .'[82] Article 1106.2 provides an exception in respect of the last of these where the requirement is 'to meet generally applicable health, safety or environmental standards-related measures, as defined in Article 915'.[83] Article 1106.3 also prohibits a party from 'conditioning the receipt or continued receipt of an advantage, in connection with investments in its territory of investors of a Party or of a non-Party' on compliance with the first four of the requirements listed in Art 1106.1.[84]

This article raises an important issue as to whether a measure is to be judged on its face or by whether it creates a *de facto* performance

---

77 Paragraph 87.
78 See, also, *Waste Management v Mexico* (Arb (AF)/00/3), award, 30 April 2004. The tribunal made a similar finding in respect of breaches of a contract between the Mexican state body and a US waste disposal firm.
79 Sub-paragraph (a).
80 Sub-paragraph (b).
81 Sub-paragraph (c).
82 Sub-paragraph (f).
83 Article 915 is in Chapter Nine which contains NAFTA's equivalent of the WTO TBT Agreement.
84 All performance requirements listed in paras 1 and 3 are prohibited, whether imposed on investors of a party or not. However, only investors of a party have the right to challenge breaches of the provision.

requirement, as was argued by the investor in *Ethyl Corp v Canada*. The tribunal in *Pope & Talbot v Canada* opted for the former alternative. Pope and Talbot had argued that Art 1106 had been violated because the Export Control Regime required the investment to export a given level of goods that was 'lower than that which the Investment would export if it were not force to pay export fees on exports above its fee-free allocation'. They also argued that the Regime penalised softwood lumber producers for under-utilisation of export quotas, thereby creating a *de facto* requirement to export up to quota levels.

The tribunal held that Art 1106 had to be analysed in the light of the ordinary meaning of its terms, particularly in the light of para 5 which provides that paras 1 and 3 do not apply to any requirements other than those listed therein. No claim under Art 1106.1(a) had been made out. Although the regime might deter exports to the US, that did not amount to a 'requirement' for establishing, acquiring, expanding, managing, conducting or operating a foreign-owned business in Canada.[85] Nor had a claim been made out under Art 1106.1(e), which prohibits a party from imposing restrictions on sales of goods or services 'in its territory that such investment produces or provides by relating such sales in any way to the volume or value of its exports or foreign exchange earnings'. The phrase 'sales of goods in its territory' referred to sales made in Canada for use or consumption within Canada, and not to export sales to the US. As the regime imposed no restrictions or limitations on *domestic* sales of softwood lumber, there was accordingly no breach of this provision.[86]

7.5. Article 1110. Expropriation

Article 1110(1) provides that:

> No Party shall directly or indirectly nationalise or expropriate an investment of an investor of another Party in its territory or take a measure tantamount to nationalisation or expropriation of such an investment except:
>
> (a) for a public purpose;
> (b) on a non-discriminatory basis;
> (c) in accordance with due process of law and article 1105(1); and
> (d) on payment of compensation in accordance with paragraphs 2 to 6.[87]

---

85 Paragraph 75.
86 A similar 'effects'-based interpretation of Art 1106 was also rejected in *SD Myers v Canada*. However, Dr Schwarz in his separate opinion, dissented on this point, on the ground that any breach must be looked at as a matter of substance not form. The practical effect of the ban required Myers to dispose of the waste in Canada.
87 Paragraphs 2 and 3 provides for compensation in accordance with the 'Hull Formula'.

It should be noted that the four conditions for a lawful expropriation set out in headings (a) to (d) are cumulative. Therefore, an expropriation which was for a public purpose was non-discriminatory and made in accordance with due process of law and the international standards referred to in Art 1105.1 would still be unlawful if made without payment of compensation.

7.5.1 What constitutes expropriation or a measure 'tantamount to expropriation'?

Once the investor has cleared the threshold issue of what constitutes an 'investment', which has already been discussed, it remains to be considered what type of governmental conduct can constitute either expropriation or 'a measure tantamount to nationalization or expropriation'.[88] The award in *Pope & Talbot v Canada* gives some useful pointers as to what will and will not amount to expropriation for the purposes of Chapter Eleven. The investor based its claim on losses it had suffered by reason of restrictions on lumber exports to the US by its wholly owned Canadian company, pursuant to the operation of the Softwood Lumber Agreement between the US and Canada. The investor argued for a wide reading of Art 1110, alleging that there would be expropriation whenever a governmental act was used to deny *some* benefit to property. The words 'tantamount to expropriation' should be construed to cover a measure beyond the sort of outright taking or creeping expropriation that was recognised under customary international law. So long as a measure, even if it were non-discriminatory, substantially interfered with the investment of a foreign investor, then there would be a violation of Art 1110. The tribunal concluded that Pope and Talbot's access to the US market did constitute a property interest subject to protection under Art 1110 and that 'the scope of that article does cover non-discriminatory regulation that might be said to fall within an exercise of a state's so-called police powers'.[89] The tribunal, however, rejected Canada's position that 'mere interference is not expropriation: rather, a significant degree of deprivation of fundamental rights of ownership is required'.[90]

---

88   See, further, Durnberry, P, 'Expropriation under NAFTA Chapter 11 Investment Dispute Settlement Mechanism: Some Comments on the Latest Case Law' (2001) 4(3) Int ALR 96, pp 96–104; Weiler, T, 'NAFTA Chapter 11 Jurisprudence: Coming Along Nicely' (2003) 9 South Western Journal of Law and Trade in the Americas 245; 'Arbitration under the NAFTA; Remedies for Poor Regulatory Treatment' (2000) 6 Int'l Trade Law and Regulation 84, pp 84–128; 'Regulatory Reform Obligations under International Law' (2000) 24 JWT 71; and 'A First Look at the Interim Merits Award in SD Myers, Inc v Canada: It is Possible to Balance Legitimate Environmental Concerns with Investment Protection?' (2001) 24 Hastings Int'l Law and Comp L Rev 173.

89   Paragraph 96.

90   Paragraphs 87–88.

The tribunal then went on to rule that the phrase 'measure tantamount to nationalisation or expropriation' in Art 1110 did not broaden 'the ordinary concept of expropriation under international law to require compensation for measures affecting property interests without regard to the magnitude or severity of that effect'. The problem for Pope & Talbot was to identify an expropriation. The tribunal observed that:

> The sole 'taking' that the Investor has identified is interference with the Investment's ability to carry on its business of exporting softwood lumber to the US. While this interference has, according to the Investor, resulted in reduced profits for the Investment, it continues to export substantial quantities of softwood lumber to the US and to earn substantial profits on those sales.[91]

The applicable test was whether the interference alleged was 'sufficiently restrictive to support a conclusion that the property has been "taken" from the owner'.[92] Such a definition was coterminous with that adopted under customary international law. The phrase 'tantamount' meant nothing more than 'equivalent' and did not extend Art 1110 beyond the limits of customary international law on expropriations.

In *S D Myers v Canada*, the claim under Art 1110 was also unsuccessful. The tribunal observed that 'regulatory conduct by public authorities is unlikely to be the subject of legitimate complaint under Art 1110 of the NAFTA, although the tribunal does not rule out that possibility'.[93] It then continued:

> Expropriations tend to involve the deprivation of ownership rights: regulations a lesser interference. The distinction between expropriation and regulation screens out most potential cases of complaints concerning economic intervention by a state and reduces the risk that governments will be subject to claims as they go about their business of managing public affairs.[94]

The closure of the border here had been temporary, whereas an expropriation usually 'amounts to a lasting removal of the ability of an owner to make use of its economic rights although it may be that, in some contexts and circumstances, it would be appropriate to view a deprivation as amounting to an expropriation, even if were partial or temporary'.[95] The tribunal construed

---

91   Paragraph 101.
92   Paragraph 102.
93   Paragraph 281.
94   Paragraph 282.
95   Paragraph 283. The position is similar to that under US takings law. See *Tahoe-Sierra Preservation Council Inc v Tahoe Regional Planning Agency* 535 US 302, 122 SCt 1465 (2002), where a 32-month moratorium on development of all land around Lake Tahoe was held not to give rise to a total takings claim.

the word 'tantamount' as 'equivalent' and agreed with the finding in *Pope & Talbot* that it cannot logically mean more than 'expropriation'. The word was inserted to cover:

> 'creeping expropriation' rather than to expand the accepted international definition of 'expropriation.' On the facts there was no expropriation as all that happened was than an opportunity was delayed; Canada realised no benefit from the measure and there was no transfer of property or benefit directly to others.

One of the arbitrators, Dr Schwarz, issued a separate opinion in which he devoted considerable attention to the ambit of Art 1110. Expropriations tended to involve unjust enrichment of a public authority at the expense of an investor and to upset an owner's 'reasonable expectations concerning what belongs to him, in law and fairness'. In contrast, property owners should reasonably expect regulation of the way in which their property is used. 'It generally does not amount to an unfair surprise'.[96] On the facts, Dr Schwarz was sympathetic to the classification of the measure as one that was 'tantamount to expropriation', given the loss of goodwill as a property interest and the arbitrary and discriminatory nature of the measure. However, he refrained from making such a finding, which would make no practical difference to the damages to which Myers would be awarded,[97] whereas a finding of expropriation might contribute to public misunderstanding about this decision and the wider implications of NAFTA.

A more expansive interpretation of 'tantamount to expropriation' was to be provided by the tribunal in *Metalclad v Mexico*,[98] the only case to date in which a claim under Art 1110 has succeeded. The facts are somewhat similar to those in *Tecmed v Mexico*. Metalclad is a Delaware corporation whose wholly owned subsidiary, Eco-Metalclad, a Utah corporation, was in turn the sole owner of all the shares in Econsa, a Mexican corporation. In 1993, Econsa bought another Mexican company, Coterin, with a view to acquiring, developing and operating its hazardous waste transfer station and landfill in Guadalcazar, for which it owned permits and licences. The regulatory background at the time of the purchase was that the federal government of Mexico had authorised Coterin to construct and operate a hazardous waste transfer site in Guadalcazar and agencies of the federal government, INE and SEMARNAP, had granted Coterin a federal permit to construct and operate a landfill site. The state government had also granted Coterin a state land use permit to construct the landfill, subject to the condition that the project conform to various specifications and technical requirements. The permit

---

96 Paragraphs 211–13.
97 Given the tribunal's finding that the measure was in breach of both Arts 1102 and 1105.
98 *Metalclad v* Mexico (ICSID (Additional Facility) Case No ARB/(AF)/97/1), 30 August 2000.

stated that the licence did not prejudge the rights or ownership of the applicant, nor did it authorise works, construction or the functioning of business or activities. Additionally, the state governor had given Metalclad the impression he would support the project if studies confirmed the site as suitable or feasible and if the environmental impact was consistent with Mexican standards. A building permit was still required from the muncipality, although officials of the federal government led Metalclad to believe this was a mere formality.

Against this background, Metalclad began construction of the landfill site in May 1994. There was, however, considerable local opposition to the landfill site. In October 1994, the Muncipality ordered all building work to cease due to absence of a municipal construction permit. The following month, however, Metalclad resumed construction of the site and then obtained an additional federal construction permit from INE. The site was completed in March 1995, but it was prevented from opening by local demonstrators. In November 1995, Metalclad and two of SEMARNAP's sub-agencies reached an agreement, the *convenio*, which allowed the landfill to be operated subject to Metalclad submitting an action plan to correct deficiencies identified in an environmental audit prepared earlier in the year. However, the state governor publicly denounced the *convenio* shortly after it was announced. The muncipality then denied the construction permit and commenced *amparo* proceedings before the Mexican courts who granted an injunction barring Metalclad from performing any landfill operations. On 2 January 1997, Metalclad initiated Chapter Eleven proceedings under Art 1117, on behalf of Coterin, as the enterprise. On 23 September 1997, the state governor, on his final day in office, issued an Ecological Decree declaring a Natural Area for the protection of rare cactus over land which comprised the area of the landfill. In May 1999, the *amparo* was dismissed and the injunction lifted.

The tribunal found that there had been a breach of both of Arts 1105 and 1110. Its reasoning was founded on the assumption that the transparency obligations imposed by NAFTA generally by Art 102.1 more concretely in Chapter Eighteen should be read into Chapter Eleven. The tribunal held that a consequence of these obligations was that there should be no room for doubt or uncertainty as to the legal requirements affecting investors.[99] Once the authorities of the central government became aware of any scope for misunderstanding or confusion, they came under a duty to ensure the correct position was promptly determined and clearly stated. The tribunal referred to the lack of a transparent and predictable framework for Metalclad's business planning and investment.[100] In coming to this conclusion, the tribunal, having heard conflicting evidence as to Mexican law, concluded that the municipality had exceeded its authority in refusing the permit. Its authority extended

99 Paragraph 76.
100 Paragraph 99.

only to matters relating to the safe operation of the site whereas its decision had been based on the wider issue of whether the site should be operating in the first place, an issue which fell to be decided by the federal government. The manner in which the municipality had reached its decision was also administratively flawed.

These failings on the part of both the municipality and the federal government meant that Coterin had effectively and unlawfully been prevented from operating the landfill site. This constituted a measure 'tantamount to expropriation' and Metalclad was awarded the costs of its investment, reduced to take account of the remediation costs of the landfill site.[101] The tribunal observed that:

> . . . expropriation under NAFTA includes not only open, deliberate and acknowledged takings of property, such as outright seizure or formal or obligatory transfer of title in favour of the host state, but also covert or incidental interference with the use of property which has the effect of depriving the owner, in whole or in significant part, of the use or reasonably-to-be-expected economic benefit of property even if not necessarily to the obvious benefit of the host State.[102]

This formulation is in terms wider than that used in *SD Myers v Canada* and *Pope & Talbot v Canada* in that it appears to recognise that partial takings can constitute expropriation. If so, this goes beyond the position under customary international law[103] and appears to set out a *lex specialis* under NAFTA on expropriation, contrary to what was said by the tribunal in *Pope and Talbot v Canada*. The tribunal also supported its findings on Art 1110 by reference to *Biloune v Ghana Investment Centre*,[104] where an investor in Ghana had begun work on renovating a restaurant prior to getting a building permit, in reliance on a representation from an official of a government-affiliated entity. This was held to have amounted to an expropriation in that the totality of the circumstances had had the effect of causing the irreparable cessation of work on the project. The tribunal also justified its finding on the alternative ground that the Ecological Decree, which had the effect of barring forever the operation of the landfill, also amounted to an expropriation. It observed that the motivation or intent behind the measure need not be considered.[105]

---

101 The tribunal, however, rejected Metalclad's claim for future profits because the landfill had never been operative. This method of assessment could be adopted only once an investment had been operated for a sufficiently long time to establish a performance record.
102 Paragraph 104.
103 The *Metalclad* formulation was, however, referred to with approval by the tribunal in *CME v Czech Republic*.
104 *Biloune v Ghana Investment Centre* (1993) 95 ILR 183, pp 207–10.
105 Paragraph 109.

The implementation of the decree would, in and of itself, constitute an act tantamount to expropriation.[106]

These observations were to prove significant when the award came up for review in British Columbia. Judge Tysoe found that the tribunal's finding of a breach of Art 1110 had been infected by its error of importing transparency obligations into its analysis of Art 1105. Although the tribunal had referred to the decision in *Biloune*, it had not relied independently on the cases to find that there had been expropriation prior to the Ecological Decree:

> The tribunal simply relied on *Biloune* as support for the conclusion it had already made that there had been an expropriation (which conclusion was based, at least in part, on the concept of transparency).[107]

However, Judge Tysoe held that the finding of a violation of Art 1110 could still stand by reference to the tribunal's secondary finding concerning the effect of the Ecological Decree. Once the primary finding was set aside, this then became the governing finding.[108] Although the tribunal had adopted an extremely broad definition of expropriation[109] which was 'sufficiently broad to include a legitimate rezoning of property by municipality or other zoning authority',[110] this definition amounted to a question of law with which the court was not entitled to interfere, unless it was patently unreasonable: which it was not.

One element in all the definitions of 'expropriation' adopted by the tribunals in these cases is the protection of the 'reasonable expectations' of an investor. This will require an analysis at the regulations already in place at the time the investor made its investment. An investor will not be able to claim that an expropriation has been effected by reason of regulations already in existence at such time. In *GAMI v Mexico*, the tribunal held, in the context of a claim under Art 1105, that an investor must accept the regulatory background in force when the investment is made.[111] The question that needs to be addressed is whether subsequent changes to this background can trigger the

---

106 Paragraph 111.
107 *Biloune*, moreover, was distinguishable on two grounds. First, the investor's restaurant had been partially destroyed by government officials. Secondly, the investor had been deported from Ghana and prevented from returning.
108 Paragraph 84.
109 The definition included 'covert or incidental interference with the use of property which has the effect of depriving the owner, in whole or in significant part, of the use or reasonably-to-be-expected economic benefit of property'.
110 Paragraph 99.
111 Final award, 15 November 2004. See, too, *Feldman v Mexico* (Case No ARB (AF) 99/1), award, 16 December 2002. Furthermore, expectations generated by an informal waiver of regulations relating to exports of cigarettes from Mexico could not form the basis of an expropriation when the authorities decided to enforce the regulations.

operation of Art 1110. Is the investor entitled to assume that regulatory regime in force at the time the investment is made will remain unaltered throughout the lifetime of the investment?

This issue is likely to prove critical in the recent suit against the US commenced by the Canadian mining company, *Glamis Gold* which shows that the issue may be more complex than at first seems to be the case.[112] Glamis is a Nevada corporation which owns Glamis Gold, a Canadian corporation, which, in turn owns Glamis Imperial, a Nevada corporation. Chapter Eleven proceedings have been commenced in relation to losses it claims to have sustained as a result of: (a) failure on the part of the Department of the Interior, under both the Clinton and Bush administrations, to approve its gold mining claims in the California desert; and (b) legislation introduced by California at the end of 2002 which would have subjected all new and pending mining claims to reclamation requirements that would be unfeasible, both economically and technically.

Glamis Gold committed some $13 million in developing its mining project on federal lands in the California desert following the California Desert Protection Act 1994 which resulted from a congressional review of land use on federal lands. The Act created various wilderness areas, but explicitly ruled out any buffer zones around them. The land Glamis proposed to mine fell well outside the closest of these wilderness areas. The claim raises the issue of whether Glamis Gold had a reasonable expectation that no further restrictions on mining operations in the California desert would be introduced in the foreseeable future. It also raises the issue of whether, if this were not the case, there has still been an expropriation of their investment for the purposes of Art 1110.

Finally, it should be noted that the intent behind the measure, although highly relevant to a claim under Art 1102, and possibly under Art 1105 as well, has not been a feature of the various tribunal's interpretations of Art 1110.[113] However, the following passage from the final award in *Methanex v USA* contains a hint that discriminatory intent may sometimes have a part to play in the analysis of Art 1110. The tribunal, considering the phrase 'tantamount to expropriation', stated that:

> ... as a matter of international law, a non-discriminatory regulation for a public purpose, which is enacted in accordance with due process and which affects, inter alios, a foreign investor is not deemed

112 *Glamis Gold v US*, claim filed, 9 December 2003.
113 If a measure is motivated by an intent to discriminate against foreign investors, then this will have an impact on the threshold issue of whether the measure is one 'relating to' the investor or the investment. In its award on jurisdiction, the tribunal in *Methanex v USA* held that a measure would not 'relate to' investors who were *indirectly* affected thereby. However, the tribunal recognised that the position would be different if there were evidence of discriminatory intent behind the measure. The investor in *SDMI v Canada* was in just such a position.

expropriatory and compensable unless specific commitments had been given by the regulating government to the then putative foreign investor contemplating investment that the government would refrain from such regulation.[114]

This suggests that a measure whose effect was insufficiently severe to be ordinarily regarded as expropriatory could, nonetheless, support a claim under Art 1110 if it was actuated by discriminatory intent or was not for a public purpose. It also suggests that even if such a measure was non-discriminatory and for a public purpose, it could form the basis of a claim under Art 1110 if it entailed a breach of a stabilisation clause. This formulation is at odds with the effects based criterion of expropriation applied under customary international law. It is submitted that a violation of a stabilisation clause which adversely impacts on the alien's investment, but is not sufficiently serious in its effect to amount to an appropriation, should give rise to a claim under Art 1105 instead.[115] Unlike the position with Art 1110, the tribunal would then be able to take into account legitimate policy objectives in deciding whether or not there had been a violation of Art 1105.

7.6 Exceptions to Chapter Eleven obligations

Tribunals have stressed that public policy considerations can inform the analysis of provisions such as Arts 1102 and 1105 and lead to the finding that a measure based on legitimate grounds of environmental protection has not violated such provisions. However, the position is somewhat different with Art 1110. Its wording clearly mandates the payment of compensation for an expropriation notwithstanding that the measure in question is for a public purpose. Therefore, in a claim under Art 1110, arising out of a measure of environmental protection that amounts to an expropriation, it will be important to establish whether there are any exceptions, either in Chapter Eleven itself, or elsewhere in NAFTA, the respondent NAFTA party might rely on in such an eventuality.

7.6.1 Article 1114. Environmental measures

This provides:

1.   Nothing in this Chapter shall be construed to prevent a Party from adopting, maintaining or enforcing any measure *otherwise consistent with this Chapter* that it considers appropriate to ensure that

114 *Methanex v USA*, final award, 3 August 2005. Chapter IV D, para 7.
115 It was the context of Art 1105, that this point was raised in *Waste Management v Mexico (resubmitted claim)*, final award, 30 April 2004, para 98.

investment activity in its territory is undertaken in a manner *sensitive to environmental concerns*. (emphasis added).

2. The Parties recognize that it is inappropriate to encourage investment by relaxing domestic health, safety or environmental measures. Accordingly, a Party should not waive or otherwise derogate from, or offer to waive or otherwise derogate from, such measures as an encouragement for the establishment, acquisition, expansion or retention in its territory of an investment of an investor. If a Party considers that another Party has offered such an encouragement, it may request consultations with the other Party and the two Parties shall consult with a view to avoiding any such encouragement.

The highlighted words illustrate the potentially limited effect of the exception in para 1. First, there is the weakness of the wording 'sensitive to environmental concerns'. Secondly, the words 'otherwise consistent with this Chapter' subordinate the exception to the general principles of investor protection to be found in Chapter Eleven.[116] As the wording of Art 1110 specifies that expropriations can only be justified if they are both for a public purpose and accompanied by suitable compensation, it is likely that Art 1114.1 will not derogate from this. Article 1110.1 does not prevent a party from introducing an expropriatory measure 'to ensure that investment activity in its territory is undertaken in a manner sensitive to environmental concerns'. The reference to 'public purpose' clearly allows this, *provided* that compensation is paid to the investor.

This interpretation is tacitly borne out by the findings of the tribunal in *Metalclad v Mexico* – the only occasion on which Art 1114.1 has been considered in a Chapter Eleven award. The tribunal dealt briefly with the issue in the context of the claim under Art 1105 when it observed that the conclusion of the *Convenio* and the issuance of the federal permits showed that Mexico was satisfied that Metalclad's project was consistent with, and sensitive to, environmental concerns.[117] When the award came up for review, Judge Tysoe noted that:

> . . . although the Tribunal did not mention Article 1114(1) in connection with the Ecological Decree, it did comment on the Article earlier in the Award . . . In any event, any error by the Tribunal in this regard is not patently unreasonable.[118]

Significantly, Judge Tysoe made no reference to the tribunal's failure to

---

116 The wording here is similar to that in the *chapeau* of GATT, Art XX.
117 Paragraph 98.
118 Paragraph 104.

refer to the possible application of Art 1114.1 to the claim under Art 1110. This confirms the analysis stated above, that Art 1114.1 has no application to such claims. As regards Art 1114.2, this is not designed to act as an exception to Chapter Eleven, but rather as hortatory provision directed at preventing a 'race to the bottom' whereby the NAFTA parties compete for investment by relaxing environmental and public health measures. The only outcome contemplated by this provision is the establishment of 'consultations' in the event that one NAFTA party believes that another party is offering such inducements.

7.6.2 Article 1112

This provides that: 'In the event of any inconsistency between a provision of this Chapter and a provision of another Chapter, the provision of the other Chapter shall prevail to the extent of the inconsistency.' This might suggest that Chapter Eleven is subject to the sanitary and phyto-sanitary (SPS) provisions to be found in Chapter Seven and to the technical barriers to trade (TBT) provisions to be found in Chapter Nine, both of which are very similar to those found in the equivalent WTO agreements. However, for the same reasons given above in relation to Art 1114.1, it is likely that there would be no 'inconsistency' between a measure complying with Chapters Seven and Nine and an obligation to compensate under Art 1110, given the reference in the latter to a 'public purpose'.

The wording of these chapters is also such that it is unlikely that they apply to suits under Chapter Eleven in any event. Chapter Seven begins by stating that it 'applies to *trade* in agricultural goods and to sanitary and phytosanitary measures' (emphasis added). Chapter Nine begins as follows: 'This Chapter applies to any standards-related measure of a Party, other than those covered by Chapter Seven, Subchapter B (Sanitary and Phytosanitary Measures), that may, directly or indirectly, *affect trade in goods or services* between the Parties, and to measures of the Parties relating to such measures' (emphasis added). It is, therefore, likely that the effect of the emphasised words is such as to restrict Chapter Seven to disputes arising under Chapter Three, relating to trade, and to restrict Chapter Nine to disputes arising under Chapter Three and Chapter Twelve, which relates to the provision of cross-border services.[119]

---

119 Such an argument may, however, be inconsistent with the finding of the tribunal in *SD Myers v Canada* that a measure may give rise to proceedings under Chapter Eleven, as well as forming the basis of a potential state-to-state claim based on the violation of another NAFTA chapter.

7.6.3 Article 103

This reaffirms the parties' existing rights and obligations to each other under GATT whilst providing for the primacy of NAFTA in the event of inconsistency between the provisions of the two agreements. Article 2101, 'General Exceptions', then specifically incorporates GATT, Art XX and its interpretative notes into NAFTA for the purposes of Part Two (Trade in Goods), except to the extent that a provision of that part applies to services or investment, and Part Three (Technical Barriers to Trade), except to the extent that a provision of that part applies to services. On general principles of construction, therefore, the exceptions contained in GATT, Art XX would not appear to apply to claims brought under Chapter Eleven. Although the tribunal in *SD Myers v Canada* did apply an analysis similar to that brought to bear on Art XX by WTO panels, in assessing whether or not a measure was actually violative of Arts 1102 and 1105, it did not do so by reference to Art 2101, nor was such an analysis brought to bear on the claim under Art 1110. This is not surprising, given that Art 1110 mandates compensation even where an expropriation has been made for a 'public purpose'.

7.6.4 Article 104

This provides for the primacy of the CITES Convention 1973, the Montreal Convention 1987 in the event of any inconsistency between the specific trade obligations set out therein and the provisions of NAFTA. Similar provision is made as regards the Basel Convention 1989 'upon its entry into force for Canada, Mexico and the US'.[120] Article 104 goes on to provide that the obligations in these treaties shall prevail to the extent of inconsistency with NAFTA, subject to the proviso that 'where a Party has a choice among equally effective and reasonably available means of complying with such obligations, the Party chooses the means that is least inconsistent with the other provisions of this Agreement'. This wording invites an analysis of the 'measure' similar to that brought to bear on the *chapeau* to GATT, Art XX by panels in references under the WTO.

7.7 Quantum

Article 1110 explicitly subjects expropriation claims under Chapter Eleven to the full compensation standard of the 'Hull formula'. Paragraph 2 requires compensation to be 'equivalent to the fair market value of the expropriated investment immediately before the expropriation took place'. Further,

---

120 Thus in *SD Myers v Canada* Art 104 had no application because at the time the measure was introduced the US had not ratified the Basel Convention 1989.

compensation should not reflect any change in value 'occurring because the intended expropriation had become known earlier'. Valuation criteria are to include 'going concern value, asset value (including declared tax value of tangible property) and other criteria, as appropriate to determine fair market value'. Paragraph 3 then requires that compensation be paid without delay and is fully realisable.

However, where an investment has not had time to build up a track record before it is expropriated, it will be difficult for the tribunal to make any award in respect of future lost profits. In *Metalclad v Mexico*, the tribunal rejected Metalclad's claim for $90,000,000 calculated by reference to a discounted cash flow analysis of future profits so as to establish the fair market value of Coterin. Because the landfill had never been operative, it would be too speculative to assess its potential future profits by this method. A similar objection defeated the further claim for an extra $20 million to $25 million to cover the general negative impact the Coterin episode was said to have had on its overall business operations. Other unrelated factors may well have affected Metalclad's share price. Instead, the tribunal awarded Metalclad the costs of its investment, but reduced these to just under $17 million to take into account the following factors. First, costs incurred in 1991 and 1992 prior to 1993 in which Metalclad acquired Coterin should be discounted. Secondly, bundling costs, whereby Metalclad had aggregated its earlier costs in connection with other possible landfill sites in Mexico, should be discounted. Thirdly, account should be taken of remediation costs of the landfill site title to which would pass from Coterin to Mexico on payment of the award.

Where there is a breach of a provision of Chapter Eleven, other than Art 1110, NAFTA gives no guidance as to how compensation for breach of its provisions should be assessed, although Art 1135 (3) excludes the possible award of punitive damages. In *SD Myers v Canada*, the tribunal held that the 'fair market value' formula contained in Art 1110 would not always be appropriate for assessing damages for breaches of other provisions of Chapter Eleven, stating that:

> Expropriations that take place in accordance with the framework of Article 1110 – that is, expropriations that are conducted for a public purpose, on a non-discriminatory basis and in accordance with due process of law – are 'lawful' under Chapter 11 provided that compensation is paid in accordance with the . . . fair market value of the asset . . . formula. Under other provisions of Chapter 11, the liability of the host Party arises out of the fact that the government has done something that is contrary to the NAFTA and is 'unlawful' as between the disputing parties. The standard of compensation that an arbitral tribunal should apply may in some cases be influenced by the distinction between compensating for a lawful, as opposed to an unlawful, act. Fixing the fair market value

of an asset that is diminished in value may not fairly address the harm done to the investor.[121]

Instead, the tribunal turned for guidance to the *Chorzow Factory* decision, applying the principle of restitution that the PCIJ had stated as being applicable to unlawful takings. The enquiry under Chapter Eleven was more akin to that applied in assessing damages in tort or delict.[122] The aim was to put the innocent party in the position it would have been in had the measure not been passed.[123] Nothing in Chapter Eleven limited the recovery made by an investor to the losses it had actually sustained in the state imposing the measure. SDMI would, therefore, be entitled to recovery in respect of losses it had sustained in the US as a result of the closure of the border to PCB exports. In its subsequent award on damages the tribunal applied these principles, in a detailed analysis of the evidence as to what SDMI's position would have been had Canada not closed the US border when it did, and awarded it the substantial sum of $6,050,000.[124] However, the tribunal rejected, as too speculative, SDMI's additional claims for the loss of the chance to make profitable use of the profits that it would have received but for the border closure.

7.8 Recent US responses to NAFTA jurisprudence

In 2004, the US concluded Free Trade Agreements with Australia, Chile, Central America (CAFTA), Morocco and Singapore, all of which are based on the provisions of NAFTA. However, in response to concerns generated by the developing jurisprudence on Art 1110, they all contain an annex providing a shared understanding as regards the expropriation provisions.[125] It is stated that these are 'intended to reflect customary international law of States with respect to expropriation'. The shared understanding recognises that the expropriation provisions deal with two situations, direct and indirect expropriations. As regards the latter, it goes on to provide explicit criteria to decide 'where an action or series of actions by a Party has an effect equivalent to direct expropriation without formal transfer of title or outright seizure'. The shared understanding continues as follows:

   (a) The determination of whether an action or series of actions by a Party, in a specific fact situation, constitutes an indirect expropriation,

---

121 Final Award, para 308.
122 For this reason it was inappropriate to refer to the concept of foreseeability as it appears in the law of contract in relation to the assessment of which losses are too remote to be awarded by way of damages.
123 Paragraph 159.
124 *SD Myers v Canada*, damages award, 21 October 2002.
125 As does the US new model BIT.

requires a case-by-case, fact-based inquiry that considers, among other factors;

(i)   the economic impact of the government action, although the fact that an action or series of actions by a Party has an adverse effect on the economic value of an investment, standing alone, does not establish that an indirect expropriation has occurred;

(ii) the extent to which the government action interferes with distinct, reasonable, investment-backed expectations; and

(iii) the character of the government action.

(b) Except in rare circumstances, non-discriminatory regulatory actions by a Party that are designed and applied to protect legitimate public welfare objectives, such as public health, safety and the environment, do not constitute indirect expropriations.[126]

These provisions go a long way towards meeting concerns that the NAFTA jurisprudence has expanded the scope of expropriation beyond the norms of customary international law. Sub-heading (b) is particularly useful in reaffirming the rights of parties to regulate for legitimate public welfare objectives without triggering an obligation to compensate for an indirect expropriation. However, it is significant that this wording is limited to 'non-discriminatory' regulatory actions. A potential uncertainty exists as to what will constitute the 'rare circumstances' in which such regulation will mandate compensation. The shared understanding also contains useful clarification of the type of rights that are capable of being expropriated by providing that: 'An action or a series of actions by a Party cannot constitute an expropriation unless it interferes with a tangible or intangible property right or property interest in an investment.' Uncertainty remains as to which party's domestic law is to determine the issue of whether there has been a 'tangible or intangible property right or property interest' that has been interfered with.

7.9 Conclusion

NAFTA has now been in force for 13 years. Predictions that Chapter Eleven suits would act to 'chill' environmental regulation have not been borne out by the awards that have come out of the investor-state procedure. Tribunals have been at pains to stress their sensitivity to bona fide environmental

126 Cf. Canada's updated model Foreign Investment Promotion and Protection Agreement (FIPA) which 'incorporates a clarification of indirect expropriation which provides that, 'except in rare circumstances, non-discriminatory measures designed and applied to protect legitimate public welfare objectives, such as health, safety and the environment, do not constitute indirect expropriation and are not subject, therefore, to any compensation requirements'.

measures. In deciding whether a measure has violated a provision of Chapter Eleven, tribunals have taken pains to take into consideration any legitimate policy considerations behind a measure that has an adverse impact on the investor of another NAFTA party. The 'effects-based' analysis of Art 1106, argued for by the investor in *Ethyl Corp v Canada*, was rejected by the tribunal in *Pope & Talbot*. In the same award, the tribunal emphasised that its analysis of Art 1105 did not entitle it to 'substitute its judgment on the choice of solutions [as regards the "stumpage dispute" under the Softwood Lumber Agreement] for Canada's, unless that choice can be found to be a denial of fair and equitable treatment'. In *SD Myers v Canada*, the tribunal took pains to show how legitimate environmental concerns would inform the issue of whether or not a foreign investor was in 'like circumstances' with a domestic comparator. In *Methanex v USA*, the tribunal took a similar approach and rejected the argument that 'like circumstances' be construed in accordance with the trade law jurisprudence that had emerged from Art III of GATT which uses rather different wording with regard to the issue of 'likeness'.

A potential problem, however, still exists in relation to Art 1110, given the requirement that even a lawful expropriation, for a public purpose, still requires payment of compensation. Of course, this merely restates the position under customary international law, and the first enquiry should be whether the Chapter Eleven jurisprudence has gone beyond the norms of customary international law on expropriation. To do this, one must analyse the factors, referred to by tribunals in the Chapter Eleven awards discussed above, as being determinative of whether a measure falls under Art 1110.

First, there must be a substantial interference with the economic use of the investment. If all that has occurred is that there has been a reduction in the profitability of the investment, there can be no claim under Art 1110, although, as in *SD Myers v Canada* a claim may still succeed under other provisions of Chapter Eleven, such as Arts 1102 and 1105. The interference must generally be permanent. However, as the tribunal observed in *SD Myers v Canada*, a temporary interference of sufficiently long duration may amount to expropriation.

Secondly, the measure must interfere with the investor's reasonable expectations. The investor will have to accept the regulatory structure in force at the time the investment is made. The issue will then be whether subsequent changes to that structure amount to an 'unfair surprise' so as to constitute an expropriation. If the area in which the investment is made is already highly regulated, the investor may reasonably anticipate further regulation, including regulation which ultimately prevents it from making further economic use of its investment. In theory, such regulation should not give rise to a claim under Art 1110. A tribunal would be able to find that the regulation did not constitute an expropriation or a measure tantamount to an expropriation because the expectation of a future worsening in the regulatory environment would outweigh the severity of a measure's effect on the investor. In practice, much would depend on the advance notice given to the investor before such regulation came into force.

Thirdly, the discriminatory intent of a measure may also be taken into account, although it is not entirely clear whether non-discriminatory measures that have an unexpected and drastic effect upon an investment may nonetheless form the basis of a claim under Art 1110. It is likely that the intent behind a measure is not so much related to any 'police powers' exception, but rather to the question of whether a particular measure amounts to an 'unfair surprise' and frustrates the legitimate expectations of the investor. The discriminatory nature of the measure is also a factor to be taken into account in determining whether a measure is one 'relating to' an investor who is indirectly affected thereby.

Fourthly, a measure which benefits the state at the expense of the investor is more likely to be regarded as expropriatory than one which involves no such transfer of benefit. However, expropriation may still occur even in the absence of such a transfer of benefit. Such a finding is also possible under the norms of customary international law, as evidenced by the partial award in *CME v Czech Republic*.

Fifthly, the fact that property is expropriated for a public purpose does not absolve a party from the obligation to compensate. This follows naturally from the language of Art 1110 itself and is also consistent with the position under international law, as set out in *Cia del Desarollo de Santa Elena SA v Republic of Costa Rica*.[127]

Sixthly, measures that have only an indirect, consequential, effect on an investor will not, in the absence of proof of discriminatory intent, form the basis of a Chapter Eleven claim for they will not constitute measures 'relating to' the investor or the investment. The finding of the *Methanex* tribunal in this respect will screen out most cases where loss is sustained due to a party's omissions. Again, this is paralleled by the decisions in *Olguin* and *Sea-Lands*.

All of these factors have featured in the process determining the norms of expropriation under customary international law as well as the norms applicable to claims for deprivation of possessions' under Art 1 of the First Protocol of the European Convention on Human Rights. It would therefore seem that the tribunal in *Pope and Talbot* was correct in its observation that Art 1110, in particular its reference to measures 'tantamount to expropriation', did not intend to go beyond what constituted expropriation under customary international law. Although, the tribunal's formulation in *Metalclad* appears to go beyond these limits, covering regulatory takings that would not form

---

127 However, the references in the *Tecmed* award to the European Convention on Human Rights jurisprudence on 'proportionality' in assessing claims for breach of First Protocol, Art 1 of the Convention, suggest that at international law the motive behind a measure and the manner of its implementation are both factors to be taken into account in considering whether or not a measure amounts to a compensable expropriation.

the basis of an expropriation claim under customary international law, it should be recalled that on the facts both the measures in question had the effect of depriving the investor permanently of any future economic use of its landfill site.

However, the problem with Chapter Eleven and claims for expropriation lies with its wide definition of 'investor' and 'investments' in Art 1139. It is this which has the capacity to expand the scope of a claim under Art 1110 beyond the bounds of what would constitute an expropriation under customary international law. First, the definitions in Art 1139 of investment, particularly the reference to 'indirect' control of an enterprise, allow investors to bring claims in situations where there might be a lack of jurisdiction in state-to-state claims under the rule in *Barcelona Traction*. Secondly, claims may be made in respect of loss of goodwill or denial of market access, of the sort which were denied in the *Oscar Chinn* case.

Once market access is treated a distinct category of property, though, it becomes far easier to categorise regulatory interference as amounting to an expropriation. Imagine, for instance, a Chapter Eleven claim based on facts similar to those in *Pinnacle v United Kingdom*, but where the party affected was a foreign, rather than a domestic, investor. The foreign investor might very well succeed in claiming in respect of an expropriation under Art 1110, even though there would have been no 'property' capable of taking so as to support a state-to-state claim for expropriation under customary international law. Once the right to make a living by de-boning cattle heads is capable of being viewed as an investment, the measures preventing the continuance of this occupation can now be regarded as 'tantamount to expropriation'. Article 1110 would then mandate compensation, no matter that the measure was non-discriminatory and motivated by the most urgent considerations of public health protection. The only limiting factor in this process is the interpretation of the words 'relating to' in Art 1101 adopted in *Methanex*, which would generally preclude a claim being brought by downstream suppliers who were indirectly affected by the measure.[128]

In contrast, legitimate public welfare considerations may be taken into account in assessing whether the same measure would entail a violation of the national treatment obligation of Art 1102 or the minimum standards obligations to be found in Art 1105. In deciding this question the tribunal in *SD Myers v Canada* found it legitimate to take account of factors similar to those which determine the application of the exceptions to be found in GATT, Art XX. However, once 'market access' is treated as an 'investment', it becomes

---

128 If this initial NAFTA analysis of 'investor' and 'investment' were brought to bear on claims under European Convention on Human Rights, First Protocol, Art 1, many instances of regulatory interference would be shifted from the 'control of use' category to that of 'deprivation of possessions', for which compensation would generally be required.

increasingly likely that trade restrictions will generate investor-state suits under Chapter Eleven. Trade disputes will, therefore, no longer remain under the control of the NAFTA state parties. The decision in *SD Myers v Canada* makes it clear that the existence of state-to-state arbitration under Chapter Twenty does not preclude trade restrictions generating parallel proceedings under Chapter Eleven of the restriction has an effect on an investment or investor. This may well lead to different results arising in parallel arbitrations under Chapter Eleven and Chapter Twenty, or under the WTO dispute settlement procedure. The measure might fall within the scope of NAFTA, Chapter Seven, which deals with SPS measures, and yet a claim for expropriation might still succeed under Art 1110 due to the lack of any equivalent exception based on public welfare considerations in respect of expropriations.

Chapter 8

Multinational corporations and environmental liability (1). US litigation: jurisdictional issues

Since the Bhopal gas explosion of the night of 2/3 December 1984, an increasing number of claims have been brought against multinational corporations in respect of environmental damage caused by the activities of their subsidiaries in the developing world.[1] The Bhopal explosion itself gave rise to litigation before the federal court in New York and then before the courts in India. Although the claims were settled in 1989 a fresh batch of litigation is still proceeding through the federal court in New York. The same court has also been faced with claims against a New York parent corporation in respect of pollution in Ecuador from an oil pipeline operated by a consortium in which its fourth level subsidiary was a participant.[2] Claims have been brought in Australia arising out of pollution caused by the collapse of a tailings dam in a copper mine in Papua New Guinea,[3] in Quebec, following the rupture of a dam of the effluent treatment plant of a gold mine in Guyana,[4] and in the UK, in respect of death and personal injury claims by employees of overseas subsidiaries of parent companies based in England.[5] Such claims raise difficult issues as to the applicable principles of tort law that govern the responsibility of a parent corporation for the acts or omissions of its subsidiary.

---

1 See, generally, Joseph, S, *Corporations and Transnational Human Rights Litigation*, 2004, Oxford: Hart Publishing; Tromans, S, 'Multinational Companies and Environmental Liability', *International Business Lawyer*, November 1998; Ward, H, 'Governing Multinationals. The Role of Foreign Direct Liability', Royal Institute of International Affairs Briefing Paper February 2001, www.eldis.org/static/DOC8831.htm (accessed 4 April 2007); Blumberg, P, 'Asserting Human Rights Against Multinational Corporations under United States Law' (2002) 50 American Journal of Comparative Law 493; Anderson, M, 'Transnational Corporations and Environmental Damage: Is Tort Law the Answer' (2002) 41 Washburn Law Journal 399.
2 *Aguinda v Texaco Inc* 142 F Supp 2d 534 (SDNY 2001).
3 *Dagi v BHP (No 2)* [1997] 1 VR 428. See, also, Prince, P, 'Bhopal, Bougainville and OK Tedi: Why Australia's *Forum Non Conveniens* Approach is Better' (1998) 47 ICLQ 573.
4 *Recherches Internationales Quebec v Cambior Inc* [1998] QJ No 2554, 14 August 1998.
5 *Connelly v RTZ Corporation plc and Ritz Overseas Ltd* [1998] AC 854 and *Lubbe v Cape Industries plc* [2001] Lloyd's Rep 383.

The activities of multinational corporations abroad have given also given rise to US litigation based on alleged complicity in human rights abuses committed by foreign governments in connection with projects involving the multinational corporation. This litigation has generally been pursued through the federal courts, using the Alien Tort Claims Act 1789 (ATCA).[6] This category is epitomised by the ATCA litigation against Unocal in the federal courts in respect of its involvement in the Yadana oil pipeline project in Myanmar in the 1990s. The claim arose out of Unocal's alleged complicity in human rights abuses by the Myanmar military committed during the course of the project. These abuses generated a parallel tort claim in the state courts of California. As well as raising issues as the principles that determine the responsibility of a parent corporation for the acts or omissions of its subsidiary, these claims raise the additional problem of linking the subsidiary with the human rights abuses that have been committed by the foreign government with whom it was engaged in a joint venture.

However, what is remarkable about this history of litigation against multi-national corporations is the almost total absence of any decision on the merits of the claims. Instead, the battleground has been jurisdictional. The typical pattern is that the foreign claimant commences proceedings in the parent corporation's jurisdiction. The parent corporation then seeks to stay the proceedings on the grounds of *forum non conveniens*. After these proceedings the claim is usually settled.[7] This is well illustrated by 'Forum non Conveniens in America and England: "A rather fantastic fiction"',[8] in which Professor David Robertson of the University of Texas School of Law attempted to discover the subsequent history of each reported transnational case dismissed under *forum non conveniens* from *Gulf Oil v Gilbert* in 1946 to the end of 1984. He found that less than 4 per cent of cases dismissed under the doctrine of *forum non conveniens* ever reach trial in a foreign court. Data was received on 55 personal injury cases and 30 commercial cases. Only one of the personal injury cases and two of the commercial cases actually reached trial in a foreign court.

First, however, it is important to establish why claimants in these cases choose to proceed in the jurisdiction in which the parent company is located rather than having recourse to the courts of the jurisdiction in which the harm occurred. The obvious advantages of what is sometimes referred to as 'forum shopping' are the obtaining of a more favourable legal environment as regards key procedural matters such as discovery; the likelihood of obtaining a higher award of damages (particularly if the case comes before a US jury) than would be the case where the claim to be heard in the courts of the

---

6   ATCA is sometimes referred to as the Alien Tort Statute (ATS).
7   If the claim is not stayed, the settlement is likely to be larger.
8   (1987) 103 LQR 398, p 419.

claimant's home jurisdiction. Thus, in the *Bhopal* case, the assets of the subsidiary, UCIL, at the time of the litigation were estimated to be no more than $39 million, which would clearly be inadequate for the purpose of meeting any judgment against it given the likely size of any ultimate award of damages.[9] In contrast, the parent, Union Carbide, was estimated to hold some $200 million of liability cover[10] and assets of $500 million realised from its recent restructuring.[11]

However, the perjorative epithet of 'forum shopping' overlooks one reason why it is imperative that such claims be brought in the foreign forum if the claimant is to make *any* recovery at all. Usually, the foreign subsidiary will have insufficient assets to meet any eventual judgment in full. The claimant must therefore direct its fire at the parent company which in most cases will have sufficiently deep pockets to satisfy any judgment in full. Proceeding against the parent company in the foreign jurisdiction, though, entails the very real risk that such a judgment would be ultimately unenforceable. Under the general principles of private international law, for such a judgment to be enforceable, the defendant would have had to have submitted to the jurisdiction of the foreign court. Alternatively, it would have had to be 'present' in the jurisdiction at the time the proceedings were started. Unless and until the parent corporation agrees to submit to the jurisdiction of the claimant's home jurisdiction, the claimant has no alternative but to commence proceedings before the courts of the parent's jurisdiction.

8.1 Establishing jurisdiction over the defendant

The first hurdle for the plaintiff will be in bringing suit against the defendant in one of the state or federal courts of the US. 'Transitory' tort claims, that is, claims involving torts committed outside the US, may be brought before the state courts, provided the actions impugned would constitute a tort in the foreign state. Alternatively, 28 USC, s 1332 allows claims to be brought before the federal courts in 'diversity cases'. These are claims involving 'controversies between ... citizens of different states' where the amount claimed exceeds $75,000.[12] The law applied in a diversity case is the law of the state in which the action was filed.[13] Claims under ATCA may be brought only in the federal courts, although this does not preclude bringing a parallel claim on the same facts, but pleaded in tort, before a state court. This dual approach was adopted by the plaintiffs in the Unocal litigation.

---

9 'India to speed up Bhopal claim', *The Guardian*, 14 May 1968.
10 'Union Carbide agrees tentative Bhopal deal', *Financial Times*, 24 March 1986.
11 *The Times*, 22 January 1986, p 17.
12 Diversity jurisdiction will not exist where one or more of the co-plaintiffs is a US citizen, nor will it exist where the plaintiffs are stateless.
13 *Erie Railroad Co v Tompkins* 304 US 64, 58 SCt 817, 82 L Ed 1188 (1938).

The defendant must also be served in accordance with the requirements of 'due process' stipulated in the Fifth and Fourteenth Amendments of the US Constitution. Service may be based on the defendant's presence within the jurisdiction, its domicile within the jurisdiction, or its consent to the service of proceedings. Where none of these requirements is satisfied, the defendant may be served if dealings or affiliations with the forum jurisdiction which make it reasonable to require it to defend a lawsuit there.

In *International Shoe Co v Washington*,[14] the Supreme Court set out four principles to assess whether or not there existed minimum contacts to justify subjecting the defendant to the jurisdiction of the forum. First, jurisdiction is permissible when the defendant's activity in the forum is continuous and systematic and the cause of action is related to that activity. Secondly, sporadic or casual activity of the defendant in the forum does not justify assertion of jurisdiction on a cause of action unrelated to that forum activity. Thirdly, a court may assert jurisdiction over a defendant whose continuous activities in the forum are unrelated to the cause of action sued upon when the defendant's contacts are sufficiently substantial and of such a nature as to make the state's assertion of jurisdiction reasonable. This is known as 'general jurisdiction'. Fourthly, even a defendant whose activity in the forum is sporadic, or consists only of a single act, may be subject to the jurisdiction of the forum's courts when the cause of action arises out of that activity or act. This is known as 'specific jurisdiction'.[15]

These principles have been considered in two cases involving claims under ATCA 1789. In 1998, in *Unocal (1998)*,[16] Paez J heard a challenge to jurisdiction brought by the defendant Total SA, a French corporation that was part of the consortium involved in the Yadana project. Total SA had been served under California's long-arm statute on jurisdiction in respect of the plaintiffs' claim under ATCA 1789. The service of proceedings, however, had not conformed to the requirements of due process. Total SA had no direct contacts with the US beyond the listing its stock on various exchanges and promoting sales of stock in the US. Nor were its indirect contacts sufficient to warrant service under California's long-arm statute on jurisdiction. Its contract with Unocal, a Californian corporation, was an insufficient basis for specific jurisdiction. Those contracts were made out of the jurisdiction, and were subject to the laws of England, Bermuda or Myanmar. The oil from the Yadana project would not go to the US and Unocal's presence was not an essential element to enable the project to go ahead. Total was far from

---

14 *International Shoe Co v Washington* 326 US 310, 66 SCt 154, 90 L Ed 95 (1945).

15 Dismissal for lack of personal jurisdiction falls under Fed R Civ P 12(b)(2), under which the plaintiff bears the burden of establishing a prima facie case that the court has personal jurisdiction over a defendant.

16 *Unocal (1998)*. 27 F Supp 2d 1174 (CD Cal). Affd 248 F 3d 915 (9th Cir 2001).

under-capitalised and had agreed to take on the Yadana project before seeking bids from potential partners.

Nor could due process as regards 'general jurisdiction' be established through the presence in California of Total's subsidiary corporations. These could not be treated as Total's alter egos. Total was an active parent corporation involved directly in decision-making about its subsidiaries' holdings, but its control was not so extensive as to render the subsidiaries 'mere instrumentalities'. Neither could the subsidiaries be regarded as Total's agents. A finding of agency for this purpose, as opposed to a finding of agency in the context of a parent company's substantive liability for the acts of its subsidiaries, was subject to the following test. Had the subsidiary performed services that were sufficiently important to the parent corporation that, without the subsidiary, the parent's own officials would have had to perform substantially similar services? Paez J found that there was no evidence to support such a conclusion. The inclusion of information of facts about Total's subsidiaries in Total's annual reports was immaterial as consolidation of the activities of a subsidiary into the parent's reports was a common business practice.

A contrasting result was reached in *Wiwa*.[17] The ATCA claim alleged that Shell Nigeria, under the direction of the defendants, Royal Dutch, a Netherlands corporation, and Shell Transport, an English holding company, had instigated, orchestrated, planned and facilitated human rights abuses by the Nigerian Government in suppressing opposition to oil exploration and development in the Ogoni region. The validity of service on the defendants depended on whether the defendants had been 'present' in New York through their Investment Relations Office (IRO) which was run by Mr Grapsi. Unlike Paez J in *Unocal 1998*, the circuit court for the Second Circuit held that the IRO's activities in the jurisdiction had been sufficiently important to justify a finding of agency.[18] Both Mr Grapsi and the IRO, while nominally part of Shell Oil, devoted all their time to the business of the defendants who also fully funded the IRO to the tune of $500,000 per annum. Although the IRO was not directly involved with the core functions of the defendants' business – the operation of an integrated international oil business – its work in maintaining good relationships with existing and potential investors was of meaningful importance. New York, as the site of the most important US stock market, was the obvious place to conduct these activities. The IRO's services went beyond activities necessary to maintain a listing on the New York Stock Exchange and involved their expenditure of substantial sums of money in cultivating the defendants' relationship with the New York capital markets.

---

17 *Wiwa v Royal Dutch Petroleum Co* 226 F 3d 88 (2d Cir 2000).
18 See, also, *Presbyterian Church of Sudan v Talisman Energy* 244 F Supp 2d 289 (SDNY 2003) (*Talisman*). A similar analysis was applied here by Schwarz J, in finding that the Canadian defendant could be served in New York because of significant operations conducted for it there by its wholly owned subsidiary.

The defendants' contacts with New York were, therefore, more than minimal and they would not be greatly inconvenienced in being required to litigate in New York.

8.2 Forum non conveniens

Once a plaintiff has managed to commence proceedings against the defendant in a US forum, it faces the prospect of the defendant applying for the case to be dismissed on grounds of *forum non conveniens*. In 1946, the Supreme Court in *Gulf Oil Corp v Gilbert* set out the principles that should be applied to the issue of *forum non conveniens* in federal courts.[19] These principles are also generally applied in the state courts.[20] After the defendant has established that there exists an adequate alternative forum, the court should then undertake a balancing exercise involving two factors. First there are the private interests of litigants, principally the ease and cost of access to documents and witnesses. In most litigation against multinational parent corporations, these factors will weigh heavily in favour of dismissal of the suit. Secondly, there are the public interest factors, such as the interest of the forum state, the burden on the courts, and notions of judicial comity.

In 1981, in *Piper Aircraft v Reyno*,[21] these principles were applied for the first time to a claim involving foreign plaintiffs and where the wrong complained of had occurred outside the US. The court added a gloss to the *Gilbert* principles by suggesting that little deference should be given to the plaintiff's choice of forum in a US court in such circumstances. In *Wiwa*, the circuit court for the Second Circuit noted that: 'While any plaintiff's selection of a forum is entitled to deference, that deference increases as the plaintiff's ties to the forum increase.' This was because '. . . the greater the plaintiff's ties to the plaintiff's chosen forum, the more likely it is that the plaintiff would be inconvenienced by a requirement to bring the claim in a foreign jurisdiction'. For these purposes, the plaintiffs only needed to be US residents, and did not also have to be resident in the Southern District of New York where they had filed suit.[22]

Forum non conveniens operates whether the claim be based on principles of tort law or on ATCA. In *Wiwa*, the circuit court reversed the district court's dismissal on grounds of *forum non conveniens* in favour of the courts of the

---

19 *Gulf Oil Corp v Gilbert* 330 US 501, pp 508–9, 67 SCt 839, pp 843–4, 91 L Ed 1055 (1947).
20 However, this has not invariably been the case. In *Dow Chemicals v Castro Alfaro* (1990) 786 SW 2d 674, the Supreme Court of Texas held that *forum non conveniens* formed no part of the law of Texas. Legislation was subsequently introduced to reverse this position.
21 *Piper Aircraft v Reyno* 454 US 235 (1981).
22 A foreign plaintiff will be treated in the same way where there is a treaty between the US and the country of the foreign plaintiff which accords its nationals access to US courts equivalent to that provided to US citizens. ATCA claims may also be treated in the same way.

UK and remanded the case to the district court for a more careful examination of the *forum non conveniens* factors. It stated that in passing the Torture Victims Protection Act 1991 (TVPA) 'Congress has expressed a policy of US law favoring the adjudication of such suits in US courts'. However, TVPA has not nullified 'or even significantly diminished' the doctrine of *forum non conveniens*:

> The statute has, however, communicated a policy that such suits should not be facilely dismissed on the assumption that the ostensibly foreign controversy is not our business. The TVPA in our view expresses a policy favoring our courts' exercise of the jurisdiction conferred by the ATCA in cases of torture unless the defendant has fully met the burden of showing that the *Gilbert* factors tilt strongly in favour of trial in the foreign forum.[23]

Subsequently, in both *Flores v SPCC*[24] and *Aguinda v Texaco Inc*,[25] it has been held that ATCA claims enjoy no special immunity from the effects of the doctrine. The statement in *Wiwa* is really no more than a caution against 'facile' dismissals on the ground of the foreign nature of the controversy and a reminder that where torture is involved, the US does have a public interest in hearing the case. However, that interest is still capable of being outweighed by other factors in the case that point to the dismissal of the case in favour of the courts of the alternative. The circuit court then added that the issue of *forum non conveniens* was not settled by 'adding to the mix' the failure of the district court to take into account the US residence of two of the plaintiffs and the interests of the US in hearing claims based on allegations of torture, given the enactment of the TVPA.

> If the defendant advanced substantial interests supporting dismissal in favor of a British forum we would either remand to the District Court for reconsideration, or, if the defendant's interests were sufficiently substantial, sustain the dismissal notwithstanding our identification of interests in favor of retention that the District Court did not consider.

8.2.1 Identifying an available alternative forum

Before the court begins to weigh the private and public interests in favour of dismissal, it must first be satisfied of the adequacy of the courts in the alternative forum. This will usually be the place of the plaintiff's residence, or the place where the wrong was committed. In *Bank of Credit and Commerce*

---

23 *Wiwa v Royal Dutch Petroleum Co* 226 F 3d 88 (2d Cir 2000) 106.
24 *Flores v SPCC* 253 F Supp 2d 510 (SDNY 2002), 343 F 3d 140 (2d Cir 2003).
25 *Aguinda v Texaco Inc* 142 F Supp 2D 534 (SDNY 2001) (*Aguinda (2001)*).

International (Overseas) Ltd v State Bank of Pakistan,[26] it was said that an alternative forum is generally regarded as adequate when: (1) the defendant is subject to the service of process there; and (2) the forum permits litigation of the subject matter of the dispute. Claims by the plaintiffs that they will face financial hardship by having to litigate in the alternative forum do not bear on the issue of adequacy, but, rather, are taken into account at the stage at which the court balances the private and public interests in connection with the retention of the suit.[27]

As regards the first requirement, a stay will only be granted where the defendant agrees to accept the jurisdiction of the alternative forum, although it can delay giving such agreement to the time of the hearing. This was one of the conditions which Judge Keenan attached to the stay of the New York proceedings arising out of the Bhopal disaster in *In re Union Carbide Corp Gas Plant Disaster at Bhopal (Union Carbide)*.[28] In 1987, the circuit court upheld Judge Keenan's stay but lifted the last two conditions.[29] In *Aguinda v Texaco*, though, Judge Rakoff stayed proceedings brought against Texaco in New York without requiring Texaco to accept service of proceedings in Ecuador, the alternative forum.[30] The circuit court then vacated and remanded. Ecuador could not be an alternative forum because the defendant had not submitted to its jurisdiction.[31]

As regards the second requirement, there are various reasons why a claim may not be litigated in the alternative forum. The first is that the type of claim brought before the US forum would not be cognisable in the alternative forum. In *Sarei v Rio Tinto*,[32] Morrow J held that Australia was not an adequate forum because the ATCA claims were not cognisable there, in that the Australian courts did not recognise independent tort claims based on violations of customary international law. In *Presbyterian Church of Sudan v Talisman Energy (Talisman)*,[33] Schwarz J rejected the notion that Sudan was an adequate alternative for claims arising out of the alleged complicity of a Canadian defendant corporation in the genocidal activities of Sudan's Islamic government against its non-Islamic population in the south of the country, where its oil reserves were located. The plaintiffs were also able to

---

26 *Bank of Credit and Commerce International (Overseas) Ltd v State Bank of Pakistan* 273 F 3d 242, p 246 (2d Cir 2001).

27 *Murray v British Broadcasting Corp* 81 F 3d 287, pp 292–3 (2d Cir 1996).

28 *In re Union Carbide Corp Gas Plant Disaster* F Supp 842, 809 F 2D 195 (2d Cir 1987) (SDNY 1986) (*Union Carbide*).

29 Judge Keenan also required that Union Carbide agree to honour the judgment of the Indian courts, and to use US discovery rules in the Indian proceedings. In 1987 the circuit court upheld Judge Keenan's stay but lifted these two conditions: 809 F 2d 195 (2d Cir 1987).

30 *Aguinda v Texaco* 945 F Supp 625 (SDNY 1996).

31 *Jota v Texaco* 157 F 3d 153 (2d Cir 1998).

32 *Sarei v Rio Tinto* 221 F Supp 2d 1116 (CDCal).

33 *Presbyterian Church of Sudan v Talisman Energy* 244 F Supp 2d 289 (SDNY 2003) (*Talisman*).

produce evidence showing the system of Islamic law in place in Sudan accorded greatly reduced legal rights to non-Muslims.[34] However, it is not necessary that the claim be pleaded in exactly the same way in the alternative forum, for otherwise a case based on US common law principles could never be dismissed in favour of the courts of a civil law jurisdiction. In *Flores v SPCC*,[35] Peru was held to be an alternative forum, even though its courts did not award punitive damages.

A claim may also be rendered non-cognisable by 'retaliatory legislation' introduced in the alternative forum with the specific intent of rendering that forum no longer available. This occurred in *Martinez v Dow Chemicals*.[36] The plaintiffs were agricultural workers in several different countries who claimed in respect of injuries sustained as a result of exposure to a pesticide manufactured by the defendants. Their claims before a Texas court were dismissed for *forum non conveniens*. They then attempted to recommence suit in Costa Rica, Honduras and the Philippines but found that retaliatory legislation had the effect of preventing their claims being heard there, given their decision to file suit first in the US. Barbier J held that in such circumstances their claims should not be dismissed on grounds of *forum non conveniens*. This issue also came before Judge Rakoff in *Aguinda (2001)*, where he was faced with Ecuador's Law 55. This had been introduced in 1998 in an attempt to block off a *forum non conveniens* challenge by depriving the plaintiffs of a right of suit in Ecuador as a result of their election to proceed in New York. Judge Rakoff thought it unlikely that Law 55 would be applied to a suit commenced before it came into force but imposed a condition on the stay that would allow the New York proceedings to be resumed if a court of last review in Ecuador did subsequently prevent the plaintiffs from bringing their claims in Ecuador due to the operation of Law 55. A few months before the US circuit court for the Second Circuit upheld Judge Rakoff's dismissal of the suits, on 16 August 2002, Law 55 was to be declared unconstitutional by the Ecuadorian Constitutional Court.

A foreign forum will not be an available alternative jurisdiction if the plaintiff can show that corruption in the courts there is so pervasive that it will prove practically impossible for the claim to be litigated there. Since *Bridgeway Corp v Citibank*,[37] plaintiffs have been allowed to rely on US State Department Country Reports as evidence of this issue. However, the court is not bound to rely on these reports and in two cases has concluded that the courts of the foreign jurisdiction do constitute an available alternative forum.

---

34 Schwarz J also doubted whether Canada could be regarded as an alternative forum given that there seemed no possibility of an action there being based on violations of the law of nations.
35 *Flores v SPCC* 253 F Supp 2d 510 (SDNY 2002), 343 F 3d 140 (2d Cir 2003).
36 *Martinez v Dow Chemicals* 219 F Supp 2d 719 (ED La 2002).
37 *Bridgeway Corp v Citibank* 201 F 3d 134 (2d Cir 2000).

In *Aguinda (2001)*, the plaintiffs referred to the State Department reports on Ecuador for 1999 and 2000 which had described Ecuador's legal and judicial systems as 'politicized, inefficient and sometimes corrupt' as regards 'human rights practices'. Judge Rakoff, however, noted that these conclusions did not relate to claims for environmental pollution, like the one before the court. The plaintiffs' claims were the subject of intense public scrutiny and political debate in Ecuador and he concluded that Ecuador was an available alternative forum in which they could be heard.[38] As regards the financial hardships faced by a plaintiff in an alternative jurisdiction, it was noted in *Murray v British Broadcasting Corp*[39] that the authorities were divided on whether this would cause that forum to be deemed unavailable. However, the court agreed with the majority view that this factor did not go to the issue of the availability of an alternative forum, but was merely one of the factors to be taken into account in determining the balance of convenience between that forum and the US forum. This approach has been followed as regards ATCA claims in both *Aguinda (2001)* and *Sarei v Rio Tinto* in which the absence of a class action procedure was held not to render an alternative forum unavailable.

8.2.2 Balancing the private interest and public interest factors

Having established that there exists an adequate alternative forum, the court will now proceed to weigh the private and public interests in favour of retaining or vacating the suit in the US jurisdiction. Under *Gulf Oil Corp v Gilbert*,[40] the 'private interest' factors include the relative ease of access to sources of proof; the cost of obtaining the attendance of willing witnesses; the availability of compulsory process for obtaining attendance of unwilling witnesses; the possibility of viewing the relevant premises, and other such practical concerns. However, in most environmental suits against a multinational corporation, these factors will weigh heavily against the retention of the suit, even if the plaintiff's choice of US forum is not subject to the 'lesser deference' discount set out in *Piper Aircraft v Reyno*.

As regards the public interest factors, the Supreme Court in *Piper Aircraft v Reyno* synthesised the *Gulf Oil Corp v Gilbert* factors as follows: the local interest in having localised controversies decided at home; the interest in having the trial of a diversity case in a forum that is at home with the law that must govern the action; the avoidance of unnecessary problems in conflicts of

---

38 A similar conclusion on this issue was reached in *Flores v SPCC* 253 F Supp 2d 510 (SDNY 2002), 343 F 3d 140 (2d Cir 2003), in which reliance was placed on those affidavits that showed how the judicial system in Peru had improved since President Fujimori left power in November 2000.

39 *Murray v British Broadcasting Corp* 81 F 3d 287, p 292 (2d Cir 1996).

40 *Gulf Oil Corp v Gilbert* 330 US 501, p 508, 67 SCt 839 (1947).

law or in the application of foreign law; and the unfairness of burdening citizens in an unrelated jurisdiction with jury duty. In considering these factors the court would need to strike a balance between the interests of the home and host states. In the two major cases arising solely out of environmental harm, the interests of the host state in regulating activity within its jurisdiction has been held to outweigh the interest of the US as the home state. However, these competing interests are likely to be weighed differently where the claim involves alleged complicity of a subsidiary corporation in human rights abuses by a foreign government.

8.2.3 Forum non conveniens and environmental claims

The first, and most notorious claim, is that arising out of the Bhopal disaster. In *Union Carbide*, Judge Keenan dismissed the suit on the grounds of *forum non conveniens*. The suit had an overwhelming connection with India.[41] Most of the material witnesses and documentation were situated in India, and not the US. This was also the case as regards most of the documents bearing on the design, safety, start-up and operation of the plant, as well as the safety training of the plant's employees. Much of this documentation would require translation from Hindi or other Indian languages, and would require translation before a US court. Similar language problems would also exist as regards the majority of witnesses. There would be considerable transportation costs if the parties attempted to bring hundreds of Indian witnesses to the US, whereas there were only a few US witnesses, most of them Union Carbide employees. An Indian court would also be in a better position to direct and supervise a viewing of the Bhopal plant, which was sealed after the accident.

In contrast, Judge Keenan found that the suit had very little connection with the US. Union Carbide's participation in the design, construction and operation of the plant was limited. Any involvement it may have had in plant operations had ended long before the accident. In 1973, under agreements negotiated at arm's length with its subsidiary, UCIL, Union Carbide had provided a 'process design package' for constructing the plant. Although some of its technicians had also been used to monitor the progress of UCIL in detailing the design and erecting the plant, the terms of the agreements, which were controlled by the Indian Government, prevented Union Carbide from exercising any authority to 'detail design, erect and commission the plant'. Instead, this was done independently between 1972 and 1980 by a team of Indian engineers, acting under the supervision of UCIL. The vital parts of the Bhopal plant, including its storage tank, monitoring instrumentation, and vent gas scrubber, were manufactured by Indians in India. Some 40 UCIL employees received safety training at UCC's plant in West

---

41 *In re Union Carbide Corp Gas Plant Disaster* (*Union Carbide*) F Supp 842, 809 F 2D 195 (2d Cir 1987) (SDNY 1986).

Virginia, but these constituted only a small fraction of those employed at the plant. Between 1980 and 1984, more than 1,000 Indians were employed at the plant, but only one American was employed there, until 1982. No Americans visited the plant for more than one year prior to the accident, and during the five-year period before the accident the communications between the plant and the US were almost non-existent.

The public interest factors also weighed heavily in favour of trial in India, as that was where the accident and the relevant events had taken place. The victims, over 200,000 in number, were almost entirely Indian citizens and located in India. Indian law, as the *lex situs*, would govern the case and India had a strong interest in having these claims heard in its own courts, under its standards, rather than under US standards. For years India had treated UCIL as an Indian national, subjecting its construction and operation of the plant to intensive regulations and governmental supervision. Indian officials had conducted regular on-site inspections of the plant, and had approved its machinery and equipment, including its facilities for storage of the lethal methyl isocyanate gas that escaped, so causing the disaster. India, therefore, had a deep interest in ensuring compliance with its safety standards, particularly as its law, as the law of the place where the tort occurred, would undoubtedly govern the case. In contrast, a long trial of the 145 cases in New York would involve both jury hardship and heavy expense. The trial would pose numerous practical difficulties in tasks such as the language difficulties in understanding the extensive relevant Indian regulations, as well as the laborious process of hearing scores of witnesses through interpreters.

The litigation proceeded quickly to an interlocutory judgment on 17 December 1987 when Deo J[42] awarded interim compensation of US$270 million, on the basis that Union Carbide would end up being found liable under *Rylands v Fletcher*. Its liability, as a parent company, would be by virtue of the control it had over its subsidiary through its majority holding in it.[43] On 4 April 1988, Seth J in the Madhya Pradesh High Court upheld the interim award of damages, on the same grounds, but reduced the amount to US$195 million.[44] On 14/15 February 1989, while its challenge to Seth J's decision was still pending before the Indian Supreme Court, Union Carbide settled with the Indian Government for US$470 million. Many of the Indian claimants then petitioned for the review of the settlement as being too low, but on 22 December 1989 the Supreme Court upheld the Bhopal Act 1985 as constitutional.[45] A second wave of litigation was commenced in the early

42 Unreported.
43 Applying *DHN Food Distribution Ltd v Tower Hamlets London Borough Council* [1976] 1 WLR 852.
44 Again unreported.
45 Doubts have been expressed as to whether a final judgment in the Indian courts on the grounds relied on in the interlocutory judgements would have been enforceable before a US court.

1990s against Union Carbide and its President, Warren Anderson, alleging *inter alia* breaches of ATCA in relation to the operation of the Bhopal plant. The ATCA claims were dismissed as having been precluded by the terms of the 1989 Bhopal Settlement and the fact that under India's Bhopal Act 1985 the Indian Government had assumed to itself exclusive rights to represent victims of the gas explosion.[46]

The second claim involving environmental damage is *Aguinda v Texaco Inc*.[47] The claims arose out of environmental damage and personal injuries that were alleged to have arisen out of negligent management of oil pipelines in Ecuador in the 1960s and 1970s. The pipelines ran over land owned by the government of Ecuador and were operated by a consortium in which a fourth tier subsidiary of Texaco, Tex-Pet, participated until 1992. Two class actions were brought against Texaco in New York, its home state. The first, *Aguinda v Texaco*, was filed on behalf of inhabitants of Oriente region of Ecuador and the second, *Jota v Texaco*, was filed on behalf of residents of Peru in respect of alleged downstream pollution from the consortium's activities in Ecuador. The case was initially dismissed by Judge Rakoff on the grounds of *forum non conveniens*,[48] but the circuit court then vacated and remanded on the grounds that Ecuador could not be an alternative forum because the defendant had not submitted to its jurisdiction.[49] Texaco subsequently agreed to submit to the jurisdiction of the courts of Ecuador in respect of the *Aguinda* plaintiffs and in Peru or Ecuador in respect of the *Jota* plaintiffs.

The claims then came before Judge Rakoff for the second time. Once again he stayed proceedings on the grounds of *forum non conveniens*. His decision was subsequently upheld by the circuit court. The private interest factors pointed heavily towards Ecuador. The contaminated sites in the Ecuadorian rain forest could easily be viewed by a court in Ecuador. All the plaintiffs, as well as all members of their putative classes, some 55,000 in number, resided in eastern Ecuador or nearby areas of Peru, all of their alleged personal and property injuries occurred there, and virtually all witnesses to the manner in which such injuries occurred resided there, along with all the relevant medical and property records. Ecuador was also the location of both the documentary and testamentary evidence of the allegedly negligent acts and decisions taken by the consortium. In contrast, access to this evidence would be more difficult if the case were to go ahead in New York. There would also be considerable language problems with the variety of different dialects spoken by the different class members. A further difficulty would be that the claims would be covered by Ecuadorian law. It was also significant that

---

46 *Bano v Union Carbide* 273 F 3d 120 (2d Cir 2001).
47 *Aguinda v Texaco Inc* 142 F Supp 2D 534 (SDNY 2001) (*Aguinda (2001)*).
48 *Aguinda v Texaco* 945 F Supp 625 (SDNY 1996).
49 *Jota v Texaco* 157 F Supp 153 (2d Cir 1998).

neither the government of Ecuador, nor the state-run oil company that owned and controlled the consortium for most of the relevant period, were parties to the New York litigation. They could, however, be joined in any similar suit brought in Ecuador.

In contrast, Judge Rakoff found that the case had very little to do with the US. Texaco's only involvement was its indirect investment in its fourth-tier subsidiary, Tex-Pet, which was not a party to the litigation, and whose activities in the consortium had occurred almost exclusively in Ecuador. All of the consortium's key activities, including the decisions and practices here at issue, were managed, directed, and conducted by consortium employees in Ecuador. No material decisions as to the activities and practices of the consortium were made by persons in the US, let alone by Texaco employees. Texaco, like Union Carbide in the *Bhopal* case, was very much a 'hands off' parent corporation. In this capacity Texaco had exercised some general oversight over the expenses and revenues of its subsidiaries. However, it had exercised no control or direction over the key matters of pipe design, waste disposal, and the allegedly negligent practices of the consortium that were in issue in the case. Indeed, one of the plaintiffs' own witnesses affirmed that Texaco had no involvement in drilling wells in Ecuador. From time to time Tex-Pet would request technical information from US-based Texaco personnel on topics such as the maximum safe levels of salt and oil in water and how to clean up oil spills. The data would then be forwarded to the consortium for its use and decision-making. However, Texaco never got involved with decisions made by the consortium as to what action to take on the basis of this information.

8.2.4 Forum non conveniens and human rights claims

Where the plaintiff brings a claim relating to human rights abuses it claims to have suffered in a foreign jurisdiction, the US courts have showed a more accommodating attitude to the plaintiff's difficulties in proceeding in an alternative forum. In *Wiwa v Royal Dutch Petroleum Co*,[50] the circuit court observed that *forum non conveniens* dismissals in torture cases were a huge setback to the plaintiff. The plaintiff would need to start again in the courts of another nation and obtain not only new counsel, but also, maybe, a new residence. The plaintiff could generally not sue in the place where the abuse had taken place, due to dangers it would face in returning there. It would face difficulty in suing in the courts of other nations, which would find such suits time consuming, burdensome and difficult to administer. Such suits might also embarrass the government of the forum in which suit had been brought. 'Finally, because characteristically neither the plaintiff nor the defendant are

---

50 *Wiwa v Royal Dutch Petroleum Co* 226 F 3d 88 (2d Cir 2000).

ostensibly either protected by the domestic law of the forum nations, courts often regard such suits as "not our business".'

In *Wiwa*, the defendants argued that England was the alternative forum, rather than Nigeria, where the alleged abuses had occurred. England was not an obviously better suited foreign forum than the courts of New York. There was no substantial physical evidence that was difficult or expensive to transport as had in *Union Carbide*. For a non-party witness, trial in New York would not be significantly more inconvenient than for a trial in England.[51] The extra costs of shipping documents and flying witnesses to New York, rather than London, would not be excessively burdensome, given the defendant's vast resources. Any inconvenience would be fully counter-balanced by the cost and inconvenience to the plaintiff of having to reinstigate litigation in England, especially given their minimal resources compared to the defendants' vast ones. The court noted that the plaintiffs had obtained excellent pro bono counsel in New York and had no guarantee of getting equivalent representation in London without incurring substantial expenses.[52] There was also the cost to a US resident plaintiff of being uprooted to England for the duration of the trial and being required to replicate in England the large amounts of time, money and energy already expended on the suit in the US.

Wiwa is a potentially hopeful decision for plaintiffs pursuing transnational claims against multinational corporations in the US courts for two reasons. First, the decision of the circuit court recognises that in appropriate circumstances the US does have an interest in having its courts hear certain claims regarding human rights violations, even though those violations have occurred in other jurisdictions. Secondly, the decision appears to treat very seriously the disparity in economic resources between the plaintiff and the defendant. However, the effect of the decision is likely to be limited to torture cases. For a start, the US public interest in such cases was expressly stated to have derived from the fact that in 1991 Congress saw fit to pass the Torture Victims Protection Act (the TVPA). Moreover, in such cases the nature of the claim makes it unlikely that the place where the violations occurred will be considered an adequate alternative forum, due to the risks likely to be faced by the plaintiff in litigating there. This removes a powerful private interest factor in favour of the defendant, the desirability of having the claim heard in the jurisdiction in which the alleged wrong occurred. On the facts of *Wiwa* the inconvenience to the defendant in litigating in New York as opposed to London would be considerably less than in cases in such as *Union Carbide* where the alternative forum would be the jurisdiction in which the disaster

51 The second defendant was in any case, Dutch. The fact that Nigeria was a member of the Commonwealth was of no particular significance. These factors argued equally against dismissal in favour of the courts of the Netherlands.

52 Footnote 13.

occurred and in which the bulk of the evidence was located, including evidence that would be difficult or impossible to remove to another jurisdiction.

A similar decision was reached in *Sarei v Rio Tinto*. The defendants argued that either Australia or Papua New Guinea would be a more appropriate forum for hearing a case involving allegations of human rights abuses during the 10-year civil uprising on Bougainville. The plaintiffs objected to Papua New Guinea as an alternative forum because of the risk to their personal safety if they were forced to litigate there. Given that the plaintiffs and other Bougainvilleans had been engaged in a civil war with the Papua New Guinea Government for the past 10 years, this was a well-founded apprehension.[53] This factor did not prevent Papua New Guinea from being regarded as an available alternative jurisdiction. It did, however, tip the balance of private interest factors in favour of retention of the suit, together with the doubts raised as to whether the plaintiffs would be able to identify counsel willing to represent them on a contingency fee basis in Papua New Guinea.

However, where the plaintiffs claim is wholly based on an environmental tort, without any accompanying allegations of other human rights abuses, their chances of resisting the defendant's application to dismiss on grounds of *forum non conveniens* will be slim. Cases such as *Union Carbide* and *Aguinda* are predicated on the lack of a strong US connection, both as regards private and public interest factors, to counteract the strong pull of the jurisdiction in which the claim arose. In particular, those cases have emphasised the 'hands-off' nature of the relationship between the US parent and its foreign subsidiary, manifesting the tacit assumption that in such circumstances the parent would not incur liability under US law. The assumption remains tacit because dismissal of the case on grounds of *forum non conveniens* guarantees that this issue of substantive US law remains unaddressed. This then paves the way for a finding that the claim will be subject to the law of the jurisdiction in which the harm occurred and that the host jurisdiction will have an overwhelming public interest in hearing the case because of its interest in regulating activities within its territory that may cause environmental harm. This approach is also said to avoid charges of 'economic imperialism' by recognising the right of the host nation to decide on what balance to strike between environmental protection and economic development. Looked at from this perspective, it is not surprising that US courts have decided that such cases are 'not our business' and that US jurors should not be burdened with hearing them.

However, the circuit court in *Wiwa* recognised that US courts did have an interest in hearing allegations of torture that had been committed in foreign jurisdictions. Although that interest was specifically derived from the fact

---

53 In *Doe I v Exxon Mobil Corp* 393 F Supp 2d 20 (DDC 2005), this factor prevented tort claims from being stayed on the ground of *forum non conveniens*.

that Congress had seen fit in 1991 to pass the TVPA, it is possible to construct a strong US interest in hearing foreign environmental tort claims against US parent corporations, notwithstanding the lack of an international law dimension or of any US legislation equivalent to the TVPA. With such claims the interest of the state of the host jurisdiction in regulating environmental harm within its territory cannot be looked at in isolation from the wider issue of the ultimate accountability of foreign parent corporations. These are outside its jurisdiction and are more effectively controlled by the courts of their home jurisdiction. These are the courts in which the process of developing new principles of law to regulate the global activities of multinational enterprises need to be developed and yet this process is continually stillborn by the dismissal of such suits on the grounds of *forum non conveniens*.

These considerations were articulated at length by Judge Doggett in *Dow Chemicals v Castro Alfaro*.[54] The claim arose out of allegations that, that while working on Standard Fruit's banana plantation in Costa Rica, the plaintiffs had sustained injuries as a result of being required to handle the pesticide dibromochloropropane (DBCP). The plaintiffs alleged that its manufacturer, Dow, had supplied the pesticide to the owners of the plantation, Standard Fruit, after its use within the US had been banned by the EPA. The majority of the Texas Court of Appeal decided that the doctrine of *forum non conveniens* no longer formed part of the law of Texas. Judge Doggett, however, went further with a comprehensive assault on the whole basis of the doctrine, particularly as it applied to environmental tort claims brought against US multinational corporations. The fact that the chemical had been manufactured in Texas gave the courts of Texas a strong interest in hearing the case and comity would not be achieved by allowing US multinational corporations to adhere to a double standard when operating abroad. Potential exposure to domestic litigation was likely to prove the most effective means of encouraging US multinational corporations to raise the standards employed in their overseas activities. A further domestic interest was the fact that although DBCP had been banned from use within the US, traces of the chemical could be present in foods imported from countries, such as Costa Rica, which still permitted its use, and so would prove a potential health to US consumers.

A similar recognition of US interests in such claims can be seen in *Doe v Exxon Corp*.[55] Oberdorfer J, in giving leave to amend an ATCA claim so that it could be pleaded as a tort claim under the diversity jurisdiction set out in 28 USC, s 1332, analysed the applicable law in the tort claim against a US multinational corporation involving alleged complicity in human rights

54 (1990) 786 S W 2d 674.
55 *Doe v Exxon Corp (Plaintiffs' motion to amend complaint)*, unreported, 2 March 2006, WL 516744 (DDC).

abuses in Indonesia. He held that the US had an overriding interest in applying its own law to the defendants, which were all US companies. US law provided for punitive damages which would be particularly appropriate if the aim was to provide sanctions against the defendants. 'Ultimately, the United States, the leader of the free world, has an overarching, vital interest in the safety, prosperity, and consequences of the behavior of its citizens, particularly its super-corporations conducting business in one or more foreign countries.'

It would seem, therefore, that the interests of the home nation in hearing such cases have been somewhat underplayed. However, if the home nation does have an equally compelling interest in hearing the case as does the host nation, is that outweighed by the risks of 'docket congestion'? Decisions such as *Aguinda* assume that this risk is real even in the absence of any substantiating empirical evidence. In any event, the risk is minimised by the fact that jurisdiction still has to be established over the defendant in the home jurisdiction. This will not happen if the defendant has no connection whatsoever with that jurisdiction. However, if it does have the necessary connection, either because it conducts business or is incorporated there, then it is not unreasonable that claims against it should be heard in that jurisdiction. The proper screening procedure for fanciful claims is not *forum non conveniens*, but rather the procedure for striking out claims that are frivolous and vexatious.

This interest of the home state will be strengthened if it has accepted the OECD Guidelines for Multinational Enterprises (the Guidelines). These are recommendations addressed by governments to multinational enterprises. The revised Guidelines were adopted in Paris on 27 June 2000 by the governments of the 30 member countries of the OECD (which includes the UK), as well Argentina, Brazil and Chile. In this situation, it becomes less easy to classify a suit against a parent corporation as having no connection with its home jurisdiction. The Guidelines constitute recommendations by governments to multinational enterprises and this would therefore indicate a strong public interest in having claims against such enterprises heard in their home jurisdiction courts. Of particular relevance is sub-heading 5, which recommends that the multinational enterprise 'maintain contingency plans for preventing, mitigating, and controlling serious environmental and health damage from their operations, including accidents and emergencies; and mechanisms for immediate reporting to the competent authorities'. Sub-heading 6(a) goes on to recommend that the multinational enterprise continually seeks to improve corporate environmental performance, 'by encouraging, where appropriate, such activities as: (a) Adoption of technologies and operating procedures in all parts of the enterprise that reflect standards concerning environmental performance in the best performing part of the enterprise . . .'

8.3 Other grounds for declining jurisdiction

Even if the plaintiff manages to defeat an application to stay on the grounds of *forum non conveniens*, as happened in *Sarei v Rio Tinto*, the defendants may still be able to persuade the court to stay the proceedings on the following other grounds of abstention from jurisdiction: foreign sovereign immunity; absence of an indispensable party; act of state; political question; and comity.

8.3.1 Foreign sovereign immunity

Foreign states, their agencies and instrumentalities are immune from suit under the Foreign Sovereign Immunity Act 28 USC, s 1330, ss 1602–11. The immunity also extends to servants of the foreign state.[56] As foreign sovereign immunity applies to ATCA claims, this would appear to prevent claims against state officials in respect of human rights abuses.[57] However, such claims are possible on the basis that state officials who commit such abuses have ceased to act in their official capacity.[58] Immunity may, however, be claimed by acting heads of state in respect of such claims.[59]

An exception to foreign sovereign immunity exists when the action is based on: (1) a commercial activity carried on in the US by the foreign state; or (2) an act performed in the US in connection with a commercial activity of the foreign state elsewhere; or (3) an act outside the US in connection with a commercial activity of the foreign state elsewhere and that act causes a direct effect in the US. In *Unocal (2000)* the plaintiffs argued that the Myanmar government and Myanmar Oil and Gas Enterprise (MOGE), a state corporation, fell within the third exception. Lew J rejected this argument. First, the pipeline may have been a commercial activity, but the human rights violations associated with it were not, because they derived from abuse of the state's police powers and, as such, were peculiarly sovereign in nature. Secondly, there were no direct effects in the US. The plaintiffs had provided no allegation to support their allegation that the violations reduced the cost of the project and so gave Unocal an unfair competitive advantage in the US gas market. The circuit court upheld the decision but on the second ground only. It held that Lew J had been in error on the first ground of his decision in that an abuse of police powers in connection with commercial activity could fall

---

56 *Herbage v Meese* 747 F Supp 60 (DC 1990).

57 *Argentine Republic v Amerada Hess Shipping Corp* 488 US 428 (SCt 1989). *Siderman de Blake v Republic of Argentina* 965 F 2d 699 (9th Cir 1992).

58 *In re Estate of Ferdinand E Marcos Human Rights Litigation* 978 F 2d 493 CA 9 (Hawaii 1992). Earlier dicta in *Republic of Philippines v Marcos* 665 F Supp 793, p 797 (NDCal 1987) went further in suggesting that no natural person, apart from a current head of state, might claim the benefit of sovereign immunity.

59 *Tachiona v Mugabe* 169 F Supp 2d 259 (SDNY 2001).

within the second and third exceptions. The words of these exceptions were 'in connection with' rather than 'based on'.

8.3.2 Indispensible parties

Rule 19 of FRCP provides that in certain circumstances proceedings may be dismissed because of the absence of an indispensible party. It must first be established that the absent party is necessary and unable to be joined. Section (a) provides that a party is 'necessary' if '(1) in the person's absence complete relief cannot be accorded among those already parties or (2) the person claims an interest relating to the subject matter of the action'. If an absent party is 'necessary', section (b) then directs the court to consider 'whether in equity and good conscience the action should proceed among the parties before it, or should be dismissed'. In considering this issue the court should balance: the prejudice to any party or to the absent party; whether relief could be shaped to lessen that prejudice; whether an adequate remedy, even if not complete, could be awarded without the absent party; and whether there existed an alternative forum. If the necessary party is immune, its immunity may be a compelling factor and dispense with the need to undertake a balancing inquiry.

In *Unocal (1997)*, the defendants argued that the case should be dismissed because of the absence of State Law and Order Restoration Committee (SLORC) and MOGE, who, as organs of the Myanmar state, would have been entitled to rely on the doctrine of foreign sovereign immunity. Paez J rejected this plea. If the plaintiffs could show that the defendants were joint tortfeasors, complete relief might still be awarded among the remaining parties. Even the injunctive relief sought would still be possible in the absence of SLORC and MOGE, for the plaintiffs had asked for an order that the defendants cease payments to SLORC and MOGE and cease participation in the Yadana project until the human rights violations had ceased. The defendants would be no more burdened than if SLORC and MOGE had been subject to suit. In contrast, in the 1996 *Aguinda* decision the plaintiffs, at that time, were seeking equitable relief by way of an injunction requiring a clean up of the polluted lands in Ecuador, a major alteration of the pipeline, and a commitment to future monitoring for years to come. As the state of Ecuador was by then the 100 per cent owner both of the pipeline and of the consortium, it was an indispensible party in respect of the injunctive relief sought.

8.3.3 Act of state

The doctrine of act of state precludes a US court from adjudicating claims which would require the court to invalidate a foreign sovereign's official acts within its own territory – so leading to interference with executive branch foreign policy decisions. The defendant bears the initial burden of showing that the claim involves an official act of a foreign sovereign; performed within its own territory; and a claim for relief that would require the court to declare the foreign sovereign's act invalid. The doctrine was considered in *Sarei v Rio Tinto*.[60] The ATCA claims were brought by plaintiffs from the island of Bougainville and related to violations of international law allegedly committed by the defendant and the Papua New Guinea Defence Force (PNGDF) during the 10-year civil uprising on the island. Morrow J held that the doctrine did not cover the claims in respect of war crimes and crimes against humanity. These were allegedly illegal acts and could not be regarded as the official act of a foreign sovereign. Although orders given by military commanders during wartime were commonly viewed as official sovereign acts, the actions of the PNGDF referred to by the plaintiffs in did not involve acts of legitimate warfare.

In contrast, the claims for racial discrimination, and environmental torts involving breaches of UNCLOS, did fall within the doctrine.[61] These claims involved wrongs committed directly by Rio Tinto, whereas the claims asserting war crimes and crimes against humanity involved actions allegedly committed by the PNGDF, in which Rio Tinto were allegedly complicit. If Rio Tinto's wrongs were to amount to a violation of the law of nations, it would be necessary to implicate the Papua New Guinea Government. The plaintiffs would have to prove that the government had played an integral role in building and operating the mine, and in the racial discrimination and environmental harm purportedly caused thereby. It was, therefore, very likely that the court would have to assess the legality of the government's official conduct. If the court concluded that Rio Tinto could be regarded as a state actor, so that its conduct violated the law of nations, that would, *a fortiori*, lead to a conclusion as to the invalidity of official acts of the government of Papua New Guinea relating to the operation of the mine.

If the defendant discharges the initial burden, the court will then consider four factors in determining whether or not to abstain from jurisdiction on this ground.[62] First, was there any international consensus regarding the claims in issue? In *Unocal (2002)*, the circuit court held that an allegation of a breach of an *ius cogens* norm[63] would weigh against the application of the

---

60 *Sarei v Rio Tinto* 221 F Supp 2d 1116 (CD Cal).

61 The circuit court reversed this finding as regards the claims for racial discrimination, as these involved the violation of an *ius cogens* norm and such acts could not be regarded as the official acts of a sovereign. *Sarei v Rio Tinto* F 3d 2006 WL 2242146 (9th Cir 7 August 2006).

62 The first three factors were set out in *Sabbatino v Banco Nacional de Cuba* 376 US 398, p 428 (1964). The fourth was set out in *Liu v Republic of China* 892 F 2d 1419 (9th Cir 1989).

63 An *ius cogens* norm of customary international law is one that has received such widespread acceptance among the community of nations that it binds even those states which are persistent objectors to its application.

doctrine as such norms were, by definition, supported by a high degree of international consensus.[64] In *Sarei v Rio Tinto*, Morrow J also held that there was a high degree of consensus with regard the claim for racial discrimination.[65] Secondly, what would the impact of any judgment be on US foreign relations? In addressing this question, the submission of a Statement of Interest by the US State Department is likely to be accorded very great weight. In *Unocal*, the circuit court regarded it as significant that the co-ordinate branches of the US Government had already denounced Myanmar's human rights abuses and imposed sanctions. Further, in 1997, the State Department had advised the district court that the hearing of the claims would not prejudice or impede the conduct of US foreign relations with the current Myanmar Government. In contrast, in *Sarei*, the Department of State had filed a Statement of Interest which clearly expressed the view that continued adjudication of the case would have a negative impact on US foreign relations with Papua New Guinea. Thirdly, had there been a change in government since the time of the alleged abuses? This was not the case in *Sarei*. Neither was it the case in *Unocal*, but the circuit court held that this factor on its own was not enough to justify dismissal of the claims. Fourthly, was the conduct in question undertaken for a public purpose? The circuit court in *Unocal* found it difficult to see how the alleged violations of human rights committed by the Myanmar government in relation to the Yadana project could have been regarded as in the public interest.

8.3.4 Political question

The political question doctrine derives from the US constitutional principles of the separation of powers, so as to restrict the justiciability of certain issues. However, not every case implicating US foreign relations involves a non-justiciable political question.[66] The doctrine involves an examination of the following six factors set out in *Baker v Carr*:[67]

(1) the existence of any textually demonstrable constitutional commitment of the issue to a coordinate political department;

(2) a lack of judicially discoverable and manageable standards for resolving the claims;

---

64 *Doe I v Unocal Corp* 395 F 3d 932 (9th Cir 2002) (*Unocal (2002)*).
65 No such international consensus existed as regards the environmental tort claims, except as respects the claimed violation of UNCLOS.
66 *Klinghoffer v SNC Achille Lauro* 937 F 2d 44, p 49 (2d Cir 1991) where it was stated that 'The fact that the issues . . . arise in a politically charged context does not convert what is essentially an ordinary tort suit into a non-justiciable political question . . .'
67 *Baker v Carr* 369 US 186, p 210, 82 SCt 691, 7 L Ed 2d 663 (1962).

(3) the impossibility of deciding without an initial, non-judicial, policy determination;

(4) the impossibility of a court's undertaking independent resolution without expressing lack of the respect for the co-ordinate branches of government;

(5) an unusual need for unquestioning adherence to a political decision already made;

(6) the potentiality of embarrassment from multifarious pronouncements by various departments on one question.

Morrow J in *Sarei* held that the Department of State's Statement of Interest showed that continuance of the suit in the US would fall within the fourth and sixth of these factors. It would be impossible to rule on the merits of the plaintiffs' allegations without passing judgment on the pre-war and wartime conduct of the Papua New Guinea Government. According to the Statement of Interest, this indicates such a judgment might have serious implications for the future of the peace agreement and of the foreign policy objectives of the executive. Such a judgment also placed the court in the position of announcing a view that is contrary to that of a co-ordinate branch of government, with all the attendant embarrassment that would ensue. Therefore, the entirety of the claims fell to be stayed on this ground.

In August 2006, the circuit court overruled Morrow J's decision to dismiss the claims on this ground.[68] Without the Statement of Interest, there would have been no obvious grounds to dismiss the claims on this ground. Although the Statement of Interest had to be given 'serious weight' as required by *Sosa*, the circuit court concluded that no political question was present. Even if the continuance of the case involved some risk to the peace process in Bougainville, that would not engage the last three *Baker* factors. A further example of a district court refusing to dismiss by reference to a Statement of Interest can be found in *Doe I v Exxon Mobil Corp*.[69] ATCA claims had been made against the defendant in respect of its activities in Aceh, Indonesia, and its alleged complicity in human rights abuses that were said to have been carried out there by the Indonesian security forces. The Bush administration submitted a Statement of Interest arguing that continuance of the suit would hinder US actions against Islamic terrorists in Aceh. Oberdorfer J held that the Statement of Interest justified the dismissal of the ATCA claims. *Sosa* meant that courts needed to be aware of the 'collateral consequences' of interfering with US foreign relations that the use of the statute entailed. Proper concern for Indonesia's sovereignty required the dismissal of claims against the Indonesian corporate defendant in which Pertamina, Indonesia's state-owned oil

68 *Sarei v Rio Tinto* F 3d 2006 WL 2242146 (9th Cir 7 August 2006).
69 *Doe I v Exxon Mobil Corp* 393 F Supp 2d 20 (DDC 2005). Affd 473 F 3d 345 (CADC 2007).

and gas company, had a 55 per cent holding. However, the claims could still proceed as transitory tort claims against the US corporate defendants, subject to the condition that discovery be conducted in such a manner so as to avoid intrusion into Indonesian sovereignty.

8.3.5 Comity

The doctrine of comity is based on 'the recognition which one nation allows within its territory to the legislative, executive or judicial acts of another nation'.[70] The doctrine gives the courts a discretion to defer to the laws or interests of a foreign country and decline to exercise the jurisdiction they otherwise have. The Restatement at s 403(2) sets out seven factors relating to this issue.[71] These considerations will generally overlap with those that are relevant to the public interest analysis under *forum non conveniens*. However, in *Sarei*, Morrow J, following *Hartford Fire Ins Co v California*,[72] held that the seventh factor, a conflict between the laws of the US and those of another state, was a prerequisite to a dismissal on this ground. On this basis comity justified excluding the claims for environmental damage, as Papua New Guinea in 1995 had passed legislation mandating that such claims be pursued exclusively in Papua New Guinea. In August 2006, the Circuit Court upheld this part of the decision, but, in the light of its observations regarding the role played by the Statement of Interest in the decisions to dismiss on grounds of act of state, and political question, the case was remitted to the district court for further consideration.

---

70 *Hilton v Guyot* 159 US 113, p 164, 16 SCt 139, 40 L Ed 95 (1895).
71 '(a) the link of the activity to the territory of the regulating state, i.e., the extent to which the activity takes place within the territory, or has substantial, direct, and foreseeable effect upon or in the territory; (b) the connections, such as nationality, residence, or economic activity, between the regulating state and the person principally responsible for the activity to be regulated, or between that state and those whom the regulation is designed to protect; (c) the character of the activity to be regulated, the importance of regulation to the regulating state, the extent to which other states regulate such activities, and the degree to which the desirability of such regulation is generally accepted; (d) the existence of justified expectations that might be protected or hurt by the regulation; (e) the importance of the regulation to the international political, legal, or economic system; (f) the extent to which the regulation is consistent with the traditions of the international system; (g) the extent to which another state may have an interest in regulating the activity; and (h) the likelihood of conflict with regulation by another state'.
72 *Hartford Fire Ins Co v California* 509 US 764, 113 SCt 2891, 125 L Ed 2d 612 (1993).

Multinational corporations and environmental liability (2). US litigation: substantive law

9.1 Claims under the ATCA

Unlike the position before the English courts, claims involving environmental torts in the US have been brought on two fronts. The first involves conventional principles of tort law, whilst the second involves an attempt to classify such torts as violations of norms of customary international law so as to bring the case within the ATCA, which provides that: 'The district courts shall have original jurisdiction of any civil action by an alien for a tort only, committed in violation of the law of nations or a treaty of the United States.' This Act lay dormant for nearly two centuries until 1980 when it was successfully invoked in a claim for damages in *Filartiga v Pena-Irala*.[1] The plaintiff, the sister of a Peruvian who had been tortured in Peru, successfully invoked the Act to obtain an award of damages against her brother's torturer, who was then living in Brooklyn.

The circuit court held that the Act created a cause of action based on a violation of the prohibition of torture under customary international law. However, the district court was still required to perform a traditional choice of law analysis to see whether international law, the law of the forum state, or *lex situs* applied. Subsequent cases have shown a divergence of judicial approaches to the question of the law to be applied once the plaintiff has managed to cross the initial ATCA threshold. One view has been that the court should apply international law, whereas another has been that international law was only relevant as the trigger for jurisdiction, after which the court should apply the tort laws of the forum state. Having established that the federal courts have jurisdiction over a claim based on ATCA, the question arises as to the choice of law to be applied. A variety of approaches has been suggested. In *Xuncax v Gramajo*,[2] it was stated that international law would be applied. On the other hand federal law was applied by Reinhardt J in the

---

1 *Filartiga v Pena-Irala* 630 F 2d 876 (2d Cir 1980).
2 *Xuncax v Gramajo* 866 F Supp 162, pp 182–4 (D Mass 1995).

circuit court decision in *Unocal*. Alternatively, it has been suggested that the law of the foreign *situs* might be applied where that is not out of line with international law or the policy behind ATCA.[3] In the light of the decision of the Supreme Court in *Sosa v Alvarez-Machain*,[4] which is discussed below, it is likely that ATCA claims should be determined in accordance international law.[5]

The decision in *Filartiga* has generated a flood of cases by aliens before the federal courts of the US, in which claims for compensation against individuals have been based on alleged violations of international law. In 1991, the Torture Victims Protection Act took ATCA as its inspiration in creating a cause of action under US law where under 'color of law of any foreign nation' an individual was subject to torture or extra-judicial killing. The reference to an 'individual' meant that the cause of action created was also available to US citizens, and not, as is the case with ATCA, restricted to aliens.

In 1997, Paez J in *Unocal (1997)* gave a landmark judgment in which he held that the Act could, in appropriate circumstances, also be invoked against corporate defendants.[6] In 2004, the Supreme Court considered the scope of ATCA for the first time in *Sosa v Alvarez-Machain*.[7] Until then, only a handful of dissenting judgments had challenged the view that ATCA was not only to do with the jurisdiction of the federal courts, but also created causes of action based on violations of customary international law, which were subject to a 10-year limitation period.[8] The Department of State, alarmed at the prospect of ATCA being used against anti-terrorist measures adopted by the US and its allies, submitted an amicus brief arguing that ATCA had only procedural effect and created no new causes of action.

Sosa v Alvarez Machain provided the Supreme Court with its first opportunity to review the operation of ATCA. The plaintiff's claim was based on an allegation that he had been unlawfully abducted from Mexico for 24 hours to bring him back to the US to face trial. Souter J, giving the principal majority opinion, held that the Act was jurisdictional and created no new

---

3 *Tachiona v Mugabe* 234 F Supp 2d 401, p 418 (SDNY 2002).
4 *Sosa v Alvarez Machain* 542 US 692, 124 SCt 2739 (2004).
5 Customary international law was applied in *Presbyterian Church of Sudan v Talisman Energy, Inc* 374 F Supp 2d 331 (SDNY 2005) (*Talisman (2005)*) and in *Bowoto v Chevron Corp*, 22 August 2006, unreported, 2006 WL 2455752 (NDCal). However, where such claims raise issues relating to the piercing of the corporate veil, these must be dealt with under a system of national law, usually that of the place of incorporation. *Presbyterian Church of Sudan v Talisman Energy* 453 F Supp 2d 633 (SDNY 2006) (*Talisman (2006)*).
6 *Doe I v Unocal Corp* 963 F Supp 880 (CDCal 1997) (*Unocal (1997)*).
7 *Sosa v Alvarez Machain* 542 US 692, 124 SCt 2739 (2004).
8 *Papa v United States* 281 F 3d 1004 (9th Cir 2002). ATCA itself contains no express limitation period. The circuit court chose this period of limitations for ATCA claims by analogy with the TVPA which contains an express 10-year limitation period.

causes of action. It was not, however, stillborn, as it was understood by the drafters of the Act that common law would provide a cause of action for the three violations of international law thought to carry personal liability at the time – offences against ambassadors, violation of safe conducts and piracy. No developments over the next 200 years precluded the development of common law expanding this category, but a federal court should exercise restraint in considering such a new cause of action.

Souter J referred with approval to the reference in *In re estate of Marcos* to a norm that is 'specific, universal and obligatory'[9] and in *Tel-Oren* to the fact that ATCA covered only 'a handful of heinous actions – each of which violates definable and universal and obligatory norms'.[10] He also approved the statement in *Filartiga* that: 'For the purposes of civil liability, the torturer has become – like the pirate and slave trader before him – *hostis humanis generis*, an enemy of all mankind.'[11] In fn 21 Souter J suggested that some other possible limitations on ATCA might be the application of a requirement of prior exhaustion of domestic remedies, as was required by the TVPA 1991, as well as a case-specific deference to the political branches of the US. Alvarez' relatively brief period of detention in excess of positive authority did not show a violation of any international law norm which met this standard.

Breyer J substantially agreed with Souter J, but pointed out that substantive uniformity on a norm of international law would not automatically lead to universal jurisdiction. The eighteenth-century consensus on piracy, for instance, was not only that it was wrong, but also that any nation could prosecute any pirate. Today international law sometimes reflected procedural agreement on universal jurisdiction to prosecute a subset of universally condemned behaviour – such as torture, genocide, crimes against humanity and war crimes. This procedural consensus showed that universal jurisdiction was consistent with notions of comity. Criminal jurisdiction necessarily contemplated a significant degree of civil tort recovery as well. Scalia J, with whom Thomas J agreed, dissented on the basis that the Supreme Court's decision in *Erie Railroad Co v Tompkins*[12] left the federal courts with no discretion to create federal common law.

After *Sosa*, one might have expected the federal courts to adopt a more restrictive approach to ATCA. Such an approach can be seen in *Enahoro*,[13] where it was held that claims by aliens arising out of torture could no longer be brought under ATCA, as the TVPA now 'occupied the field' and provided

---

9 *In re estate of Marcos* 25 F 3d 1467, p 1475 (CA 1994).
10 *Tel-Oren v Libyan Arab Republic* 726 F 2d 774 (CADC 1984), Edwards J, p 781.
11 *Filartiga v Pena-Iral* 630 F 2d 876, p 890 (2d Cir 1980).
12 *Erie Railroad Co v Tompkins* 304 US 64, 58 SCt 817, 82 L Ed 1188 (1938).
13 *Enahoro v Abubakar* 408 F 3d 877, pp 889–90 (7th Cir 2005).

an exclusive avenue for such claims. This has the effect of narrowing the rights of suit available to aliens as, unlike ATCA, the TVPA is expressly subject to a requirement of exhaustion of local remedies.[14] Another significant limitation has been the finding by several district courts that the issue of a private actor liability under ATCA is to be determined exclusively by reference to the principles of customary international law relating to non-state actors and that the US 'color of law' jurisprudence set out in s 1983 has no role to play.[15]

However, the district courts have not taken up other suggestions from the judgments in *Sosa* that would have led to a profound curtailment on the scope of ATCA. In 2005, in *Talisman*, Cotes J held that *Sosa* had no effect on the applicability of ATCA to claims against corporations.[16] She also held that the issue of accomplice liability of private actors in an ATCA claim continued to be determined under the principles set out by the majority of the circuit court in *Unocal (2002)*, whereby the international law principles regarding criminal liability of accomplices were applied in the context of their civil liability. In August 2006, in *Sarei v Rio Tinto*,[17] the circuit court declined to take up Souter J's suggestion that a requirement of exhaustion of local remedies be read into ATCA.

9.1.1 Environmental claims and ATCA

To come within ATCA, the claim must be made by an alien, must involve a tort and that tort must involve a 'violation of the law of nations'. There are two preliminary modes of attacking the plaintiff's claim. First, there is a challenge under the Federal Rules of Civil Procedure (FRCP) 12 (b)(1) on the ground that the plaintiffs pleaded claim discloses a lack of subject matter jurisdiction. For these purposes the allegations in the claim will be assumed to be true. Secondly, there is an application by the defendant for summary judgment. To date, plaintiffs have had singularly little success in fending off challenges to ATCA claims based on environmental torts, on the ground that these involve no violation of a rule of customary international law.

The first such claim, in 1991, in *Amlon Metals v FMC*,[18] resulted in a finding that ATCA did not cover claims arising out of the export of a contaminated consignment from the UK to the US. The plaintiffs relied first on Principle 21 of the Stockholm Principles, United Nations Conference on the

---

14 The ambit of this restriction is narrowed somewhat if the TVPA does not allow actions to be brought against corporation, as has been held by some district courts.
15 Most recently by Illston J in *Bowoto v Chevron Corp*, 22 August 2006, unreported, 2006 WL 2455752 (NDCal).
16 *Presbyterian Church of Sudan v Talisman Energy, Inc* 374 F Supp 2d 331 (SDNY 2005) (*Talisman (2005)*).
17 *Sarei v Rio Tinto* F 3d 2006 WL 2242146 (9th Cir 7 August 2006).
18 *Amlon Metals v FMC* 775 F Supp 668 (SNDY 1991).

Human Environment (adopted 16 June 1972), to which the US was a signatory. This provides that states have the responsibility of ensuring that activities within their jurisdiction or control do not cause damage to the environment of other states or of areas beyond the limits of national jurisdiction. However, Principle 21 was general in nature and set forth no specific proscriptions which could form the basis of a norm of customary international law. The plaintiffs also relied on the norm of customary international law against causing transnational pollution referred to in the Restatement (Third) of Foreign Relations Law, s 602(2) (1987):

[w]here pollution originating in a state has caused significant injury to persons outside that state, or has created a significant risk of such injury, the state of origin is obligated to accord to the person injured or exposed to such risk access to the same judicial or administrative remedies as are available in similar circumstances to persons within the state.

However, this did not constitute a statement of universally recognised principles of international law, but merely set out the existing US view of the law of nations regarding global environmental protection.

The second claim was *Beanal v Freeport McMoran Inc*,[19] which arose out of the operation of an open pit copper, gold and silver mine in Jayawinya Mountain in Irian Jaya, Indonesia. The plaintiff's ATCA claim alleged, *inter alia*, a violation of the law of nations through environmental harm. The plaintiffs relied on principle two of the Rio Declaration on Environment and Development of 13 June 1992, which provides that states have 'the sovereign right to exploit their own resources pursuant to their own environmental and developmental policies . . .', but bear a 'responsibility to ensure that activities within their jurisdiction or control do not cause damage to the environment of other states;' and on *Principles of International Environmental Law I: Frameworks, Standards and Implementation* (Sands (ed) 1995a), in which the basic principles of the polluter pays principle, the precautionary principle and the proximity principle). However, both sources failed to establish any specific norm of customary international law prohibiting intra-state pollution. Indeed, the materials relied on by the plaintiffs showed that this was a matter of national rather than international concern.

A similar finding was made in *Flores v Southern Peru Copper Corporation*[20] in respect of a claim under ATCA in respect of pollution from the defendant's mining operations in Peru. The plaintiffs attempted to reclassify their claim as one involving breaches of their rights to life and health under the following conventions. First, the Universal Declaration of Human Rights

---

19 *Beanal v Freeport McMoran Inc* 969 F Supp 362 (EDLa 1997), 197 F 3d 161 (5th Cir 1999).
20 253 F Supp 2d 510 (SDNY 2002), 343 F 3d 140 (2d Cir 2003).

(UN 1948). Article 3 states that: 'Everyone has the right to life, liberty and the security of person.' Article 25(1) states that: 'Everyone has the right to a standard of living adequate for the health and well being of himself and of his family.' Secondly, the International Covenant on Economic Social and Cultural Rights (UN 1966) which refers to '. . . the right of everyone to the enjoyment of the highest attainable standard of physical and mental health'. Thirdly, the World Charter for Nature (1982) which states that: 'I. Nature shall be respected and its essential processes shall not be impaired. II. Activities which might have an impact on nature shall be controlled, and the best available technologies that minimise significant risks to nature or other adverse effects shall be used . . .'

Haight J, whose decision was upheld by the circuit court, held such rights were too ill-defined to be capable of generating norms of customary international law. The plaintiffs had failed to establish the necessary general consensus among nations that a high level of pollution, causing harm to humans, was universally unacceptable. All that was established was a general agreement as to the value of human life, health, together with growing international concern over environmental pollution, but this was not enough to show that this concern had become a norm of customary international law. In fact, this generalised concern indicated that control of intra-national pollution was a matter which lay exclusively within the domain of each individual state, and was not therefore a matter of mutual concern betweens states. The plaintiffs had also relied on the observation in *Zapata v Quinn*[21] that ATCA 'applies only to shockingly egregious violations of universally recognised principles of international law'. The phrase had been used descriptively not prescriptively, and was no more than a recognition that only conduct that was 'shockingly egregious' was likely to attract the international consensus necessary for the creation of a norm of customary international law. However, no matter how 'shocking' or 'egregious' conduct might be, it would not found a suit under ATCA, unless it violated a norm of customary international law.

The decisions in *Beanal* and *Flores* clearly establish that there is no rule of customary international law that prohibits intra-national pollution, irrespective of whether that alleged norm is defined in relation to the pollution itself or to the effects it has on human life, health and wellbeing. The problem is the absence of any consensus of states beyond the general agreement that pollution is a 'bad thing' and the general aspiration that it ought to be reduced. Materials such as the Rio Declaration have been interpreted in such a way as to establish an international consensus in favour of leaving intra-national pollution exclusively within the domain of individual states. This militates against the development of a rule of customary international law in two ways.

---

21 707 F 2d 691, p 692 (2d Cir 1983) (*per curiam*).

First, it indicates that intra-national pollution is a matter of several, rather than mutual, concern. Secondly, it guarantees a diversity of national standards as to the levels of intra-national pollution that individual states are prepared to tolerate. This necessarily impedes the development of the requisite universal condemnation by states of any *specific* level of pollution. In an amicus brief submitted before the circuit court in *Flores*, Earthrights argued for the existence of a specific norm prohibiting intra-state pollution that entailed 'severe, long-term environmental degradation that prejudices the heath and survival of a population and that was engaged in pursuant to a systematic policy of deliberate indifference to human life and health'. They argued that such a norm could be justified by reference to the prohibitions on causing environmental damage in war that were contained in Geneva Convention 1949, Protocol Additional (I), Art 55(1). This argument was, however, not accepted by the circuit court.

The decisions have subsequently been followed in two cases. First, there is *Aguinda v Texaco*, which involved claims of both intra-national and transnational pollution following the activities in Ecuador in the 1960s and 1970s of an oil consortium in which a fourth-tier subsidiary of the defendant, Texaco, had been a participant. Judge Rakoff held that the claim fell outside ATCA in the absence of any precedent to support the allegation that the 'Consortium's oil extraction activities violated evolving environmental norms of customary international law'. Secondly, there is *Sarei v Rio Tinto*, in which the plaintiffs argued, *inter alia*, that environmental harm could amount to a breach of customary international law by reference to the right to life and health and the right to sustainable development. Morrow J held that these rights were still insufficiently specific to evidence a norm of customary international law in that the plaintiffs' evidence did not describe their parameters, nor detail what type of conduct would violate such rights. Furthermore, there was no evidence of the necessary universal recognition by states that these rights could be violated by perpetrating environmental harm, nor that the rights concerned wrongs of mutual, rather than merely several, concerns to states.

Morrow J did, however, hold that ATCA could cover claims which involved a breach of UNCLOS. The plaintiffs alleged breaches of two of its provisions relating to marine pollution from land-based sources.[22] The provisions of UNCLOS had become part of customary international law in that the convention had been ratified by 166 nations, including Papua New Guinea.

---

22 The first of these requires states to take 'all measures . . . that are necessary to prevent, reduce and control pollution of the marine environment' that involves 'hazards to human health, living resources and marine life through the introduction of substances into the marine environment'. The second requires states to 'adopt laws and regulations to prevent, reduce, and control pollution of the marine environment caused by land-based sources'.

Although the US had not ratified the convention, it had signed it. Breaches of the provisions of UNCLOS could, therefore, found an ATCA claim notwithstanding the fact that the plaintiffs had not exhausted national and international remedies.

But what of transnational pollution? The decisions in *Beanal* and *Flores* suggest that transnational pollution *might* constitute a breach of a norm of customary international law. In particular, both decisions, in contrast to that in *Amlon*, placed reliance on Third Restatement (1987), s 602. Because s 602 only referred to a rule of customary international law prohibiting transnational pollution, the courts in *Beanal* and *Flores* therefore concluded that this meant that there was no equivalent rule in relation to intra-national pollution. This would appear to weaken the effect of the finding in *Amlon* that the reference in the Restatement to a prohibition on transnational pollution only represented the US view of customary international law, but that it had not been shown that such view was universally accepted so that it actually constituted a rule of customary international law. Further, the facts of *Amlon* could be regarded as falling outside the norm articulated in the Restatement in that, following the placement of the shipment in steel drums, there was no longer a danger to the environment or human health. In *Aguinda*, Judge Rakoff overlooked the possibility that the plaintiff's transnational pollution claims might involve a breach of customary international law and so fall within ATCA. The *Trail Smelter* arbitration between the US and Canada, 1938–41, established that transnational pollution was capable of amounting to a breach of international law.[23] The pollution in *Aguinda*, unlike that in *Amlon*, would very probably come within the scope of the norm established in *Trail Smelter*. However, the plaintiffs' claim would still have been likely to fall outside ATCA as it would have been unlikely that the claim fell within the limited category of claims in which private actor liability for a breach of customary international law could be established.

9.1.2 Private actor liability under international law

Having established a violation of the law of nations, the plaintiff must then overcome the problem that most established norms of customary international law only proscribe the conduct of states rather than of private actors. An exception exists with regards a handful of *ius cogens* norms – slavery (including forced labour), genocide and war crimes.[24] Even if the plaintiff alleges a violation of such norms, it is unlikely that the violation will have been committed by the corporate defendant. Instead, such a violation is likely

---

23 *Trail Smelter (US v Canada)* (1938/1941) 3 RIAA 1905, 9 ILR 315.

24 *Ius cogens* norms are those rules of customary international law that have attained such widespread acceptance amongst states that they are binding even on states that are persistent objectors to such norms.

to have been committed by the state in which that defendant has been operating. The plaintiff will need to find some way to implicate its corporate defendant in the violations committed by the state. There are two main ways in which it can achieve this.

The first possibility is to have recourse to principles of international law regarding accomplice liability of private actors. In *Kadic v Karadzic*,[25] state action was held not to be required as regards violations of a limited category of core *ius cogens* norms of customary international law. These are the prohibitions against slavery, which now includes forced labour, genocide and war crimes.[25] Private actors who violate these norms will be liable under customary international law. They will also be liable if they are accomplices to violations committed by a state. This issue arose in the *Unocal* litigation under ATCA where the plaintiffs sought to hold Unocal liable for being an accessory to forced labour perpetrated by the Myanmar military during the construction of the Yadana pipeline in the mid-1990s. In *Unocal (2000)*, Lew J granted Unocal's application for summary judgment, holding, on this issue, that Unocal could not be liable under the international law rules on accessories as the plaintiffs had not alleged that Unocal had actually been an active participant in the forced labour perpetrated by the Myanmar military.[27]

In *Unocal (2002)*, however, the circuit court rejected this analysis.[28] The 'active participation' standard derived from war crimes cases before Nuremberg Military Tribunals involving the role of German industrialists in the Nazi forced labour program during the Second World War. This standard had been applied solely to overcome the defence of necessity invoked by the defendants, which, in the present case had not been invoked, nor could have been invoked. The law to be applied was that which had been developed in decisions of international criminal tribunals such as in *Prosecutor v Furundzija (Furundzija)*.[29] There, the International Tribunal for the former Yugoslavia had held that the *actus reus* of aiding and abetting in international criminal law requires practical assistance, encouragement, or moral support which has a substantial effect on the perpetration of the crime.[30] The assistance need not constitute an indispensible element in the perpetration of the

---

25 *Kadic v Karadzic* 70 F 3d 232 (2d Cir 1995).
26 Dicta in *Talisman* suggest that private actor liability exists in respect of *all* violations of *ius cogens* norms. This is inconsistent with *Kadic* as well as with the finding in *Wiwa* that state action was required in respect of the human rights violations in question, which included violations of *ius cogens* norms such as the prohibition on torture.
27 *Doe I v Unocal Corp* 110 F Supp 2d 1294 (CDCal 2000) (*Unocal (2000)*).
28 *Doe I v Unocal Corp* 395 F 3d 932 (9th Cir 2002) (*Unocal (2002)*).
29 *Prosecutor v Furundzija* (IT–95–17/1-T), 10 December 1998, (1999) 38 ILM 317.
30 The tribunal based its *actus reus* standard for aiding and abetting chiefly on decisions by American and British military courts and tribunals dealing with Nazi war crimes, as well as German courts in the British and French occupied zones dealing with such crimes in the aftermath of the Second World War.

crime, but did have to have a substantial effect on its commission. The test was whether the criminal act would most probably not have occurred in the same way without someone acting in the role that the accomplice had, in fact, assumed.[31] The tribunal had then defined the *mens rea* for aiding and abetting as actual or constructive knowledge that the actions of the accomplice would assist the perpetrator in the commission of the crime. However, the accomplice did not need to share the mens rea of the perpetrator, in the sense of positive intention to commit the crime, nor even to know the precise crime that the principal intended. It would be sufficient if the accused was aware that one of a number of crimes would probably be committed, and one of them is in fact committed, and he had intended to facilitate the commission of that crime. At least with respect to assistance and encouragement, the *Furundzija* standard was similar to the standard for aiding and abetting under domestic tort law.[32] The majority, however, stressed that they were not applying the *Furundzija* international criminal standard wholesale in that, given their findings on the question of knowing practical assistance and encouragement, they did not need to consider whether it would have been enough if Unocal had only given moral support to the Myanmar Military.

The majority then moved to apply the modified *Furundzija* standard to the allegations made by the plaintiffs. If these allegations were substantiated at trial, they would show that forced labour had been used in connection with the construction of the pipeline and that Unocal had given practical assistance to the Myanmar Military in subjecting the plaintiffs to forced labour, in the form of hiring the Myanmar Military to provide security and build infrastructure along the pipeline route in exchange for money or food and using photos, surveys and maps in daily meetings to show the Myanmar Military where to provide security and build infrastructure.

Furthermore, the fact that Unocal had these daily meetings with the Myanmar Military, despite its knowledge that the Myanmar Military would probably use forced labour to provide these services, may have encouraged the Myanmar Military to go ahead with using forced labour for the benefit of the project. Similarly, by paying the Myanmar Military for providing these services, Unocal would also have encouraged the use of forced labour by the Myanmar Military, if it knew that forced labour had actually been used in providing the services for which it was paying the military. This had a substantial effect on the perpetration of forced labour, in that it most probably

---

31 The tribunal also referred to International Criminal Tribunal for Rwanda's description of the *actus reus* as all acts of assistance in the form of either physical or moral support that substantially contribute to the commission of the crime. *Prosecutor v Musema* (ICTR–96–13-T), 27 January 2000, www.ictr.org (accessed 28 March 2007).

32 Thus, the Restatement (Second) of Torts, s 876 (1979) states: 'For harm resulting to a third person from the tortious conduct of another, one is subject to liability if he . . . (b) knows that the other's conduct constitutes a breach of duty and gives *substantial assistance or encouragement* to the other so to conduct himself . . .' (emphasis added).

would not have occurred in the same way had the Myanmar Military not been hired to provide security, and had Unocal not shown them where to do it. In this connection the court deemed significant the admissions of Unocal Representative Robinson that '[o]ur assertion that [the Myanmar Military] has not expanded and amplified its usual methods around the pipeline on our behalf may not withstand much scrutiny', and of Unocal President Imle that '[i]f forced labor goes hand and glove with the military yes there will be more forced labor'. Given that the district court had found that the evidence suggested both that Unocal knew of the use of forced labour and that the practice benefited the joint venturers in the pipeline project, a reasonable factfinder could also conclude that Unocal's conduct met the *mens rea* requirement.

The circuit court's decision was vacated in February 2003 and an *en banc* rehearing reordered, primarily to clarify whether international law or federal tort law was the applicable law for an ATCA claim.[33] The hearing took place in June 2004 and on 17 June was prorogued pending the result of the Supreme Court's decision in *Sosa*. In December 2004, the day before the rehearing was due to start, the claims were settled.

After *Sosa*, there have been several attempts to limit the scope of ATCA in cases involving alleged corporate complicity in human rights abuses by foreign governments. Defendants have argued against the existence of any norm of customary international law imposing civil liability on accessories, of the sort relied on by the circuit court in *Unocal (2002)*. After *Sosa*, three district courts have held that such a norm does exist, on the basis set out by the circuit court in *Unocal (2002)*,[34] whilst another district court has come to the contrary conclusion.[35] Arguments that ATCA does not cover claims against corporations have also fallen on stony ground.[36]

However, the application of the international criminal law rules on aiding and abetting may not be as favourable to ATCA plaintiffs as *Unocal (2002)* suggests. This can be seen in the recent decision of Cotes J in *Talisman (2006)*.[37] The facts of the case have many similarities to those in the *Unocal* litigation. The plaintiffs' claims were based on alleged human rights violations by the fundamentalist Islamic Government of Sudan in prosecuting a

---

33 The effect of vacating the decision is that it has no precedential effect and may not be cited on the Ninth Circuit.

34 *Presbyterian Church of Sudan v Talisman Energy, Inc* 374 F Supp 2d 331, p 341 (SDNY 2005) (*Talisman (2005)*). *In re Agent Orange Product Liability Litig* 373 F Supp 2d 7, p 53 (EDNY 2005). *Bowoto v Chevron Corp*, 22 August 2006, unreported, 2006 WL 2455752 (NDCal).

35 *In re South African Apartheid Litig* 346 F Supp 2d 538 (SDNY 2004).

36 *Presbyterian Church of Sudan v Talisman Energy, Inc* 374 F Supp 2d 331 (SDNY 2005) (*Talisman (2005)*). *In re Agent Orange Product Liability Litig* 373 F Supp 2d 7, p 53 (EDNY 2005). *Bowoto v Chevron Corp*, 22 August 2006, unreported, 2006 WL 2455752 (NDCal).

37 *Presbyterian Church of Sudan v Talisman Energy* 453 F Supp 2d 633 (SDNY 2006) (*Talisman (2006)*).

'war of genocide' or jihad aimed at the forced Islamisation of the southern Sudan. This entailed intense persecution for Christians and those practicing traditional indigenous religions, resulting in approximately 2 million deaths and the displacement of 4 million people. The plaintiffs claimed that a key feature of the civil war was its development into an 'oil war' for control of valuable petroleum resources in the south. Oil concessions were granted to foreign companies, operating through a consortium, the Greater Nile Petroleum Operating Company Ltd. (GNPOC). In 1998, Talisman, a Canadian company, started operations in Sudan, acquiring, through its subsidiaries, 25 per cent of GNPOC from another Canadian company, Arakis, which had operated in the Sudan since 1988. Talisman's responsibility under GNPOC was for exploration and production in areas inhabited primarily by the Dinka and Nuer peoples, who are Christian or practice traditional indigenous religions.

The plaintiffs contended that from the beginning there was an inextricable link between the Sudanese Government's oil development policy and its violent campaign against ethnic and religious minorities. The government saw its oil reserves as the means to acquire the military resources necessary to pursue its 'jihad' against the non-Islamic populations in the south of the country. The plaintiffs alleged that, for their part, first Arakis, and then Talisman, knew from the start that military action would be required to secure the concession for oil exploration and extraction. According to the plaintiffs the government and the members of the consortium were engaged in an 'unholy alliance' whereby, in exchange for oil concessions, the government would clear the area around the oil fields of the local population and the oil companies would the invest in dual-use infrastructure, such as all-weather roads, airfields and communications facilities. These could be used both to support exploration and to enable the government to pursue its ethnic cleansing of the local population.

Cotes J first held that there could be no claim against Talisman for a conspiracy based on allegations of its knowing participation in a forcible transfer of population by the government of Sudan. International law recognised only conspiracies to wage war and to commit genocide, neither of which had been alleged by the plaintiffs. As regards the claims that Talisman had aided and abetted the Sudanese Government in committing, genocide, torture, war crimes and crimes against humanity, these fell to be dealt with under the principles of international criminal law, which closely paralleled those of federal criminal law. In *Prosecutor v Vasiljevic*,[38] the Appeals Chamber of the International Criminal Tribunal for the Former Yugoslavia stated that the *actus reus* of aiding and abetting required that the accused had carried

---

38 *Prosecutor v Vasiljevic* (Case No IT–98–32-A), judgment, 102(i) (App Chamber, 25 February 2004).

out 'acts *specifically directed* to assist, encourage or lend moral support to the perpetration of a certain specific crime' (emphasis added) and that these had had 'a substantial effect upon the perpetration of the crime'. The *mens rea* of the crime was 'knowledge that the acts performed by the aider and abettor assist the commission of the specific crime of the principal'. To show that a defendant had aided and abetted a violation of international law, the plaintiff needed to establish five things. First, the principal had violated international law. Secondly, the defendant knew of the specific violation. Thirdly, the defendant had acted with the intent to assist that violation (that is to say the defendant specifically directed his acts to assist in the specific violation). Fourthly, the defendant's acts had had a substantial effect upon the success of the criminal venture. Fifthly, the defendant was aware that its acts assisted the specific violation. Cotes J's approach differs markedly from that of the circuit court in *Unocal (2002)* as regards the third of these requirements. The circuit court did not require the defendants to have specifically directed their acts to assist the Myanmar military in using forced labour. Instead, it was enough that Unocal knew or ought to have known that what they were doing would help the Myanmar military to do so.

The plaintiffs argued that Talisman had provided substantial assistance in the commission of crimes against humanity and war crimes law through the following: upgrading the Heglig and Unity airstrips which were then used for bombing raids on civilians by the Sudanese military; designating particular areas, in the non-Islamic parts of Sudan, for oil exploration; helping the Sudanese Government in its purchase of military equipment by its payment of royalties to the government; and giving general logistical support to the Sudanese military, such as building all-weather roads which were then used to wage the civil war.

These activities generally accompanied any natural resource development business or the creation of any industry. These acts of potential substantial assistance had no necessary or obvious criminal component. The plaintiffs' essential complaint was that Talisman should not have invested in the Sudan when it knew that the government forcibly evicting non-Muslims from lands that could be exploited for oil. To succeed, the plaintiffs would have to show that the acts of alleged substantial assistance were performed with Talisman both knowing of the criminal enterprise of the government and intending that it should succeed. There was no evidence of such intent and, indeed, Talisman had no role in many of the acts relied on by the plaintiffs. The two airstrips were operated by GNPOC and there was no evidence that Talisman had any role in operating or upgrading them. Talisman was not party to the decision to make all-weather roads, which was made by GNPOC, nor was it involved in the proposal to explore south of the river. As regards the royalty payments, it was not enough to show that Talisman believed that these were being used by the government to buy armaments. The plaintiffs also had to show evidence that Talisman had intended its royalty payments to be used for this purpose. No such evidence had been adduced. The claims would be dismissed due to the plaintiff's failure to adduce any evidence that Talisman itself performed any act of substantial assistance to the government.[39] Talisman could not be made liable indirectly through its membership of the consortium. In contrast to the consortium in *Unocal*, GNPOC was established as a corporation which excluded the operation of principles of joint venturer liability. Instead, the matter fell within the law of Mauritius, where GNPOC had been incorporated. This provided that, unless the corporate veil could be pierced, which was not the case here, Talisman, as a shareholder, would not be liable in respect of wrongs committed by the company.

9.1.3 Private actor liability under s 1983

The second means of proceeding against a private actor in respect of breaches of customary international law is by reference to s 1983, 'Civil action for deprivation of rights', which provides:

> Every person who, under color of any statute, ordinance, regulation, custom, or usage, of any State . . . subjects, or causes to be subjected, any citizen of the United States or other person within the jurisdiction thereof to the deprivation of any rights, privileges, or immunities secured by the Constitution and laws, shall be liable to the party injured in an action at law, suit in equity, or other proper proceeding for redress . . .

Section 1983 will apply where there is a violation of any norm of international law and there has been state action on the part of the defendant. This requires the defendant to establish a linkage between the defendant and the violations of international law committed by the state in which it was operating.

Where the alleged violations have been committed by the corporate defendant, then, unless they involve the handful of norms for which private actor liability exists under international law, the plaintiff will have to establish state action on the part of the defendant when it committed those violations. Where the wrong has been committed by the corporate defendant, the plaintiff will need to find some way of linking its conduct with the state in whose jurisdiction those wrongs were committed. The Tenth Circuit's 1995 decision in *Gallagher v Neil Young Freedom Concert* sets out four factors that are relevant to a finding of state action.[40] First, was there a sufficiently close

---

39 This finding is similar to that of Chaney J in the tort claims brought against Unocal before the state courts of California where she found that another member of the project, Total, had been responsible for hiring the Myanmar military to provide security.
40 *Gallagher v Neil Young Freedom Concert* 49 F 3d 1442, p 1455 (10th Cir 1995).

nexus between the state and the challenged action of the regulated entity so that the acts of the latter might fairly be treated as those of the state? Secondly, had the state so far insinuated itself into a position of inter-dependence with the private party that there was a symbiotic relationship between them? Thirdly, was the private party a wilful party in joint activity with the state or its agents? Fourthly, had the private entity exercised powers that were traditionally exclusively reserved to the state?

In *Beanal*, the plaintiffs alleged that alleged torts committed by Freeport's security personnel, constituted state action because of the presence of Indonesian troops at the time. However, the claim for state action had not been made out in that the plaintiffs had failed adequately to specify what had been the role of the Indonesian troops, whether onlookers or active participants. The more common situation is that of 'reverse state action' where the wrongs have been committed by the foreign state and the plaintiff seeks to link the defendant to those violations. In *Unocal (2000)*, where the alleged violations of international law had been committed by the Myanmar military, Lew J applied both a 'joint action' and 'proximate cause' test. Because there was no evidence that Unocal participated in or influenced the unlawful conduct, or that it conspired with the government of Burma, Lew J held there was no proof of joint action.[41] It was not enough that Unocal and the Myanmar Government shared an interest in ensuring the profitability of the project was not sufficient to prove that Unocal was a state actor. Nor did Unocal's conduct fall within the 'proximate cause' test, as there was no evidence that Unocal controlled the Myanmar Government's decision to commit violations of international law.

In *Sarei v Rio Tinto*, Morrow J applied this test to Rio Tinto's potential liability for war crimes allegedly committed by the PNGDF during the Bougainvaille civil war, in instituting a blockade of the island in violation of the Geneva Conventions which apply to 'armed conflict(s) of an international character'. The plaintiffs' allegations went significantly further than those made in Unocal. The mine was a joint venture between Rio Tinto and PNG and waging war against the Bougainville Resistance Army was necessary to reopen the mine. In particular they asserted that Rio Tinto had threatened to withdraw its investment unless something was done to enable the mine to be opened again. The plaintiffs also alleged that Rio had continuously encouraged continuation of the blockade and that at one meeting in 1990 one top Rio manager had urged continuation of the blockade to 'starve the bastards

---

41 At pp 1306–7. See, too, *Aguinda v Texaco*, where Judge Rakoff held that the discovery in the case that had already taken place established overwhelmingly that no act taken by Texaco in the US bore materially on the pollution-creating activities of which the plaintiffs complained. This was not a case, then, where the US was specifically used as a base from which to direct violations of international law visited on some foreign site.

out some more, and they will come around'. This verbal encouragement was also backed up by Rio's supplying helicopters and other vehicles for use by the PNGDF. Morrow J held that, if proved, these facts in combination, would justify a finding that Rio Tinto had acted under 'color of law' under s 1983.

However, since the Supreme Court's decision in *Sosa*, two district courts have held that the US jurisprudence under s 1983 has no place to play in determining the liability of private actors under customary international law for the purpose of an ATCA claim. In *Doe I v Exxon Mobil Corp*,[42] Oberdorfer J stated that: 'Grafting s.1983 color of law analysis onto international law claims would be an end-run around the accepted principle that most violations of international law can be committed only by states … Recognising acts under color of law would dramatically expand the extraterritorial reach of the statute.' A similar finding was made in *Bowoto v Chevron Corp*.[43] Illston J based her decision on the requirement set out in *Sosa* that an international law norm had to be definite and accepted before it could form the basis of a cause of action under ATCA. An integral feature of international law was that it was only binding on specific defendants. Therefore, 'allowing a private party to be held liable based upon notions of "color of law" developed in this country would blur the applicability of the obligations that international law imposes'. Such expansion of the scope of ATCA would also be inconsistent with the repeated calls for judicial restraint to be found in *Sosa*. If these decisions are followed in other circuits, ATCA claims against corporations will be possible only as regards the very limited category of norms of customary international law which can be violated by a private actor. In *Bowoto*, the plaintiffs' claims in respect of aiding and abetting crimes against humanity, and genocide, fell within this category, but not their claims for torture and extra-judicial killing, which were dismissed. The circuit court in *Sarei v Rio Tinto* is, however, unclear on this point.[44] The issue arose as to whether claims for *vicarious liability* for violations of *ius cogens* norms were actionable under ATCA. It was held that they were and that the courts would draw on federal common law under which there were well-settled theories of vicarious liability. The circuit court did not specifically refer to s 1983, but its reference to federal common law is inconsistent with the district courts' finding that *Sosa* requires this issue to be determined by reference to customary international law.[45]

42 *Doe I v Exxon Mobil Corp* 393 F Supp 2d 20 (DDC 2005).
43 *Bowoto v Chevron Corp*, 22 August 2006, unreported, 2006 WL 2455752 (NDCal).
44 *Sarei v Rio Tinto* F 3d 2006 WL 2242146 (9th Cir 7 August 2006).
45 However, as Illston J pointed out in *Bowoto v Chevron Corp* (22 August 2006), the plaintiffs' claims against Rio Tinto in respect of war crimes and crimes against humanity would fall under the norms of customary international law norms that are binding on private actors.

9.2 Other statutory avenues for human rights claims

9.2.1 Torture Victims Protection Act 1991

In 1991, Congress extended to US citizens the right hitherto enjoyed by aliens under ATCA of making civil claims in the federal courts in respect of human rights abuses. However, the TVPA, although it overlaps with ATCA, contains the following important differences. First, it does not extend to all torts committed in violation of the law of nations, but only applies to acts of torture and extra-judicial killings. Secondly, these must occur 'under actual or apparent authority, or color of law, of any foreign nation' against both aliens and US citizens. This would preclude private actor liability based on the principles of customary international law of the type recognised by the circuit court in *Unocal (2002)*, which is more generous to plaintiffs than the way in which the 'state action' requirements of s 1983 have been interpreted. Thirdly, TVPA contains a 10-year limitation period, unlike ATCA which has none (although in *Papa*, it was held that ATCA claims should be subject to the same limitation period as claims under TVPA). Fourthly, TVPA, unlike ATCA, explicitly requires the plaintiff to have exhausted domestic remedies. The burden of proof in establishing this falls on defendant and in many instances it will be difficult to satisfy, given the likelihood of retaliatory action against a plaintiff who commenced suit against his torturers in the place where he had been tortured. Fifthly, TVPA gives a right to claim against 'individuals' which may preclude claims against corporations. The law on this point is unclear. The district courts have taken the view that 'individuals' does not comprise corporations, in *Beanal v Freeport McMoran*, and *Doe I v Exxon Mobil Corp.*[46] The contrary position has been taken in *Sinaltrainal v Coca Cola*[47] and *Estate of Rodriguez v Drummond.*[48]

9.2.2 USC, s 1331

USC, s 1331, which gives federal courts jurisdiction over matters arising under the Constitution and federal laws, might also form the justification for basing a suit on a breach of a norm of customary international law which is sufficiently universal to form the basis of a right of action under federal common law. In *Bodner v Banque Paribas*,[49] it was held that US

---

46 *Doe I v Exxon Mobil Corp* 393 F Supp 2d 20 (DDC 2005).
47 *Sinaltrainal v Coca Cola* 256 F Supp 2d 1345, p 1359 (SD Fla 2003).
48 *Estate of Rodriguez v Drummond* 256 F Supp 2d 1250, pp 1266–7 (WD Al 2003).
49 *Bodner v Banque Paribas* 114 F Supp 2d 117, p 127 (EDNY 2000). As US citizens they could not have recourse to ATCA. Neither, given the nature of the violation of customary international law, could they have recourse to the TVPA.

citizens could sue a French bank in respect of the looting of their possessions in the Second World War, which constituted a war crime. In contrast, in *Xuncax v Gramajo*,[50] it was held that federal law gave rise to no autonomous right to sue for breaches of customary international law. After *Sosa* it is likely that this is the correct approach. However, if there is a violation of a norm of customary international law that is as well established as the norms existing in 1789, it is possible that it might confer a right of suit on a US plaintiff, who could not have recourse to ATCA, in the event that the norm in question did not generate a right to sue under the TVPA.

9.2.3 *Racketeer Influenced and Corrupt Organisations Act*

The Racketeer Influenced and Corrupt Organisations Act (RICO) 18 USC, s 1962 (2002) was enacted to deal with organised crime, but has potential application to alleged criminal conspiracies involving corporations in their dealings with foreign governments. Paragraph c states:

> It shall be unlawful for any person employed by or associated with any enterprise engaged in, or the activities of which affect, interstate or foreign commerce, to conduct or participate, directly or indirectly, in the conduct of such enterprise's affairs through a pattern of racketeering activity, or collection of unlawful debt.

The plaintiff must satisfy one of two tests when it is claiming in respect of extra-territorial acts. The first is the conduct test. Did the conduct within the US directly cause the loss? The second is the effects test. Did the predominantly foreign transaction have substantial effects within the US? In *Unocal (2002)*, the circuit court held that the plaintiffs' claims for forced labour created a potential RICO claim, in that freedom to make personal and business decisions about the use of one's labour could be regarded as a property right. However, the facts fell outside both tests. The transfer of monies and technical support by Unocal to Myanmar could not be seen as part of an alleged pattern of extortion outside the US. These were mere preparatory acts and were far removed from the alleged fraud. Nor were there any effects in the US in that there was no evidenced that Unocal's activities in Myanmar had given it an unfair competitive advantage in the US market.[51] In contrast, in *Wiwa*,[52] the evidence on this point was stronger and the plaintiffs

---

50 *Xuncax v Gramajo* 866 F Supp 162, pp 182–4 (D Mass 1995).
51 Although no mention was made of the point by the circuit court, it is probably significant that, as found in the challenge to jurisdiction in *Unocal (1998)*, the majority of oil coming from the Yadana project was likely to be sold in South East Asia.
52 *Wiwa v Royal Dutch Petroleum Co* No 96 Civ 8386(KMW), 2002 WL 319887 (SDNY 28 February 2002).

were held to have adequately pled a RICO claim based on the effects test. The alleged 'enterprise' was a conspiracy between the defendants, the Nigerian military and an unaffiliated company, Willbros, West Africa. The alleged racketeering acts were murder, arson, extortion and bribery which caused relevant damage to the plaintiffs by forcing them to abandon their property and businesses. Unlike the situation in *Unocal*, these alleged acts had an effect within the US in that 40 per cent of the oil extracted from Ogoniland was exported to the US and the defendants hoped to obtain a competitive advantage from their alleged racketeering actions by obtaining the benefit of lower production costs.

9.3 Tort claims

Following the decisions in *Beanal, Flores* and *Aguinda*, most pollution claims against a US corporation will have to be based exclusively on common law tort principles. As is the case in English litigation, the big problem facing the plaintiffs will be that of finding a way to make a parent company liable in respect of the negligence of its subsidiary. Shareholder liability is limited to the amount of unpaid share capital, a principle that applies equally to corporate groups where a parent company holds the majority, or even the totality, of shares in a subsidiary. This is the case notwithstanding that the principle was established before the emergence of corporate groups. Indeed, Blumberg has pointed out that in the US the principles of limited liability were established at a time when, in most states, corporations were actually prohibited from owning shares in other corporations.[53] However, US law provides three possible avenues of derivative liability by which the faults of the subsidiary can be attributed to the parent.

9.3.1 Alter ego

The corporate veil will be disregarded when the subsidiary is held to have been the 'alter ego' in which case parent and subsidiary will be treated as one. In *Seymour v Hull & Moreland Engineering*,[54] the federal test for piercing the corporate veil on this ground was said to involve three general factors: 'the amount of respect given to the separate identity of the corporation by its shareholders, the degree of injustice visited on the litigants by recognition of the corporate entity, and the fraudulent intent of the incorporators. Federal decisions naturally draw upon state law for guidance in this field'.[55]

---

53 Blumberg, P, *The Multinational Challenge to Corporation Law*, 1993, Oxford: Oxford University Press.
54 *Seymour v Hull & Moreland Engineering* 605 F 2d 1105, p 1111 (9th Cir 1979).
55 The third factor, however, is not universally accepted as state law.

As regards the first factor, officers of a parent corporation may be involved in the supervision of a subsidiary corporation without incurring liability for the parent corporation, provided they act within the bounds of corporate formalities. In *US v Bestfoods*,[56] the Supreme Court considered that 'monitoring of the subsidiary's performance, supervision of the subsidiary's finance and capital budget and articulation of general policies and procedures' all constituted examples of appropriate parental involvement as well as holding that liability would not be imposed on a parent merely because its directors also served as directors of the subsidiary. As regards the second factor, the inability of the subsidiary to meet its liabilities will not be enough to trigger a finding of alter ego.

It has, therefore, proved very difficult to establish derivative liability on this ground. This is illustrated by *Bowoto v Chevron*.[57] Chevron Nigeria Limited (CNL) operated a joint venture with the Nigerian National Petroleum Company, the Nigerian state oil company. The case arose out of claims that CNL had recruited the Nigerian military and police to fire at protesters on an oil platform and to open fire on a village from Chevron helicopters, flown by Chevron pilots, as well as using Chevron sea trucks to transport the military to a village where they then fired on the inhabitants. The sole issue at this stage of the proceedings was the extent of a parent corporation's responsibility for the acts of its subsidiaries. The defendants were both Chevron Texaco Corporation (CVX)[58] and its wholly owned subsidiary, Chevron Overseas Petroleum, Inc (COPI).[59]

The first incident occurred on 28 May 1998 when a number of Nigerians staged a protest on Chevron's Parabe oil platform. The Nigerian military and police opened fire at the protestors, killing two of them. The plaintiffs alleged that CNL, acting in concert with defendants, had recruited the Nigerian military and police to end the protest in this manner and also that CNL's management and security forces were involved in the subsequent detainment and torture of Bola Oyinbo, one of the leaders of the protest movement. The second and third were the Opia and Ikenyan incidents, which occurred on 4 January 1999. The plaintiffs alleged that a helicopter flown by Chevron pilots and transporting Nigerian military and/or police had overflown the community of Opia and opened fire on the villagers, killing one person and injuring others. The helicopter then flew to the Ikenyan community where similar abuses were allegedly committed. According to the plaintiffs, 30 minutes later, CNL sea trucks, containing CNL personnel and Nigerian military, approached Opia and opened fire on the villagers, killing several people.

---

56 *US v Bestfoods* 524 US 69 (1998), 118 SCt 1876.
57 *Bowoto v Chevron* 312 F Supp 2d 1229 (NDCal 2004).
58 Formerly, the Chevron Corporation.
59 Subsequently, Chevron Texaco Overseas Petroleum, Inc (CTOP).

The soldiers then disembarked from the sea trucks and set fire to buildings and livestock, killing another person.

Illston J held that the alter ego theory did not apply on the facts alleged by the plaintiffs. The doctrine involved a two-pronged test. First, the plaintiff must show that the subsidiary was a mere instrumentality of the parent. The mere fact that officers of a parent corporation were involved in the supervision of a subsidiary corporation was not sufficient to attribute liability to the parent corporation. There would be no veil-piercing in respect of typical acts of parent corporation officers which fell within the bounds of corporate formalities, such as supervising the acts of the subsidiaries; receiving regular reports from the subsidiaries; creating general policies and procedures which the subsidiaries must follow; and overseeing the financial management of the subsidiaries. Officers of a parent might also simultaneously act as officers of the subsidiary without their actions in that capacity being attributable to the parent corporation. Secondly, it must show that observing the corporate form would achieve an inequitable result. The plaintiffs were unable to show any evidence on this point. The inability of plaintiffs to recover for their losses was not a sufficient inequity to justify overlooking the corporate form.[60]

9.3.2 Agency

Secondly, the subsidiary may be found to have acted as the agent of the parent in respect of the particular action giving rise to the claim. Unlike the 'alter ego' theory, a finding of agency does not detract from the separate corporate personalities of the parent and subsidiary The Restatement (Second) of Agency, 14M states:

> . . . a subsidiary may become an agent for the corporation which controls it, or the corporation may become the agent of the subsidiary. In some situations, a court may find that the subsidiary has no real existence or assets, that its formal existence is to cloak a fraud or other illegal conduct. As in a similar situation in which an individual is the offender, it may be found that the parent company is the real party to a transaction conducted by the illusory subsidiary and responsible for its transactions as a principal.

Unlike liability under the alter-ego or veil-piercing test, agency liability does not require the court to disregard the corporate form. The Restatement has likewise noted the distinction between veil-piercing and agency theories of liability.[61]

---

60 A third possible requirement was that incorporation had been undertaken in bad faith, of which there was no evidence here
61 Restatement (Second) of Agency, Appendix S, 14M, Reporter's Notes at 68 (1958).

In *Bowoto v Chevron*, Illston J set out the factors that would support a finding of derivative liability based on agency. First, there must exist a close relationship or domination between the parent and subsidiary, and moreover there must also be a finding that the injury allegedly inflicted by the subsidiary, for which the parent is being held liable, was within the scope of the subsidiary's authority as an agent. As stated in *Phoenix Canada Oil v Texaco*: 'Not only must an arrangement exist between the two corporations so that one acts on behalf of the other and within usual agency principles, but the arrangement must be relevant to the plaintiff's claim of wrongdoing.'[62]

The first factor was that the defendants, COPI and CVX, had exercised more than usual control over the activities of their subsidiary, particularly as regards security. This was evidenced as follows. COPI controlled the appointment of CNL managers and lower level positions, and CNL managers simultaneously served in management positions for the defendants as well as doing work for other Nigerian subsidiaries. CNL employees were paid according to standards set by COPI and high-ranking CNL officials simultaneously performed COPI functions. The defendants set salaries for CNL representatives and had veto power over decisions made by high-level managers of CNL. The defendants closely monitored CNL's oil exploration and production, providing almost daily reports. CVX required all subsidiary companies to obtain authorisation for expenditures in excess of $100,000 and the defendants audited CNL three times a year. This close monitoring of CNL activities could be found to be well beyond the review of a subsidiary entity which a parent corporation normally performs.

> Here, defendant functioned as a multi-national corporation in which CNL played a significant role. Defendant had much more than the usual degree of control over CNL's operations, and particularly in setting security policy. The revolving door of managers and directors at the highest levels between CNL and defendants is dramatic evidence of the close relationship that was shared and can be viewed as further evidence of an agency relationship.

Significantly, this high level of control was particularly apparent in the area of security. The Corporate Security Group determined the security policies for CNL and other subsidiaries and influenced CNL policy on security. Prior to the May incident, it held meetings in London, attended by CNL's public affairs manager Sola Omole, regarding possible developments in the Nigerian political climate and how those developments would affect CNL. It evaluated evaluated CNL security in the wake of the attacks during which period the defendants had extensive communications with the plaintiffs during the Parabe and Opia/Ikenyan incidents. The defendants and CNL had regular

---

62 *Phoenix Canada Oil v Texaco* 842 F 2d 1466, pp 1477–8 (3d Cir 1988).

communications regarding security measures before and after the attacks with an extraordinarily high volume of phone calls between defendants' personnel in the US and CNL on 27 May 1998, the first day of the occupation of the Parabe platform. Defendants' security, international and public affairs staff was the contact point for CNL during the communications. Corporate security had frequent communications with CNL regarding Iijaw unrest and CNL's intended response to it.

Another relevant factor was that CNL had engaged in activities in Nigeria that, but for its presence there, the defendants would have had to undertake themselves.[63] Apart from the very close relation between parent and subsidiary as evidenced above, there was the fact that the CVX annual report portrayed the defendants as part of an integrated operation with CNL.[64] The importance of CNL to the defendant's business was shown by the fact that CNL's oil production represented 20 per cent of COPI's earnings. There was also significant evidence that the defendants viewed unrest in Nigeria as directly affecting CNL's oil production, and their own revenues.[65] Taken together, this evidence could support a finding of agency based on the fact that CVX and CTOP, the US-based defendants, had exercised more than the usual degree of direction and control which a parent exercises over its subsidiary. Such agency would also directly relate to the plaintiffs' causes of action, which alleged that defendants were significantly involved in security matters and benefited directly from CNL's oil production, which was made possible, or at least protected by the military's wrongful use of force to quell local unrest. The plaintiffs also contended that defendants and CNL increased their revenues both through the military's response to Nigerian unrest and through their cover-up in the US of the events after they occurred.

Even if CNL had acted outside the scope of its authority, the defendants could still be liable by ratifying its conduct through the subsequent 'cover up'. This could be evidenced by conflicting statements the defendants made to the media about CNL's involvement in the attacks, such as reporting that the

---

63 *Gallagher v Mazda Motor of America, Inc* 781 F Supp 1079, pp 1083–4 (EDPa 1992). This is a factor which is also relevant to the question of whether jurisdiction can be established by serving the defendant's subsidiary. However, the factor appears to be stronger in establishing agency in this context than is the case when substantive liability is in issue where it is only one of a number of factors that will establish agency.

64 In particular, the annual report described CVX as 'an international company that, through its subsidiaries and affiliates engages in fully integrated petroleum operations, chemical operations and coalmining in the United States and approximately 90 countries'.

65 Chevron's 1997 annual report stated: 'In certain locations . . . political conditions have existed that may threaten the safety of employees and the company's continued presence in those countries. Internal unrest or strained relations between a host government and the company or other governments may affect the company's operations. Those developments have, at times, significantly affected the company's operations and related results and are carefully considered by management when evaluating the level of current and future activity in such countries.'

military had approached Chevron to provide transportation to the platform and that CNL did not own helicopters or boats. The defendants also seemed to have made contradictory statements about CNL's ownership of the helicopters and boats used to transport the Nigerian military to the platform. Most of defendants' statements took great pains to suggest that the helicopters and boats were not CNL's to loan to the Nigerian military, but rather property of the joint venture.

9.3.3 Single economic entity

Thirdly, in limited circumstances the corporate veil may be pierced when the courts find that parent and subsidiary have acted as a single economic entity, the so-called theory of enterprise liability. In *The Amoco Cadiz*,[66] Judge McGarr held that Standard Oil was responsible for the tortious acts of two of its wholly owned subsidiaries which had resulted in an oil spill from a tanker. These were Transport, the nominal owner of the vessel, and AIOC, which exercised complete control over its operation, maintenance and repair, as well as over the selection and training of its crew. The basis of Standard's liability for the defaults of these two subsidiary companies was that it 'exercised such control over its subsidiaries . . . that those entities would be considered to be mere instrumentalities of Standard' and that as an integrated multinational corporation Standard would be responsible for the tortious acts of its wholly owned subsidiaries and instrumentalities.[67] These findings were not challenged when the case was subsequently appealed. However, the decision goes against the whole tenor of US decisions on veil-piercing, and, furthermore, is imprecise as to exactly which facts will justify a finding that the subsidiary was a mere instrumentality. In *Bowoto v Chevron Corp*, in which *The Amoco Cadiz* was not cited, Illston J declined to apply an integrated enterprise theory to the issue of veil-piercing.[68]

9.3.4 Direct liability

Apart from piercing the corporate veil, the parent might also be held liable in respect of its own primary breach of duty, rather than vicariously in respect of the breach of its subsidiary. As is the case with English law, this question involves uncharted areas of tort law, particularly as regards the question of

---

66 *The Amoco Cadiz* [1984] 2 Lloyd's Rep 304, esp p 338F, 43–6. Affd 954 F 2d 2179 (7th Cir 1992).

67 Judge McGarr also found that Standard was also personally liable because it had initially been involved in and controlled the designing, construction, operation and management of the vessel which it had treated as its own.

68 Such a theory had been applied in specific statutory contexts, principally those relating to the liability of employers, but it could not be imported without examination into different contexts involving the issue of veil-piercing.

whether a parent company will ever owe supervisory duties in relation to the activities of a foreign subsidiary.

The general principles were reviewed by the Supreme Court in *US v Bestfoods* in 1998.[69] Proceedings were brought under Comprehensive Environmental Response, Compensation, and Liability Act of 1980 (CERCLA), s 107(a)(2) against CPC International Inc, the parent corporation of the defunct Ott Chemical Co (Ott II), for the costs of cleaning up industrial waste generated by Ott II's chemical plant. Section 107(a)(2) authorises suits against, among others, 'any person who at the time of disposal of any hazardous substance owned or operated any facility'. The question arose as to whether Ott II's parent corporation could be viewed as an 'operator' under CERCLA. The district court held that this would be the case where it had exerted power or influence over its subsidiary, by actively participating in, and exercising control over, the subsidiary's business during a period of hazardous waste disposal. CPC was therefore held liable because it had selected Ott II's board of directors and populated its executive ranks with CPC officials, and another CPC official had played a significant role in shaping Ott II's environmental compliance policy. The circuit court reversed the decision on the grounds that a parent company could only be held directly liable under s 107(a)(2) if it actually operated its subsidiary's facility in the stead of the subsidiary, or alongside of it, as a joint venturer. A parent corporation's liability for operating a facility ostensibly operated by its subsidiary depended on whether the degree to which the parent controls the subsidiary and the extent and manner of its involvement with the facility amounted to an abuse of the corporate form sufficient to warrant piercing the corporate veil.

The Supreme Court, for whom Souter J gave judgment, rejected the direct liability analysis of the district court, which had mistakenly focused on the relationship between parent and subsidiary, and premised liability on little more than CPC's ownership of Ott II and its majority control over Ott II's board of directors. The issue of direct liability by the parent had to be kept distinct from its possible derivative liability for its subsidiary's operation of the facility. Instead, the analysis should have focused on the relationship between CPC and the facility itself, that is to say on whether CPC 'operated' the facility, as evidenced by its direct participation in the facility's activities. The circuit court, however, had been unduly restrictive in limiting direct liability under CERCLA to a parent's sole or joint venture operation. The parent could also 'operate' a facility when joint officers or directors conducted the affairs of the facility on behalf of the parent; or agents of the parent, with no position in the subsidiary, managed or directed activities at the subsidiary's facility. Norms of corporate behavior were crucial reference

---

69   *US v Bestfoods* 524 US 69 (1998), 118 SCt 1876.

points for: (a) determining whether a dual officer or director had served the parent in conducting operations at the facility; and (b) distinguishing a parental officer's oversight of a subsidiary from his control over the operation of the subsidiary's facility. The district court's opinion had identified both an agent who had played a conspicuous part in dealing with the toxic risks emanating from the plant's operation, and some evidence that these activities were eccentric under accepted norms of parental oversight of a subsidiary's facility. Accordingly, the case was referred to the lower courts for re-evaluation and resolution.

However, it is significant that the Supreme Court's approach focuses on positive involvement by the parent in the activity of the subsidiary that goes beyond established norms of corporate behaviour. Where the problem is parental inactivity then it is very unlikely that any duty of care will come into existence. This issue arose indirectly in the following two decisions on *forum non conveniens*. Judge Keenan in *In re Union Carbide Corp Gas Plant Disaster* held that India was the *lex loci delicti* without providing any detailed analysis of the underlying substantive tort law. Judge Keenan assumed that the critical witnesses would be those in India connected with the operation of the plant. This assumption downplayed the potential importance of those persons resident in the US who would give evidence as to the degree of control Union Carbide exercised over the activities of its subsidiary. Judge Keenan's assumption appears to have been predicated on the arm's length relations that existed between Union Carbide and its Indian subsidiary.[70] A similar approach can be seen in *Aguinda v Texaco Inc*,[71] where Judge Rakoff noted that all the evidence was in Ecuador or nearby areas of Peru. No US connection was established by the mere fact that a member of the consortium operating in Ecuador was a fourth tier subsidiary of Texaco. This reflects a tacit assumption that the parent would not incur any direct liability in respect of a failure to supervise the overseas activities of its subsidiary.[72]

It is, however, possible that a parent corporation might be liable for the defaults of its subsidiary even in the absence of any direct involvement by the parent corporation in the activities of the subsidiary, by reference to

---

70 Judge Keenan's approach is perhaps explicable when one recalls that the *Bhopal* case was pleaded on the basis of both primary and vicarious liability. Whatever the evidence required for the former, the Indian witnesses crucial to the latter would tip the balance in favour of India as the appropriate forum for the action.

71 *Aguinda v Texaco Inc* 142 F Supp 2d 534 (SDNY 2001) (*Aguinda 2001*).

72 This view of Texaco's potential liability as parent company also seems to have informed Judge Broderick's initial order of discovery as to whether Texaco in fact directed activities in Ecuador from the US. The approach is similar to that adopted by Illston J in *Bowoto v Chevron Corp*, 22 August 2006, unreported, 2006 WL 2455752 (NDCal), where she held that the parent company could not be directly liable as it had not directed the acts of its Nigerian subsidiaries. Any liability would have to be indirect, based on a lifting on the corporate veil by application of the concepts of agency or alter ego.

the principle whereby a party is liable for the defaults of its independent contractors when they are engaged in inherently dangerous activity.[73] Applying this principle, Oberdorfer J in *Doe v Exxon Corp (Plaintiffs' motion to amend complaint)*[74] held that the plaintiffs had adequately alleged that the US corporate defendants knew or had to reason to know that paying the Indonesian military personnel to provide security for defendants' pipeline posed a danger to others as evidenced by the alleged history of human rights abuses by Indonesian soldiers. The defendants' motion to dismiss the plaintiffs' transitory tort claim in the state of District Columbia was, therefore, denied. However, the case involved independent contractors and it is uncertain whether the principles applied to the employer-contractor relationship would be applied that the parent-subsidiary relationship. With environmental torts there is also the issue of the threshold at which the subsidiary's overseas activities could be regarded as inherently dangerous.

9.4 The chain of attribution in the Unocal litigation

A critical issue in litigation against multinational corporations for environmental torts is the chain of attribution linking the domestic parent corporation with its foreign subsidiary. Where the claim involves complicity in human rights the chain is more complex due to the need to link the foreign subsidiary with the actual perpetrators of the abuse. This complex issue of attribution arose in the Unocal litigation. This arose out of allegations or forced labour, rape, torture and murder by the Myanmar military during the construction of a gas pipeline pursuant to a project involving various overseas investors, including two subsidiary companies of Unocal. The Yadana project involved two projects. The first involved gas exploration by a joint venture consisting of a Unocal subsidiary, MOGE, Total SA, and a Thai company, PTTEP. The second involved the onshore and operation construction of the gas pipeline. This was the responsibility of the Myanmar Gas Transportation Company (MGTC) in which a Unocal subsidiary, Unocal International Pipeline Corp, held a 28 per cent interest. The Myanmar military had been hired to provide security for the pipeline project. Two parallel cases were brought, the ATCA claim in the federal courts, and a tort claim in the Superior Court of California.[75]

The first step in the chain of attribution was to link the Myanmar military with the pipeline project. The circuit court, in the ATCA proceedings, assumed that the Myanmar military, having been engaged to provide security

---

73 Restatement (Second) of Torts, s 411 (1965).
74 *Doe v Exxon Corp (Plaintiffs' motion to amend complaint)*, unreported, 2 March 2006, WL 516744 (DDC).
75 These proceedings are unreported.

for the pipeline project, had acted as agents for MGTC. In the California proceedings, Chaney J held that the military could not be regarded as the alter ego of MOGE, the Myanmar state entity that was one of the joint venturers in the gas exploration project. It could, however, be regarded as the agent of the joint venturers. A principal would be liable for the intentional torts of his agent committed within the scope of the employment, which depended on whether the principal could have foreseen the wrongdoing of the agent. An agency relationship might be precluded if the joint venture lacked the legal right to control the military's activities. If this were the case, then the military would have acted as an independent contractor which the joint venture had directed to accomplish certain tasks, including security and the preparation of roads and helipads. The joint venture would incur liability because it should have recognised that the methods adopted by the military were likely to cause harm, given the military's well-known human rights record.

The second step was to link the pipeline project with the gas project. The minority judgment in the circuit court was given by Reinhardt J, who decided the case on the basis of federal, rather than international, law.[76] He held that the following evidence would enable a reasonable trier of fact to find that the joint venture was responsible for the pipeline project as well as the gas exploration project: MGTC was an under-capitalised shell corporation which maintained no independent offices and relied only on the employees of the joint venture; Unocal would share revenues and costs of both the drilling and transportation components of the Yadana project; one of Unocal's business managers had stated that 'the [Yadana] project is an entirety . . . although there may appear to be two different businesses . . . this is an illusion'. Observing that '[t]here is substantial evidence in the record that MGTC was the alter ego of the joint venture, in which case Unocal would be responsible for torts committed by its co-venturer, the Myanmar military, in the course of the pipeline construction company's activities', he held that the plaintiffs' claim of joint venture liability should proceed to trial.

In the California Superior Court, Chaney J, for similar reasons, also held that there was enough prima facie evidence to raise a case that there was a single Yadana project. Even if there had been two projects, the gas exploration project could still be regarded as a joint venturer with MGTC, provided its corporate veil could be pierced, so as to allow its activities to be attributed

---

76 Although the majority based their decision on the application of international law, they did note, at fn 20, that claims under federal law based on joint venture, agency, negligence and recklessness theories, to determine a defendant's tort liability in respect of wrongs committed by a third party, might have been viable on the facts of the cases. 'Moreover, on the facts of other ATCA cases, joint venture, agency, negligence, or recklessness may in fact be more appropriate theories than aiding and abetting.' This is most likely a reference to other cases involving violations of the law of nations that do require state action.

to the joint venturers.[77] The plaintiffs had produced the following evidence to show that MGTC was under-capitalised and could therefore be treated as the alter ego of the gas exploration project: when MGTC was capitalised, the cost of pipeline construction was estimated at $580 million; the shareholders made only nominal capital contributions, including Unocal's share of $30,000; Unocal had to submit its annual report to ensure MGTC's solvency; MGTC was financed by cash calls; and the parent companies of MGTC shareholders were required to guarantee payments for bid packages of goods and services to the Yadana project.

The third step was to link Unocal with its subsidiary companies that were involved in each of the two projects. The majority in the circuit court addressed this issue rather briefly.[78] There were four possible ways of linking Unocal with its subsidiary in the pipeline project. First, the subsidiary might be regarded as Unocal's alter ego. Secondly, it might be regarded as Unocal's agent. Thirdly, MGTC might be regarded as the alter ego of the gas exploration project which would allow its liability to be attributed amongst the joint venturers, one of whom was Unocal. Fourthly, Unocal might be liable in respect of its own conduct in connection with the pipeline project. The majority of the circuit court found that Unocal might be liable on either the first or the fourth of these theories.[79] The following evidence would allow a reasonable factfinder to conclude that the Unocal Pipeline Corp and the Unocal Offshore Co were alter egos of Unocal: their under-capitalisation; the direct involvement in and direction of their business by Unocal President Imle, Unocal CEO Beach, and other Unocal officers and employees.[80] An alter ego finding would not lead to a finding that Unocal was vicariously liable for the torts of the Myanmar military. Rather, it would lead to a finding that Unocal was liable, based on its own actions, and on those of its alter ego subsidiaries, in violating the law of nations by allegedly aiding and abetting the Myanmar military in perpetrating forced labour.

77 In contrast, in *Talisman (2006)*, the plaintiffs were unable to rely on joint venture principles because they had not pleaded evidence that would allow a finding that the corporate veil of GNPOC should be pierced.

78 Reinhardt J did not refer to this third issue of attribution.

79 In *Sarei v Rio Tinto*, this issue of the attributability of the acts of a subsidiary, BCL, to the parent corporation, Rio Tinto, received virtually no analysis. Many of the allegations which enabled Morrow J to find that Rio Tinto fell within the colour of law jurisprudence of s 1983 dealt with acts by employees of BCL, rather than Rio Tinto, and yet these were treated as evidencing conduct by Rio Tinto. The only material on this issue is a brief reference at the start of the case to the corporate structure of the Rio Tinto group which refers to the fact that Rio Tinto Ltd, Australia held a majority holding in BCL, which, although it had been reduced, still stood at 53.6 per cent in 1998.

80 Cf. the ATCA claim in *Wiwa v Royal Dutch Petroleum Co* No 96 Civ 8386(KMW), 2002 WL 319887, *13 n 14 (SDNY, 28 February 2002), where the district court held that the parent corporation, by its direct involvement in, and direction of, its subsidiary's activities, could be liable in tort by a finding that the subsidiary had acted as its agent.

In contrast, Chaney J, in a more extended analysis of this issue in the tort claims, found that the plaintiffs had not alleged evidence that would support a finding that Unocal's subsidiaries in the two projects could be regarded as its alter egos. Although there was some commingling of funds among the defendants and their subsidiaries, the subsidiaries controlled their own assets and the corporate formalities had been observed. Unocal had not exercised inappropriate control over the subsidiaries' daily operations through the companies' sharing of officers, directors, employees and offices. The subsidiaries were adequately capitalised and none was a shell, nor was ownership concealed. Appropriate arm's length relationships had been maintained between parents and subsidiaries. There had been no wrongful diversion of assets and the subsidiaries had not been created to transfer an existing liability. Furthermore, the plaintiff's assertion that, if there were no veil-piercing, the subsidiaries would be left without the means to satisfy existing and potential creditors was not enough to show that there would be injustice in the absence of veil-piercing.

However, these alter ego findings did not preclude a finding that the subsidiaries may have acted as Unocal's agents. The factual findings that led to the court deciding not to pierce the corporate veil did not decide the issue of agency. The main factual sub-issue in the alter ego analysis was the degree of control exercised by the parent over the subsidiary. This would need to be re-examined because a lesser degree of control would suffice to establish a finding of agency. The plaintiffs' failure to prove eradication of the subsidiaries' separate personalities did not preclude them from proving the defendants controlled specific aspects of the Yadana project to an extent beyond that permissible by a mere owner.

Apart from derivative liability, there was the possibility that Unocal might be liable on the basis of its own actions. The circuit court based its finding on this basis, as well as on an alter ego basis, although its very brief analysis of the issue does not disclose why it made this alternative finding.[81] The issue was examined in greater depth by Chaney J in the tort claims in the Superior Court of California. The first potential head of liability would be for aiding and abetting. This required knowledge that a tort had been, or was to be, committed, coupled with acts done with the intent of facilitating the commission of that tort. Unocal's day-to-day involvement with the military in the management of the pipeline project did not show it had acted with the intent of facilitating the commission of the Myanmar military's torts.

---

81 In the circuit court Reinhardt J held that the plaintiffs might also have a viable claim against Unocal under the common law theory of recklessness or reckless disregard based on the allegation that they had suffered harm due to Unocal's disregard of the risk of unreasonable harm to the plaintiffs caused by their decision to use the military for pipeline security, a risk of which they were, or should have been, aware.

The district court, in the ATCA proceedings, had made it clear that the evidence relied on by the plaintiffs did not suggest Unocal sought to employ forced or slave labor. Instead, the joint venturers expressed concern that the Myanmar Government was utilising forced labour in connection with the project, and the military tried to conceal its use of forced labour. It was not enough that the joint venturers had benefited from the use of forced labour.

There were also two other obstacles to imposing liability on this ground. First, the allegations that Unocal had provided maps to the military, and was aware that Total and TMEP were providing food, trucks, a bulldozer and possibly payment to the military for security, did not amount to the substantial assistance required as the *actus reus* of aiding and abetting.[82] At no stage had Unocal made a significant contribution to the plaintiffs' injuries. Secondly, Unocal's negotiations for, and entry into, the project had not had such effect, as Total would have proceeded with the project in any event, even without Unocal.[83] Unocal's participation in the project would have been unlikely to affect the operation of the pipeline.[84] Even if Unocal had protested to the Myanmar Government, and threatened to withdraw its investment, or had actually carried out such a threat, the military's abuses would still have continued. Unocal had not been responsible for hiring the military. It was Total who was responsible for pipeline security.

The second head of claim was in respect of five intentional tort causes of action: battery, assault, false imprisonment, intentional infliction of emotional distress and conversion. The evidence in the ATCA claim before Lew J in *Unocal (2000)*[85] suggested that Unocal knew that forced labour was being utilised and that the joint venturers benefited from the practice. This created a triable issue of fact on the *mens rea* element of the torts. The claims could not proceed, however, because the Myanamar military, and not Unocal, was the actor as to the intentional tort causes of action.

The third head of claim was that of negligence. The plaintiffs needed to establish the existence of a duty of care owed to them by Unocal. A person owed no duty to control the conduct of a third person to prevent him from causing physical harm to another, in the absence of a special relationship between the defendant and the plaintiff or the person whose conduct needed to be controlled. A special relationship would not exist unless the defendant

---

82 In contrast, the circuit court in the ATCA case subsequently found that Unocal's involvement did amount to substantial assistance in that, without it, the military's abuses would probably not have occurred in the same way.

83 This factual analysis derives from the findings in *Doe v Unocal Corp* 248 F 3d 915, p 925 (9th Cir 2001) (*Unocal (1998)*).

84 *Doe v Unocal Corp* 67 F Supp 2d 1140, p 1147 (CD Cal 1999).

85 *Doe I v Unocal* 110 F Supp 2d 1294, p 1310 (CD Cal 2000). Chaney J's decision on this point came before the decision of the circuit court in *Unocal (2002)*.

had the ability to control the third party and here Lew J in *Unocal (2000)* had found that Unocal did not have control over the Myanmar military. However, there might also have been a duty of care not to place another person in a situation in which the other person was exposed to an unreasonable risk of harm through the reasonably foreseeable conduct of a third person. Where the defendant had made the plaintiffs' position worse and has created a fore-seeable risk of harm from the third person, then a duty of care to prevent foreseeable harm would arise from conduct which contributed to, increased or changed the risk of harm that would otherwise have existed. While there was a possibility that Unocal's investment perpetuated the risk, there was no evidence that Unocal's investment placed plaintiffs in a risky situation or *created* a risk of harm from the Myanmar military. Accordingly, the negligence claims were dismissed.[86]

9.5 Applicable law

A variety of approaches have been demonstrated to the question of the law to be applied in respect of torts committed outside the US. Restatement (Second) of Conflict of Laws, s 145 states that the applicable law is that of the jurisdiction with the most significant relationship to the occurrence and the parties. In determining this, various factors are listed as being relevant, such as the needs of the international legal system; the relevant polices of the forum state; the relevant polices of other interested states; the justified expectations of the parties; certainty; predictability; uniformity; and the ease in determining the relevant law. However, several courts have simply assumed that the law of the *situs* will apply, as was the case in *Re Union Carbide* and *Aguinda v Texaco*. Other courts have applied the law of the forum if it has an interest in the outcome of the case. A recent example is provided by *Doe v Exxon Corp (Plaintiffs' motion to amend complaint)*,[87] where Oberdorfer J held that US courts have an interest in controlling the overseas activities of US companies.

However, foreign law will not apply where it conflicts with public policy in the forum. In the *Unocal* proceedings before the state court in California, Chaney J rejected Myanmar law as being radically indeterminate and there-fore assumed it to be not out of harmony with Californian law, which she proceeded to apply. Had Myanmar law barred tort claims based on allega-tions of forced labour, Chaney J would not have applied it, as this would

---

86 Chaney J also dismissed the parallel negligence claims against Unocal directors, Imle and Beach in the absence of any evidence that the activity of the Myanmar military was under their control and that they had negligently failed to take action to avoid the harm.

87 *Doe v Exxon Corp (Plaintiffs' motion to amend complaint)*, unreported, 2 March 2006, WL 516744 (DDC).

have been contrary to public policy. It is possible that this argument could also be used in the reverse situation where the law of the *situs* is more, rather than less, generous to the plaintiffs than that of the US forum. An example might be where that law attributes the actions of a subsidiary company to its parent in circumstances in which a US court would maintain the corporate veil.

Chapter 10

Actions against multinational corporations before English courts

To date, most environmental and human rights litigation against multi-national corporations has taken place before the US courts. However, in recent years this type of litigation has also started to come before the English courts, as well as those of other Commonwealth countries, such as Australia and Canada. Not surprisingly, the underlying legal framework of this type of litigation has many similarities with that applied by the courts of the US, as the claims have all arisen within a common law system. There are, though, two important differences between the litigation in the US and litigation before the English courts. First, England has no equivalent of ATCA 1789. Secondly, the European Court of Justice's 2004 decision in *Owusu v Jackson*[1] has established that Art 2 of the Brussels Regulation 2001 precludes the use of *forum non conveniens* to dismiss proceedings in a member state in which the defendant is domiciled. This means that a UK parent corporation which is sued in the English courts may no longer stay proceedings on this ground. This has profound implications for the future of this type of litigation, given that most US claims end up being dismissed on this ground.

10.1 Establishing jurisdiction

The first step in bringing a claim against a UK parent company in respect of environmental torts committed by its foreign subsidiary will be to effect service of proceedings on the parent company. The position is governed by EC Regulation 44/2001 (Brussels Regulation), Art 2, formerly the Brussels Convention 1968.[2] This provides that suit is to be brought against the defendant in its state of domicile. In *Group Josi Reinsurance Co SA v Universal General Insurance Co*,[3] the ECJ held that the plaintiff is entitled to rely on this

---

1 *Owusu v Jackson* (Case C–281/02) [2005] ECR I–1383.
2 The regulation came into force on 1 March 2002 and made various changes in the application of the Brussels and Lugano Conventions within the EC, save as regards Denmark. Unless otherwise stated, no changes were made to the provisions referred to in this chapter.
3 *Group Josi Reinsurance Co SA v Universal General Insurance Co* (Case C–412/98) [2001] QB 68.

provision, even though its own domicile might be in a state that is not a member of the EC. Where the defendant is a corporation, Art 60.1 provides that a company 'or other legal person or association of natural or legal persons' is domiciled 'at the place where it has its: (a) statutory seat, or (b) central administration, or (c) principal place of business'. For the purposes of the UK and Ireland, 'statutory seat' is defined by Art 60.2 as 'the registered office or, where there is no such office anywhere, the place of incorporation or, where there is no such office anywhere, the place of incorporation or, where there is no such place anywhere, the place under the law of which the formation took place'. Therefore, a company incorporated in a part of the UK but which has no other connection with the UK would be domiciled in the UK for the purposes of Art 2. So, also, would a company which was not incorporated in the UK, but which was effectively run from the UK.[4]

As an alternative to suing a defendant in its place of domicile, Art 5.3 of the Brussels Regulation gives the plaintiff the option of proceeding in the courts of another member state 'at the place where the harmful event occurred'. The meaning of these words was considered in *Bier BV v Mines de Potasse D'Alsace SA*,[5] in which the French defendant was alleged to have polluted the Rhine in France which had carried the pollutants into the Netherlands where they were said to have caused damage to a horticultural business based there. The ECJ held that Art 5.3 applied either to the place where the wrong was committed or the place where the injury was sustained. Accordingly, the plaintiff was entitled to bring its claim in the courts of the Netherlands. These provisions would give a claimant who was suing a parent company with a domicile in England the right to proceed either in England or in the foreign jurisdiction in which the damage occurred, provided that jurisdiction that of another member state.

10.2 Declining jurisdiction

10.2.1 Forum non conveniens

Once the claimant has established jurisdiction through service of proceedings, the defendant may apply to stay proceedings on the grounds of *forum non conveniens*. The general principles to be applied in applications to stay on this ground were set out in *The Spiliada*.[6] If another forum is more

---

4 Service of an oversea company with a branch in England and Wales is governed by Companies Act 1985, s 694A (inserted with effect from 1 January 1993) and s 695. Alternatively, CPR, r 6.2(2) permits service under CPR, r 6.5(6). Unlike s 694A, this provision does not require that the service of process be 'in respect of the carrying on of the business of the [English] branch'.
5 *Bier BV v Mines de Potasse D'Alsace SA* (Case 21/76) [1978] QB 708.
6 *Spiliada Maritime Corp v Cansulex* [1987] AC 460.

appropriate for the hearing of the action a stay will be granted, unless, to do so, would cause injustice to the plaintiff.[7] The second limb of *Spiliada* has enabled plaintiffs to see off *forum non conveniens* challenges in several actions brought against a UK parent corporation, involving allegations of personal injuries suffered as a result of unsafe working conditions adopted by the foreign subsidiary.[8]

However, the scope of the doctrine has been drastically reduced by the decision of the ECJ in *Owusu v Jackson*[9] to the effect that a defendant that is sued in its place of domicile, pursuant to Art 2 of the Brussels Regulation, is not entitled to have those proceedings stayed, even where the alternative forum is outside the EC.[10] Actions against UK parent companies will, therefore, fall within Art 2 of the Brussels Regulation and will no longer be subject to being stayed on the grounds of *forum non conveniens*. However, there may be some cases where the claimant seeks to proceed against a company that falls outside Art 2. Where the defendant is not domiciled in a jurisdiction subject to the Brussels Regulation, Art 4 of the Regulation preserves the domestic rules regarding jurisdiction, including *forum non conveniens*. Unless the defendant can be served in accordance with the provisions relating to service of oversea companies, the claimant will need to obtain leave to serve it out of the jurisdiction. This could happen, for example, where a claimant wishes to sue a foreign corporation, which might be the subsidiary of an English parent, in respect of alleged complicity in human rights abuses by agencies of a foreign government. The matter is governed by CPR, r 6.20. The claimant will have to bring itself within the provisions relating to tort in heading (8).[11] The most likely way it can do this is if it has relocated to the UK where it has suffered subsequent mental illness consequent upon the original human rights violations it suffered in the foreign jurisdiction.[12] The court will exercise its discretion on grounds similar to those applied with *forum non conveniens*, but with the burden of proof falling on the claimant not the defendant.

---

7 'Public interest' considerations of the sort applied in the US under the *Gilbert* test have no place to play in the analysis of *forum non conveniens* under English law. *Lubbe v Cape plc (No 2)* [2000] 1 WLR 1545.
8 *Ngcobo v Thor Chemicals Ltd, The Times*, 10 November 1995. *Sithole v Thor Chemicals Ltd* [2000] WL 1421183. *Connelly v RTZ Corporation plc and Ritz Overseas Ltd* [1998] AC 854. *Lubbe v Cape plc (No 2)* [2000] 1 WLR 1545.
9 *Owusu v Jackson* (Case C–281/02) [2005] ECR I–1383.
10 Thus overruling the Court of Appeal's decision on this point in *Re Harrods (Buenos Aires) Ltd.* [1992] Ch 72.
11 If the claim is brought against a UK parent corporation, the claimant may seek leave to serve out of the jurisdiction as against a foreign subsidiary under CPR, r 6.20(3) as a 'necessary or proper party'.
12 This was the basis on which leave to serve out of the jurisdiction was granted in *Al-Adsani v Govt of Kuwait* (1995) 100 ILR 465, *Times*, 29 March 1996.

The doctrine of *forum non conveniens* still exists in other Commonwealth jurisdictions and has twice been invoked in cases involving environmental tort claims against a domestic parent company of a multinational enterprise. In Canada, in *Recherches Internationales Quebec v Cambior Inc*,[13] the proceedings were stayed on this ground due to the fact that the preponderance of evidence was located in Guyana where the damage occurred. In Australia, however, it is considerably more difficult to stay on this ground due to the decision of the High Court of Australia in *Voth v Manildra Flour Mill*[14] that the doctrine will operate only if it is established that Australia is a 'clearly inappropriate' jurisdiction for the litigation. The decision may explain the fact that in *Dagi v BHP (No 2)*,[15] a claim arising out of pollution caused by the collapse of a tailings dam in a copper mine in Papua New Guinea, the defendants did not seek to dismiss the Australian proceedings on this ground.

10.2.2 Act of state

Apart from the doctrine of *forum non conveniens*, a suit before an English court may also be dismissed by reference to the act of state doctrine which prevents the courts from adjudicating on the legality of the official acts of a sovereign. This doctrine, however, has considerably narrower ambit than its US equivalent. As expressed by Lord Wilberforce in *Buttes Gas & Oil Co v Hammer (No 3)*,[16] its basis is the non-justiciability of certain issues, rather than the potential embarrassment that their adjudication might cause to the British Government. The case involved a defamation action between oil companies which would have required the determination of an international maritime boundary dispute involving four countries, as well as on the actions of a number of states involved in the dispute. The plaintiffs' claims were non-justiciable in that there were no established principles of international law by which the English courts could determine this issue.

10.2.3 Sovereign immunity

State Immunity Act 1978, s 1 provides that: 'A State is immune from juridiction from the jurisdiction of the courts of the United Kingdom except as provided in the following provisions of this Part.'[17] Notwithstanding the

---

13 [1998] QJ No 2554, 14 August 1998.
14 *Voth v Manildra Flour Mill* (1990) 171 CLR 538, HCA.
15 *Dagi v BHP (No 2)* [1997] 1 VR 428.
16 *Buttes Gas & Oil Co v Hammer (No 3)* [1982] AC 888.
17 Such as the exception under s 3 in respect of commercial transactions entered into by a state, and the exception under s 5 in respect of claims against a state in respect of death or personal injury, or damage to or loss of tangible property, caused by an act or omission in the UK.

fact that torture is recognised as a *ius cogens* norm of customary international law,[18] and that the UN Convention against Torture and Other Cruel, Inhuman and Degrading Punishment 1984, expressly grants universal criminal jurisdiction against torturers, the Court of Appeal in *Al Adsani v Govt of Kuwait*[19] held that the 1978 Act precluded a civil suit being brought against a foreign state for breach of this norm. The decision was subsequently upheld by a majority decision of the ECHR.[20]

In *Propend Finance Pty v Sing*,[21] the Court of Appeal held that this immunity extended to servants and agents of the state. Subsidiaries who collude with abusive conduct by overseas governments are unlikely to be regarded as agents and therefore will fall outside the scope of sovereign immunity in any event. However, there is a danger that the greater the involvement of the subsidiary in the human rights' violations committed by the foreign government, the greater the likelihood that the subsidiary will be regarded as a *de facto* agent of that government. A claim based on accessory liability must therefore be pleaded carefully so that the allegations of complicity are not so strong that they lead to a finding that the subsidiary had acted as the agent of the foreign sovereign.

The US courts have allowed ATCA claims to be brought against government officials who are alleged to have committed breaches of norms of customary international law. In such circumstances, such government officials may not rely on sovereign immunity. By committing breaches of customary international law, they will have acted outside the scope of their authority and can no longer be regarded as acting on behalf of the state. The UK courts, however, have refused to recognise any such an exception. In *Jones v Govt of Saudi Arabia*,[22] an attempt was made to argue that an exception to the principles set out in the 1978 Act existed when a civil claim in respect of torture was brought against an individual state official, as opposed to a state. The argument succeeded before the Court of Appeal where Mance LJ held that a state's immunity was *ratione personae*, whereas that of an official was *ratione materiae* only. However, the House of Lords overruled the decision, on the grounds that the 1984 Convention against Torture provides no exception to the principle of sovereign immunity in relation to civil proceedings. Torture is defined by Art 1 of the Convention as the infliction of pain or suffering 'by or at the instigation of or with the consent or acquiescence of a public official or other person acting in an official capacity'.

---

18 This is a rule of customary international law that has received sufficiently widespread acceptance as to be binding even on those states that do not accept it.
19 *Al Adsani v Govt of Kuwait* (1995) 100 ILR 465, *Times*, 29 March 1996
20 *Al Adsani v UK* (2002) 34 EHRR 11.
21 *Propend Finance Pty v Sing* (1997) 111 ILR 611.
22 *Jones v Govt of Saudi Arabia* [2004] EWCA Civ 1394, [2005] QB 699; [2006] UKHL 26, [2006] 2 WLR 1424.

This posed an insurmountable problem for the claimants. To bring their claim within the Convention they had to show that the torture was official, whilst simultaneously arguing the contrary position, to defeat the claim to immunity. The Convention deals with civil proceedings in Art 14.1 which provides: 'Each State Party shall ensure in its legal system that the victim of an act of torture obtains redress and has an enforceable right to fair and adequate compensation, including the means for as full rehabilitation as possible.' Their Lordships held that this only required a state to grant a civil remedy in respect of torture committed within its jurisdiction. The English courts were not, therefore, required to provide the claimants with a civil remedy in respect of torture which they claimed to have suffered in Saudi Arabia.

10.3 Tort liability

Claims arising out of environmental damage will be based on the overseas activities of the subsidiary company. The claims are likely to be based on the negligence of the subsidiary in these overseas activities. Claims might also be based on nuisance or on *Rylands v Fletcher*,[23] or equivalent actions in the jurisdiction in which the harm occurred.[24] The claimant will need to establish a link between the subsidiary and the parent that will enable the liability of the former to be attributed to the latter. There are two ways in which the parent company can be linked with the activities of its foreign-based subsidiary. The first is to make the parent derivatively liable for the defaults of its subsidiary. The second is to find the parent primarily liable for a breach of a primary duty of care owed by it towards the claimants.

10.3.1 Derivative liability. 'Piercing the veil'

Since *Salomon v Salomon*,[25] the English courts have upheld the principle that a company is a legal entity distinct from that of its shareholders. Shareholder liability is limited to the amount of unpaid share capital. The principle applies equally to corporate groups where a parent company holds the majority, or even the totality, of shares in a subsidiary. This is the case notwithstanding that the principle was established before the emergence of corporate groups.[26] There are, however, limited situations in which the

---

23 *Rylands v Fletcher* (1865) 3 H&C 774.
24 Where the claimant attempts to base its claim on the conduct of the foreign subsidiary, rather than on that of its UK parent, it is likely that the tort law to be applied will be that of the jurisdiction in which the subsidiary was operating.
25 *Salomon v Salomon* [1897] AC 22.
26 Blumberg, P, *The Multinational Challenge to Corporation Law*, 1993, Oxford: Oxford University Press.

courts will ignore this artificial personality and trace back to the underlying economic reality as far as justice requires. This process of 'piercing the corporate veil' is used by the courts only in exceptional circumstances and to date there have been no decisions in which an English court has used it in a tort case.[27]

The courts will disregard the corporate form where the interests of justice require them to do so, particularly if the corporate form is being used as a vehicle for fraud. This is a wide and potentially far-reaching judicial discretion. The authorities, however, show that the courts have been far readier to use it in favour of corporations rather than against them. For example, in *DHN Estates v Tower Hamlets LBC*,[28] the Court of Appeal gave as one of its reasons for allowing the loss suffered by the parent to be included when assessing compensation due to the landowner subsidiary, the fact that the companies formed a 'single economic unit'.[29]

However, under English law, when a corporation relies on the doctrine of separate corporate personality as a defence the courts have been far less willing to make use of their discretion. Unless there is clear evidence of a fraudulent use of the corporate form, the courts will continue to respect the separate legal identities of corporate defendants. Moreover, the category of fraud is very narrowly defined. It is limited to the use of corporate personality to avoid existing contractual obligations as in *Jones v Lipman*,[30] where a vendor sought to avoid a sale of his house to the plaintiff by transferring it to a company incorporated for the purpose of purchasing the house. However, the corporate form must have been used with the express intention of avoiding an existing obligation. In contrast, in *Electric Light and Power Supply Co Ltd v Cormack*,[31] the New South Wales Supreme Court refused to grant an injunction where the defendant had contracted to use only the plaintiff's power in his business for two years and had then sold his business to another company, of which he was manager, which used another source of power. There was no evidence that the defendant had sold his business to avoid his obligations. A sale of a business where the vendor knows that there are still outstanding claims against it will not, in itself, constitute fraud. Although the decision in *Creasey v Breachwood*[32] seems to have been based on such a basis, it has since been disapproved by the Court of Appeal in *Ord v Belhaven*

---

27 For a more general discussion of this topic, see Gallagher, L and Ziegler, P, 'Lifting the corporate veil in the pursuit of justice' (1990) JBL 292.

28 *DHN Food Distribution Ltd v Tower Hamlets LBC* [1976] 1 WLR 852.

29 Similar reasoning underlay the US decision of McGarr J in *The Amoco Cadiz* [1984] 2 Lloyd's Rep 304, esp pp 338F, 43–6. Affd 954 F 2d 2179 (7th Cir 1992).

30 *Jones v Lipman* [1962] 1 WLR 832.

31 *Electric Light and Power Supply Co Ltd v Cormack* (1911) 11 SR (NSW) 350.

32 *Creasey v Breachwood* [1993] BCLC 481.

33 *Ord v Belhaven Pubs* [1998] 2 BLC 607.

Pubs,[33] where it was stressed that the transaction must have been motivated by the desire to avoid pre-existing claims.[34]

However, the use of the corporate form to minimise the incidence of future liabilities is perfectly legitimate and in such cases the veil will not be pierced. Any doubt on this issue was removed by the decision of the Court of Appeal in *Adams v Cape Industries plc*.[35] The case involved an attempt to enforce in England a default judgment obtained in Texas against Cape, an English based multinational corporation involved in the asbestos industry, and Capasco, its English-based marketing subsidiary. Cape had supplied asbestos from its South African mining subsidiary, Egnep, to US customers via its wholly owned Illinois subsidiary, the North American Asbestos Company (NAAC). Workers at an asbestos factory in Texas suffered illness as a result of their exposure to the asbestos. They sued various parties, including Cape, Capasco, NAAC and Egnep. The first batch of litigation, the Tyler 1 cases, was settled for US$20 million of which the Cape group contributed US$5.2 million.

By the time the second batch of litigation, the Tyler 2 cases, began, Cape avoided its mistake in the Tyler 1 proceedings in voluntarily submitting to the court's jurisdiction. Instead, it took no part in the Tyler 2 proceedings and was content to suffer judgment in default against it. Cape knew that obtaining a judgment was only half the story; enforcing it would be another matter altogether. To frustrate the ultimate enforcement of any Texas judgment against it, Cape had to eliminate its presence in the jurisdiction at the time the Tyler 2 actions commenced. Its absence from the jurisdiction at this time would subsequently enable it to argue that the general principles of private international law precluded the enforcement of any such judgment in any country, such as the UK, which lacked reciprocal arrangements with the US for the enforcement of judgments.

In order to eliminate its 'presence' from Texas, Cape put NAAC into liquidation and conducted its business through a new company, CPC, set up with Cape money, but which had no formal corporate link with Cape. The only way the Tyler 2 claimants could hope to enforce their judgment in England was by proving that, first through NAAC, and then through CPC, Cape had been present in the jurisdiction.

In this they were to prove unsuccessful. The Court of Appeal refused to pierce the corporate veil of either company on the grounds of fraud. There was no fraud if a group of companies chose to use the doctrine of separate corporate personality in such a way as to minimise its group exposure to

---

34 Where a defendant corporation attempts to divest itself of its assets after proceedings have been brought against it, the claimant may also seek to reverse such transfers pursuant to Insolvency Act 1986, s 423. An application under this section was made in the second set of proceedings against Thor Chemicals in *Sithole v Thor Chemical Holdings Ltd* [2000] WL 1421183.

35 *Adams v Cape Industries plc* [1990] Ch 433.

future liabilities. What is striking is that these future liabilities were not just some distant hypothesis. The success of the Tyler 1 actions showed that these future liabilities were a very real present factor and it was this which caused Cape to reorganise in the US. It is but a small step from prohibiting the use of corporate personality to avoid subsisting contractual obligations to prohibiting its use to avoid tort suits which you know are about to materialise. Nonetheless, the Court of Appeal refused to take this small step and its decision confirms the latitude the English courts have allowed to corporations in their use of the corporate form as a tool of claims-evasion. As for *DHN v Tower Hamlets London Borough Council*, this was distinguished almost to vanishing point on the grounds that it involved the wording of a specific statute and set down no general principle of law.[36]

10.3.2 Derivative liability. Agency

Alternatively, the courts may choose to side-step the veil by creative use of the concept of agency. If a subsidiary company can be regarded as having acted as agent for a parent company, the parent will be held vicariously liable for the defaults of the subsidiary. However, the courts have proved far more willing to make a finding of agency when it is for the benefit of the parent company. In *Smith, Stone and Knight Ltd v Birmingham Corporation*,[37] a local authority compulsorily acquired premises occupied by the subsidiary company. For the parent to succeed in an action for compensation for loss of business it would have to show that the subsidiary was its agent in conducting business on the premises. Atkinson J pointed to a variety of factors which pointed to agency. The parent had treated the subsidiary's profit as its own. It had appointed the directors conducting the business of the subsidiary and had directed all that was done within the subsidiary. It had maintained effectual and constant control over the subsidiary.[38] This reasoning bears a striking similarity to those used in the Indian courts in the interlocutory decisions in the *Bhopal* case, to justify the piercing of the corporate veil in an action *against* the parent corporation.[39] However, the decision has subsequently been distinguished by the Court of Appeal in *Rayner (JH) (Mincing Lane) Ltd v Department of Trade and Industry*,[40] as a case peculiar to its facts, involving no general principle of law.

36 The decision had previously been distinguished on the grounds that it involved a wholly owned subsidiary. *Woolfson v Strathclyde Regional Council* [1978] 38 P & CR 521.

37 *Smith, Stone and Knight Ltd v Birmingham Corporation* [1939] 4 All ER 116.

38 This reasoning bears a striking similarity to those used in the Indian courts in the interlocutory decisions in the *Bhopal* case, and, also, by Judge McGarr in *The Amoco Cadiz*, to justify the piercing of the corporate veil in an action *against* the parent corporation.

39 And, also, by Judge McGarr in *The Amoco Cadiz*.

40 *Rayner (JH) (Mincing Lane) Ltd v Department of Trade and Industry* [1989] 1 Ch 72, esp pp 189–90, affd [1990] 2 AC 418.

In *Adams v Cape Industries plc*, the plaintiffs made an unsuccessful attempt to use agency reasoning against Cape. CPC and, to a lesser extent NAAC, had both been conducting some business of their own in Texas and were therefore not wholly involved in acting for Cape. As for the business they had conducted for Cape, that was not enough to make them Cape's agents. Neither company had ever had the power to enter contracts on behalf of Cape, nor had they ever purported to do so. In the words of Buckley LJ in *Okura & Co Ltd v Forsbacka Jernverks Aktiebolag,* Cape would have been operating 'through' NAAC and CPC, but not 'by' them.[41] They could not, therefore, be acting as Cape's agents. After *Adams v Cape Industries plc,* therefore, the English courts will only disregard the corporate form where it is used to avoid existing legal obligations, or where one company has the power to contract on behalf of another, thereby justifying a finding of agency.

10.3.3 Direct liability

If the parent company is not vicariously liable for the defaults of its subsidiary, it might still incur liability in respect of a duty of care owed to the plaintiff arising out of its own act. Three claims have been brought before the courts of the UK, in the last 15 years, against UK parent companies in respect of industrial injuries allegedly sustained by employees of its foreign subsidiaries in the course of their employment. All were pleaded on the basis of the parent's primary liability. The first two involved allegations that the duty was created by the active involvement of the parent in the harmful activities of its subsidiary.[42] In *Ngcobo v Thor Chemicals Ltd*[43] and *Sithole v Thor Chemicals Ltd,*[44] claims were made by South African plaintiffs in respect of injuries they had sustained while working for the defendant's subsidiary company in Natal. The English parent company had been engaged in the manufacture and reprocessing of mercury-based chemicals in England, but following sustained criticism of its operations by the Health and Safety Executive it relocated these processes to Natal where it established a plant run by a wholly owned subsidiary. The chairman of the parent company was employed by the subsidiary company to design and set up the new plant. The

---

41 *Okura & Co Ltd v Forsbacka Jernverks Aktiebolag* [1914] 1 KB 715, p 721.
42 This was also the basis on which the Australian court in *CSR Ltd v Wren* (1997) 44 NSWLR 463 found that a parent company, whose employees were used by the subsidiary company to direct the way in which its operations were conducted, owed a duty of care to the employees of its subsidiary. In contrast, in *James Hardie & Co Pty Ltd v Hall* (1998) 43 NSWLR 554, there had been no such active involvement in the subsidiary's operations by its parent. The parent's power to control its subsidiary was held to be insufficient to create a duty of care on the parent in relation to the subsidiary's employees.
43 *Ngcobo v Thor Chemicals Ltd, The Times,* 10 November 1995.
44 *Sithole v Thor Chemical Holdings Ltd* [2000] WL 1421183.

plaintiffs alleged that the South African company dealt with the problem of mercury contamination by testing the blood and urine of their workers and temporarily laying off those with excessive levels of mercury until such time as those levels had reduced. In 1994, two actions on behalf of 20 workers were begun against the parent company and its Chairman, by now the only director.[45]

The second claim, *Connelly v RTZ Corporation plc and Ritz Overseas Ltd*,[46] was advanced on the basis of the following allegations: that RTZ, the parent company, had devised the policy on health, safety and the environment adopted by RUL, its subsidiary in Namibia; or had advised RUL as to the contents of the policy. Further, it alleged that employee/s of RTZ had implemented the policy and supervised health, safety and/or environmental protection at the mine operated by RUL at which the plaintiff worked.[47]

In contrast, the third case, *Lubbe v Cape plc (No 2)*,[48] was pleaded on the basis of a duty to supervise arising out of a combination of knowledge of a defect in the operations of a subsidiary and the ability to rectify it, seems to have formed the basis of the primary duty alleged in three recent cases involving. The plaintiffs' claim was reformulated as follows:

> Whether a parent company which is proved to exercise de facto control over the operations of a (foreign) subsidiary and which knows, through its directors, that those operations involve risks to the health of workers employed by the subsidiary and/or persons in the vicinity of its factory or other business premises, owes a duty of care to those workers and/or other persons in relation to the control which it exercises over and the advice which it gives to the subsidiary company?

The manner in which the claim was formulated was not challenged either by the defendant or by the courts in the *forum non conveniens* proceedings. In the House of Lords, Lord Bingham of Cornhill noted that in this connection one of the issues that would have to be considered the defendant's responsibility as a parent company for ensuring the observance of proper standards of health and safety by its overseas subsidiaries. His Lordship observed that:

> Resolution of this issue will be likely to involve an inquiry into what part the defendant played in controlling the operations of the group, what its

---

45 The actions were settled out of court in April 1997 for £1.3 million. A third action was brought in 1998 on behalf of another 21 workers which settled out of court in October 2000 for £270,000 plus legal costs.

46 *Connelly v RTZ Corporation plc and Ritz Overseas Ltd* [1998] AC 854.

47 These issues of substantive liability were never to be determined as Mr Connelly's claim against the English parent company was subsequently held to have been made out of time.

48 *Lubbe v Cape plc (No 2)* [2000] 1 WLR 1545.

directors and employees knew or ought to have known, what action was taken and not taken, whether the defendant owed a duty of care to employees of group companies overseas and whether, if so, that duty was broken. Much of the evidence material to this inquiry would, in the ordinary way be documentary and much of it would be found in the offices of the parent company, including minutes of meetings, reports by directors and employees on visits overseas and correspondence.[49]

The primary duty of care owed by a parent company could also be analysed by reference to the circumstances in which an employer is held to owe a non-delegable primary duty of care in respect of the activities of an independent contractor. This relationship is the closest to that pertaining between a parent company and its subsidiary. The employer will owe a duty of care in selecting a reasonably competent contractor, but after that will generally come under no additional duty of care in respect of the contractor's activities. The fact that the employer still has the underlying power to control the contractors' acts is, in itself, insufficient to lead to any larger duty of care. Most people are content to allow the contractor get on with their task. *Daniel v Metropolitan Rly*[50] shows that employers are quite entitled do just that. Works were being done over a railway line which entailed heavy iron girders being placed upon the walls running alongside the line. This type of work had been carried out manually by the contractors for the past 20 years. They then decided to use a mechanical monkey-wrench whose jerky movement gave them less control of the operation. Consequently, a girder fell and injured the plaintiff who was travelling in a train which happened to be passing underneath at the time. The employer was held to owe no duty of care to the plaintiff. The evidence showed that it was entitled to assume that the work was in the hands of competent workmen who would take all necessary care to see that no accident took place. In *D&F Estates Ltd v Church Commissioners for England*,[51] the House of Lords confirmed that an employer generally owes no duty to supervise the activities of an independent contractor.

There are, however, a limited number of circumstances in which the employer may come under a more extensive duty of care. For example, in *D&F Estates Ltd v Church Commissioners for England*, Lord Bridge considered the situation where the main contractor had actually chosen to supervise the sub-contractor's work and then come to know of defects in it. In these circumstances, the main contractor, if he condoned the negligence of

---

49 [2000] 2 Lloyd's Rep 383, 390.
50 *Daniel v Metropolitan Rly* [1871] LR 5 HL 45.
51 *D&F Estates Ltd v Church Commissioners for England* [1989] AC 177.

the sub-contractor, would 'no doubt make himself potentially liable for the consequences as a joint tortfeasor'.[52]

Special features inherent in the work are also factors which itself can the duty of the employer beyond the basic duty of taking reasonable care in employing a competent contractor. The work may be hazardous to third parties unless specific information held by the employer is divulged to the contractor. Hence in *Distillers Co (Biochemicals) Ltd v Thompson*,[53] the duty extended beyond engaging a reasonably competent body to market the drug in Australia to giving that body warnings about the hazards of the drug. The warnings had to be given by the manufacturer as they depended on information within its sole domain.[54] Without the warnings the Australian firm, no matter how competent they were in the general pharmaceutical sphere, would not be reasonably competent to market this drug.

An analogous situation occurred in *Stevens v Brodribb*,[55] a decision of the Australian High Court. There two sets of independent contractors, 'sniggers' and 'truckers' were used in a logging operation. During the loading of logs onto a truck a 'snigger' was injured by the negligence of a 'trucker'. Despite the hazardous nature of the work, no liability was found to attach to the employer. The employer did owe a duty, to set up a safe system of work within which the two sets of contractors could interact, but that had not been breached. There was no additional duty in relation to the operation of that safe system, once it was in place. The case is similar to the *Distillers* case in that the nature of the duty owed is based on the fact that the operation performed by the contractor could not be performed safely without a particular contribution from the defendant, which could only be provided by the defendant. In *Stevens v Brodribb*, that contribution was the setting up of a safe system of work, in *Distillers* it was the passing on of information relating to the drug to be marketed. Both factors were within the exclusive domain of the defendant and without them neither contractor could be said to be 'reasonably competent' to do the work entrusted to it.

Stevens v Brodbribb might suggest that in some circumstances a parent company owes a duty to ensure that its subsidiary adopts a safe system of working. However, this argument was rejected by an Australian court in *James Hardie & Co Pty Ltd v Hall*.[56] The claim arose out of the death of an employee due to exposure while working for a New Zealand subsidiary

---

52 At p 209D.
53 *Distillers Co (Biochemicals) Ltd v Thompson* [1971] AC 458.
54 See also *Castree v ER Squibb* [1980] 2 All ER 589, where a machine imported from West Germany caused injury whilst being operated in England. The tort was held to have been committed not when the machine was made but when it was marketed in England without proper warning as to its defects.
55 *Stevens v Brodribb* [1986] 160 CLR 16.
56 *James Hardie & Co Pty Ltd v Hall* (1998) 43 NSWLR 554.

of the defendant. Sheller JA held that the defendant had not engaged the subsidiary to do work for them and there was no need for them to give directions as to when and where the plaintiff worked, or to co-ordinate his activities with those of others.[57] The plaintiff could look to the subsidiary company, as occupier of the factory, to provide him with a safe system of work.

Another exception to the general rule relating to the employment of independent contracts exists where the contractor is engaged to conduct extra-hazardous activities. The nature of the risk with extra-hazardous substances or processes is that hazard can be reasonably expected even in the hands of competent contractors. It is this factor which imposes an antecedent duty on the employer for the acts of the contractor. As such it is a category of liability peculiarly apt to attach to new technologies, such as flash-light in *Honeywill & Stein Ltd v Larkin Bros (London's Commercial Photographers) Ltd*,[58] where adequate safety measures have yet to be evolved due to the process itself still being something of an unknown quantity.

However, the exception is a limited one as can be seen in *Rainham Chemical Works v Belvedere Fish Guano Co*,[59] a case with some superficial resemblance to the Bhopal disaster. Two individuals with a government contract to manufacture munitions transferred their business to a limited company which they controlled and of which they were the directors. An explosion occurred due to negligence in the storage of a chemical, DNP, which formed part of the munitions process. DNP in isolation was a fairly stable component of explosives, unless exposed to heat. It was stored next to flammable material. A fire broke out in the DNP storehouse, spread to the flammable material adjacent which in turn generated enough heat to cause the DNP to explode. The House of Lords held that the directors as individuals were not liable in negligence for the acts of the company in storing the DNP.[60] They had neither directed the company to commit the act which caused the damage, that is to say to store DNP in a negligent fashion, nor did they owe an antecedent duty in relation to the storage of DNP. The reasons for this finding appear most clearly in Younger LJ's judgment in the Court of Appeal.[61] After first stressing that the directors had no suspicion of risks in the storage as opposed to the manipulation of DNP, Younger LJ continued:

> Nor, as I have shown, is there any real risk in such storage. DNP is not a wild beast, dangerous unless kept under lock and key. At the worst it is

---

57 At p 583.
58 *Honeywill & Stein Ltd v Larkin Bros (London's Commercial Photographers) Ltd* [1934] 1 KB 191, p 200.
59 *Rainham Chemical Works v Belvedere Fish Guano Co* [1921] 2 AC 465.
60 They were, however, liable for the explosion under *Rylands v Fletcher* as they had remained the tenants of the factory where it occurred, the lease prohibiting any sub-letting.
61 *Rainham Chemical Works v Belvedere Fish Guano Co* [1920] 2 KB 487, p 520.

even now only shown to be mischievous if placed among highly inflammable materials, and then only under very exceptional circumstances. Isolated it is quite stable.

This analysis has the effect of denying the existence of a non-delegable duty in respect of substances which may become hazardous when placed in proximity with certain other substances. However, it was an analysis rejected by the majority of *Burnie Port Authority v General Jones Pty Ltd*,[62] where the action in *Rylands v Fletcher* was assimilated with negligence. A fire on premises occupied by the appellant was caused by the negligence of its independent contractor in carrying out unguarded welding operations in close vicinity to stacked cardboard cartons of Isolite, an insulating material which burns ferociously once brought into sustained contact with a flame. The majority held that the appellant was liable in both negligence and under *Rylands v Fletcher*. The nature of the activity carried out on its land and the attendant risks determined the extent of the duty of care owed by the respondent to the appellant. Mason CJ continued:

> It follows that the relationship of proximity which exists in the category of case into which *Rylands v Fletcher* circumstances fall contains the central element of control which generates, in other categories of case, a special 'personal' or 'non-delegable' duty of care under the ordinary law of negligence. Reasoning by analogy suggests, but does not compel, a conclusion that that common element gives rise to such a duty of care in the first-mentioned category of case. There are considerations of fairness which support that conclusion, namely, that it is the person in control who has authorised or allowed the situation of foreseeable potential danger to be imposed on the other person by authorising or allowing the dangerous use of the premises and who is likely to be in a position to insist upon the exercise of reasonable care. It is also supported by considerations of utility: 'the practical advantage of being conveniently workable, of supplying a spur to effective care in the choice of contractors, and in pointing the victim who is easily discoverable and probably financially responsible'.[63]

An advantage of this broad approach is that it allows the question of negligence to be decided without reference to compartmentalised rules about liability for the acts of contractors and for dangerous substances.[64] This is

---

62 *Burnie Port Authority v General Jones Pty Ltd* (1994) 120 ALR 42.
63 See above, at 63. The quotation is from Thayer, 'Liability without fault' (1916) Harvard Law Review 801, p 809.
64 This approach would rule out a situation such as occurred in *Rainham*, where the defendant could be liable under *Rylands v Fletcher*, but not in negligence.

highlighted by the different approaches of the majority and the minority to the facts. The majority found the respondent negligent, even though Isolite only became particularly hazardous due to the 'collateral negligence' of the contractors in storing it in cardboard containers in an area in which welding work was being carried on. Mason CJ said:

> If X engages an independent contractor to separately move two chemicals which will cause a major explosion if they come into contact with one another, into separate storage areas, there may be no real risk of injury or damage at all if the independent contractor does what he or she is engaged to do. The activity is, however, obviously fraught with danger unless special precautions are taken to ensure that the independent contractor does not, through 'collateral' negligence, transport the two chemicals together and in a way which causes contact between them.[65]

It is possible that liability for extra-hazardous operations is strict. This was considered *obiter* as a possibility in *Honyewill*,[66] but runs counter to the tendency of English law in cases such as *Read v Lyons*[67] of restricting the ambit of *Rylands v Fletcher* and was rejected by the Australian High Court in *Stevens v Brodribb*. It is more likely that liability is vicarious, as was suggested by the Court of Appeal in *Alcock v Wraith*,[68] a case where a contractor damaged a party wall. Alternatively, the liability may be a personal one arising out of breach of a non-delegable primary duty of care. Support for this can be derived from *Hughes v Percival*,[69] where the defendant engaged contractors to do works on his house which shared a party wall with that of the plaintiff. Although the contract required the contractor to obtain the defendant's consent to any variation in the schedule of works, the workmen nonetheless cut into the party wall which caused the plaintiff's house to fall. The defendant was held liable for the acts of the contractors. Not only should he have specifically warned them not to cut into the party wall, but he should have taken steps to ensure his instructions were being carried out.[70]

---

65 See above, pp 68–9. In contrast, Brennan J, at p 85, held that there was no negligence because although the appellant had authorised both storage of Isolite in the roof void and welding in the roof void, 'neither of those activities might have been expected to cause damage ... provided [the contractors] performed the work without negligence'. This analysis is very similar to that by which Younger LJ categorised DNP as non-hazardous in *Rainham*.

66 *Honeywill & Stein Ltd v Larkin Bros (London's Commercial Photographers) Ltd* [1934] 1 KB 191, p 200.

67 *Read v Lyons* [1947] AC 156.

68 *Alcock v Wraith, The Times*, 23 December 1991.

69 *Hughes v Percival* [1883] 8 App Cas 443, esp pp 446–7.

70 See also Lord Colonsay in *Daniel v Metropolitan Rly* [1871] LR 5 HL 45, p 63: '... if the operation was one, which according to previous knowledge and experience, however carefully performed was likely to lead to mischief, I think it would then have been incumbent on the railway company *to foresee it and to take precautions against it*' (emphasis added).

10.3.4 How would the English courts have dealt with the Bhopal disaster?

The ambit of the current English law on the primary liability of a parent company for the acts of its foreign subsidiary will now be tested by an analysis of how an English court might deal with a claim with facts such as those in the *Bhopal* case, with the modification that the action was being directed at an English, rather than a US, parent corporation. The *Bhopal* case was settled before it came to trial, and the exact cause of the disaster still remains unclear.[71] However, three possible causes will now be examined from the perspective of English law on the primary duties of care owed by a parent company.[72]

First, there is the allegation that the storage system of MIC in proximity to water was inherently unsafe. This allegation was based on the opinion of Dr Chris Pietersen, the only independent expert to be given access to the plant and to have carried out an investigation into the causes of the disaster. This points to a potential liability on the parent company by reference to an employer's non-delegable duty in relation to extra-hazardous work carried out by a sub-contractor. As against this, there is the fact that Union Carbide's plant in Norfolk, Virginia had operated without any problems, suggesting an operational problem rather than a design fault. Furthermore, if the proximity of MIC to water were only likely to cause problems if the plant were poorly maintained, then on the analysis adopted by the Court of Appeal in *Rainham* that would argue against the operation of the plant as constituting an extra-hazardous activity.[73] However, the plaintiffs also alleged that a contributory cause of the leak was the parent company's cost-cutting decision to shut off the refrigeration unit on the ill-fated tank of methyl-isocyanate, thus allowing the gas to warm from zero degrees Celsius to the more volatile ambient temperature.[74] If substantiated, this would establish that the parent company's involvement in its subsidiary's activities had made the plant extra-hazardous.

Secondly, the plaintiffs alleged that Union Carbide had been aware of safety problems at the Bhopal plant for some years prior to the disaster and yet had failed to respond to its Indian subsidiary's requests for help in putting

---

71 Muchlinski, P, 'The Bhopal case: controlling ultrahazardous industrial activities undertaken by foreign investors' (1987) 50 MLR 545. Baughen, S, 'Multinationals and the export of hazard' (1995) 58 MLR 54.

72 Unless otherwise stated, the facts set out below are taken from Catliff, N, 'Sabotage and the B-Word', *The Guardian*, 1 March 1991, p 29.

73 In addition, the plant's initial design was subsequently modified by the Indian subsidiary, although the modification was approved both by the parent company and by the Indian Government.

74 Anderson, M, 'Transnational Corporations and Environmental Damage: Is Tort Law the Answer?' (2002) 41 Washburn Law Journal 399, p 416.

matters right.[75] In particular, Union Carbide had allegedly failed to respond to its own safety audits in 1982 and 1984 which had noted problems with the MIC unit from where the disaster was to originate. Using either Lord Bridge's dictum in *D&F Estates* or the *Distillers* duty to warn, a duty might well arise out of the combination of the parent corporation's actual knowledge of safety defects and its power to ensure their remedy.

Thirdly, one theory attributes the disaster to human and technical failure during a routine cleaning operation when failure to maintain and close a series of valves while flushing the system resulted in the overflow of water into the storage tank.[76] This would point to negligence by the subsidiary alone, rather than to any breach of a primary duty by its parent. However, if the parent had become aware of these negligent working practices, a duty might still arise under Lord Bridge's dictum in *D&F Estates*.

10.3.5 'Soft law' international instruments and direct liability

Another consideration that the English courts might take into account in developing this uncharted area of tort law, are two sets of international guidelines relating to the conduct of multinational enterprises. First, there are the OECD Guidelines for Multinational Enterprises (the Guidelines), which are recommendations addressed by governments to multinational enterprises. The revised Guidelines were adopted in Paris on 27 June 2000 by the governments of the 30 member countries of the OECD (which includes the UK), as well Argentina, Brazil and Chile. Chapter I states that these are joint recommendations by OECD governments, and those of several non-OECD states, to multinational enterprises and provide 'principles and standards of good practice consistent with applicable laws'. However, chapter I then goes on to state that: 'The Guidelines are recommendations jointly addressed by governments to multinational enterprises' and 'Observance of the Guidelines by enterprises is voluntary and is not legally enforceable.' An innovation in the 2000 Guidelines was the establishment of National Contact Points to which complaints about the operation of a multinational enterprise could be directed.

Given the paucity of law relating to the possible duty of care owed by a parent company in respect of the activities of a subsidiary, it is possible that the English courts might take account of these 'soft law' provisions in

---

75 On 24 December 1981, a phosgene leak from the plant resulted in one death and three hospitalisations. A further leak on 9 February 1982 led to a further 25 hospitalisations. Cassels, J, 'The Uncertain Promise of Law. Lessons from Bhopal' (1991) 29 Osgoode Hall Review 1, p 5, fn 4.
76 Cassels, J, op. cit., p 4, fn 1.

establishing when such a duty of care might arise. This would be a way round the fact that under English law a claim in negligence cannot generally be founded on the defendant's failure to act. Although the observation of the Guidelines is stated to be 'voluntary and not legally enforceable', the Guidelines do reflect 'principles and standards of good practice' which have been recommended by OECD members, including the UK Government. In these circumstances, it would seem somewhat perverse for an English court not to take account of recommendations by the UK Government when it came to working out the applicable principles of tort law in the uncharted area pertaining to the potential direct liability of parent companies in respect of the activities of their subsidiaries. Some support for such an approach may be derived from the *BATCO* case in 1979 when the fact that a parent company had explicitly stated that its policies were informed by the Guidelines was one of the factors considered by a Dutch court in granting an injunction to prevent the parent from closing its Amsterdam factory.[77]

The Guidelines contain several recommendations that could usefully inform the analysis of an English court as to the extent of a parent company's primary duty of care. Chapter V deals with the environmental obligations of enterprises and recommends that enterprises should:

1. Establish and maintain a system of environmental management appropriate to the enterprise, including:

    (a) Collection and evaluation of adequate and timely information regarding the environmental, health, and safety impacts of their activities;
    (b) Establishment of measurable objectives and, where appropriate, targets for improved environmental performance, including periodically reviewing the continuing relevance of these objectives; and
    (c) Regular monitoring and verification of progress toward environmental, health, and safety objectives or targets.

3. Assess and address in decision-making, the foreseeable environmental, health, and safety-related impacts associated with the processes, goods and services of the enterprise over their full life cycle. Where these proposed activities may have significant environmental, health, or safety impacts, and where they are subject to a decision of a competent authority, prepare an appropriate environmental impact assessment.

---

77 *BATCO*, Amsterdam Commerce Chamber of the Court of Amsterdam Court of Appeals, 21 June 1979 (NJ 1980, 71). The parent company had failed to consult with employees before closing the factory, contrary to recommendations contained in the 1976 version of the Guidelines.

4. Consistent with the scientific and technical understanding of the risks, where there are threats of serious damage to the environment, taking also into account human health and safety, not use the lack of full scientific certainty as a reason for postponing cost-effective measures to prevent or minimise such damage.

5. Maintain contingency plans for preventing, mitigating, and controlling serious environmental and health damage from their operations, including accidents and emergencies; and mechanisms for immediate reporting to the competent authorities.

6. Continually seek to improve corporate environmental performance, by encouraging, where appropriate, such activities as:

    (a) Adoption of technologies and operating procedures in all parts of the enterprise that reflect standards concerning environmental performance in the best performing part of the enterprise . . .

7. Provide adequate education and training to employees in environmental health and safety matters, including the handling of hazardous materials and the prevention of environmental accidents, as well as more general environmental management areas, such as environmental impact assessment procedures, public relations, and environmental technologies.

Many of these recommendations, such as those in paras 5 and 7, call on the parent company to take a proactive role in supervising the activities of its foreign subsidiary. Paragraph 6(a) would be of particular interest in the situation where a parent company sanctions the operation by its subsidiary of exported technology in a foreign jurisdiction under laxer health and safety provisions than were applied to the operation of that technology in its home jurisdiction.[78]

Where a claim is based on corporate complicity in human rights abuses committed by a foreign state the courts might draw guidance as to the duty of care owed by both the parent company and its subsidiary by reference to the provisions of Chapter II. These recommend that enterprises take fully into account:

> . . . established policies in the countries in which they operate, and consider the views of other stakeholders. In this regard enterprises should. 1. Contribute to economic, social and environmental progress with a view

---

78 In this context, the courts might also take account of the recommendation in Chapter IV(4) that multinational enterprises 'take adequate steps to ensure occupational health and safety in their operations'.

to achieving sustainable development. 2. Respect the human rights of those affected by their activities consistent with the host government's international obligations and commitments.

Paragraph 11 also recommends that enterprises 'abstain from any improper involvement in local political activities'.

The second soft law instrument that an English court might consider in delineating the scope of a parent company's primary duty of care is the UN's Draft Norms for Transnational Corporations adopted in 2003.[79] Paragraph 14 sets out the environmental obligations of transnational corporations[80] as follows:

> Transnational corporations and other business enterprises shall carry out their activities in accordance with national laws, regulations, administrative practices and policies relating to the preservation of the environment of the countries in which they operate, as well as in accordance with relevant international agreements, principles, objectives, responsibilities and standards with regard to the environment as well as human rights, public health and safety, bioethics and the precautionary principle, and shall generally conduct their activities in a manner contributing to the wider goal of sustainable development.[81]

In addition, para 7 requires transnational corporations to 'provide a safe and healthy working environment as set forth in relevant international instruments and national legislation as well as international human rights and humanitarian law'.

The broader issue of compliance with human rights is addressed in section C, 'Security of Persons', which provides:

---

79 Draft Norms on the Responsibilities of Transnational Corporations and Other Business Enterprises with Regard to Human Rights, E/CN.4/Sub.2/2003/12 (2003).
80 Paragraph 20 defines a 'transnational corporation' as 'an economic entity operating in more than one country or a cluster of economic entities operating in two or more countries – whatever their legal form, whether in their home country or country of activity, and whether taken individually or collectively'.
81 Paragraph (g) of the draft commentary on the norms provides:

> Transnational corporations and other business enterprises shall take appropriate measures in their activities to reduce the risk of accidents and damage to the environment by adopting best management practices and technologies. In particular, they shall use best management practices and appropriate technologies and enable their component entities to meet these environmental objectives through the sharing of technology, knowledge, and assistance, as well as through environmental management systems, sustainability reporting, and reporting of anticipated or actual releases of hazardous and toxic substances. In addition, they shall educate and train workers to ensure their compliance with these objectives.

3. Transnational corporations and other business enterprises shall not engage in nor benefit from war crimes, crimes against humanity, genocide, torture, forced disappearance, forced or compulsory labour, hostage-taking, extrajudicial, summary or arbitrary executions, other violations of humanitarian law and other international crimes against the human person as defined by international law, in particular human rights and humanitarian law.[82]
4. Security arrangements for transnational corporations and other business enterprises shall observe international human rights norms as well as the laws and professional standards of the country or countries in which they operate.

10.4 Civil liability in respect of violations of customary international law

The UK has no statute such as ATCA 1789. It is, however, possible that violations of customary international law create causes of action under common law. In *Trendtex Trading Corp v Central Bank of Nigeria*,[83] Lord Denning MR stated that international law formed part of the common law of England.[84] However, to incorporate customary international law into domestic law is not a straightforward matter. In *Maclaine Watson v Dept of Trade and Industry*,[85] which arose out of the collapse of the Tin Council, one of the issues before the Court of Appeal was whether there was a rule of international law that states who were members of international organisations could be sued in respect of liabilities incurred by such organisations. Both Kerr LJ and Nourse LJ agreed that there was indeed such a rule, but differed as to how it would have effect under domestic law. Nourse LJ was of the view that the rule would simply be transposed into national law, whereas Kerr LJ thought that the question was whether a state could be sued for the debts of an international organisation under national law, to which the answer was 'no'. The issue was not reconsidered when the case came before the House of Lords where the decision was based on an analysis of treaty rights rather than the application of customary international law.

The sceptical approach of Kerr LJ has subsequently informed decisions relating to the invocation of international law to provide a defence to criminal

82 Significantly, para 3 requires a transnational corporation not to benefit from violations of the listed norms of customary international law, even if it does not actually engage in such violations.
83 *Trendtex Trading Corp v Central Bank of Nigeria* [1977] QB 529.
84 This issue is analysed in detail in the 'Report on Civil Actions in the English Courts for Serious Human Rights Violations Abroad' by the International Law Association Human Rights Committee (2001) EHLR 129. However, the discussion on *forum non conveniens* predates the decision in *Owusu v Jackson*.
85 *Maclaine Watson v Dept of Trade and Industry* [1988] 3 All ER 257.

charges under domestic law. In *Hutchinson v Newbury Magistrates Court*,[86] the divisional court held that, although 'waging aggressive war' was a crime under international law, it could not be relied to provided a defence to domestic criminal proceedings due to uncertainty as to how the incorporation of international law would work in the domestic system. Recently, the House of Lords has held in *R v Jones (Margaret)*[87] that international law does not afford a defence in criminal proceedings, whilst stressing that it was making no finding as regards its potential role in civil proceedings. Historically, the courts may have recognised breaches of international law, such as piracy, violations of safe conduct and the rights of ambassadors, as creating domestic crimes. However, since *R v Knuller*,[88] the courts had refused to create any new criminal offences. That was entirely a matter for Parliament. The fact that conduct had achieved the level of a crime under international law did not mean that the same conduct would be a crime under domestic law. Thus the international prohibition on torture did not give the courts of the UK criminal jurisdiction over torture committed outside the jurisdiction. That required the additional step of the implementation of Criminal Justice Act 1998, s 134.

It seems, however, that some violations of customary international law may form the basis of a distinct cause of action under English law. In both *Al Adsani* and *Jones v Govt of Saudi Arabia*, the claimants based their claims not only on conventional intentional torts, but also on a violation of the international prohibition against torture. The significance of pleading the claim on this basis, and not merely in tort, can be seen in the Court of Appeal's decision in *Jones v Govt of Saudi Arabia* that servants or agents of a state ceased to be able to rely on sovereign immunity when they had committed torture, whereas they could still rely on it to defeat an ordinary domestic tort claim. Although the House of Lords overruled this finding, their Lordships made no comment on whether a violation of the international prohibition on torture gave rise to a cause of action separate from that arising under domestic tort law.

It would, therefore, seem that there is still some scope for arguing a claim on the basis of a breach of a violation of a norm of customary international law. This raises the question of whether norms of customary international law might also create causes of action. The issue could become important if in future claims were to be brought before the English courts arising out of facts similar to those in the US litigation in *Unocal*. The advantage to a claimant in arguing its claim in this way would be to take advantage of the rules of customary international law that relate to the imposition of aiding and abetting liability on non-state actors. English law does not allow a party

---

86 *Hutchinson v Newbury Magistrates Court* (2000) ILR 499.
87 *R v Jones (Margaret)* [2006] UKHL 16, [2007] 1 AC 136.
88 *R v Knuller* [1973] AC 435.

who aids and abets a tort to incur civil liability.[89] To be a joint tortfeasor a party must procure the tort or be part of a common venture with the tort feasor. Facilitation will be insufficient to ground liability.

However, the rules of customary international law as to when a private actor may incur criminal liability in respect of aiding and abetting may have a wider scope than the English law on joint tortfeasors. The US cases such as *Unocal*, which were discussed in the previous chapter, disclose the following pattern. The foreign subsidiary is alleged to have known of the human rights violations of its foreign partner, to have benefited from them and to have done nothing to prevent it. It is also alleged to have provided substantial assistance to the party that actually commits the violations, through provision of dual-use services that are capable both of benefiting the commercial joint venture while at the same time enabling the foreign state party to perpetrate violations of the law of nations. Yet there is no suggestion that the foreign subsidiary has procured the violations, nor that the violations form part of the common purpose of the subsidiary and its foreign state partner. Therefore, it is unlikely that the subsidiary would be found liable as a joint tortfeasor. The circuit court in *Unocal (2002)*,[90] however, held that in such circumstances international law would impose criminal liability on the defendant for aiding and abetting forced labour, and that criminal liability would also entail civil liability.[91]

This factor, therefore, provides a reason why claimants may still seek to rely on a cause of action deriving from a breach of customary international law as generating a cause of action an attractive option.[92] It could be argued that a cause of action is generated whenever there is a violation of one of those norms of customary international law in which liability is imposed on non-state actors. These are the prohibitions against slavery (including forced labour), piracy, genocide, and crimes against humanity. The claimant would then have to convince an English court that the universal criminal jurisdiction that is created in respect of violations of these norms also justifies the imposition of civil liability. However, such an approach is unlikely to commend itself to the English courts. Three steps are needed to get to reach the

---

89 'Mere facilitation of the commission of a tort by another does not make the defendant a joint tortfeasor and there is no tort of "knowing assistance" nor any direct counterpart of the criminal law concept of aiding and abetting: the defendant must either procure the wrongful act or act in furtherance of a common design or be party to a conspiracy', Rogers, W, *Winfield and Jolowicz on Tort*, 16th edn, 2002, London: Sweet and Maxwell, at 21.2.

90 *Doe I v Unocal Corp* 395 F 3d 932 (9th Cir 2002) (*Unocal (2002)*).

91 However, Cotes J's approach to this issue in *Presbyterian Church of Sudan v Talisman Energy* 453 F Supp 2d 633 (SDNY 2006) (*Talisman (2006)*). interprets the aiding and abetting principles of international criminal law in a manner that is very close to the English rules on civil liability of joint tortfeasors.

92 However, a claim against a UK parent corporation would still require the finding of a sufficient attributional link between it and its subsidiary.

same result as that reached by the majority of the circuit court in *Unocal (2002)*. First, the foreign state must violate a norm of international law which gives rise to liability for non-state actors. Secondly, the facts must be such as to lead to the imposition of criminal liability on the non-state actor, as an aider and abetter of such violation. This link in the chain now looks decidedly threadbare after the decision of the House of Lords in *R v Jones (Margaret)*[93] that new criminal offences can be created by Parliament alone. Thirdly, the imposition of criminal liability under international law automatically translates into civil liability. The problem, here, is that the only evidence for the existence of such a norm is the ATCA jurisprudence of US federal courts on this issue. It is likely that such a claim would be dismissed on grounds of act of state as being non-justiciable in the absence of any clear rules of customary international law.

An alternative ground for finding a company liable for its involvement in a project with a foreign government, which violates norms of customary international law in the course of the execution of that project, is by reference to partnership law. If the business relations between the company and the foreign government constitute a partnership, Partnership Act 1890, s 10 will make a partner liable in respect of torts committed 'in the course of business' by another of the partners.[94] There would be no need for it to have had any knowledge of the violations. All that would be required would be for the torts to have occurred 'in the course of business'. If the violations only occur because the military are in the area because of the pipeline project the answer would be 'yes'. The situation would be analogous to that, in *Dubai Aluminium v Salaam*,[95] where the House of Lords held that partners of a firm of solicitors could be held liable under s 10 in respect of a liability in dishonest assistance incurred by one of the partners who, while doing work for the partnership, helped a client to breach its fiduciary obligations to a third party. Similarly, the allegations in *Unocal* that the violations occurred while the Myanmar military were providing security for the pipeline, are of a type that would lead to an English court finding that such acts had occurred 'in the course of business'.

However, the discussion so far assumes that the partnership is subject to English law. The defendant is likely to argue that the applicable law is that of the jurisdiction in which the partnership was formed, particularly if that law makes it more difficult to make a partner vicariously liable for the torts of

---

93 *R v Jones (Margaret)* [2006] UKHL 16, [2007] 1 AC 136.
94 If, however, the partnership is conducted through a company in which the joint venturers are shareholders, as in *Talisman (2006)*, the matter will fall within company law rather than partnership law. The shareholders would be liable for the wrongs committed by the company only if the corporate veil could be pierced, under the law of the country in which the company had been incorporated.
95 *Dubai Aluminium v Salaam* [2002] UKHL 48, [2003] 2 AC 366.

another partner than is the case under English law. The English courts will still apply English law, as the law of the forum, as far as it relates to procedure. They will, therefore, have to establish whether the foreign law on partnership pleaded by the defendant is procedural or substantive. On this point, *Cheshire and North's Private International Law* states that:

> ... the foreign rule must not be dismissed as procedural if [so to do] would impose a liability that does not exist by the law governing the transaction; but if it merely requires the enforcement in a particular manner of an admitted liability, it must be dismissed as a rule affecting only the mode of process.[96]

10.5 Applicable law

For torts committed after 11 May 1996, the position is governed by the provisions of the Private International Law (Miscellaneous Provisions) Act 1995. Section 11(1) provides that in cases involving personal injury or death, the law to be applied is that of the country in which the claimant was when it sustained injury or death. In cases with facts like those in *Lubbe v Cape plc (No 2)*,[97] this would point to the application of South African law. However, s 12 allows for the displacement of the law provided for in s 11 if the law of another country is substantially more appropriate, given various factors connecting the proceedings with another jurisdiction. These are factors relating either to the parties, the events constituting the tort or any circumstances or consequences of those events. In a case like *Lubbe* which was pleaded on the basis of the wrongdoing of the parent company itself, this would shift the balance back to England, as this would be the place where the tort, arising out of the acts of the parent company, had been committed. In contrast, where an environmental tort claim is argued on the basis that the corporate veil should be pierced, the applicable law analysis becomes more complicated. The focus on the wrongdoing of the subsidiary would not displace the application of the law of the country in which the claimant had suffered injury or death, as this would also be the country connected with the wrongful acts of the subsidiary. However, English law would still have to be applied to the issue of whether the corporate veil could be pierced so as to make the parent company liable for the wrongs of the subsidiary.

There are two situations in which the courts will not apply a foreign law, notwithstanding that this is indicated by the application of the analysis undertaken under s 11 and s 12. First, s 14(3)(a) provides that a foreign law will not applied if to do so would involve a 'conflict with principles of public

---

96 North and Fawcett, *Cheshire and North's Private International Law*, 13th edn, 1999, London: Lexis Nexis Butterworths, pp 80–1.
97 *Lubbe v Cape plc (No 2)* [2000] 1 WLR 1545.

policy'. The application of the law of another jurisdiction, such as India, that made it easier to disregard the separate corporate personalities of parent and subsidiary companies might well be regarded as involving such a conflict, in that it might have the effect of discouraging multinational corporations from having a presence in England. Lord Hoffmann in his dissenting judgment in *Connelly v RTZ* was clearly unhappy with the prospect of a multinational company being amenable to suit in England by reason of its activities any-where in the world, merely by reason of the presence of its parent company in the jurisdiction.[98] Similar arguments of public policy were articulated by the Lord Chancellor's Department in September 1998 when it wrote to senior lawyers to propose reversing the decision by legislation, reasoning that 'because multinational companies based in England would be exposed to actions that would more properly be conducted abroad, they may as a result be more reluctant to have a presence in England'.[99] Conversely, s 14(3)(a) may lead to the disapplication of the law of the foreign jurisdiction where it provides an immunity to the defendant from civil liability in respect of the events forming the basis of the claim. The foreign state might, for example, have granted an immunity to human rights violators or may have passed legislation such purporting to exempt the defendant from liability for an environmental tort.[100]

Secondly, s 14(3)(b) provides that nothing in Part III of the Act shall affect 'any rules of evidence, pleading or practice' or authorise 'questions of pro-cedure in any proceedings to be determined otherwise than in accordance with the law of the forum'. The House of Lords in *Harding v Wealands*[101] has recently held that this provision retains the existing common law rules whereby the law relating to the quantification of damages in tort claims is regarded as procedural, and subject to the law of the forum.

10.6 Conclusion

At first glance, US law presents a far richer field of jurisprudence than its UK equivalent. Not only is there the rediscovery of ATCA in *Filartiga* and its continued, if circumscribed role, after the decision in *Sosa*, there is also the enactment of the TVPA in 1991. In the field of tort law, US courts have proved far more willing than the English courts to make a finding that a

---

98 [1998] AC 854, HL, p 876.
99 Ward, H, 'Foreign Direct Liability: Exploring The Issues', paper given to workshop held at the Royal Institute of International Affairs in London on 7 and 8 December 2000, www.chathamhouse.org.uk/pdf/briefing_papers/governing_multinationals.pdf (accessed 8 April 2007).
100 An instance of such legislation is the OK Tedi Mine Continuation (Ninth Supplemental) Act 2001 of Papua New Guinea.
101 *Harding v Wealands* [2006] UKHL 32, [2006] 3 WLR 83. See Scott, A, 'Substance and Procedure and Choice of Law in Torts' [2007] LMCLQ 44.

subsidiary corporation has acted as the agent of its parent. However, the extensive case law regarding the accountability of multinational corporations in respect of environmental and human rights abuses resulting from their overseas activities has generated very little real success for plaintiffs. Environmental claims will rarely fall within ATCA. To date, almost all such claims have fallen at the jurisdictional hurdle of *forum non conveniens*, due to the fact that the bulk of the evidence is likely to be located in the jurisdiction in which the damage occurred, as well as a desire to avoid 'docket congestion' in the US courts. The most that can be achieved by commencing proceedings in the US would seem to be the obtaining of the defendant's agreement to accept service of proceedings in the *lex situs*. This led to some limited success in the Bhopal litigation where this condition was attached to the dismissal of the suit in New York and exposed Union Carbide to liability under a judgment of the Indian courts, which led in turn to the settlement endorsed by the Bhopal Act 1989. It remains to be seen whether a similar turn of events will follow from the remission of the *Aguinda* claims to the courts of Ecuador.

There is also the fact that since *Sosa*, the scope of finding private actor liability under ATCA has been substantially reduced in two respects. First, there are decisions such as that of Illston J in *Bowoto v Chevron Corp* to the effect that this issue can no longer be decided by reference to the domestic US 'color of law' jurisprudence deriving from s 1983. It is true that most ATCA cases have failed to disclose allegations that would satisfy the demanding threshold set by s 1983. However, there are some cases, such as *Sarei v Rio Tinto*, where the allegations, if substantiated, would lead to a finding of private actor liability under s 1983. In future, such claims would have to be pleaded as conventional tort claims, unless they involved violations of that limited class of *ius cogens* norms in respect of which a private actor could be held criminally liable for aiding and abetting. Secondly, the scope of criminal liability of non-state actors in respect of aiding and abetting seems rather narrower after the decision of Cotes J in *Talisman (2006)* than had appeared to be the case after the decision of the majority of the circuit court in *Unocal (2002)*.

Even those claims that do fall within the ambit of ATCA or TVPA remain vulnerable to dismissal on one of the various grounds of abstention. The only unequivocal success to date is the *Unocal* litigation where the plaintiffs' success in fighting off the defendant's initial jurisdictional challenges led to the conclusion of a settlement. Cases such as *Aguinda v Texaco* show that ATCA claims enjoy no immunity from being dismissed on the grounds of *forum non conveniens*. Even when this hurdle is surmounted, the plaintiff's joy is likely to be shortlived as the claim is still vulnerable to being dismissed on other grounds such as act of state, political question or comity. The risk would be that the Department of State would submit a statement of interest objecting to the continuance of the suit because of its capacity to interfere with US foreign relations, an increasingly common occurrence under the

Bush administration. The district court judge would then feel bound to dismiss on one of these grounds, as was the case with Morrow J in *Sarei v Rio Tinto*. However, the recent decision of the circuit court in this case shows that an objection from the Department of State should not necessarily lead to the dismissal of the claim on such grounds. A similar degree of judicial independence was shown by Oberdorfer J in *Doe v Exxon* in refusing to dismiss tort claims, involving a US corporation's relationship with the Indonesian security forces in Aceh, on this ground. The politically charged nature of the claim, though, did lead to a finding that the claim should not proceed under ATCA, as this would require a US court to make findings as to the legitimacy of acts of the Indonesian state. The decision raises the question of whether similar cases in future would have better prospects of being heard before the US federal courts if they were brought as conventional tort claims under the diversity jurisdiction provided by 28 USC, s 1332.

In the UK, by way of contrast, there have been few claims involving multinational corporations, but the success rate has been much higher. The plaintiffs successfully beat off the *forum non conveniens* challenge in three case involving industrial injuries caused by alleged poor working conditions in a subsidiary's overseas plant. Following the decision of the European Court of Justice in *Owusu*, such litigation is likely to be even more successful in the future as *forum non conveniens* will no longer be a ground for dismissing a claim against a defendant corporation that is situated in the UK under Brussels Regulation 2001, Art 2. Furthermore, such claims are far less likely to be dismissed on grounds of act of state than would be the case in the US.

However, the scope of sovereign immunity is wider in the UK than in the US. The decisions in *Propend* and *Jones v Govt of Saudi Arabia* have firmly shut the door on any actions being taken against agents of a foreign state in respect of their human rights violations. What has yet to be seen in the English courts, though, is any suit against a multinational corporation in respect of accessory liability, of the kind seen in the US in *Unocal, Wiwa* and *Talisman*. Such a suit would have to be based on a violation of customary international law rather than on general tort law, given the very limited scope of accessory liability under English tort law. Such claims have been successfully pleaded, alongside conventional tort claims, both in *Al Adsani* and in *Jones*. What remains to be seen is whether the English courts, faced with such a claim, would follow the lead of their US counterparts, and develop principles of accessory liability in civil cases by reference to the jurisprudence established in criminal cases under international tribunals.

A final word of caution needs to be added. Whether the claim is brought in tort, or is brought for a violation of norms of customary international law, there still remains the problem of attributing the acts or omissions of an overseas subsidiary company to the parent company. In both the US and in the UK the legal tools exist for attributing liability where a parent has been *actively* involved in the wrongful conduct of its subsidiary which has led to the claimants' death or personal injury. The courts in the US have achieved this result by way of agency, and it seems likely, given the pleadings in cases like *Connelly* and *Lubbe*, that the English courts would reach a similar result by reference to the primary duty of care incumbent on a parent corporation. However, under both legal systems it would prove difficult to establish liability on a parent in the event that it had failed to supervise the activities of a subsidiary with whose activities it had very much an arm's-length relationship. The courts, however, could justify expanding the scope of the parent company's primary duty of care by reference to the recommendations in the OECD Guidelines on Multinational Enterprises, particularly those in Chapter V, which could be used to fashion a proactive primary duty of care in respect of the environmental consequences of the enterprise's operations.

Chapter 11

Alternative approaches to transnational pollution

Transnational pollution comes in two forms. First, there is obvious transnational pollution which arises when polluting activities in a state cause damage in the territory of a neighbouring state. Secondly, there is the corporate transnational pollution of the sort analysed in the previous chapters. This involves a multinational enterprise, where the parent company is based in one state, usually in the developed world, and damage is caused in another state, usually in the developing world, through the operations of one of its subsidiary companies.

Transnational pollution of the first type can involve a violation of a norm of customary international law. The *locus classicus* is the *Trail Smelter* arbitration that took place between Canada and the US from 1937 to 1941.[1] The US and Canada arbitrated a dispute arising out of the operations of a smelter in Trail, Canada. The US claimed in respect of damage suffered in its territory due to sulphur dioxide fumes emitted from the smelter, arguing that the height of the stacks increased the area affected within its territory. The tribunal held that international law prevented a state from using or permitting the use of its territory so as to cause injury by fumes to the territory of another state. The threshold of liability was that the injury must be serious in its consequences and established by clear and convincing evidence. The tribunal award damages to the US on a market value approach and ordered Canada to prevent the smelter from causing any future damage to US territory.

The decision is an isolated one, however, and leaves many questions unclear, such as the threshold issue of how serious the pollution must be so as to give rise to a state-to-state claim under customary international law. Furthermore, the singularity of the award reflects a general reluctance of states to have recourse to international law in such cases of transboundary pollution. For example, no claims were made against the Soviet Union in respect of the Chernobyl disaster of 1986 which led to the dispersal of radioactive

---

1 (1938/1941) 3 RIAA 1905, 9 ILR 375.

material throughout Europe. A major factor behind this diffidence must be a realisation that a state making such a claim is equally likely to find itself as a respondent to such a claim in the future. Instead, states have preferred to leave this issue to civil liability claims involving private actors.

The problem is that transnational pollution claims are not easily handled by private litigation. The previous chapters have shown that such litigation gives rise to difficult issues of jurisdiction and applicable law, with matters being complicated by the used of the corporate form to shield a wealthy parent company from the defaults of it under-capitalised foreign subsidiary. Similar problems arise as regards ship-source pollution, which involves the phenomenon of the one-ship company whose vessel flies a flag of convenience. This mirrors the problem of multinational corporations who seek to relocate their hazardous activities to jurisdictions in the developing world which apply a laxer regulatory regime than that pertaining in their domestic jurisidiction. Many flag states in the developing world have failed to address seriously their regulatory obligations as regards vessels flying their flags. In addition, the use of a one-ship company will mean that there may be insufficient assets to meet any judgment resulting from the spill. I shall now examine how international conventions have dealt with these problems, first as regards regulation aimed at avoiding ship-source pollution, and then from the perspective of ensuring adequate compensation in the event of such pollution.

11.1 International regulation of ship-source pollution

11.1.1 MARPOL

The International Maritime Organisation (IMO) is the main organisation for providing internationally recognised common standards in the maritime sphere.[2] The IMO is responsible for the main international convention regulating marine oil pollution. This is MARPOL, which was substantially amended in 1978 to facilitate its entry into force. Its detailed regulations are contained in its annexes.[3] Annex I deals with oil pollution and Annex II with chemical pollution. These annexes bind all parties (the others are optional). MARPOL's approach relies mainly of the formulation of technical measures to limit oil discharges. In 1992, in the wake of the *Exxon Valdez* spill, it

---

2 Examples of these are the International Convention on Load Lines 1966, the Convention on International Regulations for Preventing Collisions at Sea 1972, the Safety of Life at Sea Convention 1974 whose 1978 Protocol contain additional features applicable to oil tankers and other large vessels, and the International Safety Management Code 1998.

3 The first international convention to regulate marine pollution was the London Convention for the Prevention of Pollution of the Sea by Oil 1954. This has largely been replaced by MARPOL, although 40 states still adhere to it.

instituted a requirement that new vessels have double hulls. Its concern is with oil discharges that take place en route, more than 50 miles form land. It also designates special areas where more stringent standards apply, amounting to a virtual prohibition on discharges. MARPOL is not confined to oil pollution and extends to other types of ship-based pollution, such as the bulk carriage of noxious liquids, harmful substances and disposal of garbage from ships.

MARPOL's enforcement scheme requires the co-operation of coastal states, flag states, coastal states, and port states. It has instituted a system of certification, inspection and reporting which impose two obligations on flag states. The first is that of ensuring periodic inspections of vessels flying their flag. The second is a responsibility for issuing an 'international oil pollution prevention certificate' which provides prima facie evidence that the ship complies with MARPOL requirements. Such a certificate must be accorded the same validity by other state parties as they would accord to their own certificates. Additionally, ships are also subject to inspection by port states, pursuant to their pre-existing jurisdiction to regulate the entry of vessels into their ports. This is known as 'port state control' and is the principal means of securing enforcement with MARPOL standards. Port state control has been facilitated by the development of a series of regional schemes based on the 1982 Paris Memorandum of Understanding which covers 17 states in Western Europe, as well as Canada, and which provides for an annual inspection by each administration of at least 25 per cent of incoming foreign vessels.

Article 5 contains the following grounds for inspection: to determine whether the vessel possesses a valid certificate; to determine the vessel's condition when there are 'clear grounds' to show that it is not in 'substantial compliance' with its certificate; where there are clear grounds to believe that the master and crew were not familiar with essential shipboard measures relating to the prevention of oil pollution.[4] If a vessel is found not to be in compliance with MARPOL requirements, the port state must not allow her to sail, unless her sailing would not present an unreasonable threat of harm to the marine environment. Instead, the vessel must be kept in port until suitably repaired. Where serious deficiencies are identified, port states have power to detain vessels or ban them from ports in the region. In less serious cases, the port state must report the violation to the flag state or initiate its own prosecution if the non-compliance amounts to a violation of its own municipal law. However, the port state must not unduly delay vessels.

Under Art 6 inspection can also be used to adduce evidence that the vessel has violated her obligations in respect of oil discharges. Unlike Art 5, this provision does not require there to be 'clear grounds' for suspecting a violation. If a violation is indicated the port state must report to the flag state. Any party, including a coastal state, may request inspection by the port state if

---

4 This ground was introduced in 1996.

there is evidence of harmful discharges 'in any place'. Port states may apply these provisions, as a condition of port entry, to vessels flagged with non-parties to MARPOL, but must ensure they give no more favourable treatment to non-parties than they do to vessels flying the flag of MARPOL state parties.[5]

MARPOL, Art 4.1 contemplates that the responsibility for regulating and prosecuting violations will lie primarily with flag states. Where there is sufficient evidence of a violation, it is incumbent on the flag state to prosecute, even if the violation occurs on the High Seas or within the jurisdiction of another state. Flag states in developing countries have, however, a poor record of enforcement.[6] Article 4.2 also provides for prosecution by port states,[7] although Art 9.3 specifies that jurisdiction 'shall be construed in the light of international law in force at the time of application or interpretation of the present Convention'.

11.1.2 Enforcement jurisdiction under international law

The jurisdiction of port states to prosecute, therefore, depends upon the principles of customary international law and of UNCLOS.[8] UNCLOS, Art 211.2 requires flag states to have in place regulations which have 'at least the same effect' as 'generally accepted international rules and standards'. As 94 per cent of world tonnage flies the flag of a MARPOL state party, Annexes I and II constitute these 'generally accepted international rules and standards'. This requires all states to have MARPOL standards as a minimum floor, but does not preclude the adoption of more onerous standards. Article 217 requires flag states to take measures necessary for the implementation and enforcement of international rules and standards as well as mandating the investigation of violations and the bringing of appropriate proceedings, and imposing a duty to act on request of other states when they report a violation.

Article 211.4 allows coastal states, in the exercise of their sovereignty over their territorial sea, to 'adopt laws and regulations for the prevention, reduction and control of marine pollution from foreign vessels, including vessels exercising the right of innocent passage'. There is no express limitation that such law must be based on 'generally accepted international rules and standards'. However, such laws and regulations must not hamper the right of

---

5 Article 5.4.
6 In 1992, the IMO set up a Flag State Implementation Committee to provided guidelines as to the responsibilities of flag states. However, there is no mechanism for compelling flag states to fulfil their regulatory obligations.
7 '... any violation ... within the jurisdiction of any party to the Convention shall be prohibited and sanctions shall be established thereby under the law of that Party'.
8 UNCLOS came into force on 16 November 1994 and, as of 4 April 2007, has been ratified by 153 states.

innocent passage of foreign vessels.[9] UNCLOS' rules on innocent passage are
to be found in Part III. This contains Art 21 which sets out the legislative competence of coastal states in relation to innocent passage of vessels through
their territorial sea. This gives coastal states the right to designate environmentally protected, or particularly sensitive sea areas, to control navigation
routes for purposes of safety and protection of the environment, to prohibit
polluting discharges from vessels, without being limited to 'generally accepted
international rules and standards'.[10] However, such standards do limit the
coastal state's right to regulate the construction, design, equipment and man-
ning standards for vessels. Where a coastal state has claimed an exclusive
economic zone under UNCLOS, Art 211.6 permits it to apply 'generally
accepted international rules and standards' in respect of that zone.

Coastal states' rights of enforcing the legislation and regulations referred
to in Art 211 is dealt with in Art 220. Paragraph 1 authorises coastal states to
take proceedings against a vessel which is voluntarily within its port, or off-
shore terminal, in respect of such violations within its territorial sea or its
exclusive economic zone. Where a vessel is in the territorial sea, and there are
clear grounds that there has been a violation there of legislation or regulation
of the sort referred to in Art 211.4, the coastal state may undertake physical
inspections of the vessel.[11] Where such violation has occurred in the exclusive
economic zone, the coastal state's powers as regards a vessel in its territorial
sea or exclusive economic zone is more limited. In such circumstances the
coastal state is limited to being able to require such vessel 'to give information
regarding its identity and port of registry, its last and its next port of call and
other relevant information required to establish whether a violation has
occurred'.

If, however, there are clear grounds for believing that such violation has
resulted 'in a substantial discharge causing or threatening significant pollution
of the marine environment', the coastal state 'may undertake physical inspection of the vessel for matters relating to the violation if the vessel has refused
to give information or if the information supplied by the vessel is manifestly
at variance with the evident factual situation and if the circumstances of the

---

9 This is defined in Art 19. Passage will cease to be innocent in the event of 'wilful and serious'
   pollution. This does not cover accidental pollution and will have a very limited impact on
   operational pollution which, though 'wilful', is rarely 'serious'.
10 In *R (on the application of Intertanko) et al v The Secretary of State for Transport* (Case No
   CO/10651/2005) [2006] EWHC 1577 (Admin), Hodge J referred to the European Court of
   Justice the question of whether Directive 2005/35, which requires Member States to impose
   stricter criminal standards as regards discharges at sea of polluting substances than are
   provided for by MARPOL, is contrary to the provisions of UNCLOS, to the extent that the
   directive requires member states to apply the measure within their territorial sea and exclusive
   economic zone.
11 Article 220.2.

case justify such inspection'.[12] In extreme circumstances, the coastal state may institute proceedings, including detention of the vessel, in respect of such violations. There must be 'clear objective evidence' that such a violation of the type has resulted in a 'discharge causing major damage or threat of major damage to the coastline or related interests of the coastal State, or to any resources of its territorial sea or exclusive economic zone'.[13]

As regards port states, Art 211.3 requires that they give due publicity to entry conditions and inform the IMO, but it assumes that they have full autonomy in determining the substance of such conditions, as is the position under customary international law. Article 218.1 also grants port states the express power to investigate and prosecute violations wherever they have occurred, including the High Seas and the coastal zones of another state, but only at the request of the affected coastal state. Article 219 requires port states that to prevent the sailing of vessels that are 'in violation of applicable international rules and standards relating to seaworthiness of vessels and thereby threatens damage to the marine environment'.

In a pollution emergency, a coastal state may need to act outside its territorial waters or exclusive economic zone. Such intervention may be justified by necessity or, more doubtfully, by invoking the principle of self-defence. The matter falls under the Convention on Intervention on the High Seas in Cases of Oil Pollution Casualties 1969, which in 1973 was extended to deal with other forms of pollution. This is limited to maritime casualties and permits no measures against government vessels or warships. A high intervention threshold is set in that there must be 'grave and imminent danger' which results in 'major harmful consequences'. UNCLOS, Art 221 assumes that coastal states have a right to intervene in such circumstances,[14] providing there is 'actual or threatened damage'. Intervention depends on what is necessary for protection of coastal states and must be proportionate. Military intervention of the type applied by the UK in response to the 1967 *Torrey Canyon* spill is unlikely to satisfy this requirement. The appropriate response by the coastal state will usually be to require affected vessels to accept salvage services.

Where a state becomes aware of imminent or actual pollution of the marine environment, UNCLOS, Art 198 requires it to give immediate notification to other states likely to be affected. UNCLOS and the regional sea agreements require states to co-operate in dealing with such pollution. The Convention on Oil Pollution Preparedness Response and Co-Operation 1990 (COPPR) was the IMO's response to the *Exxon Valdez* spill in 1989. Article 7 obliges parties to respond to requests for assistance from states likely to be affected by oil pollution. Major incidents are to be notified to the IMO.

---

12 Article 220.5.
13 Article 220.6.
14 So, too, does the 1989 Salvage Convention, Art 9.

Under Art 12 the IMO is given responsibility for co-ordinating and facilitating co-operation on various matters and, on request, is to provide technical assistance and advice to states dealing with major oil pollution incidents. The 2000 Protocol extends these principles to pollution from hazardous and noxious substances. COPPR, Art 3 requires flag states to ensure their vessels have on board an oil pollution emergency plan that conforms with IMO provisions.

11.2 Civil liability conventions on oil pollution

The *Torrey Canyon* spill in 1967 highlighted four problems with leaving the question of compensation for oil spills to national laws. First, the need to prove negligence by the shipowner. Secondly, the lack of recovery under national systems for environmental mitigation and reinstatement costs. Thirdly, the unwillingness of local courts to assume jurisdiction over non-national vessels. Fourthly, the likelihood that the shipowner might have limited assets and be unable to satisfy any judgment in full.

The result was a new international convention, the CLC, which entered into force in June 1975. The convention represented a compromise between the various interests involved in and affected by the carriage of oil by sea, and was drafted against the background of the customary international law rights of navigation of flag state vessels. The companion to CLC was the International Convention on the Establishment of an International Fund for Compensation for Oil Pollution Convention 1971 (Fund Convention) which came into force in 1978. This created the Fund, financed by levies on receivers of oil cargoes to provide additional compensation in circumstances in which compensation would not available under the CLC, in particular when the claim exceeded the CLC limitation figure. Fund Convention, Art 2.2 provides that the Fund shall be recognised in each contracting state as a legal person, capable of assuming rights and obligations, and of being a party in legal proceedings before the courts of that contracting state.[15]

The CLC's aim was to set out a system of uniform international rules to make available adequate compensation to persons who suffered damage caused by pollution resulting from the escape or discharge of oil from ships. In the 1980s, cargo interests perceived that shipowners' liability was lagging behind rising mitigation costs and inflation and therefore shifting the burden onto them through the Fund. Shipowners for their part worried about the ease with which some national courts were breaking their right to limit. In 1984, an IMO Conference reviewed the operation of the CLC and the Fund.

---

15 The CLC and the Fund Convention, respectively, were supplemented by two voluntary supplementary agreements by tanker owners, Tanker Owners Voluntary Agreement Concerning Liability for Oil Pollution (TOVALOP) (1969–97) and Contract Regarding an Interim Supplement to Tanker Liability for Oil Pollution (CRISTAL) (1971–97).

This proposed raising the limits of liability and making them harder to break as well as the explicit recognition of the environment as falling within the scope of pollution damage under CLC. A further recommendation was that the geographical scope of the conventions be extended beyond the territorial seas of contracting states, made possible by the modifications to customary international law effected by UNCLOS.

US ratification, however, was not forthcoming. The *Exxon Valdez* spill in 1989 caused the US to take unilateral action in implementing the Oil Pollution Act 1990 which imposed stronger duties of care on shipowners, allowed claims against operators and opened up the possibility of unlimited liability. In 1992, the IMO reduced the entry into force requirements to facilitate adoption of the amendments without US ratification. Although many states have adopted the 1992 CLC, a significant number still adhere to the 1969 CLC. The 1992 protocols also saw the creation of a new Fund with higher overall claim limits. From 16 May 1998, members of the 1992 Fund ceased to retain membership of the 1971 Fund and on 24 May 2002 the 1971 Fund ceased to be in force. To become a party to the Fund, a state must now become a party to the 1992 CLC.

11.2.1 Liability regime

The CLC tackled the problems of establishing liability in negligence by adopting a system of strict liability subject to limited exceptions. CLC, Art III.1 applies a strict liability regime to shipowners 'for any pollution damage caused by oil which has escaped or been discharged from the ship as a result of the incident'. The 1992 protocols expanded the definition of 'ship' in Art I to cover:

> . . . any sea-going vessel and seaborne craft of any type whatsoever constructed or adapted for the carriage of oil in bulk as cargo, provided that a ship capable of carrying oil and other cargoes shall be regarded as a ship only when it is actually carrying oil in bulk as cargo and during any voyage following such carriage unless it is proved that is has no residues of such carriage of oil in bulk.[16]

The 1992 protocols also extended the definition of 'oil' so as to cover 'any persistent hydrocarbon mineral oil such as crude oil, fuel oil, heavy diesel oil and lubricating oil, whether carried on board a ship as cargo or in the bunkers of such a ship'.

Article III.2 allows the shipowner to avoid liability in three situations. First, where the shipowner proves that the damage resulted from an act of war,

---

16 The 1969 CLC defined 'ship' as 'any sea-going vessel and any seaborn craft of any type whatsoever, actually carrying oil in bulk as cargo'.

hostilities, civil war, insurrection or a natural phenomenon of an exceptional, inevitable and irresistible character. Secondly, where the shipowner proves the damage was wholly caused by an act or omission done with intent to cause damage by a third party. Thirdly, where the shipowner proves that the damage was wholly caused by the negligence or other wrongful act of any government or other authority responsible for the maintenance of lights or other navigational aids in the exercise of that function.

Article III.4 operates so as to channel all claims for compensation for pollution damage against the owner into the CLC and excludes any claim under the CLC or otherwise against the servants or agents of the owner.[17] The 1992 protocols extended these 'channelling' provisions to encompass the following:

(b) the pilot or any other person who, without being a member of the crew, performs services for the ship;
(c) any charterer (howsoever described, including a bareboat charterer), manager or operator of the ship;
(d) any person performing salvage operations with the consent of the owner or on the instructions of a competent public authority;
(e) any person taking preventive measures;
(f) all servants or agents of persons mentioned in subparagraphs (c),(d) and (e) unless the damage resulted from their personal act or omission, committed with the intent to cause such damage, or recklessly and with knowledge that such damage would probably result.[18]

An essential element of the political compromise that resulted in the CLC is the provision of an overall limitation of liability for the shipowner in respect of claims under the CLC.[19] The channelling provisions mean that the shipowner has to be sued under the CLC and will therefore need a separate limitation provision from the general right to limit for maritime claims which is afforded to him under the 1957 and the 1976 Limitation Conventions. CLC 1969, Art V entitled the shipowner to limit liability under the CLC unless the

17 Article III(5), however, preserves the shipowner's rights of recourse against third parties, whilst Art III.3 deals with contributory negligence by the claimant.
18 Article VIII contains a time bar provision, providing for the extinguishment of rights under the CLC 'unless an action is brought thereunder within 3 years from the date when the damage occurred. However, in no case shall an action be brought after 6 years from the date of the incident which caused the damage. Where this incident consists of a series of occurrences, the 6-year period shall run from the date of the first such occurrence'.
19 Article V.8 provides that the shipowner may also limit in respect of claims for 'expenses reasonably incurred or sacrifices reasonably made' where these have been voluntarily incurred by the shipowner to prevent or minimise pollution damage. Such claims rank equally with other claims against the limitation Fund.

incident had occurred with the actual fault or privity of the shipowner.[20] The 1992 protocols amended this provision so that the shipowner would lose its right to limit only 'if it is proved that the pollution damage resulted from his personal act or omission, committed with the intent to cause such damage, or recklessly and with knowledge that such damage would probably result'. This makes it extremely difficult for a claimant to establish that a shipowner should lose its right to limit. However, as against that, the 1992 protocols substantially increased the overall limitation figure.[21] Article V now provides a limitation figure of 3 million special drawing rights (SDRs) for a ship not exceeding 5,000 units of tonnage, to which amount, for ships exceeding this figure, an additional 420 SDRs per unit of tonnage is imposed, up to an overall maximum of 59.7 million SDRs.

A shipowner can constitute a limitation fund 'either by depositing the sum or by producing a bank guarantee or other guarantee, acceptable under the legislation of the contracting state where the fund is constituted, and considered to be adequate by the court or another competent authority' with a court in any of the contracting states which is given jurisdiction over the action under Art IX. The fund, once established, is available for distribution among the claimants on a pro rata basis.[22] If, before the fund is distributed, either the owner, his servants or agents, or any person providing him with insurance or other financial security, pays compensation for pollution damage as a result of the incident in question, then under Art V(5) that person obtains subrogation rights against the fund to the extent of the rights against the limitation fund that would have been exercisable by the person who has received such compensation. These subrogation rights might also be claimed by other parties who had made such payments, but only to the extent that such subrogation rights are allowed under the applicable national law.[23] Under Art 9 the fund obtains a right of subrogation in respect of 'any rights in respect of the damage which the recipient has, or but for the payment would have had, against any other person'.

Once a shipowner has constituted a limitation fund, Art VI provides that no person having a claim for pollution damage arising out of that incident may exercise any right against any other assets of the owner in respect of such claim. Secondly, if a ship, or other property of the shipowner, has been arrested in respect of the claim, that property must be released by the court or

---

20 Article V.2.
21 The initial limits in respect of any one incident were an aggregate amount of 2,000 francs for each ton of the ship's tonnage, subject to an overall limit of 210 million francs.
22 Article.V.11 extends the right to constitute a limitation fund to the insurer or other person providing financial security, subject to the same conditions and effect as if the fund were constituted by the owner. However, this right will subsist even in the event that the owner has lost the right to limit, but the constitution of the fund in such circumstances will be without prejudice to the rights of any claimant against the owner.
23 Article V.6.

other competent authority of any contracting state. If security has been provided to avoid arrest, it must be returned to the shipowner. However, these provisions apply only if the claimant had access to the court administering the fund and the fund was actually available in respect of its claim.

The fund's liability is dealt with by Art 4 of the Fund Convention, which provides that the fund is liable for pollution damage in the territory of each contracting state where the claimant has been unable to obtain full compensation under the 1992 CLC for one of the following three reasons. First, the shipowner has escaped liability by reliance on one of the exceptions permitted under the CLC. Secondly, the shipowner is financially incapable of meeting its CLC liabilities and has inadequate liability insurance. Thirdly, the damage exceeds the shipowner's liability under the CLC. A claim might also be made on the fund in respect of '[e]xpenses reasonably incurred, and sacrifices reasonably made, by the owner voluntarily to prevent or minimise pollution damage'.

Article 4.2 affords three defences to the fund. The first is where damage was suffered in a non-member state. The second is where the pollution damage resulted from an act of war or was caused by a spill from a warship. The third is where the claimant was unable to prove a causal link between its loss and a spill from one or more ships of the type that are potentially liable under the CLC. Under Art 4.3 the fund is also entitled to reduce or extinguish its liability if it can prove the pollution damage resulted wholly or partly '(a) from anything done or omitted to be done with intent to cause damage by the person who suffered the damage, or (b) from the negligence of that person'. However, no such exoneration applies 'where the pollution damage consists of the costs of preventive measures or any damage caused by such measures'.[24]

The fund's overall limitation figure under the 1992 protocols was initially fixed at 135 million SDRs, including the sum actually paid by the shipowner or its insurer, with a tacit acceptance procedure for raising the limits. In accordance with this procedure on 1 November 2003, the 2000 Protocol came into force raising the limit to 203 million SDRs, applicable to incidents on or after that date. It also contains a provision that if three states contributing to the fund receive more than 600 million tonnes of oil per annum, there should be a further increase to 300.704 million SDRs.

An additional tier of compensation is provided by the 2003 Protocol which came into force on 3 March 2005. This establishes a Supplementary Fund with an overall limit of 750 million SDRs for each incident for pollution damage in the territory of the state parties to the protocol.[25] It will only cover

---

24 Article 6 provides that an action against the fund must be commenced three years after the claim against the fund arose and not later than six years after 'the occurrence, or first of the occurrences, resulting in the discharge or escape, or (as the case may be) in the relevant threat of contamination, by reason of which the claim against the fund arose'.

25 As of 1 November 2006 the protocol has been ratified by 20 states.

334 International Trade and the Protection of the Environment

claims for incidents which occur after the protocol has entered into force for the state concerned. The financing of this extra tier of compensation falls on the oil industry. To redress this imbalance, the International Group of P & I Clubs, whose 13 members provide liability insurance to 98 per cent of the world's tanker fleets, introduced, on 20 February 2006, two voluntary agreements: the Small Tanker Oil Pollution Indemnification Agreement 2006 (STOPIA 2006) and the Tanker Oil Pollution Indemnification Agreement (TOPIA 2006). Oil spills covered by these agreements will still be dealt with by the 1992 Fund and the Supplementary Fund, but the funds will then be indemnified by the shipowner under the agreements. The limitation under STOPIA 2006 is 20 million SDR for tankers up to 29,548 gross tonnage for damage in 1992 Fund member states. Under TOPIA 2006, the Supplementary Fund is indemnified for half the amount it has paid in respect of incidents involving ships covered by the agreement.

11.2.2 Recoverable damage

CLC 1969, Art 1.6 defined 'pollution damage' as 'loss or damage caused outside the ship carrying oil by contamination resulting from the escape or discharge of oil from the ship, wherever such escape or discharge may occur . . .' It also applied to the costs of preventive measures[26] and further loss or damage caused by preventive measures. This original definition was susceptible to a variety of interpretations which caused problems in the following three cases. The first arose from the grounding of the *Antonio Gramsci* in 1979 off Ventspils in the Baltic Sea. The USSR made a claim for the estimated costs for environmental damage which went beyond demonstrable economic loss. Claims against the shipowner under the CLC would have absorbed most of the shipowner's limitation fund, which would then have implications for the Fund (to which the USSR was not a party). As a result, in 1980 the fund assembly adopted Resolution Three which provided, 'the assessment of compensation to be paid by IOPC Fund is not to be made on the basis of an abstract quantification of damage in accordance with theoretical models'.[27]

This has subsequently justified the fund in consistently rejecting claims for environmental compensation which is not related to quantifiable economic loss. In particular, the following three claims were all were rejected by the fund due to the abstract manner in which they were formulated: the *Patmos* spill in 1985, for which 5,000 million lire was claimed; the *Haven* spill in 1991,

---

26 Defined in Art I.7 as 'any reasonable measures taken by any person after an incident has occurred to prevent or minimize pollution damage'.
27 See, generally, Mason, M, 'Transnational compensation of oil pollution damage: examining changing spatialities of environmental liability', 2002, London: LSE Research Online, http://eprints.lse.ac.uk/archive/00000570 (accessed 11 April 2007).

for which 100,000 million lire was claimed; the *Evoikos* spill in 1997, for which $3.2 million was claimed. The Italian Government reacted by pursuing its environmental claims through its national courts, leading to the acceptance by the Italian Court of Appeal of a claim which included non-use environmental values assessed by expert testimony. The fund appealed and the case was settled out of court in a settlement in which the fund made it clear it neither accepted such claims nor made payments in respect of them (IOPC 1994). Italy's deferred adoption of the 1992 protocols until the *Patmos* and *Haven* claims had been resolved. In comparison, under the US Oil Pollution Act 1990, such claims would have been admissible under prescribed assessment methods.

A related issue is whether claims can be brought by the state as trustee for the public, both nationally and locally. The Italian courts in the *Patmos* held that the 1969 CLC did not distinguish between private and public property damages. A state could bring environmental compensation claims in its capacity as public trustee, even in the absence of direct public ownership, and its right of action extended beyond claims for economic loss. The fund, while accepting that public bodies can be legitimate claimants, has not, however, accepted trusteeship claims divorced from quantifiable elements of economic damage.

In response to concerns that liberal interpretations of Art 1.6 by national courts were undermining the uniform application of the CLC, the 1992 protocols amended the provision by inserting the following, 'provided that compensation for impairment of the environment other than loss of profit from such impairment shall be limited to costs of reasonable measures of reinstatement actually undertaken or to be undertaken'. This is an implicit recognition that claims purely in respect of impairment to the environment fall within the scope of the CLC, but can also be seen as a limitation on previous liberal interpretations of this provision by national courts. In particular, the redrafting of Art 1.6 made clear that claims for the impairment of the environmental fell outside the CLC, unless the impairment had caused loss of profit or the claim was for reasonable measures of reinstatement.

The US in the Oil Pollution Act 1990 has taken a far wider approach to the type of recovery that can be made in respect of 'pure' environmental damage that occurs consequent to an oil spill. Unlike the position under the CLC, such claims are not limited to clean up and restoration costs. Section 2702(b)(A) allows recovery for 'damages for injury to, destruction of, loss of, or loss of use of, natural resources, including the reasonable costs of assessing the damage, which shall be recoverable by a United States trustee, a State trustee, an Indian tribe trustee, or a foreign trustee . . .' These claims require a federal or state trustee to conduct a natural resources damage assessment. Section 2706 (D) provides that the measure of natural resource damages under this heading is: '(a) the cost of restoring, rehabilitating, replacing, or acquiring the equivalent of, the damaged natural resources;(b) the diminution in value of those natural resources pending restoration; plus (c) the reasonable cost of assessing those damages'.

Four methodologies have been employed to value the purely environmental damage that occurs with the loss of the affected area as a public resource in the period between the spill and the recovery of the affected area. First, there is travel cost methodology where individuals' travel costs to the damaged area are used as proxy for the price of 'services' provided by that area. Secondly, there is hedonic pricing methodology by which the demand for non-marketed natural resources is estimated indirectly by analysis of commodities that are traded in a market. Thirdly, there is unit value methodology in which pre-assigned monetary values for various types of non-marketed recreational or other experiences by the public are used to value a specific resource. Fourthly, there is contingent valuation methodology in which a group of interviewees is asked how much they would, theoretically, be prepared to pay to enjoy a benefit from, or how much they would want to receive to tolerate damage to a resource. The resulting sum is then multiplied by the number of persons presumed to be affected by the knowledge that the resource was damaged. The problem is that all these methodologies are essentially speculative exercises in giving value to a loss which is incapable of valuation.

Following the *Erika* break-up in 1999, France, within the 1992 Fund Working Group, urged the incorporation into the 1992 Fund Claims Manual the concept of compensation for environmental damage as a violation of state rights over collective marine assets, along the lines of the compensation methodology to be found in Oil Pollution Act (OPA) 1990, s 2706.[28] It called for the CLC to be amended to permit claims for introducing 'identical' or 'equivalent' ecological attributes in an adjacent marine area should reinstatement at the damage site be physically or economically infeasible.

In response, the International Tanker Owners Pollution Federation (ITOPF) argued that the problem was that after a clean-up operation only time would enable the natural recovery of a damaged habitat. In the interim another similar habitat within the general area might be improved or a new one created by engineering. This approach is known as habitat equivalency analysis. Because it rarely benefits the damaged habitat directly it could not be regarded as 'reinstatement' as envisaged under the 1992 CLC and Fund Conventions. Instead, it amounted to interim compensation for loss of use and services while the damaged habitat was recovering naturally. While the concept might have merit on land where there might never be natural recovery of an isolated area, this was not the case in the sea. Furthermore, in many cases it would be ecologically unsound to introduce different species

---

28 France referred to UNCLOS, Art 235(3), which requires states to assure 'prompt and adequate compensation in respect of all damage caused by pollution of the marine environment'.

into an area or engineer new habitats, thereby upsetting the natural balance of the existing ones.[29]

ITOPF argued that 'reasonable reinstatement' should be defined as follows. First, there should be a high probability that the measures would significantly accelerate the natural recovery of a damaged habitat or population. Secondly, the proposed measures should be technically feasible. Thirdly, the measures should not themselves result in the degradation of other habitats or in adverse consequences for other natural resources. Fourthly, the cost of the proposed programme should be proportionate to the extent and duration of the damage.[30] This last criterion was necessary to take account of the finite amount of compensation available under the CLC and the fund so that if the total of established claims were to exceed the maximum available, all claims would have to be prorated.

At the third Intersessional Working Group 2001, the French proposal was deemed to fall outside the scope of pollution damage under the 1992 CLC.[31] The working group identified practical criticisms of this approach that had been made by ITOPF, namely the ecological risks of introducing new species into areas or engineering new habitat areas, both of which could hinder the natural process by which residual oil was degraded after a spill. A more modest proposal was made by Australia, Canada, Sweden and the UK, which sought to clarify the fund's position that there must be a sufficient causal link between the spill and the remediation expense.[32] It suggested that this should cover innovative approaches, 'including measures taken at some distance (but still within the general vicinity of) the spill so long as it can be demonstrated that they would actually enhance the recovery of the damaged components of the environment'. At its meeting in October 2001, the fund decided not to accept the proposal, but referred the issue back to the working group.[33]

11.2.3 Jurisdiction

The CLC was drafted with deference to the sovereign rights of contracting states and therefore both it and the fund applied to pollution damage caused in or impacting on the territory of member states, including their territorial sea.[34] Accordingly, CLC 1969, Art II provided that it should apply 'exclusively to pollution damage caused on the territory including the territorial sea of a Contracting State and to preventive measures taken to prevent

29 Paragraph 6.5.
30 Paragraph 6.11.
31 92FUND/A.6/4, 92FUND/WGR.3/9 (2001), pp 32–3.
32 92FUND/A.6/4/5 (2001).
33 92FUND/A.6/28 (2001).
34 UNCLOS, Art 3 sets this at 12 miles.

or minimize such damage'. The 1984 IMO Conference saw lobbying for the recognition of the rights over the exclusive economic zone (EEZ) accorded to coastal states by UNCLOS, Part V.[35] In response, the 1992 protocols amended Art II (a) (ii) to provide that the CLC should apply:

> ... in the exclusive economic zone of a Contracting State, established in accordance with international law, or, if a Contracting State has not established such a zone, in an area beyond and adjacent to the territorial sea of that State determined by that State in accordance with international law and extending not more than 200 nautical miles from the baselines from which the breadth of its territorial sea is measured.

Outside the territorial seas and EEZs, international law is founded on the principle of open access and the near exclusive jurisdiction of flag states over vessels. The IOPC 1992 Claim Fund Manual states that responses to an oil spill in these areas would qualify for compensation only if they succeeded in preventing or reducing pollution damage within the territorial sea or EEZ of a contracting state. Such spills are rare and difficult to respond to practically, other than by relying on natural dispersal.

Article IX.1 deals with the jurisdiction of contracting states by requiring CLC actions which have resulted in pollution damage in the territory, or territorial sea, of a contracting state, or states, to be brought only in the courts of that contracting state, or states. A contracting state also has jurisdiction over a claim arising out of preventive measures taken in its territory, or territorial sea. Contracting states are required to ensure that their courts possess the necessary jurisdiction to entertain such actions for compensation.[36] After constitution of the limitation fund, the court of the state in which the fund had been constituted acquires exclusive competence to determine all matters relating to the apportionment and distribution of the fund.[37] Article X then requires contracting states to recognise final judgments given by courts with jurisdiction under Art IX, unless the judgment be obtained by fraud or where the defendant was not given reasonable notice and a fair opportunity to present his case. Such judgments are to be enforceable in each contracting state as soon as the formalities required in the state had been complied with, but the merits of the case were not to be re-opened.[38] The 1992 protocols amended the reference in Art IX to the 'territory' of a contracting state so that it now includes 'the territorial sea or an area referred to in Article II'.

---

35 Article 56.1(b)(iii) gives coastal states jurisdiction over the protection and preservation of the marine environment in their EEZ which is defined by Art 57 as extending to 200 nautical miles from the baselines from which the breath of the territorial sea is measured.

36 Article IX.2.

37 Article IX.3.

38 Article X(2).

Fund Convention 1992, Art 7 requires actions against the fund to be brought in a court that is competent under the provisions of CLC 1992, Art IX. Article 7.4 gives the fund a right to intervene in such proceedings. Article 7.3 provides for the court in which the shipowner is sued under the 1992 CLC to have exclusive jurisdiction over the fund. If proceedings are brought in a state that is a party to the 1992 CLC but not to the 1992 Fund, then the fund can be sued at its headquarters or before any court of any state party to the fund which is competent under CLC 1992, Art IX.

11.2.4 Compulsory insurance

Compulsory insurance, along with the establishment of a second-tier of compensation through the fund, is a critical component of the CLC in ensuring that there are sufficient funds to satisfy CLC claims. Article VII requires compulsory insurance of liabilities[39] arising under the CLC to be taken out by the owner of a ship registered in a contracting state and carrying more than 2,000 tons of oil in bulk as cargo up to the applicable limitation figure. Ships must carry a certificate attesting that insurance or other financial security is in force in accordance with these provisions. The certificate must issued or certified by the appropriate authority of the state of the ship's registry after determining that the insurance requirements of Art VII had been complied with. The certificate must be carried on board the ship and a copy deposited with the authorities who keep the record of the ship's registry. Claims for compensation for pollution damage may be brought directly against the liability insurer.[40]

Contracting states which are flag states must not permit their vessels to trade without such a certificate.[41] Similarly, contracting states which are port states must ensure, under their national legislation, that vessels, wherever registered, which actually carry more than 2,000 tons of oil in bulk as cargo have the insurance required by Art VII in force at the time such vessels enter or leave a port in their territory, or at the time such vessels arrive at or leave an off-shore terminal in their territorial sea.

11.3 Other international civil liability conventions

Apart from the CLC and Fund Conventions, the following other international civil liability conventions are in force. First, there are conventions concerning

---

39 Article VII (9) provides that 'any sum provided by insurance or by other financial security maintained in accordance with paragraph 1 of this Article shall be available exclusively for the satisfaction of claims under this Convention'.
40 Article VII contains provisions as to when the insurer who is sued directly may rely on the shipowner's defences and right to constitute a limitation fund.
41 Providing those vessels fall within Art VII.

the peaceful use of atomic energy. The principal convention is the International Atomic Energy Agency Convention on Civil Liability for Nuclear Damage 1963 (Vienna Convention) which came into force on 12 November 1977. Liability is channelled to the operator, which can be a state as well as an individual, and is strict, subject to limited exceptions.[42] The convention requires the operator maintain liability insurance and allows direct action to be taken against the insurer. The operator's liability is limited to US$5 million per nuclear incident. Jurisdiction lies exclusively with the courts of the contracting party in whose territory the incident occurred have exclusive jurisdiction over claims under the convention. A similar European regime is applied under the OECD Convention on Third Party Liability in the Field of Nuclear Energy 1960 (Paris Convention), which came into force on 1 April 1968 and was amended by protocols of 1964 and 1982. The Joint Protocol Relating to the Application of the Vienna Convention and the Paris Convention (Vienna) 1988 (Joint Protocol) which came into force on 27 April 1992 combines the two conventions into one expanded liability regime. Parties to the Joint Protocol are treated as though they were parties to both conventions and a choice of law is provided to determine which of the two conventions should apply to the exclusion of the other in respect of the same incident.

Potential conflicts with the maritime conventions on shipowners' liability are dealt with by the Convention Relating to Civil Liability in the Field of Maritime Carriage of Nuclear Material (Brussels) 1971 (Nuclear Convention), which came into force on 15 July 1975. This exonerates a person otherwise liable for damage caused in a nuclear incident if the operator of the nuclear installation is also liable for such damage by virtue of either the Paris Convention 1960 or the Vienna Convention 1963, or national law of similar scope of protection.

There is also the Space Objects Convention (Convention on International Liability for Damage Caused by Space Objects 1972, London, Moscow, Washington), which came into force on 1 September 1972. This provides for absolute liability on the part of the launching state, or states, for damage caused by space objects, either on the surface of the earth or to aircraft flight, subject to limited exceptions.[43] The convention covers the traditional heads of damage of loss of life, personal injury, impairment of health and damage to property. The convention has given rise to one claim, *Cosmos 954 (Canada v USSR)*.[44] This arose from the re-entry of a Soviet satellite which broke up on re-entry, spreading radioactive debris over a remote area of Canada. The dispute centred on the level of damages in respect of the

---

42 These are: an act of armed conflict; or war; or by the gross negligence of the person suffering the damage; or from an act or omission of such person done with the intent to cause damage.
43 A state will not be liable if the damage was caused by the gross negligence or from an act or omission done with intent to cause damage on the part of the claimant state.
44 *Cosmos 954 (Canada v USSR)* (1979) 18 ILM 899.

clean up operation mounted by Canada. Although environmental damage, per se, is not covered by the convention, the clean-up operation was necessary to prevent future harm. The claim was eventually settled on payment of $3 million.

Mention should also be made of the Salvage Convention 1989, which makes various contributions to the protection of the maritime environment. The most notable of these is the provision for the award of 'special compensation' under Art 13 where the salvage prevents or minimises substantial physical damage to the environment in coastal waters. If, however, the salvors fail to save the ship or minimise the pollution, they will not be entitled to a salvage award. Instead, their claim will be limited to one in respect of their expenses under the 'safety net' provisions of Art 14. In addition, Art 8.3 imposes a duty of care on salvors to prevent or minimise damage to the environment during salvage operations.

There also three international civil liability conventions which are not currently in force. First, there is the International Convention on Liability and Compensation for Damage in Connection with the Carriage of Hazardous and Noxious Substances by Sea 1996 (HNS Convention). This was drawn up to apply a regime similar to that applied under the CLC, to non-oil pollution from hazardous and noxious substances. Liability, which is strict, is channelled to shipowners who carry HNS cargoes, subject to the familiar CLC defences.[45] However, the HNS Convention does not apply to damage caused by certain radioactive materials or to pollution damage falling under the CLC. The HNS Convention contains tonnage based limitation provisions, up to a maximum aggregate amount of 100 million SDRs, with death and personal injury claims taking priority over other claims for the first two-thirds of the limitation fund, thereafter sharing equally with other claims.[46] Ships registered in a state party must maintain insurance against HNS liabilities. The convention also provides for the establishment of a fund, with an overall limit of 250 million SDRs.

Secondly, there is the Bunker Oil Pollution Convention 2001. This covers bunker spills from ships which are not bulk oil carriers, and which, therefore, fall outside both the CLC regime. The CLC again forms the model for the regime applied by the convention. However, the convention contains no separate provision for limitation of liability and claims thereunder will fall to be limited under either the 1957 or the 1976 Limitation of Liability Convention.

Thirdly, there is the Basel Protocol on Liability and Compensation for

---

45 Article 7 adds a new defence where shipper's failure to provide information about the hazardous and noxious nature of the cargo has cause the damage, wholly or in part, or has led the shipowner not to obtain compulsory HNS liability insurance.

46 Unlike CLC claims, HNS claims are not excluded from the Limitation Convention 1976. An HNS claim, therefore, will involve two parallel limitation regimes. However, the 1996 protocols to the Limitation Convention 1976 will give a state party the option to exclude HNS claims from the ambit of the 1996 protocols.

Damage 1999 (Basel Protocol), adopted on 10 December 1999. It covers the transboundary movement and disposal of hazardous wastes and other wastes which are regulated by the Basel Convention 1989.[47] Article 2 defines damage in a similar way to that adopted by the CLC. Article 4 imposes strict liability on the notifier, the party exporting the waste, until the disposer has taken possession of the waste. Thereafter the disposer becomes liable. Both the notifier and the disposer must insure against these liabilities. The notifier is exonerated if it can prove that the damage was: (a) the result of an act of armed conflict, hostilities, civil war or insurrection; (b) the result of a natural phenomenon of exceptional, inevitable, unforeseeable and irresistible character; (c) wholly the result of compliance with a compulsory measure of a public authority of the state where the damage occurred; or (d) wholly the result of the wrongful intentional conduct of a third party, including the person who suffered the damage.

Limitation of liability is to be left to national law, although Annex B provides a schedule of minimum limitation figures. Apart from the strict liability imposed on the notifier and the disposer, Art 5 imposes fault based liability on any person in respect of 'damage caused or contributed to by his lack of compliance with the provisions implementing the Convention or by his wrongful intentional, reckless or negligent acts or omissions'. Article 6 requires 'any person in operational control of hazardous wastes and other wastes at the time of an incident' to take 'all reasonable measures to mitigate damage arising therefrom'. The protocol contains no provision for the creation of a fund of the sort seen in the CLC, but contains an enabling provision enabling the Conference of the Parties to keep this issue under review.

11.4 EC Environmental Liability Directive 2004

Another approach to environmental liability is the public law approach adopted in 1980 in the US – CERCLA.[48] CERCLA allows claims to be made against potentially responsible parties[49] for clean-up costs, lost public use

---

47 This came into force on 5 May 1992 and regulates the transboundary shipment of waste, by operating a system of 'prior informed consent' for transboundary shipments between contracting parties.[47] Trade with non-parties is generally prohibited under Art 4.5. In 1995, the Basel Ban Amendment was added to the Basel Convention, prohibiting the export of all hazardous waste, even that destined for recycling, from OECD countries to non-OECD countries. This will come into force when it has received the necessary number of ratifications. However, parties who have already ratified regard themselves as morally bound by it.

48 42 USC, ss 9601–75.

49 The following can be a 'potentially responsible party'. First, the current owners and operators of a facility at the time of clean-up. Secondly, the owners and operators of a facility at the time the hazardous substances where disposed of. Thirdly, persons arranging for transport and disposal of hazardous substances (or generators of hazardous waste). Fourthly, transporters of hazardous substances.

and/or and natural resource damages imposes liability for natural resources damage caused by hazardous substances. Civil claims for property damage, personal injury and economic loss fall outside CERCLA and must be brought in tort. Liability is strict and applies retroactively where historical pollution continues to be a threat. Liability is triggered on proof of injury to the resource, namely, an observable adverse change in a natural resource that is directly or indirectly the result of the discharge. CERCLA allows a potentially responsible party to rely on the defences of an act of God, an act of war and an act or omission of a third party, but liability may still be incurred even though the loss was due to actions which may have been lawful at the time they were taken. Public trustees are designated to act on behalf of the public interest to recover for natural resource damages are recovered by public trustees who have a wide discretion in assessing the value of natural resource damages. It falls to the federal EPA to oversee environmental clean-up and remediation operations. Liability in respect of natural resource damages is limited to US$50 million. A trust fund, the 'Superfund', was established to pay for removal and remediation when no responsible party can be found. This was initially set at $1.6 billion, but was increased to $9 billion in 1986.

A limited version of such a regime is now being introduced into the EU through the Environmental Liability Directive 2004/35, which Member States are required to implement by 30 April 2007.[50] The directive was prompted by the Donana incident in 1998 in which severe damage was sustained in a Spanish national park, due to the release of toxic sludge following a breach in a dam containing waste from a mine. The directive aims to put in place an EU-wide framework for environmental remediation, by setting out two complementary public law regimes, neither of which will, have retroactive effect, to require remediation of environmental damage by polluters.[51] The directive operates a purely public law regime and does not give private parties any right of compensation.[52]

The directive starts by defining 'environmental damage', in Art 1, so as to encompass three heads of damage.[53] First, there is 'damage to protected species and natural habitats, which is any damage that has significant adverse effects on reaching or maintaining the favourable conservation status of such habitats or species'. The scope of such damage is limited to that sustained by species and habitats protected under the Wild Birds Directive, Directive 79/409 and the Habitats Directive, Directive 92/43, although Member States may designate other species 'for equivalent purposes' as those laid

---

50 The directive was introduced under Art 175 of the EC Treaty and is based on the application of the 'polluter pays' principle, set out in Art 174.
51 The directive contains a national safeguard clause which allows Member States to introduce more stringent national legislation.
52 Article 3.3. This provision is without prejudice to national legislation.
53 'Damage' is defined as 'a measurable adverse change in a natural resource or measurable impairment of a natural resource service which may occur directly or indirectly'.

down in these two directives. Secondly, there is water damage.[54] Thirdly, there is land damage.[55]

Article 3.1(a) then sets out the first liability regime under which strict liability is imposed on operators[56] who professionally conduct risky, or potentially risky, activities which include, *inter alia*, the following activities listed in Annex III:

- industrial and agricultural activities requiring permits under the 1996 Integrated Pollution Prevention and Control Directive, Directive 96/61;
- waste management operations;
- water and air pollution caused by production, storage, use, and release of dangerous chemicals;
- transport, use, and release of gmos regulated under the Contained Use Directive, Dir. 90/ 219 and the Deliberate Release Directive, Directive 2001/18.

The second liability regime is set out in Art 3.1(b). This is a fault-based regime which covers all professional activities, including those outside Annex III, where these activities have caused damage to protected species and habitats protected under the Birds Directive 1979 and the Habitats Directive 1992. Article 4.1 allows an operator the following defences in respect of either liability regime. The first is where the environmental damage or imminent threat thereof is caused by 'an act of armed conflict, hostilities, civil war or insurrection' and the second is where it is caused by 'a natural phenomenon of exceptional, inevitable and irresistible character'. Article 4.4 also excludes claims which fall under existing international civil liability conventions on maritime and nuclear pollution fall outside the directive, as these fall to be dealt with under their respective conventions.

Article 8.3 also relieves an operator of liability where it can prove that the environmental damage or imminent threat thereof was either 'caused by a third party and occurred despite the fact that appropriate safety measures were in place' or 'resulted from compliance with a compulsory order or

---

54 This is 'any damage that significantly adversely affects the ecological, chemical and/or quantitative status and/or ecological potential, as defined in Dir 2000/60/EC, of the waters concerned, with the exception of adverse effects where Article 4(7) of that Directive applies'.

55 This is 'any land contamination that creates a significant risk of human health being adversely affected as a result of the direct or indirect introduction, in, on or under land, of substances, preparations, organisms or micro-organisms'.

56 Article 2.6 defines an 'operator' as 'any natural or legal, private or public person who operates or controls the occupational activity or, where this is provided for in national legislation, to whom decisive economic power over the technical functioning of such an activity has been delegated, including the holder of a permit or authorisation for such an activity or the person registering or notifying such an activity'.

instruction emanating from a public authority other than an order or instruction consequent upon an emission or incident caused by the operator's own activities'. Article 8.4 then proceeds to allow Member States to grant to an operator two further exceptions. These may apply where the operator demonstrates that he or she was not at fault or negligent and that the environmental damage was caused by:

(a) an emission or event expressly authorised by, and fully in accordance with the conditions of, an authorisation conferred by or given under applicable national laws and regulations which implement those legislative measures adopted by the EC specified in Annex III, as applied at the date of the emission or event;
(b) an emission or activity or any manner of using a product in the course of an activity which the operator demonstrates was not considered likely to cause environmental damage according to the state of scientific and technical knowledge at the time when the emission was released or the activity took place.

There is no upper limit of liability for an operator under either of these regimes[57] and there is no requirement for operators to obtain liability insurance. In the event that they cannot meet the costs of remediation, there is no obligation that the Member State in question must effect the remediation of such 'orphan damage' instead. The two liability regimes require public authorities to identify liable polluters and to ensure that such operators undertake, or finance, the necessary preventive and remedial measures contemplated by the directive. The remediation required will depend upon the type of damage. Pollution of the soil will require decontamination of the affected areas so that they no longer pose a significant further risk to human health. Damage to species and habitats may require enhancement of nearby sites, or even sites at some distance from the affected area, which have an equivalent environmental value.

In assessing competing options for remediation, public authorities must balance the following factors: the effect of an option on public health and safety; the benefits of an option for the overall environment; the costs and implementation time of an option; the likelihood of an option's success; the possibility of future and collateral damage; the distance to the damaged site; social, economic, cultural concerns and other relevant factors specific to the locality. Citizens and non-governmental organisations have the right to request the competent national authorities to take action against actual or

---

57 However, Art 4.3 provides that the directive is without prejudice to the right of the operator to limit his liability in accordance with national legislation implementing the Convention on Limitation of Liability for Maritime Claims 1976 (LLMC).

threatened pollution falling within the directive, submitting their observations backed up supporting evidence. If the authorities do not act, their decision may be challenged in the national courts by judicial review. However, Member States are allowed not to apply these procedures where there is an imminent threat of damage but no damage has yet occurred.

The directive is a welcome attempt to address environmental remediation throughout the EU on a comprehensive, unified basis. However, the directive does have several shortcomings. A general point of criticism is its failure to require operators to carry liability insurance, thereby leaving it up to public authorities in Member States to pick up the bill for remedying 'orphan damage' where the operator has insufficient funds. In this connection, the interpretation of the term of 'operator' is likely to prove significant as regards possible attempts to make recovery from parent companies in respect of operations of their subsidiaries. The scope of the directive as regards biodiversity damage is also limited by its reference to the Wild Birds Directive 1979 and the Habitats Directive 1992.

There are also potential uncertainties and loopholes regarding the treatment of the transport and use of GMOs under the directive. First, it is uncertain whether the definition of 'operator' will cover the biotechnology company that supplies the GM seed, or the farmer that uses it. This will be a difficult issue to assess, given that the use of GM seeds is usually heavily prescribed by the terms set out in the licensing agreements required by their suppliers. Secondly, the scope of the directive may be severely undermined by the optional defences under Art 8.4. As use of GMOs will require the authorisation referred to in Art 8.4(a), this exception would allow the operator to avoid the strict liability regime. Instead, liability would be based on fault, but unlike the fault regime in Art 3.1(b) there would be a reversal of the burden of proof, so that it would be for the operator to prove an absence of fault, and damage would not be limited to damage sustained by protected habitats and species. It is likely that the operator would be able to show an absence of fault if it can prove that it has used the GMO in strict accordance with the terms of the authorisation. Thirdly, damage to land is limited to damage which causes a significant risk to human health. This would not cover biodiversity damage, such as caused by cross-pollination from a GM crop. Such damage would only fall within the directive if it fell within the scope of the Habitats Directive 1992. Fourthly, Annex III does not cover all uses of GMOs. It does not cover the Food and Feed Regulations, Regulation 1829/30, under which approval may be given for GM crops and foods intended for use as food or animal feed within the EU. Nor would it cover the use of GM plants and animals in laboratories, as the Contained Use Directive, Directive 90/219, applies only to GM micro-organisms. Liability in respect of such uses would, therefore, fall under the fault based regime in Art 3.1(b), but only in respect of damage to protected habitats and species.

11.5 Conclusion

The CLC is generally regarded as having been successful in addressing the problem of affording adequate compensation to those who suffer loss as a result of maritime accidents involving the carriage of oil. Oil spills still happen, but at least there is a mechanism in place for ensuring adequate compensation. However, the exclusion of pure environmental loss from the CLC and Fund Conventions has been regarded by some as their major shortcoming, as has the fact that their geographical ambit does not extend onto the high seas. The problem is that, pure environmental loss is, by definition, unquantifiable. Unlike land-based contamination, there is no practical way of ensuring that the wrongdoer remediates the pollution damage. In most cases, natural dispersal will be the most effective means of remediation. Pollution of the high seas also poses evidential problems in identifying the ship responsible for the pollution. Putting a price on pure environmental loss is a speculative exercise that amounts to an award of punitive damages which can only be justified by reference to its deterrent effect.

Could a civil liability convention along the lines of the CLC provide a solution to the problem of making multinationals accountable for environmental harm caused by their operations in the developing world? One must first consider exactly what constitutes the nature of the problem. The analysis of the litigation in the previous chapters might suggest that the core of the problem is the inability to obtain compensation for loss or damage consequent upon environmental torts. However, this is only a secondary part of the underlying problem which is the failure of developing countries to apply adequate regulatory regimes to control the way in which hazardous activities within their jurisdictions are undertaken. Any international approach to this problem must be directed at avoiding future Bhopals, rather than being limited to providing compensation in the event of future Bhopals.

This would entail a twin track approach. A regulatory convention equivalent to MARPOL would be needed together with a liability convention, equivalent to the CLC, which at least doubles the difficulties inherent in developing any international convention solution to the problem. The key feature of the MARPOL regime that regulates oil pollution is that it allows for enforcement of its provisions by port states and not just flag states. This back-up regime of port state control is in practice a far more effective means of ensuring compliance with MARPOL than reliance on flag states who have the primary duty of enforcement, but often lack the means or the will to discharge that duty. However, with a global regime directed at hazardous activities it is difficult to envisage who would play the key back-up role played by port states in the maritime sphere. Secondly, one must consider who such conventions would be aimed at. One simple way to devise such a convention would be for countries in the developed world to adopt a convention allowing the tort claims against multinationals to be subject to a regime of 'enterprise liability' which disregarded the corporate formalities between parent companies and their subsidiaries. However, apart from the fact that it is inconceivable that the political will could currently be found to devise such a convention, this type of approach would fail to address the problem of environmental harm caused by domestic operators. Indeed, one possible unintended consequence of such an approach might be to discourage investment in the developing world by multinational corporations and so lead to lower environmental standards.

A more promising direction for any proposed convention would be to address the hazardous activities that are likely to cause pollution, with resultant environmental claims. A regime could be envisaged whereby global operational standards were applied to such activities, accompanied by a civil liability regime based on the CLC with strict liability, subject to an overall limit per claim, compulsory insurance, and the creation of a fund to soak up unsatisfied claims. Such an enterprise would, however, be fraught with difficulties. There would be the problem of defining the activities that would fall within the scope of the new conventions. This is likely to cover a far wider range of activities that the carriage of bulk oil to which the CLC is addressed. Then there is the likely objection from developing countries that such a convention would see the imposition on them of standards from the developed world and so cut back on their competitive advantage in the global economy. There is also the question of who is to pay for all this raising of standards. Placing the costs on the developing countries would be clearly unacceptable. That means that the costs would have to be borne by the developed countries, both through financial contributions to establish the administrative structure of any regulatory regime as well as the creation of any second-tier layer of compensation through a fund, and through the transfer of environmentally sound technology. Then there would be the problem of 'free riding' by non-parties. This would need to be dealt with by trade sanctions which would then run into a conflict with GATT, particularly as such sanctions would, in most cases, need to be justified by reference to PPM criteria. The conclusion must be, therefore, that no such international convention is likely to be forthcoming in this area, at least so long as environmental pollution in the developing world does not lead to spillover damage in the developed world. Until then, inhabitants of the developing world will continue to suffer as a result of their country's decision that development is best achieved by participating in the 'race to the bottom'. When large scale environmental disasters occur, mass litigation in a jurisdiction in the developed world will still seem the best way of obtaining compensation.

Index

For Product Safety Concerns and Information please contact our EU
representative GPSR@taylorandfrancis.com
Taylor & Francis Verlag GmbH, Kaufingerstraße 24, 80331 München, Germany

www.ingramcontent.com/pod-product-compliance
Ingram Content Group UK Ltd.
Pitfield, Milton Keynes, MK11 3LW, UK
UKHW021623240425
457818UK00018B/712